The World Organisation Against Torture (OMCT) coordinates the activities of the SOS-Torture Network, which is the world's largest coalition of non-governmental organisations fighting against torture and ill-treatment, arbitrary detention, extrajudicial executions, forced disappearances, and other serious human rights violations. OMCT's growing global network currently includes 282 local, national, and regional organisations in 92 countries spanning all regions of the world. An important aspect of OMCT's mandate is to respond to the advocacy and capacity-building needs of its network members, including the need to develop effective international litigation strategies to assist victims of torture and ill-treatment in obtaining legal remedies where none are available domestically, and to support them in their struggle to end impunity in states where torture and ill-treatment remain endemic or tolerated practices. In furtherance of these objectives, OMCT has published a *Handbook Series* of four volumes, each one providing a guide to the practice, procedure, and jurisprudence of the regional and international mechanisms that are competent to examine individual complaints concerning the violation of the absolute prohibition of torture and ill-treatment. This *Practitioner's Handbook* on Article 3 of the European Convention on Human Rights is the first of the series.

ARTICLE 3 OF THE EUROPEAN CONVENTION ON HUMAN RIGHTS
A PRACTITIONER'S HANDBOOK

AUTHORS
Uğur Erdal and Hasan Bakırcı

SERIES EDITOR
Boris Wijkström

First Printing: July 2006
© 2006 World Organization Against Torture (OMCT)
ISBN 2-88477-110-7

COVER ILLUSTRATION: Veronica de Nogales Leprevost
www.damdenogales.com

World Organisation Against Torture (OMCT)
P.O. Box 21
8, rue du Vieux Billard
CH-1211 Geneva 8
Switzerland

Tel: +41 (0)22 809 4939
Fax: +41 (0)22 809 4929
E-mail: omct@omct.org or handbook@omct.org
http://www.omct.org

DIRECTOR OF PUBLICATIONS: Eric Sottas

Article 3
of the European Convention on Human Rights

Uğur Erdal &
Hasan Bakırcı

A PRACTITIONER'S HANDBOOK

OMCT Handbook Series Vol. I

Series Editor: Boris Wijkström

Note to Readers

This *Practitioner's Handbook* constitutes a capacity-building tool which is meant to support NGOs, advocates, lawyers, and indeed, the victims of torture themselves, in developing effective litigation strategies before the European Court of Human Rights in respect of violations of Article 3 of the European Convention on Human Rights. As such, OMCT has striven for comprehensive coverage of the relevant areas of substance and procedure but also for clarity and accessibility. OMCT is continuously looking for ways to improve its materials and enhance their impact. Please help us do this by submitting your comments on this book, preferably in English or French, at: handbook@omct.org

Readers are also invited to visit our website (www.omct.org) featuring a page devoted to the *Handbook* which contains further reference materials including electronic versions of all of the *Handbook's* appendices.

ACKNOWLEDGEMENTS

This publication was made possible by the European Commission, and was supported by the Government of Switzerland and the Deutsches Institut für Menschenrechte.

I would like to thank Victoria Lee for her indefatigable editorial assistance and critical feedback on multiple drafts of this *Handbook*. I am also deeply indebted to Aubra Fletcher whose keen editorial eye saved us from the many errors which inevitably insinuate themselves into a text of this length. I also wish to recognize the following for their assistance with legal and thematic research during various stages of the project: Giulia Grazioli, Sanne Rooseboom and Yvonne Troya.

I would like to thank Agnes van Steijn, case lawyer at the Registry of the European Court of Human Rights, for reading several drafts of the *Handbook* and for making many useful comments to the authors. I am also grateful to the many other case lawyers of the Registry who generously provided ideas and feedback in their discussions with the authors.

I am grateful to the following lawyers who very kindly permitted us to include documents drafted by them as appendices to this *Handbook*: Roeland Böcker of the Ministry for Foreign Affairs of the Netherlands, for the Government's observations submitted to the Court in the case of *Van der Ven v. the Netherlands*; Professors Kevin Boyle and Françoise Hampson, the applicants' legal representatives in the case of *Akkum and Others v. Turkey*, for the observations submitted to the Court on behalf of the applicants; Philip Leach, Cihan Aydın and Reyhan Yalçındağ, the applicant's legal representatives in the case of *Kişmir v. Turkey*, for the observations submitted to the Court on behalf of the applicant; Judge Egbert Myjer, Nico Mol, Peter Kempees, Agnes van Steijn and Janneke Bockwinkel for allowing us to include their article *Submitting a Complaint to the European Court of Human Rights: Eleven Common Misconceptions*; and finally, Maxim Ferschtman, for the sample request for an interim measure under Rule 39 of the Rules of Court.

I am grateful to the third party interveners (NGOs) in the case of *A and Others v. Secretary of State for the Home Department and A and Others (FC) and another v. Secretary of State for the Home Department*, and in the case of *Ramzy v. The Netherlands*, for permission to reproduce their submissions in the appendices.

I would like to thank Roderick Liddell, Head of External Relations and Communication at the European Court of Human Rights, for allowing us to reproduce various documents available on the Council of Europe's website which appear in several of the *Textboxes* and Appendices of this *Handbook*.

Finally, my thanks to Veronica de Nogales Leprevost for contributing the cover illustration for the *OMCT Handbook Series.*

Boris Wijkström
Series Editor
July 2006

DISCLAIMER

The views expressed in this book are solely those of the authors and do not represent those of the European Court of Human Rights or any other institution.

TABLE OF CONTENTS

APPENDICES

PREFACE

I welcome the publication of what is certain to be a most useful contribution to better practice before the European Court of Human Rights in cases alleging violations of the Article 3 prohibition of torture and inhuman or degrading treatment or punishment under the European Convention on Human Rights. It is written by persons with extensive inside experience of the Court's work.

At first sight, one might wonder why another 'how to' book on the Court is necessary. In fact, the Court has developed such an extensive case law on both substance and procedure, potential applicants or their lawyers will be well served by this article-specific work. This is particularly apposite in the context of Article 3 violations: torture and other prohibited ill-treatment generally occur far from the public eye, in secret, dark places where the victim has no control over the circumstances and where the ensuing physical and psychological trauma make access to justice more difficult even after the torture stops. Moreover, it is a commonplace observation that public officials who commit torture are careful to cover up their tracks and usually have ample means at their disposal to do so. As a consequence, litigating a case under Article 3 presents special evidential and other challenges for the victim. In this connection, the comprehensive treatment the *Handbook* accords to the 'establishment of facts' and other procedural and evidential challenges peculiar to Article 3 complaints will be especially helpful. In fact, a review of the current state of the literature reveals that while increasing attention is being focused on the development of the Court's Article 3 jurisprudence, and indeed the jurisprudence on torture of international tribunals generally, there is little which treats these developments specifically from the perspective of an applicant wishing to seek justice before the Strasbourg Court.

The definitional aspects are an especially important element of substance. In the past, the Court has inexplicably insisted on maintaining an approach which sees 'torture' as involving even more pain or suffering than is inherent in the notion of inhuman treatment, apparently because of the 'special stigma' associated with torture. Today, however, it is becoming increasingly common for the Court, in finding violations of Article 3, not to specify which aspect of the Article was violated. The extensive discussion in this *Handbook* of Article 3 severity threshold issues usefully draws out the practical implications of this trend.

The scope of subject-matter is also noteworthy, ranging as it does from brutal interrogation methods through inhumane conditions of detention to arbitrary methods of expulsion. The treatment of interim measures is of great significance in Article 3 cases, particularly those involving attempts to avoid extradition or deportation to a country where their mental or physical integrity could be at risk.

Practitioners should be immeasurably assisted by the appendices that provide an accessible guide to best practice before the Court in Article 3 cases.

Professor Sir Nigel Rodley KBE
Chair, Human Rights Centre
University of Essex
July 2006

TABLE OF CASES

Barbato v. Uruguay, Human Rights Committee Communication No. 84, 1981, § 9.6

Batı and Others v. Turkey, nos. 33097/96 and 57834/00, 3 June 2004

Baybaşin v. the Netherlands (dec.), no. 13600/02, 6 October 2005

Bayram and Yıldırım v. Turkey, (dec.) no. 38587/97, 29 January 2002

Beard v. the United Kingdom [GC], no. 24882/94, 18 January 2001

Bekos and Koutropoulos v. Greece, no. 15250/02, 13 December 2005

Bensaid v. the United Kingdom (dec.), no. 44599/98, 25 January 2000

Bensaid v. the United Kingdom, no. 44599/98, 6 February 2001

Berdzenishvili v. Russia (dec.), no. 31697/03, 29 January 2004

Biç v. Turkey (dec.), no. 55955/00, 2 February 2006

Bilgin v. Turkey, no. 23819/94, 16 November 2000

Birutis and Others v. Lithuania (dec.), nos. 47698/99 and 48115/99, 7 November 2000

Blečić v. Croatia [GC], no. 59532/00, 8 March 2006

Bosphorus Hava Yolları Turizm ve Ticaret Anonim Şirketi (Bosphorus Airways) v. Ireland [GC], no. 45036/98, 30 June 2005

Boyle and Rice v. the United Kingdom, nos. 9659/82 and 9658/82, 27 April 1998

Bozinovski v. the former Yugoslav Republic of Macedonia (dec.), no. 68368/01, 1 February 2005

Buldan v. Turkey (dec.), no. 28298/95, 4 June 2002

Buldan v. Turkey, no. 28298/95, 20 April 2004

Bulut and Yavuz v. Turkey (dec.), no. 73065/01, 28 May 2002

Büyükdağ v. Turkey, no. 28340/95, 21 December 2000

C.R. v. the United Kingdom, no. 20190/92, 22 November 1995

Calvelli and Ciglio v. Italy [GC], no. 32967/96, 17 January 2002

Camberrow MM5 AD v. Bulgaria (dec.), no. 50357/99, 1 April 2004

Campbell and Cosans v. the United Kingdom, nos. 7511/76 and 7743/76, 25 February 1982

Caralan v. Turkey (dec.), no. 27529/95, 14 November 2002

Cardot v. France, no. 11069/84, 19 March 1991

Chahal v. the United Kingdom, no. 22414/93, 15 November 1996

Charzyński v. Poland (dec.), no. 15212/03, 1 March 2005

Christine Goodwin v. the United Kingdom [GC], no. 28957/95, 11 July 2002

Corsacov v. Moldova, no. 18944/02, 4 April 2006

Council of Civil Service Unions and others v. the United Kingdom, no. 11603/85, Commission decision of 20 January 1987

Cruz Varas and Others v. Sweden, no. 15576/89, 20 March 1991

Cyprus v. Turkey [GC], no. 25781/94, 10 May 2001

Çakıcı v. Turkey, no. 23657/94, Commission Report of 12 March 1998

Çelik v. Turkey, no. 23655/94, Commission decision of 15 May 1995

Çelik and İmret v. Turkey, no. 44093/98, 26 October 2004

Hilal v. the United Kingdom, no. 45276/99, 6 March 2001

Hirst v. the United Kingdom (no. 2) [GC], no. 74025/01, 6 October 2005

The Holy Monasteries v. Greece, nos. 13092/87 and 13984/88, 9 December 1994

Hudson v. former Yugoslav Republic of Macedonia (dec.), no. 67128/01, 24 March 2005

Hugh Jordan v. the United Kingdom, no. 24746/94, 4 May 2001

I.I.N. v. the Netherlands (dec.), no. 2035/04, 9 December 2004

İçyer v. Turkey (dec.), no. 18888/02, 21 January 2006

Ilaşcu and Others v. Moldova and Russia (dec.), no. 48787/99, 4 July 2001

Ilaşcu and Others v. Moldova and Russia [GC], no. 48787/99, 8 July 2004

İlhan v. Turkey [GC], no. 22277/93, 27 June 2000

Immobiliare Saffi v. Italy [GC], no. 22774/93, 28 July 1999

Incal v. Turkey, no. 22678/93, 9 June 1998

Indelicato v. Italy, no. 31143/96, 18 October 2001

Iochev v. Bulgaria, no. 41211/98, 2 February 2006

Iordachi and Others v. Moldova (dec.), no. 25198/02, 5 April 2005

İpek v. Turkey (dec.), no. 25760/94, 14 May 2002

İpek v. Turkey, no. 25760/94, 17 February 2004

Ireland v. the United Kingdom, no. 5310/71, 18 January 1978

Issa v. Turkey, no. 31821/96, 16 November 2004

Iwańczuk v. Poland, no. 25196/94, 15 November 2001

Jabari v.Turkey, no. 40035/98, 11 July 2000

Jeličić v. Bosnia and Herzegovina (dec.), no. 41183/02, 15 November 2005

Jørgensen v. Denmark (dec.), no. 31260/03, 9 June 2005

K.C.M. v. the Netherlands, no. 21034/92, Commission decision of 9 January 1995

K.K.C. v. the Netherlands, no. 58964/00, 21 December 2001

K. and T. v. Finland [GC], no. 25702/94, 12 July 2001

Kalantari v. Germany, no. 51342/99, 11 October 2001

Kalashnikov v. Russia (dec.), no. 47095/99, 18 September 2001

Kalashnikov v. Russia, no. 47095/99, 15 July 2002

Kalın, Gezer and Ötebay v. Turkey, nos. 24849/94, 24850/94 and 24941/94, 28 October 2003

Kanlıbaş v. Turkey, no. 32444/96, 8 December 2005

Kaplan v. Turkey, no. 31830/96, Commission decision of 20 May 1998

Karabardak and Others v. Turkey (dec.), no. 76575/01, 22 October 2002

Karner v. Austria, no. 40016/98, 24 July 2003

Keenan v. the United Kingdom, no. 27229/95, 3 April 2001

Khashiyev and Akayeva v. Russia, nos. 57942/00 and 57045/00, 24 February 2005

Khudoyorov v. Russia, no. 6847/02, 8 November 2005

Kişmir v. Turkey (dec.), no. 27306/95, 14 December 1999

Moldovan and Others v. Romania, nos. 41138/98 and 64320/01, 12 July 2005

Mouisel v. France, no. 67263/01, 14 November 2002

Moyá Alvarez v. Spain (dec.), no. 44677/98, 23 November 1999

Murat Demir v. Turkey, no. 879/02, 2 March 2006

N. v. Finland, no. 38885/02, 26 July 2005

Nachova and Others v. Bulgaria [GC], nos. 43577/98 and 43579/98, 6 July 2005

Nasimi v. Sweden (dec.), no. 38865/02, 16 March 2004

Nazarenko v. Ukraine, no. 39483/98, 29 April 2003

Ndangoya v. Sweden (dec.), no. 17868/03, 22 June 2004

Nee v. Ireland (dec.), no. 52787/99, 30 January 2003

Nehru v. the Netherlands (dec.), no. 52676/99, 27 August 2002

Nevmerzhitsky v. Ukraine, no. 54825/00, 5 April 2005

Nielsen v. Denmark, judgment of 2 September 1959, Yearbook II (1958-1959), p. 412 (454)

Norris v. Ireland, no. 10581/83, 26 October 1988

Nuray Şen v. Turkey (2), no. 25354/94, 30 March 2004

Nurmagomedov v. Russia (dec.), no. 30138/02, 16 September 2004

Oğur v. Turkey [GC], no. 21594/93, 20 May 1999

Ohlen v. Denmark, no. 63214/00, 24 February 2005

Orhan v. Turkey, no. 25656/94, 18 June 2002

Osman v. the United Kingdom, no. 23452/94, 28 October 1998

Ostrovar v. Moldova, no. 35207/03, 13 September 2005

Öcalan v. Turkey [GC], no. 46221/99, 12 May 2005

Özbey v. Turkey (dec.), no. 31883/96, 8 March 2001

Özgür Kılıç v. Turkey (dec.), no. 42591/98, 24 September 2002

Özkan and Others v. Turkey, no. 21689/93, 6 April 2004

P.G. and J.H. v. the United Kingdom, no. 44787/98, 25 September 2001

Pauger v. Austria, no. 24872/94, Commission decision of 9 January 1995

Paul and Audrey Edwards v. the United Kingdom (dec.), no. 46477/99, 21 February 2002

Papachelas v. Greece [GC], no. 31423/96, 25 March 1999

Papon v. France (no. 2) (dec.), no. 54210/00, 15 November 2001

Peers v. Greece, no. 28524/95, 19 April 2001

Philis v. Greece, no. 28970/95, Commission decision of 17 October 1996

Philis v. Greece, nos. 12750/87, 13780/88 and 14002/88, 27 August 1991

Poltorachenko v. Ukraine, no. 77317/01, 18 January 2005

Poltoratskiy v. Ukraine, no. 38812/97, 29 April 2003

Price v. the United Kingdom, no. 33394/96, 10 July 2001

Pretty v. the United Kingdom, no. 2346/02, 29 April 2002

Quaresma Afonso Palma v. Portugal (dec.), no. 72496/01, 13 February 2003

Soering v. the United Kingdom, no. 14038/88, 7 July 1989

Sokratian v. the Netherlands (dec.), no. 41/03, 8 September 2005

Soto Sanchez v. Spain (dec.), no. 66990/01, 20 May 2003

Starodub v. Ukraine (dec.), no. 5483/02, 7 June 2005

Sunday Times v. the United Kingdom (former Article 50), no. 6538/74, 6 November 1989

Süheyla Aydın v. Turkey, no. 25660/94, 24 May 2005

Sürek v. Turkey (no. 2) [GC], no. 24122/94, 8 July 1999

Şükran Aydın and Others v. Turkey (dec.), no. 46231/99, 26 May 2005

T. v. the United Kingdom [GC], no. 24724/94, 16 December 1999

T.A. v. Turkey, no. 26308/95, 9 April 2002

Tahsin Acar v. Turkey (preliminary objection) [GC], no. 26308/95, 6 May 2003

Tanrıkulu v. Turkey [GC], no. 23763/94, 8 July 1999

Tauira and 18 others v. France, no. 28204/95, Commission decision of 4 December 1995

Tekin v. Turkey, no. 22496/93, Commission Report of 17 April 1997

Tekin v. Turkey, no. 22496/93, 9 June 1998

Tepe v. Turkey (dec.), no. 31247/96, 22 January 2002

Thampibillai v. the Netherlands, no. 61350/00, 17 February 2004

TI v the United Kingdom, no. 43844/98, 7 March 2000

Timurtaş v. Turkey, no. 23531/94, 13 June 2000

Toğcu v. Turkey (strike out of the list), no. 27601/95, 9 April 2002

Toğcu v. Turkey, no. 27601/95, 31 May 2005

Tomasi v. France, no. 12850/87, 27 August 1992

Tuquabo-Tekle and Others v. the Netherlands (dec.), no. 60665/00, 19 October 2004

Tyrer v. the United Kingdom, no. 5856/72, 25 April 1978

Ükünç and Güneş v. Turkey, no. 42775/98, 18 December 2003

Ülke v. Turkey, no. 39437/98, 24 January 2006

Valašinas v. Lithuania, no. 44558/98, 24 July 2001

Van der Graaf v. the Netherlands (dec.), no. 8704/03, 1 June 2004

Van der Ven v. the Netherlands, no. 50901/99, 4 February 2003

Van Houten v. the Netherlands, no. 25149/03, 29 September 2005

Varbanov v. Bulgaria, no. 31365/96, 5 October 2000

Vayiç v. Turkey (dec.), no. 18078/02, 28 June 2005

Vijayanathan and Pusparajah v. France, nos. 17550/90 and 17825/91, 27 August 1992

Vilvarajah and Others v. the United Kingdom, nos. 13163/87, 13164/87, 13165/87, 13447/87 and 13448/87, 30 October 1991

Vogl and Vogl v. Austria (dec.), no. 50171/99, 23 October 2001

Walker v. the United Kingdom (dec.), no. 34979/97, 25 January 2000

Whiteside v. the United Kingdom, no. 20357/92, Commission decision of 7 March 1994

Wilson, National Union of Journalists and Others v. the United Kingdom, nos. 30668/96,

30671/96 and 30678/96, 2 July 2002

Winterwerp v. the Netherlands, no. 6301/73, 24 October 1979

Worm v. Austria, no. 22714/93, 29 August 1997

Worm v. Austria, no. 22714/93, Commission decision of 27 November 1995

Yasin Ateş v. Turkey, no. 30949/96, 31 May 2005

Yaşa v. Turkey, no. 22495/93, 2 September 1998

Yavuz v. Turkey, no. 67137/01, 10 January 2006

Young, James and Webster v. the United Kingdom (former Article 50), nos. 601/76 and 7806/77, 18 October 1982

Yöyler v. Turkey, no. 26973/95, 24 July 2003

Z. v. the United Kingdom, no. 29392/95, 10 May 2001

Zarakolu v. Turkey, no. 32455/96, 27 May 2003

Zarakolu v. Turkey (dec.), no. 37061/97, 5 December 2002

Zeynep Avcı v. Turkey, no. 37021/97, 6 February 2003

INTRODUCTION

The purpose of this *Handbook* is to provide practical advice to persons wishing to bring a case to the European Court of Human Rights under Article 3 of the European Convention on Human Rights. Article 3 of the Convention prohibits the use of *torture or inhuman or degrading treatment or punishment* by Contracting Parties. This prohibition is absolute, allowing for no derogation or exceptions under any circumstances. The European Court has held that the Article 3 prohibition enshrines "one of the fundamental values of the democratic societies making up the Council of Europe."[1]

The *Handbook* is intended for advocates and practitioners of varying levels of experience including those who have little or no prior experience of litigating cases in Strasbourg. Indeed, applicants themselves should be able to use it to lodge an application with the Court. Naturally, the risks of oversimplification had to be avoided particularly in relation to some of the more complex areas of substance and procedure. It is hoped that the more experienced readers will find the *Handbook* useful as a reference tool, especially on such issues as the evidential rules and the establishment of facts, which, in the opinion of OMCT, have not traditionally received the attention they deserve and which have not previously been the subject of article-specific treatment.

Although the focus of this *Handbook* is Article 3, the analyses it contains should in theory enable a prospective applicant to formulate an application under any Article of the Convention. Nevertheless, due to its article-specific nature, all the substantive and procedural areas covered here are discussed in the context of the Court's Article 3 jurisprudence. In this connection, ample use has been made of the Court's judgments concerning ill-treatment to illustrate the operation of procedural rules and the application of substantive law to factual scenarios. Additionally, special emphasis has been placed on giving practical and strategic litigation advice in relation to matters which may pose particular challenges to Article 3 litigants. In doing so, the authors have drawn on their own experience in the Registry of the European Court.

The *Handbook* was written at a time when significant changes to the structure and procedure of the Court were underway. They include: the expected entry into force of Protocol No. 14 which will amend certain provisions of the Convention with the aim of improving the Court's efficiency; the amended Rules of Court which entered into force on 1 December 2005; the increasing tendency of the Court to examine admissibility and merits in a joint procedure, and finally, the creation of a fifth Section on 1 April 2006. This book

---

1   *Soering v. UK*, no. 14038/88, 7 July 1989, § 88.

takes into account the changes already in place as well as those that will follow when Protocol No. 14 enters into force.

For practical reasons, a simple method of reference was employed when
referring to the decisions and reports of the European Commission of Human
Rights and decisions and judgments of the Court. Thus, the reference "*A. v.
the United Kingdom*, no. 25599/94, 23 September 1998" includes [the applicant's name] v. [the respondent State], the application number, and the date
of the judgment. The initials "GC" in square brackets in some case references
indicate that the decision or judgment was adopted by the Grand Chamber of
the Court.

Throughout this book, the European Court of Human Rights is referred to as
"the Court" or "the Strasbourg Court"; the Convention for the Protection of
Human Rights and Fundamental Freedoms as "the European Convention on
Human Rights" or "the Convention"; and the word "ill-treatment", unless
otherwise specified, is employed as a collective term for all forms treatment
prohibited by Article 3, i.e. torture, inhuman treatment and degrading treatment. Whenever inhuman or degrading *punishment* is meant, it is referred to
as such. Finally, the person lodging the application and corresponding with
the Court is referred to simply as "the applicant" even though in practice that
person may be the applicant's lawyer.

A number of documents have been appended to the *Handbook* including reference materials such as the European Convention, Protocol No. 14, Practice
Directions, and so forth. The appendices also include a model Article 3 application to which applicants may refer in formulating their own applications,
and a detailed analysis of the Court's Article 3 jurisprudence.[2] In recognition
of the important role that non-judicial preventive mechanisms play in the
struggle to eradicate torture and ill-treatment, the appendices include an article describing the mandate and working methods of the relevant European
institutions including the European Committee for the Prevention of Torture
and Inhuman or Degrading Treatment or Punishment (CPT).[3] Due to space
constraints, a number of these appendices were placed in the CD-ROM which
accompanies this book. The appendices are generally intended to be consulted in conjunction with the sections to which they relate, as explained below.

Section 1 of the *Handbook* presents an overview of the Council of Europe,
the Court, the Convention, and provides a general description of the Court's

---

2   See Appendix No. 10, "Analysis of the Court's Article 3 Jurisprudence," prepared by the Deutsches
     Institut für Menschenrechte in collaboration with OMCT.
3   See Appendix No. 11, "European Mechanisms for the Prevention of Torture and Ill-treatment", by
     Dr. Reinhard Marx, Deutsches Institut für Menschenrechte.

proceedings. The latter is intended to give the reader a bird's-eye view of these proceedings and may be particularly useful to persons who have no prior experience with the Court. Readers are referred *inter alia* to Appendix No. 5, "Submitting a Complaint to the European Court of Human Rights: Eleven Common Misconceptions", and *Textbox ii*, "Case-Processing Flowchart".

Section 2 deals with the admissibility and standing requirements of the Convention. The issue of substantiation is analysed in detail since the large percentage of applications declared inadmissible as "manifestly ill-founded" on this ground suggests that applicants are not according sufficient attention to it.

Section 3 examines the issue of interim measures and the procedures for expediting cases. The Court is currently receiving a large number of requests for interim measures under Rule 39 from persons who are subject to expulsion. This is partly a consequence of the stricter immigration and anti-terrorist measures adopted recently by many Council of Europe Member States. The Practice Directions in Appendix No. 3 and the sample request for an interim measure under Rule 39 in Appendix No. 15 may be consulted when reading this section.

Sections 4 through 6 set out the Court's procedure from the lodging of the application up to and including the admissibility stage. At the time of writing, Article 29 § 3 of the Convention stipulates that in principle admissibility decisions are taken separately from merits decisions. However, this is more the exception than the rule. At the present time, and in anticipation of the entry into force of Protocol No. 14,[4] proceedings on admissibility and merits are conducted jointly in the vast majority of cases. The Court's recent practice of joint examination has accordingly been taken into account in this *Handbook*. Relevant appendices are *inter alia*, Appendices Nos. 1, 3-6, 10, 12 - 14, 17, and 19. Relevant *Textboxes* include *Textboxes iii-x*.

Section 7 deals with the issue of just satisfaction under Article 41 of the Convention. The reader may consult the applicants' claims for just satisfaction in the case of *Akkum and Others v. Turkey* in Appendix No. 12.

Section 8 tackles the issue of friendly settlement and strike outs under Articles 37 and 38 of the Convention. Readers may consult *Textbox xi* for a concrete example of friendly settlement declarations (*Sakı v. Turkey*, no. 29359/95, 30 October 2001).

---

4   See Article 9 of Protocol No. 14.

In Section 9, the form and content of judgments, referrals to the Grand Chamber, and the execution of judgments are examined.

Section 10 provides an analysis of the obligations inherent in Article 3 of the Convention. Annex 1 of the Istanbul Protocol, i.e. the Manual on the Effective Investigation and Documentation of Torture and Other Cruel, Inhuman or Degrading Treatment or Punishment, includes the principles applicable to the effective investigation and documentation of torture and other cruel, inhuman or degrading treatment or punishment. This may be consulted in Appendix No. 7 when formulating complaints concerning the effectiveness of investigations. Appendix No. 10 contains an analysis and discussion of the Court's Article 3 jurisprudence.

Section 11 deals with the establishment of facts and other evidential issues, such as the admissibility of evidence and the burden and standard of proof that are applied in the Court's proceedings. Annex 2 of the Istanbul Protocol, mentioned above, may be found in Appendix No. 8 of the present *Handbook*. This Annex should be consulted in conjunction with Section 11 for a review of advanced medical techniques used in the diagnoses of the effects of ill-treatment.

PART I

OVERVIEW OF THE COUNCIL OF EUROPE, THE COURT, AND ITS PROCEEDINGS

OVERVIEW

1.1 The Council of Europe

Map of Council of Europe Member States

1.2 The European Court of Human Rights

Textbox i   Dates of Ratification of European Convention on Human Rights and Additional Protocols as of 31 January 2006

1.3 Protocol No. 14

1.4 The Judges and the Registry of the Court

1.4.1 The Judges

1.4.2 The Registry

1.5 Structure of the Court

1.5.1 The Grand Chamber

1.5.2 The Sections and the Chambers

1.5.3 The Committees

1.6 Instruments of the Court

1.6.1 The European Convention on Human Rights

1.6.2 The Protocols

1.6.3 The Rules of Court

1.6.4 Practice Directions

1.6.5 Decisions and Reports of the Commission and Decisions and Judgments of the Court

1.7 Summary of Proceedings Before the Court

1.7.1 First Examination of the Application

1.7.2 Applications Declared Inadmissible by a Committee

1.7.3 Examination by a Chamber

Textbox ii   Case-processing Flowchart

1.8 Legal Representation

Textbox iii   Form of Authority

1.9 Legal Aid

Textbox iv   Legal Aid Fees (applicable as from 1 January 2006)

Textbox v   Declaration of Applicant's Means

1.10 The Languages Used in the Court's Proceedings

1.11 Written Pleadings

1.12 Third Party Interventions (*Amicus Curiae*)

1.13 Costs

1.14 Hearings

1.15 Effects of the Court's Judgments

1.1 The Council of Europe

The Convention for the Protection of Human Rights and Fundamental Freedoms, more commonly referred to as the "European Convention on Human Rights" and hereinafter as "the Convention", was drafted under the auspices of the Council of Europe, an inter-governmental body set up by the Treaty of London on 5 May 1949.[5]

According to Article 1 of the Statute of the Council of Europe, the aim of the organisation "is to achieve a greater unity between its members for the purpose of safeguarding and realising the ideals and principles which are their common heritage and facilitating their economic and social progress". In pursuit of this aim, each Member State[6] resolved, in Article 3 of the same Statute, to "accept the principles of the rule of law and of the enjoyment by all persons within its jurisdiction of human rights and fundamental freedoms". This special importance which the Member States accorded to human rights – a newly emerging concept at a time when the majority of the world's States jealously guarded the sovereign privilege to deal with their citizens as they wished – was subsequently taken to a new level with the opening for signature in Rome on 4 November 1950 of the Council of Europe's Convention for the Protection of Human Rights and Fundamental Freedoms. The Convention, which was the first international legal instrument to safeguard human rights through an enforcement mechanism, entered into force on 3 September 1953.

At the time of writing, the Council of Europe has 46 Member States and is considering the membership application of Belarus.[7] Membership in the Council of Europe is contingent on ratification of the Convention and its Protocols. The Council of Europe's headquarters is located in Strasbourg, France.

The Statute of the Council of Europe established two organs – the Committee of Ministers and the Parliamentary Assembly. The Committee of Ministers, which consists of the Ministers of Foreign Affairs of the Member States, is the decision-making body of the Council of Europe. Its functions include, in

---

5   The treaty was signed by ten European States, i.e. Belgium, Denmark, France, Ireland, Italy, Luxembourg, the Netherlands, Norway, Sweden, and the United Kingdom. In August 1949, Greece and Turkey joined the Council, increasing the number of its members to twelve. Subsequent ratifications have brought the number of Member States to 46. The Council of Europe has granted observer status to the Holy See, the United States, Canada, Japan and Mexico.

6   In this *Handbook*, the term "Member State" is used for a country which is a member of the Council of Europe, whereas the term "Contracting Party" refers to a State that has ratified the Convention.

7   A current list of the Council of Europe's Member States may be consulted at http://www.coe.int/T/E/Com/About_Coe/Member_states/default.asp

particular, supervising the execution of judgments of the European Court of Human Rights. The Parliamentary Assembly is the parliamentary organ of the Council of Europe. It consists of a number of members of national Parliaments from each Member State, with a President elected each year from amongst them. The Parliamentary Assembly's functions include the election of the judges of the European Court of Human Rights from a list of three candidates submitted by each Contracting Party. Furthermore, the Parliamentary Assembly is responsible for the adoption of Conventions and additional Protocols. Another important function of the Parliamentary Assembly is to examine whether a candidate State has fulfilled the criteria for accession to the Council of Europe.

The Council of Europe is headed by a Secretary General who is appointed by the Parliamentary Assembly on the recommendation of the Committee of Ministers, for a period of five years. The Secretary General has the overall responsibility for the strategic management of the Council of Europe's work programme and budget and oversees the day-to-day running of the organisation and Secretariat. The Secretary General also has the power, under Article 52 of the Convention, to request that a Contracting Party furnish explanations relating to the manner in which its internal law ensures the effective implementation of the Convention.[8]

The office of the Council of Europe's Commissioner for Human Rights was established on 7 May 1999 by a resolution of the Committee of Ministers. That Resolution requires the Commissioner to:

* promote education in, and awareness of, human rights in the Member States;

* identify possible shortcomings in the law and practice of Member States with regard to compliance with human rights; and,

* help promote the effective observance and full enjoyment of human rights, as embodied in the various Council of Europe instruments.

The Office of the Commissioner is a non-judicial institution which does not take up individual complaints. The Commissioner cannot, therefore, accept

---

8 For example, the Secretary General exercised his powers under this Article in his request of 25 November 2005 to the Contracting Parties for information concerning allegations of CIA abductions of terror suspects involving the use of 'Council of Europe' airspace or airports. Specifically, the Secretary General asked the Contracting Parties to provide information on whether "any public official or other person acting in an official capacity has been involved in any manner – whether by action or omission – in the unacknowledged deprivation of liberty of any individual, or transport of any individual while so deprived of their liberty, including where such deprivation of liberty may have occurred by or at the instigation of any foreign agency".

any requests to present individual complaints before national or international courts, nor before national administrations of Member States of the Council of Europe. Nevertheless, he or she can draw conclusions and take initiatives of a general nature that are based on individual complaints.[9]

During discussions on the drafting of Protocol No. 14, it was agreed that the Commissioner should play a more active role in assisting the European Court of Human Rights on certain questions, particularly in cases that reveal structural or systematic weaknesses in the Contracting Parties' institutions which lead to repetitive violations of the Convention. It was thus decided to amend Article 36 of the Convention so as to enable the Commissioner to intervene as a third party in cases before the European Court of Human Rights through the submission of written comments and by taking part in hearings.[10]

Council of Europe Member States[11]

---

9   For further information see http://www.coe.int/T/E/Commissioner_H.R/Communication_Unit/
10 See Article 13 of Protocol No. 14.
11 Source: http://www.coe.int/T/e/com/about_coe/member_states/default.asp

1.2 The European Court of Human Rights

The European Court of Human Rights is the oldest, most well established and effective of the three regional human rights systems in existence today. Its judgments are binding and have the force of law in the Member States of the Council of Europe. Failure to abide by the judgments of the Court can in theory have significant political consequences for the concerned Member State, including exclusion from the Council of Europe. In reality, such sanctions have never been applied because Contracting Parties generally have a good record of compliance with the Court's judgments.

The European human rights system went through several stages of development before crystallizing in its current form as a single permanent court with its seat in Strasbourg. Initially, a three-fold mechanism was established to enforce the obligations entered into by the Contracting Parties under the Convention. Pursuant to former Article 19 of the Convention, a European Commission of Human Rights (hereinafter referred to as "the Commission") and a European Court of Human Rights were established. These two entities – together often referred to as the "Convention institutions" or "Strasbourg institutions" – were complemented by the Committee of Ministers which was entrusted with adjudicative as well as executive powers, including the power to execute the Court's judgments.

The main function of the Commission, which consisted of a number of members equal to that of the Contracting Parties, was to act as a filtering mechanism by determining the admissibility of applications brought by individuals. When the Commission found an application admissible, it placed itself at the parties' disposal with a view to reaching a friendly settlement. If no settlement was reached, the Commission would draw up a report under former Article 31 of the Convention in which it would establish the facts of the case and express an opinion on the merits. This report would be transmitted to the Committee of Ministers. Where the respondent State had accepted the compulsory jurisdiction of the Court, the Commission, and/or any Contracting Party concerned had a period of three months following the transmission of the report to the Committee of Ministers within which to bring the case before the Court for a final and binding adjudication.

Originally, individuals were not entitled to bring their cases directly to the Court; former Article 25 of the Convention enabled individuals to apply directly to the Commission only. Protocol No. 9 to the Convention, which entered into force on 1 October 1994, did provide a limited possibility for individual applicants to have their cases examined by the Court. If a case was not referred to the Court, the Committee of Ministers would exercise its quasi-judicial powers to decide whether there had been a violation of the Convention, generally adopting the conclusion reached by the Commission in its report.[12]

From 1980 onwards, the steady growth in the number of cases brought before the Convention institutions – a development caused partly by the accession of new Member States to the Council of Europe – made it difficult for the Convention system to cope, and a restructuring became necessary. In order to reform the Convention system, Protocol No. 11 was drafted and opened for signature on 11 May 1994. The aim of this Protocol was to simplify the structure of the Convention organs with a view to shortening the length of Convention proceedings and strengthening their judicial character by, *inter alia*, abolishing the Committee of Ministers' adjudicative role.[13]

Following the entry into force on 1 November 1998 of Protocol No. 11, the part-time Commission and Court were replaced by a single, permanent Court, established pursuant to Article 19 of the Convention. As will be seen below, individuals can now bring their Convention complaints directly before the Court.

The Court is presided over by its President, who is also one of the judges of the Court. The functions of the President include representing the Court and issuing practice directions.[14] The President is assisted by two Vice Presidents,[15] who are also judges. The President and his or her deputies are elected by the plenary Court for a period of three years; they may be re-elected.[16] The expression "plenary Court" means "the European Court of Human Rights sitting in plenary session",[17] i.e. a meeting attended by all the judges. The plenary Court meets at least once a year to discuss administrative matters but it does not perform judicial functions. It deals with internal administrative matters which include, *inter alia*, the adoption of the Rules of Court,[18] the election of the President and the Vice Presidents of the Court, the setting up of the Sections, and the election of the Presidents of Sections and the Registrar and his or her deputy/ies. At this stage, it is important to know that

---

12   More information on the historical background of the Convention institutions can be found at
     http://www.echr.coe.int/ECHR/EN/Header/The+Court/The+Court/History+of+the+Court/
     For a review of the practice and procedure of the Commission, see D.J. Harris, M. O'Boyle and C.
     Warbrick *"Law of the European Convention on Human Rights"*, Butterworths, 1995, (hereinafter
     referred to as "Harris, O'Boyle and Warbrick"), p. 571 *et seq.* See also M. Janis, R. Kay, A. Bradley,
     European Human Rights Law Text and Materials, Oxford University Press, 1995, p. 30.
13   More history of the reform can be found in the Explanatory Report to Protocol No. 11 at
     http://conventions.coe.int/Treaty/en/Reports/Html/155.htm
14   For information on practice directions see Section 1.6.4 below.
15   Rule 8 § 1 of the Rules of Court.
16   Article 26 of the Convention. See also Rule 8 § 1 of the Rules of Court.
17   Rule 1 (b) of the Rules of Court.
18   For information on the Rules of Court see Section 1.6.3 below.

the Court is divided into five Sections.[19] When a Section examines an application, it does so either in a formation of seven judges (a "Chamber"), or in a formation of three judges (a "Committee").[20]

The Court's powers and duties are best described by the Court itself in its case-law:

> "...its duty, according to Article 19 of the Convention, is to ensure the observance of the engagements undertaken by the Contracting States to the Convention. In particular, it is not its function to deal with errors of fact or of law allegedly committed by a national court unless and in so far as they may have infringed rights and freedoms protected by the Convention."[21]

Although the Court does not have the powers to examine *ex officio* the legislation or the functioning of the judiciary in the Contracting Parties, it can examine such issues as part of its examination of a case before it.

One of the most widely held misconceptions about the Court is that it is a court of appeal with powers to review and quash decisions and judgments of domestic courts of the Contracting Parties. The Court has no such powers; it cannot quash or revise decisions and judgments of domestic courts.[22] The reason why the Court is perceived by many as a court of appeal may be due to the fact that the Court can only examine allegations of breaches of the Convention after those allegations have first been examined by domestic courts. In other words, and as described in detail below,[23] a potential applicant must first give an opportunity to national authorities – usually its domestic court system – to remedy his or her Convention grievances by exhausting domestic remedies in the Contracting Party against which he or she wishes to lodge an application with the Court. The requirement to exhaust domestic remedies is also a logical consequence of the Convention's main aspiration to achieve a "collective enforcement" of the rights guaranteed in the Convention.[24]

---

19 The fifth Section was created on 1 April 2006.
20 See Section 1.5 below.
21 See *P.G. and J.H. v. the United Kingdom*, no. 44787/98, 25 September 2001, § 76.
22 See Myjer, E., Mol, N., Kempees, P., van Steijn, A., and Bockwinkel, J. "Introduire une plainte auprès de la Cour européenne des Droits de d'Homme: onze malentendus fréquents" in *Annales du droit luxembourgeois*, volume 14-2004, p. 11 *et seq.* (Bruyland, Bruxelles, 2005); see Appendix No. 5 for a copy of this article in English.
23 See Section 2.4 below.
24 See the Preamble to the Convention.

Textbox i   *Dates of Ratification of the European Convention on Human Rights and Additional Protocols as of 26 June 2006*[25]

Dates of entry into force

States	Convention CETS No. 005	Protocol No. 1 CETS No. 009	Protocol No. 4 CETS No. 046	Protocol No. 6 CETS No. 114	Protocol No. 7 CETS No. 117	Protocol No. 12 CETS No. 177	Protocol No. 13 CETS No. 187
Albania	02/10/96	02/10/96	02/10/96	01/10/00	01/01/97	01/04/05	
Andorra	22/01/96			01/02/96			01/07/03
Armenia	26/04/02	26/04/02	26/04/02	01/10/03	01/07/02	01/04/05	
Austria	03/09/58	03/09/58	18/09/69	01/03/85	01/11/88		01/05/04
Azerbaijan	15/04/02	15/04/02	15/04/02	01/05/02	01/07/02		
Belgium	14/06/55	14/06/55	21/09/70	01/01/99			01/10/03
Bosnia and Herzegovina	12/07/02	12/07/02	12/07/02	01/08/02	01/10/02	01/04/05	01/11/03
Bulgaria	07/09/92	07/09/92	04/11/00	01/10/99	01/02/01		01/07/03
Croatia	05/11/97	05/11/97	05/11/97	01/12/97	01/02/98	01/04/05	01/07/03
Cyprus	06/10/62	06/10/62	03/10/89	01/02/00	01/12/00	01/04/05	01/07/03
Czech Republic	01/01/93	01/01/93	01/01/93	01/01/93	01/01/93		01/11/04
Denmark	03/09/53	18/05/54	02/05/68	01/03/85	01/11/88		01/07/03
Estonia	16/04/96	16/04/96	16/04/96	01/05/98	01/07/96		01/06/04
Finland	10/05/90	10/05/90	10/05/90	01/06/90	01/08/90	01/04/05	01/03/05
France	03/05/74	03/05/74	03/05/74	01/03/86	01/11/88		
Georgia	20/05/99	07/06/02	13/04/00	01/05/00	01/07/00	01/04/05	01/09/03
Germany	03/09/53	13/02/57	01/06/68	01/08/89			01/02/05
Greece	28/11/74	28/11/74		01/10/98	01/11/88		01/06/05
Hungary	05/11/92	05/11/92	05/11/92	01/12/92	01/02/93		01/11/03
Iceland	03/09/53	18/05/54	02/05/68	01/06/87	01/11/88		01/03/05
Ireland	03/09/53	18/05/54	29/10/68	01/07/94	01/11/01		01/07/03
Italy	26/10/55	26/10/55	27/05/82	01/01/89	01/02/92		
Latvia	27/06/97	27/06/97	27/06/97	01/06/99	01/09/97		

25 Source:
http://www.echr.coe.int/ECHR/EN/Header/Basic+Texts/Basic+Texts/Dates+of+ratification+of+the+European+Convention+on+Human+Rights+and+Additional+Protocols/

States	Convention CETS No. 005	Protocol No. 1 CETS No. 009	Protocol No. 4 CETS No. 046	Protocol No. 6 CETS No. 114	Protocol No. 7 CETS No. 117	Protocol No. 12 CETS No. 177	Protocol No. 13 CETS No. 187
Liechtenstein	08/09/82	14/11/95		01/12/90	01/05/05		01/07/03
Lithuania	20/06/95	24/05/96	20/06/95	01/08/99	01/09/95		01/05/04
Luxembourg	03/09/53	18/05/54	02/05/68	01/03/85	01/07/89		
Malta	23/01/67	23/01/67	05/06/02	01/04/91	01/04/03		01/07/03
Moldova	12/09/97	12/09/97	12/09/97	01/10/97	01/12/97		
Monaco	30/11/05		30/11/05	01/12/05	01/02/05		01/03/06
Netherlands	31/08/54	31/08/54	23/06/82	01/05/86		01/04/05	
Norway	03/09/53	18/05/54	02/05/68	01/11/88	01/01/89		01/12/05
Poland	19/01/93	10/10/94	10/10/94	01/11/00	01/03/03		
Portugal	09/11/78	09/11/78	09/11/78	01/11/86			01/02/04
Romania	20/06/94	20/06/94	20/06/94	01/07/94	01/09/94		01/08/03
Russia	05/05/98	05/05/98	05/05/98		01/08/98		
San Marino	22/03/89	22/03/89	22/03/89	01/04/89	01/06/89	01/04/05	01/08/03
Serbia	03/03/04	03/03/04	03/03/04	01/04/04	01/06/04	01/04/05	01/07/04
Slovakia	01/01/93	01/01/93	01/01/93	01/01/93	01/01/93		01/12/05
Slovenia	28/06/94	28/06/94	28/06/94	01/07/94	01/09/94		01/04/04
Spain	04/10/79	27/11/90		01/03/85			
Sweden	03/09/53	18/05/54	02/05/68	01/03/85	01/11/88		01/08/03
Switzerland	28/11/74			01/11/87	01/11/88		01/07/03
The former Yugoslav Republic of Macedonia	10/04/97	10/04/97	10/04/97	01/05/97	01/07/97		01/11/04
Turkey	18/05/54	18/05/54		01/12/03			
Ukraine	11/09/97	11/09/97	11/09/97	01/05/00	01/12/97		01/07/03
United Kingdom	03/09/53	18/05/54		01/06/99			01/02/04

1.3 Protocol No. 14

Despite the changes brought about by Protocol No. 11, by the beginning of the 21st century the Court had already become unable to deal satisfactorily with its increasing case load. At the end of 2003, some 65,000 applications were pending before the Court. Moreover, the percentage of applications terminated without a ruling on the merits, usually because they were declared inadmissible, stood at more than 90%.

The second largest group of cases concerned so-called repetitive or clone cases, i.e. cases that derive from the same structural cause which has led the Court in earlier judgments to find a breach of the Convention. A typical repetitive case, for instance, concerns complaints under Article 6 regarding excessive length of domestic court proceedings. Some 60% of the 703 judgments adopted by the Court in 2003, and 35% of the 718 judgments adopted in 2004 concerned such cases.

In order to guarantee the long-term effectiveness of the Court, the European Ministerial Conference on Human Rights, held in Rome in November 2000 to mark the 50th anniversary of the signing of the Convention, called on the Committee of Ministers to "...initiate, as soon as possible, a thorough study of the different possibilities and options with a view to ensuring the effectiveness of the Court...".[26] Subsequently, the Steering Committee for Human Rights (CDDH, *le Comité directeur pour les droits de l'homme*), which was entrusted by the Committee of Ministers with the drafting of a new Protocol to help the Court overcome the difficulties it was facing, set up its own Reflection Group on the Reinforcement of the Human Rights Protection Mechanism (GDR, *Groupe de réflexion sur le renforcement du mécanisme de protection des droits de l'homme*). The CDDH sent the Committee of Ministers its final activity report in April 2004 containing the draft amending protocol to the Convention. Subsequently, the Committee of Ministers, at the 114th ministerial session in May 2004, adopted the amending protocol as well as a declaration on "Ensuring the effectiveness of the implementation of the European Convention on Human Rights at national and European levels". In that declaration, Member States recognised the urgency of the reform, and committed themselves to ratifying Protocol No. 14 within two years. The text of the amending protocol was opened for signature by Council of Europe Member States, signatory to the European Convention on Human Rights, on 13 May 2004. At the time of writing, Protocol No. 14 had been signed by all

---

26 For a fuller history of Protocol No. 14 see the Explanatory Report to that Protocol in Appendix No. 18. It can also be accessed at http://conventions.coe.int/Treaty/EN/Reports/Html/194.htm

the Contracting Parties and ratified by 41.[27] As it is an amending protocol, it needs to be ratified by all the Contracting Parties before it can enter into force. Protocol No. 14 can be consulted in Appendix No. 2.[28]

Unlike Protocol No. 11, Protocol No. 14 makes no radical changes to the control system of the Convention. Rather, its main purpose is to improve the functioning of the existing system by giving the Court the procedural means and flexibility it needs to process applications in a timely fashion, while allowing it to concentrate on the most important cases which require in-depth examination. To achieve these ends, it introduces amendments in three main areas:

- reinforcement of the Court's filtering capacity in respect of the mass of unmeritorious applications;

- a new admissibility criterion (containing two safeguard clauses) concerning cases in which the applicant has not suffered a significant disadvantage; and

- measures for dealing with repetitive cases.[29]

The changes brought about by Protocol No. 14, in so far as they fall within the scope of the present *Handbook*, will be dealt with in subsequent sections.

1.4 The Judges and the Registry of the Court

1.4.1 The Judges

The Court consists of a number of judges equal to the number of the Contracting Parties.[30] Currently there are 45 judges.[31] There is no restriction on the number of judges of the same nationality.[32] The judges sit on the Court

---

27 A *Chart of Signatures and Ratifications* is available on the Council of Europe's Web site at http://conventions.coe.int/Treaty/Commun/ChercheSig.asp?NT=194&CM=8&DF=6/5/2006&CL=ENG

28 Protocol No. 14 can also be consulted at
    http://conventions.coe.int/Treaty/Commun/QueVoulezVous.asp?NT=194&CM=8&DF=22/08/2005&CL=ENG

29 Paragraphs 35-36 of the Explanatory Report.

30 Article 20 of the Convention.

31 A current list of judges may be consulted at
    http://www.echr.coe.int/ECHR/EN/Header/The+Court/The+Court/Composition+of+the+Plenary+Court/

32 For example, the present judge elected in respect of Liechtenstein is a national of Austria.

in their personal capacity and do not represent the State Party of which they are a national, or any other State.

Judges are elected by the Parliamentary Assembly of the Council of Europe to sit for a period of six years and may be re-elected. They retire when they reach the age of 70. Following the entry into force of Protocol No. 14, however, new judges will be elected for a non-renewable term of nine years.

Pursuant to Rules 24 § 2 (b) and 26 § 1 (a) of the Rules of Court, judges are required to attend Grand Chamber and Chamber deliberations in cases introduced against the Contracting Party in respect of which they are elected.[33] In case a judge is unable to sit on the case, for reasons set out in Rule 28 of the Rules of Court, the judge in question is required to give notice to the President of the Chamber. The President of the Chamber will then invite the Contracting Party to indicate whether it wishes to appoint another judge of the Court or an *ad hoc* judge.[34]

Judges also act as judge rapporteurs and, with the assistance of Registry lawyers, examine the applications introduced with the Court.[35] The President of the Section to which the case has been assigned designates judge rapporteurs.[36] The identity of a judge rapporteur in a particular case is never disclosed to the parties.

1.4.2 The Registry

The Registry of the Court is staffed by lawyers ("legal secretaries"[37]), administrative and technical staff and translators. The task of the Registry is to provide legal and administrative support to the Court in the exercise of its judicial functions. Within the Registry there are 20 legal divisions. At the present time there are approximately 220 lawyers and 130 other support staff[38] in the legal divisions.

All Registry lawyers are employees of the Council of Europe who have been recruited on the basis of open competitions and appointed by the Secretary

---

33 For the purposes of this *Handbook*, such judges will be referred to as "national judges".
34 Rule 29 of the Rules of Court. Following the entry into force of Protocol No. 14, the President of the Court will choose a person from a list submitted by the relevant Contracting Party to sit in the capacity of judge; see Article 6 of Protocol No. 14.
35 See Section 1.7 below.
36 Rule 49 §§ 2-3 of the Rules of Court.
37 Article 25 of the Convention.
38 The organisation chart of the Registry can be consulted at
    http://www.echr.coe.int/NR/rdonlyres/F213BF94-1A48-41CE-8A43-
    70D0EDDD4EE2/0/OrganisationChart.pdf

General of the Council of Europe. Their knowledge of the national law and the language of the Contracting Party as well as their knowledge of the official languages of the Council of Europe, i.e. English and French, play a central role in their recruitment. Members of the Registry do not represent any State and they are expected to adhere to strict conditions of independence and impartiality.

The Registry lawyers are responsible for preparing case files for examination by the Court. Their responsibilities therefore include handling all communication with the applicants relating to the complaints. Most of their time, however, is spent drafting the Court's decisions and judgments under the instructions of the judge rapporteurs. Registry lawyers are also responsible for carrying out research – mostly relating to the domestic law of the Contracting Parties – on behalf of the judges and attending deliberations.

At the Head of the Registry stands the Registrar of the Court who functions under the authority of the President of the Court. The Registrar is assisted by two Deputy Registrars. They are elected by the plenary Court.[39]

1.5 Structure of the Court

Each application introduced with the Court is dealt with by one of three formations:[40] the Grand Chamber, a Chamber or a Committee. These are the so-called decision bodies of the Court.

1.5.1 The Grand Chamber

The Grand Chamber consists of 17 judges and at least three substitute judges.[41] It includes the President and the Vice Presidents of the Court, the Presidents of the Sections, and the national judge. In cases referred to the Grand Chamber pursuant to Article 30, the Grand Chamber also includes members of the Chamber that relinquished jurisdiction. However, in cases referred to the Grand Chamber under Article 43, the Grand Chamber does not include any judge who participated in the original Chamber's deliberations on the admissibility or merits of the case, except for the President of that Chamber and the national judge. The judges and the substitute judges who

---

39   Rules 15 and 16 of the Rules of Court.
40   Article 27 of the Convention.
41   Rule 24 § 1 of the Rules of Court.

are to complete the Grand Chamber in each case referred to it are designated from among the remaining judges by a drawing of lots. In the performance of its duties, the Grand Chamber is assisted by the Registrar or a Deputy Registrar of the Court.

The Grand Chamber may deal with an application in two situations. Firstly, if a case which is pending before a Chamber raises a serious question affecting the interpretation of the Convention or the Protocols, or where the resolution of a question before the Chamber might have a result inconsistent with a judgment previously delivered by the Court, the Chamber in question may, at any time before it has rendered its judgment, relinquish jurisdiction in favour of the Grand Chamber, unless one of the parties to the case objects within one month of notification of the Chamber's intention.[42] Such cases may, for example, concern issues which have not been dealt with by the Court previously. They also include cases in which the Court is considering reversing earlier case-law.

The second situation where the Grand Chamber may consider an application is when one of the parties to the case (or indeed both Parties) requests, within a period of three months from the date of delivery of the judgment, that the case be referred to the Grand Chamber.[43] Roughly speaking, this may be compared to an "appeal" in a national jurisdiction.

Finally, the Grand Chamber is also empowered to give advisory opinions on questions concerning the interpretation of the Convention and its Protocols.[44] However, at the time of writing, only one request for an advisory opinion has ever been made. It was rejected unanimously by the Grand Chamber on 2 June 2004 on the grounds that the request did not come within the Court's advisory competence.[45]

Given the fact that only cases of a rather extraordinary nature can come before the Grand Chamber, it deals with far fewer cases than the Court's Sections. For example, in 2005 the four Sections adopted a total of 1,093 judgments whereas the Grand Chamber adopted only 12. In the same period, the Grand Chamber adopted 2 admissibility decisions whereas the Sections adopted 1,420 such decisions.[46]

---

42 See Article 30 of the Convention and Rule 72 of the Rules of Court.
43 See Section 9.2 below.
44 See Articles 47-49 of the Convention.
45 For the press release concerning the Grand Chamber's decision and the links to the decision, consult http://www.echr.coe.int/Eng/Press/2004/June/DecisiononAdvisoryopinion.htm
46 See the Court's Survey of Activities 2005 at http://www.echr.coe.int/NR/rdonlyres/4753F3E8-3AD0-42C5-B294-0F2A68507FC0/0/SurveyofActivities2005.pdf

1.5.2 The Sections and the Chambers

As mentioned above, the Court is divided into five Sections. Each judge is a member of a Section. The Sections, which are set up by the plenary Court for a period of three years, are geographically and gender balanced and they reflect the different legal systems of the Contracting Parties.[47] Each Section has its own President, assisted or replaced where necessary, by a Vice President. Section Presidents are elected by the plenary Court whereas Vice Presidents are elected by the Sections themselves.[48]

However, a case brought before a Section is not dealt with by the full Section but by a Chamber of seven judges[49] formed from among the judges in the Section.[50] Each Chamber includes the Section President and the national judge concerned. The other five members of the Chamber are designated from among the remaining members of the Section. The remaining judges who are not designated as members of the Chamber sit in the case as substitute judges. Thus, depending on the parties to the cases on the agenda of a particular Section meeting, a number of different Chambers will be constituted during that meeting.

Where possible – depending on the case load of the Section – an application introduced against a particular Contracting Party will be assigned to the Section which includes among its members the judge elected in respect of that Contracting Party, i.e. the national judge. If such a course of action has not been taken, the national judge in question sits as an *ex officio* member of the Chamber.[51]

In the performance of its duties, each Section is assisted by a senior member of the Registry, i.e. the Section Registrar. Section Registrars are assisted by Deputy Section Registrars.

Sections deal with Inter-State cases[52] and cases lodged by individuals which are not clearly inadmissible.[53] They meet once a week to deliberate on the cases assigned to them. Section deliberations are confidential and are not attended by anyone other than the judges and members of the Registry.

---

47 A list showing the compositions of the five Sections may be consulted at http://www.echr.coe.int/ECHR/EN/Header/The+Court/The+Court/Composition+of+the+Sections/
48 Rule 8 §§ 1-2 of the Rules of Court.
49 After the entry into force of Protocol No. 14, and at the request of the plenary Court, the Committee of Ministers may, by a unanimous decision and for a fixed period, reduce to five the number of judges of the Chambers. See Article 6 of Protocol No. 14 amending Article 27 of the Convention.
50 Article 27 of the Convention. See also Rule 26 of the Rules of Court.
51 Rule 26 § 1 (a) of the Rules of Court.
52 I.e. cases introduced by a Contracting Party against another Contracting Party pursuant to Article 33 of the Convention. Such applications are very rare; at the time of writing, there had only been 20 such applications.
53 For admissibility and related issues, see Section 2 below.

1.5.3 The Committees

Under Article 27 § 1, Committees of three judges are established within each Section for a period of twelve months, by rotation among its members.[54] Committees deal with cases that are clearly inadmissible under one or more of the grounds set out in Article 35 and which do not require further examination. Committees cannot deal with Inter-State cases. Committees are also empowered to strike out applications pursuant to Article 37. A case can be declared inadmissible if the applicant is found to have failed to satisfy the grounds of admissibility which are set out in Article 35 of the Convention, whereas a case can be struck out of the Court's list of cases pursuant to Article 37 of the Convention if the applicant does not intend to pursue his or her application, if the matter has been resolved, or if for any other reason established by the Court it considers that it is no longer justified to continue the examination of the application.[55] Committee decisions are final and cannot be appealed. Such decisions must however be taken unanimously; if there is no unanimity amongst the three judges, the Committee will refer the case to a Chamber to decide on admissibility and, if applicable, to rule on the merits. Committees deal with the vast majority of applications lodged with the Court. In 2005 a total of 26,360 applications were declared inadmissible by Committees. During the same period, Committees also decided to strike out a total number of 416 applications.

Protocol No. 14 will bring two important changes to the composition and powers of the Committees. Single-judge formations, as well as Committees of three judges, will be authorized to deal with the type of cases currently handled by Committees of three judges, i.e. cases that appear to be clearly inadmissible.[56] Furthermore, Committees of three judges will be empowered to render merits judgments in cases where the underlying issue is already the subject of well-established case-law of the Court,[57] i.e. repetitive cases. The purpose of empowering Committees to deal with repetitive cases is to enable the Chambers to devote more time to cases that warrant in-depth examination.

---

54   See also Rule 27 § 2 of the Rules of Court.
55   For strike out related issues see Section 8.2 below.
56   When sitting in a single-judge formation, however, a judge will not examine any application against the Contracting Party in respect of which he or she has been elected; see Article 6 of Protocol No. 14.
57   Article 8 of Protocol No. 14.

1.6 Instruments of the Court

1.6.1 The European Convention on Human Rights

As pointed out earlier, the Convention entered into force on 3 September 1953. It "...represents the minimum human rights standards which could be agreed by European states more than 50 years ago" and is primarily concerned with protecting civil and political rights, rather than economic, social, or cultural rights.[58]

The Convention consists of three Sections and a total of 59 Articles. The rights and freedoms are listed in Section 1 (Articles 1-18); Section 2 (Articles 19-51) deals with the establishment of the Court as well as its duties and powers; Section 3 (Articles 52-59) contains miscellaneous provisions concerning such issues as territorial application, reservations, denunciations, signature, and ratification. The Convention is included as Appendix No. 1 of this *Handbook* and can also be accessed online.[59]

The substantive rights and freedoms guaranteed by the Convention are set out in Articles 2-14 of the Convention. They are:

Article 2 Right to life

Article 3 Prohibition of torture

Article 4 Prohibition of slavery and forced labour

Article 5 Right to liberty and security

Article 6 Right to a fair trial

Article 7 No punishment without law

Article 8 Right to respect for private and family life

Article 9 Freedom of thought, conscience and religion

Article 10 Freedom of expression

Article 11 Freedom of assembly and association

Article 12 Right to marry

Article 13 Right to an effective remedy

Article 14 Prohibition of discrimination.

---

58 P. Leach, *Taking a Case to the European Court of Human Rights*, 2nd edition, Oxford University Press, 2005 (hereinafter referred to as "Leach"), p. 5 *et seq.*

59 The Convention and its Protocols can be accessed at:
http://www.echr.coe.int/ECHR/EN/Header/Basic+Texts/Basic+Texts/The+European+Convention+on+Human+Rights+and+its+Protocols/

These Articles are declaratory in the sense that they do not, on their own, impose any obligations on the Contracting Parties. For example, Article 3 of the Convention simply states that "No one shall be subjected to torture or to inhuman and degrading treatment or punishment"; it does not expressly bestow on the Contracting Parties an obligation to ensure, for example, that no one is subjected to torture. Rather, as some commentators have stated, "[i]t is Article 1 which transforms this declaration of rights into a set of obligations for the States which ratify the Convention".[60] Pursuant to Article 1 of the Convention, Contracting Parties undertake to secure to everyone within their jurisdiction the rights and freedoms set out in the Convention. Difficulties which have arisen in establishing the boundaries of the Contracting Parties' "jurisdiction" within the meaning of this Article have been resolved by the Court in its case-law.[61]

Under Article 32, the Court's jurisdiction extends to all matters concerning the interpretation and application of the Convention and the Protocols. Because the Court regards the Convention as a "living instrument",[62] it interprets and defines Convention rights in light of present-day conditions, not conditions obtaining when it was drafted more than 50 years ago. In the same vein, the Court strives to interpret and apply the Convention "in a manner which renders its rights practical and effective, not theoretical and illusory".[63]

For instance, the Court held the following in its judgment in the case of *Christine Goodwin v. the United Kingdom*:

> "since the Convention is first and foremost a system for the protection of human rights, the Court must have regard to the changing conditions within the respondent State and within Contracting States generally and respond, for example, to any evolving convergence as to the standards to be achieved".[64]

The *Goodwin* case provides a good example of what is meant by *interpretation in light of present day conditions*. *Goodwin* concerned the legal status of transsexuals in the United Kingdom. It was the increased acceptance among Contracting Parties in respect of transsexuality which had a direct bearing on the Court's finding of a violation of Article 8 on a matter which had previously not been found to breach the Convention. Naturally, the

---

60 See C. Ovey & R. C.A. White, *Jacobs & White: The European Convention on Human Rights*, 3rd edition, Oxford University Press, 2002 (hereinafter referred to as "Jacobs & White") at p. 14 *et seq.*

61 The issue of jurisdiction within the meaning of Article 1 of the Convention will be examined in Section 2.3.2 (b) below.

62 See, among other authorities, *Mamatkulov and Askarov v. Turkey* [GC], nos. 46827/99 and 46951/99, 4 February 2005, § 121.

63 *Ibid.*

64 *Christine Goodwin v. the United Kingdom* [GC], no. 28957/95, 11 July 2002, § 74, and the cases cited therein.

evolving ethical and legal standards of the Council of Europe will have an equal bearing on Article 3. For instance, it is possible that official conduct that was formerly not considered to be severe enough to reach the threshold for a finding of a violation of Article 3 might in light of current standards be considered to constitute ill-treatment in breach of this Article. Similarly, conduct that was formerly considered to constitute merely inhuman or degrading treatment might under current standards be regarded by the Court as torture, the most severe type of breach of the Article.[65] Applicants should keep this in mind when assessing the merits of their cases, and of course, in arguing them before the Court.

1.6.2 The Protocols

Following the entry into force of the Convention in 1953, a number of Protocols have been adopted within the Council of Europe by virtue of which some of the Contracting Parties have undertaken to protect a number of additional rights and freedoms within their jurisdictions. Protocol Nos. 2, 3, 5, 8, 9, 10, 11, and 14 are Protocols which amend Convention proceedings and do not include any additional rights or freedoms. The remaining Protocols, and the rights and freedoms they guarantee, are as follows:

- Protocol No.1, which entered into force on 18 May 1954: protection of property, the right to education, and the right to free elections.

- Protocol No. 4, which entered into force on 2 May 1968: prohibition of imprisonment for debt, freedom of movement, prohibition of expulsion of nationals, and the prohibition of collective expulsion of aliens.

- Protocol No. 6, which entered into force on 1 March 1985, provides for the abolition of the death penalty but includes a provision to allow the Contracting Parties to prescribe the death penalty in their legislation in time of war or of imminent threat of war.

- Protocol No. 7, which entered into force on 1 November 1988: procedural safeguards relating to expulsion of aliens, the right of appeal in criminal matters, the right to compensation for wrongful conviction, the right not to be tried or punished twice for the same offence, and equality between spouses.

---

65 The types of treatment prohibited by Article 3 of the Convention are examined in detail in Appendix No. 10.

- Protocol No. 12, which entered into force on 1 April 2005: created a free-standing prohibition of discrimination. Unlike Article 14 of the Convention, which prohibits discrimination in the enjoyment of "the rights and freedoms set forth in the Convention", Protocol No. 12 prohibits discrimination in the enjoyment of "any right set forth by law" and not just those rights guaranteed under the Convention.

- Protocol No. 13, which entered into force on 1 July 2003: abolished the death penalty in all circumstances.

Applicants should note that the Protocols mentioned above have not been ratified by all the Contracting Parties. It follows that a complaint made under an Article of one of the Protocols against a State which has not ratified that Protocol will be declared inadmissible.[66] The table of *Dates of Entry into Force of the Convention and its Protocols,* reproduced in *Textbox i* above, should be consulted. Also, this table is regularly updated on the Council of Europe's website.[67]

1.6.3 The Rules of Court

The Rules of Court, which are frequently referred to throughout this *Handbook*, set out in greater detail than the Convention itself the organisation and the functioning of the Court as well as the Court's procedure. They are indispensable for any applicant or lawyer wishing to make an application to the Court and must be consulted before making the application and throughout the course of the proceedings. The Rules of Court are found in Appendix No. 19 and they can also be accessed online.[68]

The Rules of Court are prepared by the Court and they enter into force after their adoption by the plenary Court. The Rules of Court which are in force at the time of writing were adopted by the plenary Court on 7 November 2005 and entered into force on 1 December 2005. It must be noted that the Rules of Court are continually revised in the light of the Court's evolving practice and it is expected that they will be subjected to substantial amendments in order to facilitate the entry into force of Protocol No. 14.

---

66 The compatibility of applications with the provisions of the Convention and the Protocols will be dealt with in Section 2.3 below.

67 http://www.echr.coe.int/ECHR/EN/Header/Basic+Texts/Basic+Texts/Dates+of+ratification+of+the+European+Convention+on+Human+Rights+and+Additional+Protocols/

68 The Rules of Court may be accessed at . http://www.echr.coe.int/NR/rdonlyres/D1EB31A8-4194-436E-987E-65AC8864BE4F/0/RulesOfCourt.pdf

1.6.4 Practice Directions

The President of the Court has the power to issue practice directions in relation to such issues as the appearance of parties at hearings and the filing of pleadings and other documents.[69] Practice directions, which supplement the Rules of Court, are described by the Registry of the Court as documents "to provide guidance to the parties on various aspects of their contacts with the Court and at the same time to introduce more standardised procedures with a view to facilitating the Court's processing of the cases". Observance by applicants and their legal representatives of the practice directions will speed up the examination of their applications by avoiding unnecessary and time consuming correspondence with the Court and will prevent an application from being rejected for failure to comply with procedural requirements. These practice directions are reprinted in Appendix No. 3.[70]

To date, three practice directions have been issued. They are:

i.   the practice direction on "Requests for Interim Measures", issued on 5 March 2003;

ii. the practice direction on "Institution of Proceedings", issued on 1 November 2003; and finally,

iii. the practice direction on "Written Pleadings", issued on 1 November 2003.

1.6.5 Decisions and Reports of the Commission and Decisions and Judgments of the Court[71]

As one commentator has suggested:

> "There is no formal doctrine of precedent as such within the Convention system. The Court does not consider itself to be bound by its previous judgments, although it is in the interests of legal certainty, foreseeability and equality before the law that it should not depart, without good reason, from precedents laid down in previous cases".[72]

However, the fact remains that the Court speaks through its judgments. The development of the Court's case-law has parallels with the development of the common law in Anglo-Saxon legal systems; in formulating its judgments,

---

69   Rule 32 of the Rules of Court.
70   The practice directions are available on the Council of Europe's Web site at:
     http://www.echr.coe.int/ECHR/EN/Header/Basic+Texts/Basic+Texts/Practice+directions/
71   Although, strictly speaking, Decisions and Reports of the Commission and Decisions and Judgments of the Court are not "Instruments of the Court", it is appropriate to deal with them in this sub-section.
72   See Leach, p. 165. See also, *Beard v. the United Kingdom* [GC], no. 24882/94, 18 January 2001, § 81.

the Court – very much like a court in a common law system – reviews its previous decisions and judgments as well as the decisions of the Commission and applies them to similar situations.

Furthermore, as pointed out above, pursuant to Article 32 of the Convention, the Court's jurisdiction extends to all matters concerning the interpretation and application of the Convention and the Protocols in the course of which it takes into account present day conditions. As will be seen in subsequent parts of this *Handbook*, there is a very large body of case-law on Article 3 of the Convention. For example, the Court has read into this Article a positive obligation – which is not apparent from the wording of the Article itself – obliging Contracting Parties to carry out effective investigations into allegations of ill-treatment.[73] At first sight, Article 3 appears only to contain an obligation that a State ensure that its authorities refrain from inflicting ill-treatment, i.e. a negative obligation. Likewise, what constitutes torture, inhuman or degrading treatment or punishment can only be gathered from the case-law. Indeed, it would have been practically impossible for Article 3 to contain an exhaustive list of every conceivable form of treatment it prohibits.

For the reasons mentioned above, in every decision and judgment adopted by the Court, there will be references to, and quotations from, previous decisions and judgments of the Convention institutions. It is imperative, therefore, that practitioners acquaint themselves with the Convention case-law in order to be able to refer to pertinent decisions and judgments in support of their applications. The case-law of the Court and of the Commission can be searched with the help of the HUDOC database which is available on the Court's website.[74] In a number of Council of Europe Member States, important decisions and judgments are translated into the national language. Also, important decisions and judgments are published in English and French in the "Reports of Judgments and Decisions".[75]

Finally, it should be noted that the Court occasionally refers to decisions and judgments of other international human rights mechanisms and benefits from their experience. For example, in its judgments in the cases of *Timurtaş v. Turkey* and *Issa v. Turkey* the Court made extensive references to the jurisprudence of the Inter-American Court of Human Rights on the issue of forced disappearances and on the issue of jurisdiction, respectively.[76] Similarly, the Court's judgments also make references to the International

---

73 See Section 10.2.2 below.
74 www.echr.coe.int/echr. HUDOC is also available on CD-ROM and DVD format.
75 Published by Carl Heymanns Verlag KG.
76 See *Timurtaş v. Turkey*, no. 23531/94, 13 June 2000 § 80; *Issa v. Turkey*, no. 31821/96, 16 November 2004 § 71.

Covenant on Civil and Political Rights and the Human Rights Committee.[77] Of relevance for the purposes of the present *Handbook* is the fact that the Court also relies on reports prepared by the Council of Europe's European Committee for the Prevention of Torture and Inhuman or Degrading Treatment or Punishment (CPT) and reports prepared by non-governmental organisations (NGOs)[78] when establishing the facts of cases. For example, in cases concerning allegations of unsatisfactory prison conditions, the Court regularly relies on reports prepared by the CPT following that organisation's visits to prisons in the territory of the respondent Contracting Party.[79] Appendix No. 11 should be consulted for detailed information about the CPT.

1.7 Summary of Proceedings Before the Court

Each stage of the Convention proceedings will be dealt with in greater detail in subsequent sections of this *Handbook*. The purpose of the present section is to give the reader a general overview of these proceedings in outline form. It should be noted at the outset that although the Convention stipulates in Article 29 § 3 that, in principle, the decision on the admissibility of an application is taken separately from the decision on the merits, this is at present more the exception than the rule. At the present time and in anticipation of the entry into force of Protocol No. 14,[80] proceedings on admissibility and merits are conducted jointly in the vast majority of cases, thus saving time by omitting a separate decision on admissibility. When the Court decides to apply this "joint procedure", the parties are informed of the decision. The overview of the Court's procedure set out below takes this new practice into account.

---

77 See, most recently, *Hirst v. the United Kingdom (no.2)* [GC], no. 74025/01, 6 October 2005, § 27.
78 See, *inter alia, Van der Ven v. the Netherlands*, no. 50901/99, 4 February 2003.
79 See *Said v. the Netherlands*, no. 2345/02, 5 July 2005.
80 See Article 9 of Protocol No. 14.

Textbox ii[81]

EUROPEAN COURT OF HUMAN RIGHTS
COUR EUROPÉENNE DES DROITS DE L'HOMME

Case-processing flowchart

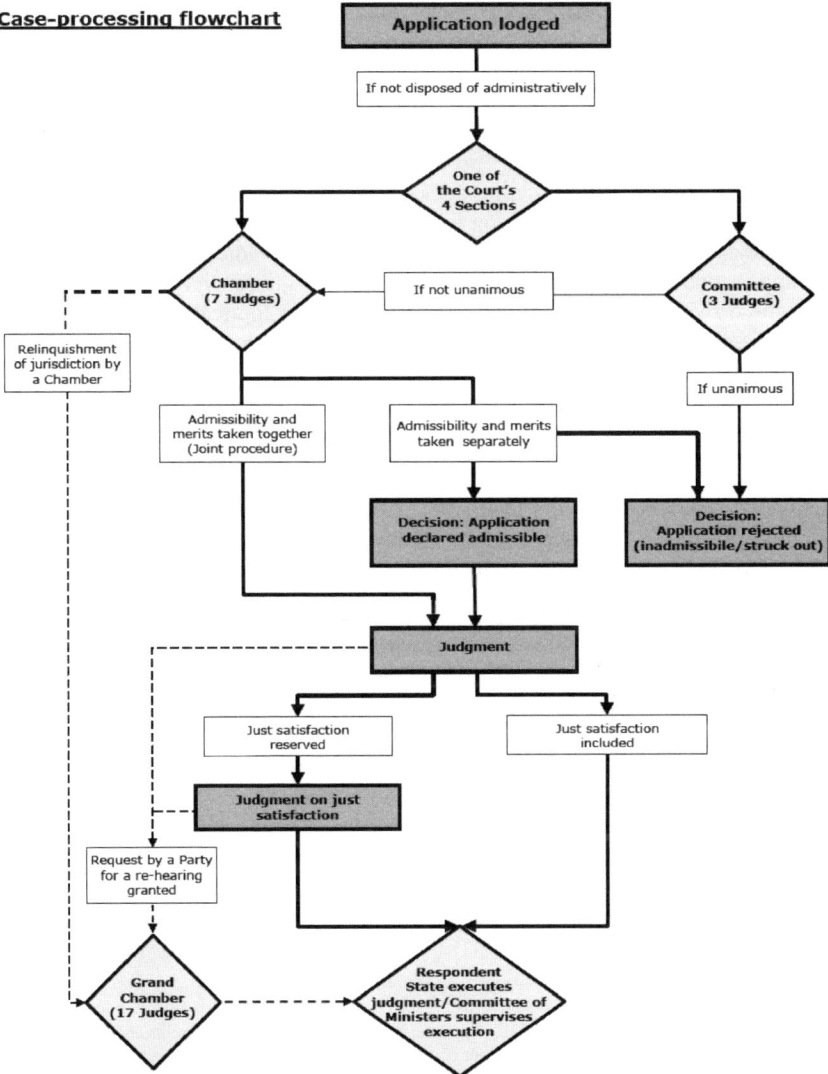

```
                        ┌─────────────────────────┐
                        │    Application lodged    │
                        └─────────────────────────┘
                                    │
                        ┌─────────────────────────┐
                        │ If not disposed of administratively │
                        └─────────────────────────┘
                                    │
                               One of
                             the Court's
                              4 Sections
```

One of the Court's 4 Sections

Chamber (7 Judges) — If not unanimous — Committee (3 Judges)

Relinquishment of jurisdiction by a Chamber

If unanimous

Admissibility and merits taken together (Joint procedure)

Admissibility and merits taken separately

Decision: Application declared admissible

Decision: Application rejected (inadmissibile/struck out)

Judgment

Just satisfaction reserved

Just satisfaction included

Judgment on just satisfaction

Request by a Party for a re-hearing granted

Grand Chamber (17 Judges)

Respondent State executes judgment/Committee of Ministers supervises execution

This flowchart indicates the progress of a case through the different judicial formations. In the interests of readability, it does not include certain stages in the procedure – such as communication of an application to the respondent State, consideration of a re-hearing request by the Panel of the Grand Chamber and friendly settlement negotiations.

---

81 Source: http://www.echr.coe.int/NR/rdonlyres/BA3F06A3-133C-4699-A25D-35E3C6A3D6F5/0/MicrosoftWordPROGRESS_OF_A_CASE.pdf

1.7.1 First Examination of the Application

Applications must be lodged using the Court's standard application form.[82] However, if there is a risk that the application cannot be prepared or completed before the end of the six-month period, it is important to note that an application may also be introduced by means of an introductory letter.[83] If an application is lodged in a document other than the Registry's standard application form and does not contain all the information required by that form, the Court will ask the applicant[84] to fill in the standard application form and send it to the Registry within six weeks together with the supporting documents. At this stage the application will also be given a number. The first digits in the application number before the forward-slash indicate the position of the application amongst the applications lodged in the same year. The digits after the forward-slash indicate the year in which the application was lodged. For example, application no. 123/05 is the 123rd application lodged in the year 2005.

If the applicant does not comply with the Court's request for a completed form and/or more information, the file will be destroyed by the Registry, i.e. it will be disposed of administratively within a year of the date of the Registry's letter because the Court will consider that the applicant has lost interest in pursuing the application. In the first six months of 2005, 9,448 applications were disposed of in this way.

Once the application is complete, it will be forwarded to the legal division of the Registry in which the lawyers who handle cases against the relevant Contracting Party are working. The application is then assigned to one of the Registry's lawyers who will be working as the case lawyer for that application. An examination of the application file will then be carried out and the application will be assigned to a decision body in one of the five Sections. In cases where the material submitted by the applicant on its own is sufficient to disclose that the application is inadmissible or should be struck out of the list[85] and also where such action can be taken "without further examination",[86] it will be registered as a "Committee case".[87] Otherwise the application will be registered as a "Chamber case", and a judge rapporteur will be appointed.[88]

---

82   Application forms may be downloaded at
http://www.echr.coe.int/ECHR/EN/Header/Applicants/Information+for+applicants/Application+form/
83   See Section 4.1 below for information on introductory letters and *Textbox vii* for a model hypothetical letter.
84   Or the applicant's lawyer if he or she is represented.
85   Rule 49 § 1 of the Rules of Court.
86   Article 28 of the Convention.
87   On 1 May 2006, 38,500 Committee cases were pending before the Court.
88   On 1 May 2006, 20,900 Chamber cases were pending before the Court. Also on 1 May 2006, 24,850 applications had not yet been allocated to a judicial formation.

1.7.2 Applications Declared Inadmissible by a Committee

If the application is registered as a Committee case, it will be dealt with by a Committee of three judges[89] who will in most cases declare the application inadmissible by a unanimous decision. The applicant will be informed of the decision by means of a letter which contains the briefest of indications as to the reasons.[90] Decisions on inadmissibility are final. If there is no unanimity amongst the judges, the application will be referred to a Chamber of seven judges within the same Section.

1.7.3 Examination by a Chamber

If the application is registered as a Chamber case, or if it is referred to the Chamber by a Committee as described above, the case will be examined by a Chamber.[91] Chamber decisions are taken by majority. The judge rapporteur assigned to the case may propose to the Chamber or to its President that notice of the application be given to the respondent Contracting Party[92] (more commonly referred to as "communication"). On average, an application may be expected to be communicated within 12 months after its introduction.[93]

If the Chamber or its President agrees to communicate the case, the Government of the State concerned will be invited to submit to the Court, usually within a period of twelve weeks, its written observations on the admissibility and merits of the case and to answer any questions which may be put to it. At the same time, the Government may also be invited to inform the Court of its position as to a possible friendly settlement of the case.[94]

Instead of communicating the case, the Chamber can also decide to declare the case inadmissible. That decision, which generally contains considerably more reasoning than the letter informing the applicant that his or her application was rejected by a Committee, will be communicated to the applicant and is final, i.e. it cannot be referred to the Grand Chamber.

---

89 As pointed out earlier, following the entry into force of Protocol No. 14, single-judge formations will deliberate and adopt such decisions. However, national judges will not have powers to deliberate such cases introduced against the Contracting Parties in respect of which they were elected.
90 See *Textbox x* for a sample letter informing the applicant of the decision of the Committee.
91 Article 29 § 1 of the Convention.
92 Rule 54 § 2 (b) of the Rules of Court.
93 See K. Reid, *A Practitioner's Guide to the European Convention on Human Rights*, 2nd edn., Sweet and Maxwell, 2004 (hereinafter referred to as "Reid"), at p. 17 *et seq.*
94 See Section 8.1 below.

If the case is communicated, the Court will forward the observations received from the Government to the applicant and will invite him or her to respond to the Government's arguments as well as to the Government's position on the issue of friendly settlement, if such a position was expressed. In addition, the applicant will be invited to submit his or her claims for just satisfaction under Article 41 of the Convention.[95] At this stage the applicant may also apply for free legal aid from the Court to cover his or her expenses or a part of them.[96]

Following the receipt of the parties' observations, the Chamber will deliberate on the case. If no friendly settlement is reached and the Chamber is of the view that the application is inadmissible, it will discontinue the joint procedure and issue a decision declaring the case inadmissible. Since such decisions are final, the parties cannot request the referral of the case to the Grand Chamber.

If, on the other hand, the Chamber considers that the application is admissible it will, under the joint procedure, immediately move on to the judgment stage. It will be presented with a draft judgment prepared on the instructions of the judge rapporteur in which the application will be declared admissible and where the Chamber concludes whether or not there has been a violation of the Articles of the Convention invoked by the applicant. Following the adoption of the judgment, the parties will have a period of three months within which to request a referral of the case to the Grand Chamber.[97] Any such request will be examined by the Panel of the Grand Chamber, whose decisions are final.

If no request for referral to the Grand Chamber has been made, the Government will be expected to pay the applicant, within three months of the date of the judgment, any amounts of just satisfaction awarded in respect of the applicant's costs and expenses and pecuniary and non-pecuniary damage. The Committee of Ministers will be responsible for the execution of the judgment.[98]

---

95 Rule 60 of the Rules of Court. See also Section 7 below.
96 Rule 91 of the Rules of Court. See also Section 1.9 below.
97 Article 43 of the Convention. See also Section 9.2 below.
98 See Section 9.3 below.

1.8 Legal Representation

The application form may be completed and submitted to the Court by the applicant him- or herself; in other words, an applicant does not have to be represented by a lawyer at this early stage of the proceedings. Legal representation will be required, however, "following notification of the application to the respondent Contracting Party",[99] i.e. after the application has been communicated. For example, in *Grimaylo v. Ukraine*,[100] the Court struck out the application from its list of cases because of the applicant's refusal to appoint a lawyer to represent him in the proceedings before the Court following the communication of the application to the respondent Government. Although Mr. Grimaylo insisted on representing himself or appointing his wife to represent him, the Court was of the opinion that a lawyer's participation was essential, given the complexity of the case from a legal and factual point of view.

As a general rule, the representative should be an advocate authorised to practise in any of the Contracting Parties and resident in the territory of one of them.[101] However, permission may be sought from the President of the Chamber allowing the applicant to represent him- or herself or for the appointment of a person other than an advocate.

Although legal representation is not required at the time of lodging the application, it is strongly recommended for a number of reasons. The most important reason, as pointed out above, is the risk that an application may be declared inadmissible by a Committee solely on the basis of the contents of the application form. Although the case lawyer in the Registry of the Court will usually give the applicant adequate opportunity to support his or her case with the necessary documentation, he or she cannot re-draft the application or the arguments set out in the application form – that is, if there are any. Indeed, it is not uncommon that application forms are submitted containing little or even no legal argumentation. Similarly, a legal representative who is retained at a later stage, after the application form has already been submitted to the Court, cannot re-draft the application or the arguments set out in the application form. As will be seen below in the section on admissibility, one of the grounds for inadmissibility is the "manifestly ill-founded" test applied to applicants' complaints.[102] An application may be deemed to be manifestly ill-founded, *inter alia*, if it is not supported by legal argumentation and/or

99   Rule 36 § 2 of the Rules of Court.
100   *Grimaylo v. Ukraine* (dec.), no. 69364/01, 7 February 2006
101   Rule 36 § 4 of the Rules of Court.
102   See Section 2.6 below.

sufficient evidence. A person without legal training may not be able to provide this. It must be emphasised here that once an application is declared inadmissible, there is virtually *nothing* an applicant can do to overturn that decision.[103]

In most countries that are parties to the Convention, a potential applicant without financial means will be able to obtain the services of a lawyer free of charge, to assist him or her with the application. Alternatively, in certain countries it may be possible to obtain legal aid from the national authorities. Furthermore, domestic legislation of some Contracting Parties allows lawyers to practise on a no-win, no-fee basis. Also in some countries, potential applicants may enter into agreements with their lawyers whereby they undertake to pay a percentage of any award made by the Court by way of just satisfaction pursuant to Article 41. Applicants may also be able to obtain legal assistance from non-governmental organisations (NGOs) with experience in human rights litigation.

In order to represent his or her client in Convention proceedings, the representative must submit to the Court a written authority or power of attorney. The Court's own standard authority form, a copy of which is reproduced below in *Textbox iii*,[104] is the most appropriate and practical one to use, but a power of attorney prepared by a notary public is also acceptable provided it expressly indicates that the advocate is authorised to represent his or her client in proceedings before the European Court of Human Rights.

If the applicant is represented, the Court will correspond with the representative and not with the applicant. Furthermore, it is the Court's policy to correspond with only one representative, even if the applicant is represented by more than one lawyer.

---

103 In some circumstances, if the reason for inadmissibility is the applicant's failure to exhaust domestic remedies, he or she may submit another application to the Court after having exhausted the relevant domestic remedy. This will only be possible, however, if the applicant does not, in the meantime, miss the deadline in domestic law to avail him or herself of that remedy. See also Section 2.4.2 (e) below.

104 It may be downloaded at
http://www.echr.coe.int/ECHR/EN/Header/Applicants/Information+for+applicants/Authority+Form/

Textbox iii   ***Form of Authority***[105]

EUROPEAN COURT OF HUMAN RIGHTS

AUTHORITY*
(Rule 36 of the Rules of Court)

I, ...

....

(name and address of applicant)

hereby authorise ....

....

....

(name, address and occupation of representative)

to represent me in the proceedings before the Europe and Court of Human Rights, and in any subsequent proceedings under the European Convention on Human Rights, concerning my application intorduced under Article 34 of the Convention against

....

(respondent State)

on ....

(date of letter of introduction)

....

(place and date)

....

(signature of applicant)

I hereby accept the above appointment

....

(signature of representative)

*   **This form <u>must</u> be competed and signed by any applicant wishing to be represented before the Court and by the lawyer or other person appointed.**

---

105   Source: http://www.echr.coe.int/NR/rdonlyres/001F1ADA-0F5A-4975-8B10-25D0C239865B/0/English.pdf

1.9 Legal Aid

If a decision has been taken to communicate the case, the Court will inform the applicant that he or she can apply for free legal aid under the Court's legal aid scheme for applicants who have insufficient means to pay for legal representation. The applicant will be invited to inform the Court as soon as possible whether an application for legal aid will be made, in which case the necessary forms will be sent to him or her. Requests for legal aid must be supported by a declaration of means, certified by the relevant domestic authorities, which will be indicated by the Court. The Court's *Declaration of Applicant's Means* form is reproduced below in *Textbox v.*

Legal aid will be granted to an applicant only where the President of the Chamber is satisfied:

(a) that it is necessary for the proper conduct of the case before the Chamber;

(b) that the applicant has insufficient means to meet all or part of the costs entailed.[106]

Legal aid may be granted to an unrepresented applicant only to cover reasonable expenses associated with the case, e.g. translation, postage, fax, stationery, etc. If the applicant is represented, the Court will also grant a specified sum in respect of the representative's fees. The Court's scale of *Legal Aid Fees* is reproduced below in *Textbox iv.*

---

106   Rule 92 of the Rules of Court; see also Rules 91, 93-96 of the Rules of Court.

Textbox iv   *Legal Aid Rates[107]*

Legal aid rates
applicable as from 1 January 2006

A. FEES AND EXPENSES   Lump sum per case

Preparation of the case

- Filing written pleadings at the request of the Court
  on the admissibility or merits of the case

- Supplementary observations at the request of the Court
  (on the admissibility or merits of the case)   € 850

- Submissions on just satisfaction or friendly settlement

- Normal secretarial expenses
  (for example telephone, postage, photocopies)

B. OTHER

1. Appearance at an oral hearing before the Court
   or attending the hearing of witnesses (including preparation)   € 300

2. Assisting in friendly settlement negotiations   € 200

3. Travelling costs incurred in connection with appearance
   at an oral hearing or hearing of witnesses
   or with friendly-settlement negotiations   according to receipts

4. Subsistence allowance in connection with appearance
   at an oral hearing or hearing of witnesses
   or with friendly-settlement negotiations   € 169 per diem

---

107   Source: Council of Europe.

Textbox v   *Declaration of Applicant's Means*[108]

DECLARATION OF APPLICANT'S MEANS

1. Name of applicant and case number:

2. Are you married, divorced or single?

3. Nature of your employment, name of employer:
   (if not at present employed, give details of your last employment)

4. Details of net salary and other net income (e.g. interest from loans and investments, allowances, pensions, insurance benefits, etc.) after deduction of tax:

5. List and value of capital assets owned by you:

   (a)   Immovable property (e.g. land, house, business premises)

   (b)   Movable property and nature thereof (e.g. bank balance, savings account, motor-car, valuables)

6. List your financial commitments:

   (a)   Rent, mortgage and other charges

   (b)   Loans and interest payable thereon

   (c)   Maintenance of dependants

   (d)   Any other financial obligations

7. What contribution can you make towards your legal representation before the European Court of Human Rights?

8. The name of the person whom you propose to assist you:
   (see Rule 94 in conjunction with Rule 36 §§ 4 and 5 of the Rules of Court)
   I certify that the above information is correct and complete.

Signed: Dated:

---

108   Source: Council of Europe.

1.10 The Languages Used in the Court's Proceedings

The official languages of the Court are English and French.[109] However, applicants may fill in the application form in one of the official languages of the Contracting Parties and may continue to correspond with the Court in that language until the communication of the application to the Contracting Party. After reaching that point all correspondence with the Court should be conducted in English or in French. Applicants may, however, seek leave from the President of the Chamber to continue to use the official language of a Contracting Party when communicating with the Court, when appearing before it at a hearing, or in drafting their observations.[110]

As a general rule, the Contracting Parties are required to communicate with the Court and to submit their observations in English or French. They may seek leave from the President of the Chamber to use their official national languages for their oral or written submissions, in which case they will be required to submit also an English or French translation of those submissions, such as observations. However, as stated above, Contracting Parties usually do submit their observations in English or French and if the applicant does not understand English or French, he or she may arrange for the translation of the observations into his or her own national language and include the expenses in the claim for just satisfaction.[111] In the alternative, he or she may ask the President of the Chamber to invite the respondent Contracting Party to provide a translation of the observations into an official language of the Contracting Party which he or she understands.[112]

Judgments and decisions of the Chambers and the Grand Chamber are handed down in English or French, and it is not the responsibility of the responding Contracting Party or of the Court to arrange for their translation.

1.11 Written Pleadings

As described in Section 1.14 below, hearings are held in only very few cases. It is for this reason that the importance of written pleadings must be highlighted since they will, in the great majority of cases, represent the only

---

109   Rule 34 § 1 of the Rules of Court.
110   Rule 34 § 3 of the Rules of Court.
111   See Section 7.2.1 (c) below.
112   Rule 34 § 5 of the Rules of Court.

opportunity for applicants to convey their arguments to the Court and to rebut the Government's counter-arguments. The first written pleading is the application, which will form the basis of the Court's consideration of the case. If the Court proceeds to communicate the application to the respondent Government, the applicant will have the opportunity to submit additional written pleadings, including the "observations" (sometimes referred to as "memorial") in reply to the respondent Government's observations on the admissibility and merits of the case.[113] The applicant may have a further opportunity to submit observations if the case is declared (partially) admissible in a separate decision. In such circumstances the Court will generally either request the parties to respond to specific questions or to submit observations on a particular issue, or it will inform the parties that it does not require any further information or observations but that it is nevertheless open to the parties to submit any additional evidence or observations they wish.[114] Although the issue of observations is discussed in subsequent parts of this *Handbook*, the present sub-section will summarise the general rules and strategic points to be kept in mind. The applicants' observations in the cases of *Akkum and Others v. Turkey*[115] and *Kişmir v. Turkey*,[116] and the respondent Government's observations in the case of *Van der Ven v. the Netherlands*[117] in Appendices Nos. 12-14, will give an idea of the form and the contents of observations submitted in the course of the Strasbourg proceedings.

It must be stressed at the outset that in preparing their observations, applicants should refer to the "Practice Direction on Written Pleadings"[118] and follow the recommendations set out therein. The time limits indicated by the Registry must always be observed. It is possible to seek an extension of the time limit and the first such request is usually granted provided that it is made within the time limit and that it is duly reasoned.

As a general rule, observations must be drafted in one of the official languages of the Court, i.e. English or French. However, as mentioned above, an applicant who has completed the application form in another language may seek leave from the President of the relevant Chamber for the continued use of that language, provided it is an official language of one of the Contracting Parties.[119] Such leave is usually given without any difficulty.

---

113 Such observations are discussed in detail in Section 5.2 below.
114 See Section 6.4 below for further information.
115 No. 21894/93, 24 March 2005.
116 No. 27306/95, 31 May 2005.
117 Cited above.
118 See Appendix No. 3.
119 Rule 34 § 3 (a) of the Rules of Court.

It is imperative that the arguments set out in observations are well structured; an unstructured, free flowing set of observations, no matter how strong the legal arguments contained therein, will frustrate the opportunity to support the case. If the applicant does not contest the facts as summarised by the Court, there is no need to set them out once more in the observations; a simple statement to the effect that the applicant agrees with the statement of facts as set out by the Court will be sufficient. Obviously, if there have been any developments (such as a new domestic court decision, a new step in the domestic investigation, or a new witness comes forward, etc.) these need to be mentioned in the observations. Furthermore, if the respondent Government has disputed the facts, the applicant should add further information and evidence to support the facts as alleged by him or herself, and further argumentation to show that his or her version of the events is more credible than that of the Government. Obviously, as the applicant will already have submitted to the Court all the evidence in support of the case, he or she may adduce further material corroborating the evidence previously submitted. For example, if the Government has disputed the accuracy or the contents of medical reports detailing injuries, the applicant should consider obtaining an independent medical opinion to counter the Government's arguments.[120]

1.12 Third Party Interventions *(Amicus Curiae)*

Persons or organisations who are not parties to a case before the Court may, in the discretion of the President of the Court, intervene in the proceedings as third parties. Such third party interventions are usually made by means of *amicus curie* briefs providing additional arguments in support of one of the parties to the case. Article 36 of the Convention provides the authority for such interventions:

> "[t]he President of the Court may, in the interest of the proper administration of justice, invite ... any person concerned who is not the applicant to submit written comments or take part in hearings".

Rule 44 of the Rules of Court governs procedures relating to third party interventions. According to this Rule, once the case has been communicated to the respondent Government, the President of the Chamber may invite or grant leave to any person concerned who is not the applicant to submit written comments or, in exceptional cases, to take part in a hearing. Requests for

---

120 See the applicant's observations in the case of *Kişmir v. Turkey*, cited above, which include a copy of an independent medical report, Appendix No. 13.

leave to intervene as a third party must be duly reasoned and submitted in writing in one of the official languages of the Court *not later than twelve weeks* after notice of the application has been given to the respondent Contracting Party. In cases before the Grand Chamber, the twelve-week period starts running from the date of notification to the parties of the decision of the Chamber under Rule 72 § 1 to relinquish jurisdiction in favour of the Grand Chamber[121] or of the decision of the panel of the Grand Chamber under Rule 73 § 2 to accept a request by a party for referral of the case to the Grand Chamber.[122] The time-limits may, in exceptional circumstances, be extended by the President of the Chamber if sufficient cause is shown. Written comments submitted under this Rule must be drafted in one of the official languages of the Court.[123] They will be forwarded to the parties to the case, who will be entitled, subject to any conditions, including time-limits set by the President of the Chamber, to file written observations in reply or, where appropriate, to reply at the hearing.

The purpose of an *amicus* intervention is to assist the Court in its deliberations on a case, or a specific issue in a case. In this connection, many NGOs have expertise or specialist information on specific human rights issues relevant to the case in which they seek to intervene, and in practice, most third party interventions are submitted by NGOs. Such information or expertise may not always be within the reach of an applicant, his or her legal representative, or indeed of the Court. A prospective third party must specify in the request for leave to intervene what added value its intervention will have for the Court's examination of the case. For example, an NGO with experience in the subject matter pertinent to the case in which it seeks to intervene could emphasise that experience. Similarly, an NGO with specialised knowledge of other human rights mechanisms may try to persuade the Court of the utility of a comparative legal analysis of a particular issue relevant to the case. In this connection it must be pointed out that the Court is frequently prepared to take account of case-law of other international and domestic courts (occasionally even of courts of countries not parties to the Convention[124]) which may serve as guidance on issues which it has not yet had occasion to consider in its own jurisprudence.[125] However, third party interventions which only discuss the jurisprudence of the European Court have marginal utility, as this is the speciality of the Court itself.

---

121   For issues relating to the relinquishment of jurisdiction by a Chamber in favour of the Grand Chamber see Section 1.5.1 above.
122   For issues relating to referral to the Grand Chamber see Section 9.2 below.
123   I.e. English and French; see Section 1.10 above.
124   See *Hirst v. the United Kingdom (No. 2)* [GC], cited above, §§ 35-39.
125   See Section 1.6.5 above.

An example of a case in which third party interventions played a role is *Nachova and Others v. Bulgaria*; *amicus* briefs were received from three non-governmental organisations, the European Roma Rights Centre (ERRC), INTERIGHTS, and Open Society Justice Initiative (OSJI).[126] The ERRC's *amicus* brief informed the Court of incidents of ill-treatment and killing of Roma by law enforcement agents and private individuals. INTERIGHTS criticised the Court's standard of beyond reasonable doubt as erecting insurmountable obstacles to establishing discrimination. The OSJI, for their part, commented on the obligation of States, in international and comparative law, to investigate racial discrimination and violence. The information and the arguments submitted by these NGOs were summarised in the judgment.[127] Whereas the information submitted by the ERRC provided background information for the Court about the problems facing Roma in Bulgaria, the arguments submitted by INTERIGHTS led the Court to explain its reliance on the standard of proof beyond reasonable doubt and to address – for the first time in its history – the criticisms which have been levelled against the Court for its insistence on this high standard of proof.[128] Finally, it cannot be excluded that the OSJI's *amicus* brief had some bearing on the Court's conclusion that "the authorities' duty to investigate the existence of a possible link between racist attitudes and an act of violence is an aspect of their procedural obligations arising under Article 2 of the Convention, but may also be seen as implicit in their responsibilities under Article 14 of the Convention taken in conjunction with Article 2 to secure the enjoyment of the right to life without discrimination."[129]

1.13 Costs

The Court does not require applicants to pay any fees at any stage of the Convention proceedings. If an applicant is successful with his or her application and the Court finds that there has been a violation of the Convention, the Court may order the respondent State to reimburse the expenses incurred by the applicant in connection with the examination of his or her Convention complaints, pursuant to Article 41 of the Convention, including lawyer's fees, translation and postage costs, and costs of attending any possible hearings in Strasbourg. In the course of the Convention proceedings, applicants

---

126   *Nachova and Others v. Bulgaria* [GC], nos. 43577/98, 43579/98, 6 July 2005, § 8.
127   See §§ 55-59 and 138-143.
128   See 11.6 for issues relating to the standard of proof in the Court's proceedings,
129   § 163.

may also apply for legal aid from the Court to cover – at least partially – their costs.[130]

1.14 Hearings

The Chamber and the Grand Chamber may hold hearings on the admissibility and/or the merits of cases in Strasbourg. Such hearings require the attendance of the parties or their representatives and sometimes also the attendance of witnesses and experts. During a hearing, the parties will present their case and arguments and answer any questions that may be put to them by the judges. However, hearings are held in only very few cases.[131] The parties are informed of the Court's decision at a subsequent date and not on the day of the hearing. Although such hearings are open to the public, the (Grand) Chamber may, of its own motion or at the request of a party or any other person concerned, decide to exclude the public and the press from all or part of a hearing in the interests of, *inter alia*, morals, public order and protection of the private life.[132]

The Court also has powers to appoint one or more of its judges to conduct an inquiry, carry out an on-site investigation, or take evidence in some other manner within the territory of the respondent Contracting Parties.[133] Although the Court uses these powers rarely, it has done so in a number of cases in order to establish the facts through the hearing of applicants, witnesses, experts, and other persons connected with the complaint.[134]

1.15 Effects of the Court's Judgments

After the Court has found a violation of the Convention and awarded just satisfaction to the injured party, it transmits its judgment to the Committee of Ministers to supervise the execution of that judgment by the respondent State in accordance with Article 46 § 2 of the Convention. The Court does not interfere with the execution process thereafter. Thus, aside from awarding monetary compensation, the Court has consistently declined to assume juris-

---

130   See Section 1.9 above and Section 7 below.
131   In 2005, 20 hearings were held by the Sections and 25 by the Grand Chamber.
132   For other reasons see Rule 63 § 2 of the Rules of Court.
133   Rule A1 of the Annex to the Rules of Court.
134   See also Section 11.3 below.

diction to order a State to carry out particular measures of reparation or to change its law or practice in any particular way so as to prevent similar violations from recurring in the future.[135]

Yet in numerous cases the Court has held that in the context of the execution of judgments pursuant to Article 46 of the Convention, a judgment in which the Court finds a violation of the Convention or its Protocols imposes on the respondent State a legal obligation not just to pay those concerned the sums awarded by way of just satisfaction, but also to choose, subject to supervision by the Committee of Ministers, the general and/or, if appropriate, individual measures to be adopted in its domestic legal order to put an end to the violation found by the Court and make all feasible reparation for its consequences in such a way as to restore as far as possible the situation existing before the breach.[136] In this connection the individual measure most commonly required for *restitutio in integrum* is the reopening of domestic legal proceedings. The need for such a measure arises primarily in respect of criminal proceedings since problems with civil proceedings can frequently be remedied through financial compensation. But a criminal conviction may need to be quashed or a retrial ordered to remedy the violation in question. For example, where an applicant has been tried and convicted by a court which is not independent within the meaning of Article 6 § 1 of the Convention,[137] or his or her right to freedom of expression under Article 10 of the Convention has been unjustifiably restricted by national law,[138] the Committee of Ministers interprets the judgments of the Court and, if necessary, exerts pressure on the respondent State with a view to forcing it to remedy the situation giving rise to a violation.

However, despite the declaratory nature of its judgments and its lack of jurisdiction to order consequential measures against a State, recent practice indicates that the Court is willing to assist the Committee of Ministers in the execution process by providing certain guidelines to the respondent States on how the consequences of a particular violation of the Convention may be

---

135 *Philis v. Greece*, nos. 12750/87, 13780/88 and 14003/88, 27 August 1991, § 79. In *Selmouni v. France*, the Court found violations of Articles 3 and 6 of the Convention on the grounds that the applicant had been subjected to acts of torture in the hands of the French police during his detention in police custody in Paris and that the proceedings in respect of his complaint against the police officers had not been conducted within a reasonable time. The Court awarded the applicant a substantial sum to cover both personal injury and non-pecuniary damage. However, it dismissed the applicant's requests concerning an order for transfer to the Netherlands (of which country he was a national) to serve the remainder of his sentence there and to specify in its judgment that the sums awarded under Article 41 should be exempt from attachment. The Court held that Article 41 did not give it jurisdiction to make such orders against a Contracting Party; see *Selmouni v. France* [GC], no. 25803/94, 28 July 1999, § 126.

136 See, for example, *Scozzari and Giunta v. Italy* [GC], nos. 39221/98 and 41963/98, 13 July 2000, § 249; *Menteş and Others v. Turkey* (Article 50), no. 23186/94, 24 July 1998, § 24; *Maestri v. Italy* [GC], no. 39748/98, 17 February 2004, § 47.

137 See, for example, *Incal v. Turkey*, no. 22678/93, 9 June 1998.

138 See, for example, *Sürek v. Turkey (no. 2)* [GC], no. 24122/94, 8 July 1999.

remedied. For example, in its judgment in the case of *Ükünç and Güneş v. Turkey* the Court, having concluded that the applicant had not received a fair trial within the meaning of Article 6 of the Convention, stated that in principle the most appropriate form of relief would be to ensure that the applicant is granted in due course a retrial.[139] In its judgment in the case of *Assanidze v. Georgia*, where the applicant was not released by the authorities of the Ajarian autonomous republic in Georgia despite his acquittal by the Supreme Court, the Court held that Georgia had to secure the applicant's release at the earliest possible date in order to put an end to the violations of the applicant's rights under Articles 5 and 6 of the Convention.[140]

Likewise, in the case of *Ilaşcu and Others v. Moldova and Russia*,[141] four Moldovan citizens brought a complaint about their treatment in the Moldovan Republic of Transniestria. They complained, *inter alia*, that they had not received a fair trial and that they were subjected to ill-treatment and inhuman prison conditions. The Court found a breach of Article 3 of the Convention on account of the ill-treatment inflicted on the applicants. It also found that the continued detention of Mr Ilaşcu by Russia and of the other three applicants by Moldova was in violation of Article 5 of the Convention. In addition to awarding the applicants a certain amount of money for pecuniary and non pecuniary damages, the Court held that any continuation of the unlawful and arbitrary detention of the three applicants would necessarily entail a serious prolongation of the violation of Article 5 found by the Court and a breach of the respondent States' obligation under Article 46 § 1 of the Convention to abide by the Court's judgment.

Coming to the cases concerning allegations of ill-treatment, there is no judgment where the Court specifically indicated, as part of just satisfaction under Article 41, a type of measure that might be taken by the respondent State to remedy the suffering of the victim of torture or other forms of ill-treatment. But, in some cases, the Court did point to certain defects in the legislation or practice of States giving rise to a systemic violation of Article 3 of the Convention. As an example, in the case of *Abdülsamet Yaman v. Turkey*,[142] which concerned the alleged torture inflicted on the applicant during his detention in police custody and where the criminal proceedings against the accused police were discontinued on the ground that the prosecution was time-barred, the Court pointed out that where a State agent has been charged with crimes involving torture or ill-treatment, it is of the utmost importance for the purposes of an "effective remedy" that criminal proceedings and

---

139 *Ükünç and Güneş v. Turkey*, no. 42775/98, 18 December 2003, § 32.
140 *Assanidze v. Georgia* [GC], no. 71503/01, 8 April 2004, § 203.
141 *Ilaşcu and Others v. Moldova and Russia* [GC], no. 48787/99, 8 July 2004, § 490.
142 *Abdülsamet Yaman v. Turkey*, no. 32446/96, 2 November 2004, § 55.

sentencing are not time-barred and that the granting of an amnesty or pardon should not be permissible. The Court also underlined the importance of the suspension from duty of the agent under investigation or on trial as well as his dismissal if he is convicted.

Similarly, in its judgment in the case of *Güngör v. Turkey*, which concerned the criminal investigation into the killing of the son of a member of the Turkish Parliament, the Court found that Turkey must take appropriate measures without delay to discharge, in accordance with the Court's judgment, its obligations to ensure that its legislation was clarified so that parliamentary immunity could no longer operate in practice to prevent prosecutions for ordinary criminal offences in cases in which members of parliament or their families were involved as possible witnesses or suspects.[143]

Mention should further be made of the fact that in some cases involving allegations of ill-treatment or other serious violations of the Convention, the parties agreed to settle their cases on the basis of friendly settlement declarations proposed by the Registry of the Court. In these declarations, the respondent Governments accepted responsibility for the alleged violation of the Convention and undertook to take necessary measures to prevent similar violations in the future and pay compensation to the victims of the violations in question.[144]

Thus, although the Court is not empowered under the Convention to order a State to carry out particular measures of reparation or to change its law or practice in any particular way, it has managed to get States to undertake these measures by way of friendly settlement judgments containing the aforementioned type of declarations. Such a situation can be illustrated by the case of *Kalın, Gezer and Ötebay v. Turkey*,[145] which concerned alleged ill-treatment inflicted on the applicants during their detention in police custody. With the assistance of the Registry of the Court, the parties respectively submitted formal declarations accepting a friendly settlement of the case. For their part, the Turkish Government accepted in the declaration that the treatment suffered by the applicants gave rise to a violation of Article 3 of the Convention. The Government also undertook to issue appropriate instructions and adopt all necessary measures to ensure that the prohibition of such acts and the obligation to carry out effective investigations would be respected in the future. It further offered to each of the applicants certain amounts of money. Following acceptance of the Government's declaration the applicants agreed

---

143 *Güngör v. Turkey*, no. 28290/95, 22 March 2005, § 111.
144 See, for example, *Sak v. Turkey*, no. 29359/95, 30 October 2001. The parties' friendly declarations in this case may be consulted in *Textbox xi*.
145 *Kalın, Gezer and Ötebay v. Turkey*, nos. 24849/94, 24850/94 and 24941/94, 28 October 2003.

to settle their case and it was subsequently struck out of the list of the Court's cases.

It is considered that serious violations of the Convention, such as violations of Articles 2 and 3, are by their very nature irreparable. Any remedy, including pecuniary compensation, will fail to be truly proportional to the gravity of the injury inflicted on the victim, particularly when the perpetrators have not been held to account for their wrongdoing. Having regard to the recent practice of the Court to provide certain guidelines to respondent States as described above, it is hoped that in its future judgments the Court will not merely award damages to victims of ill-treatment but also indicate the specific measures that might be taken by respondent States to remedy the situation giving rise to the violation, such as the (re-)opening of criminal proceedings against the perpetrators of ill-treatment.

PART II

ADMISSIBILITY

ADMISSIBILITY

2.1 Introduction

2.2 Victim Status (Article 34)

2.2.1 Summary

2.2.2 Discussion

    a) The General Rule

    b) Standing of Next of Kin in Article 2 and 3 Cases

    c) Indirect Victims

    d) Adoption of Applications of Deceased Applicants

2.3 Compatibility of the Application (Article 35 § 3)

2.3.1 Summary

2.3.2 Discussion

    a) Incompatibility *Ratione Temporis*

    b) Incompatibility *Ratione Loci*

    c) Incompatibility *Ratione Personae*

    d) Incompatibility *Ratione Materiae*

2.4 Exhaustion of Domestic Remedies (Article 35 § 1)

2.4.1 Summary

2.4.2 Discussion

    a) Only "Available" and "Effective" Remedies Need to be Exhausted

    b) Extraordinary Remedies do Not Need to be Exhausted

    c) Special Circumstances

    d) "Effective" Remedies in the Context of Article 3 Violations

        i.   Criminal Remedies

        ii. Civil and Administrative Remedies

    e) Compliance With Rules of Domestic Procedure

2.4.3 Concluding Remarks

2.5 The Six-Month Rule (Article 35 §1)

2.5.1 Summary

2.5.2 Discussion

    a) The General Rule

    b) The Date of Introduction

    c) The Starting Point of the Six-Month Period

        i.   Where Domestic Remedies Exist

EUROPEAN CONVENTION ON HUMAN RIGHTS

Article 34

Individual applications

The Court may receive applications from any person, non-governmental organisation or group of individuals claiming to be the victim of a violation by one of the High Contracting Parties of the rights set forth in the Convention or the protocols thereto. The High Contracting Parties undertake not to hinder in any way the effective exercise of this right".

Article 35

Admissibility criteria

1. The Court may only deal with the matter after all domestic remedies have been exhausted, according to the generally recognised rules of international law, and within a period of six months from the date on which the final decision was taken.

2. The Court shall not deal with any application submitted under Article 34 that:

   a. is anonymous; or

   b. is substantially the same as a matter that has already been examined by the Court or has already been submitted to another procedure of international investigation or settlement and contains no relevant new information.

3. The Court shall declare inadmissible any individual application submitted under Article 34 which it considers incompatible with the provisions of the Convention or the protocols thereto, manifestly ill-founded, or an abuse of the right of application.

4. The Court shall reject any application which it considers inadmissible under this Article. It may do so at any stage of the proceedings.

2.1 Introduction

Before lodging an application with the Court, the applicant must satisfy him or herself that the complaint is admissible. The Court's standing and admissibility rules are contained in Articles 34 and 35 of the Convention respectively. These rules constitute a formidable filtering mechanism by means of which the Court weeds out a large number of cases from its heavily overburdened docket. From the standpoint of the applicant, the admissibility rules therefore constitute the main hurdle to having a case heard in Strasbourg. A total of 26,360 applications were declared inadmissible by Committees of three judges in 2005; this figure represents almost 94% of the cases which were disposed of judicially (i.e. it does not even include cases disposed of administratively before reaching the admissibility stage). Most of the inadmissible cases were declared inadmissible because they did not comply with the exhaustion rule, the six-month rule, or both taken together. A large number of applications were also dismissed as "manifestly ill-founded" because the applicant had failed properly to substantiate his or her allegations. Therefore, the importance of strictly adhering to the Court's admissibility criteria cannot be overemphasised. In this regard, prospective applicants should pay careful attention to the Court's practice and jurisprudence on admissibility issues. Applicants should also consult and comply conscientiously with the Rules of Court[146] and pay careful attention to the Court's Practice Directions,[147] the "Notes for the guidance of persons wishing to apply to the ECHR",[148] and the "Explanatory note for persons completing the application form"[149]

In a nutshell, the Court's rules of admissibility can be expressed as follows: for an application to be considered admissible, the applicant must convince the Court that 1) he or she is a "victim", 2) that the application is "compatible" with the Convention (*ratione temporis, ratione loci, ratione materie,* and *ratione persone*), 3) that he or she has exhausted domestic remedies, 4) that the application complies with the six-month rule, 5) that the complaints are sufficiently "substantiated" on their face to disclose a violation of the Convention, and finally that the application is not 6) "abusive", 7) "anonymous", or 8) "substantially the same" as one that has been or is being considered by another international procedure of investigation or settlement.

---

146 See Appendix No. 19.
147 See Appendix No. 3.
148 See Appendix No.17.
149 See Appendix No. 4.

Virtually all of these criteria have been subject of considerable interpretation by the Court and some of them have important exceptions. Some of these exceptions apply specifically in the context of violations of Articles 2 and 3. Because the issue of admissibility is an important and complex one it is treated in some detail in this section.

The Court, through its rules of admissibility, imposes a very high standard of diligence on applicants wishing to have their "day in court" in Strasbourg. However, it is important to note that the obligation of due diligence starts well before proceedings commence in Strasbourg. In fact, due diligence needs to be exercised from the very inception of the case in the national system if it is to have a chance of succeeding before the Court: an applicant who has not presented properly documented complaints to the relevant domestic authorities on a timely basis and in compliance with domestic rules of procedure will have a difficult time convincing the European Court that his or her application merits consideration. To be sure, the principle of subsidiarity *requires* that Contracting Parties be given a proper opportunity to redress complaints through their own domestic system before being held to account internationally.

2.2 Victim Status (Article 34)

2.2.1 Summary

For purposes of the Convention, a "victim" is a natural or legal person whose Convention rights are *personally or directly affected* by a measure or act of a Contracting Party. A person who is not affected in this manner does not have standing as a victim. A person may lose his or her victim status if the violation is appropriately remedied by the Contracting Party.[151] In certain circumstances arising in the context of violations of Articles 2 and 3, the close relatives of the person affected by an act may have the requisite standing to introduce an application on behalf of that person.[152] Also, in certain circumstances, close relatives can claim to be indirect victims.[153] Subject to the

---

151 See *Eckle v. Germany*, no. 8130/78, 15 July 1982, § 66.
152 See, for example, *Salman v. Turkey* [GC], no. 21986/93, 27 June 2000, in which the wife of a man killed in police custody was able to bring an application.
153 See, for example, *İpek v. Turkey*, no. 25760/94, 17 February 2004, in which the father of two disappeared men was held by the Court to be an indirect victim on account of the disappearance of his sons. The Court found a violation of Article 3 of the Convention on account of, *inter alia*, the suffering caused to him by the disappearance.

discretion of the Court, the application of a person who dies during the pendency of Strasbourg proceedings can be adopted by a close relative.[154] The Court will not entertain abstract challenges to legislation or governmental measures (*actio popularis*); however, applicants may have standing to challenge legislation or measures which have not been applied to them if they can show that the mere existence of such legislation has a direct effect on the exercise of their Convention rights.[155]

2.2.2 Discussion

a) The General Rule

Article 34 governs the question of standing before the Court. It states that the Court may receive applications from:

> "any person, non-governmental organisation or group of individuals claiming to be the victim of a violation by one of the High Contracting Parties of the rights set forth in this Convention or the protocols thereto".

The term "person" covers not only natural persons but also legal persons, such as trade unions,[156] political parties,[157] companies[158] or other associations.[159] However, governmental organisations or State-owned companies cannot bring an application to the Court under the theory that a Contracting Party cannot complain about itself before the Court.[160]

The term "victim" denotes a person who is directly affected by a governmental act or omission. To take a clear hypothetical example: a Contracting Party that fails to provide medical assistance to a detainee who is ill, resulting in the deterioration of the detainee's health, has directly affected his or her rights under the Convention. However, there are situations where it is more difficult to establish and prove the relationship between the governmental act

---

154 See *Aksoy v. Turkey*, no. 21987/93, 18 December 1996, § 7, in which the father of a victim of ill-treatment continued the application lodged by his son who died in the course of the Court's proceedings.

155 See, for example, *Dudgeon v. the United Kingdom* (no. 7525/76, 22 October 1981) and *Norris v. Ireland* (no. 10581/83, 26 October 1988) in which the applicants were able to persuade the Court that the mere existence of legislation criminalising adult homosexual relations caused them to live in constant fear that they would one day be prosecuted and that under such circumstances, they could reasonably claim to be directly affected by the legislation and therefore be considered victims within the meaning of Article 34 of the Convention.

156 *Wilson, National Union of Journalists and Others v. the United Kingdom*, nos. 30668/96, 30671/96 and 30678/96, 2 July 2002.

157 *Refah Partisi (the Welfare Party) and Others v. Turkey* [GC], nos. 41340/98, 41342/98, 41343/98 and 41344/98, 13 February 2003.

158 *Bosphorus Hava Yolları Turizm ve Ticaret Anonim Şirketi (Bosphorus Airways) v. Ireland* [GC], no. 45036/98, 30 June 2005.

159 *The Holy Monasteries v. Greece*, nos. 13092/87;13984/88, 9 December 1994.

160 *RENFE v. Spain*, no. 35216/97, Commission decision of 8 September 1997.

and the resultant harm. For instance, in the case of *Tauira and 18 others v. France*, the applicants complained of the decision of the French Government to resume a series of nuclear tests in French Polynesia and alleged a violation of their rights under Articles 2, 3, and 8 of the Convention and Article 1 of Protocol No. 1. The Commission dismissed the applicants' complaints on the grounds that they could not claim to be victims of a violation of the provisions invoked by them because the consequences, if any, of the resumption of the nuclear tests were too remote to affect the applicants' personal situation.[161]

The Convention does not provide for an *"actio popularis"*. In other words, individuals cannot complain in the abstract about legislation or governmental acts which have not been applied to them personally through a measure of implementation, for instance, a prosecution. Therefore, if applicants wish to challenge legislation which has not been applied them, they must be able to prove that the mere existence of the legislation has a direct effect on the exercise of their Convention rights. In *Dudgeon v. the United Kingdom*[162] and *Norris v. Ireland*[163] the applicants, who were homosexuals, complained of the legislation in force in their respective countries which criminalised adult homosexual relations. The respondent Governments disputed the applicants' victim status arguing that no criminal prosecution had in fact been brought against them under the impugned legislation and that the applicants could consequently not claim to have been directly affected by the legislation. However, the Court found that the mere existence of this legislation had such a direct effect on the applicants' private lives – not least because the applicants had to live in constant fear that they might one day be prosecuted – and that under such circumstances they could reasonably claim to be directly affected by the legislation. The Court therefore considered them to be victims within the meaning of Article 25 (now Article 34).

The applicant may lose status as a "victim" if he or she has succeeded in obtaining a favourable decision from the domestic courts in respect of his or her Convention complaints. However, a decision or measure favourable to the applicant is not always sufficient to deprive him or her of "victim" status; in order for this to happen, the national authorities must have acknowledged the breach, either expressly or in substance, and then afforded redress for it.[164]

In the context of Article 3 violations, adequate redress will normally include an effective official investigation capable of leading to the identification and

---

161 *Tauira and 18 others v. France*, no. 28204/95, Commission decision of 4 December 1995.
162 *Dudgeon v. the United Kingdom*, cited above.
163 *Norris v. Ireland*, cited above.
164 *Eckle v. Germany*, cited above, § 66.

punishment of those responsible.[165] Notwithstanding this requirement, there may be situations in which the prosecution and punishment of the perpetrators is insufficient in the eyes of the Court to establish that the applicant has lost victim status. This point is well illustrated by the Court's judgment in the case of *Mikheyev v. Russia*. In *Mikheyev*, the respondent Government notified the Court – after the case had been pending before the Court for a number of years – that the police officers who ill-treated the applicant had been convicted by a domestic court of abuse of official power and sentenced to four years' imprisonment. The Strasbourg Court noted, however, that that domestic decision did not, in the circumstances of the case, affect the applicant's victim status for the following reasons:

> "In the present case, the Court notes firstly that the judgment of 30 November 2005 is not yet final, and may be reversed on appeal. Secondly, although the fact of ill-treatment was recognised by the first-instance court, the applicant has not been afforded any redress in this respect. Thirdly, the judgment of 30 November 2005 dealt only with the ill-treatment itself and did not examine the alleged flaws in the investigation, which is one of the main concerns of the applicant in the present case."[166]

b) Standing of Next of Kin in Article 2 and 3 Cases

The Court stated in *İlhan v. Turkey* that "complaints must be brought *by or on behalf of* persons who claim to be victims of a violation of one or more of the provisions of the Convention. Such persons must be able to show that they were 'directly affected' by the measure complained of" (emphasis added).[167] It follows, therefore, that an application can be introduced, for example, by a close relative of the deceased or a close relative of the disappeared. The applicant in such a case will have the requisite standing to bring complaints concerning the events which led to, or which are related to, the disappearance or the death of his or her relative. Indeed, if this was not the case, the protection provided in Article 2 of the Convention would be ineffective because, for obvious reasons, persons who are deceased or disappeared are themselves not capable of bringing complaints to the attention of the Court. Examples of Article 2 and 3 cases brought by family members include *Salman v. Turkey*, where the Court examined the application of the wife of Mr Agit Salman, who died as a result of torture during his detention in police custody.[168] Similarly, in *Timurtaş v. Turkey* the applicant father complained of the disappearance of his son who was taken away by soldiers, and invoked Articles 2,

---

165　See Section 2.4.2 (d) below.

166　*Mikheyev v. Russia*, no. 77617/01, 30 January 2006, §§ 61 and 89-90.

167　*İlhan v. Turkey* [GC], no. 22277/93, 27 June 2000, § 52.

168　*Salman v. Turkey* [GC], cited above.

5, 13, and 18 of the Convention in respect of his son and Article 3 of the Convention in respect of himself.[169]

Close relatives of deceased persons whom the Court held to have the requisite standing in Article 2 cases have included a wife,[170] a father,[171] a brother,[172] a son,[173] and a nephew.[174]

On the other hand, a close relative of a deceased person will not have the requisite standing to bring an application concerning the deceased person's right to release pending trial under Article 5 § 3 of the Convention, or right to a fair trial under Article 6 of the Convention.[175] According to the Court, the rights guaranteed by Article 5 of the Convention belong to a category of rights which are non-transferable.[176] It must be stressed, however, that complaints under Article 5 of the Convention can be brought on behalf of disappeared persons on account of their disappearance.

In ill-treatment cases, a close relative of the victim may have the requisite standing if the victim is in a particularly vulnerable position as a result of the ill-treatment. In the case of *İlhan v. Turkey*, the brother of the applicant had suffered brain damage and a long-term impairment of function as a result of being severely beaten by Turkish law enforcement officers. The applicant made it clear that he was complaining on behalf of his brother who, considering his state of health, was not in a position to pursue the application himself. The Court held that "it would generally be appropriate for an application to name the injured person as the applicant and for a letter of authority to be provided allowing another member of the family to act on his or her behalf. This would ensure that the application was brought with the consent of the victim of the alleged breach and would avoid *actio popularis* applications".[177] However, having regard to the special circumstances of the case, i.e. the mental impairment of the applicant's brother, the Court concluded that the applicant could be regarded as having validly introduced the application on his brother's behalf.[178]

---

169   See *Timurtaş v. Turkey*, cited above, § 60.
170   See *Süheyla Aydm v. Turkey*, no. 25660/94, 24 May 2005.
171   *İpek v. Turkey*, cited above.
172   *Koku v. Turkey*, no. 27305/95, 31 May 2005.
173   *Akkum and Others v. Turkey*, cited above.
174   *Yaşa v. Turkey*, no. 22495/93, 2 September 1998.
175   See *Biç v. Turkey* (dec.), no. 55955/00, 2 February 2006.
176   See *Georgia Makri and Others v. Greece* (dec.), no. 5977/03, 24 March 2005.
177   *İlhan v. Turkey* [GC], cited above, § 53.
178   *Ibid.*, § 55. The fact that an applicant is deemed to be of "unsound mind" on account of brain damage or other reasons and therefore lacks legal capacity for the purposes of national law and procedure, will not prevent him or her from exercising the right of individual application under Article 34 of the Convention; see *Winterwerp v. the Netherlands*, no. 6301/73, 24 October 1979, §§ 65-66.

c) Indirect Victims

An act or an omission may, in addition to directly victimising one or more persons, also have indirect repercussions on other persons who are closely connected to the direct victim(s). This occurs primarily in cases involving persons who are disappeared by State agents and in some deportation and expulsion cases. In such circumstances, the indirectly affected persons may bring complaints as victims in their own right.

The case of *İpek v. Turkey* concerned the disappearance of the applicant's two sons who were last seen in the hands of State security forces. The applicant alleged that he had suffered acute distress and anguish as a result of his inability to find out what had happened to his sons and because of the way the authorities had responded to his enquiries. The Court held that the question of whether a family member of a "disappeared person" is a victim of treatment in breach of Article 3 depends on the existence of special factors which give the suffering of the applicant a dimension and character distinct from the emotional distress which is inevitably caused to the relatives of a victim of a serious human rights violation. Relevant elements include the proximity of the family tie (a certain weight will attach to the parent-child bond), the particular circumstances of the relationship, the extent to which the family member witnessed the events in question, the involvement of the family member in the attempts to obtain information about the disappeared person, and the way in which the authorities responded to those attempts. The Court emphasised that the essence of such a violation did not so much lie in the fact of the "disappearance" of the family member but rather concerned the authorities' reactions and attitudes to the situation when it was brought to their attention. According to the Court, it was especially in respect of the latter that a relative could claim to be a victim of the authorities' conduct. Having found that the applicant had suffered, and continued to suffer distress and anguish as a result of the disappearance of his two sons and of his inability to find out what had happened to them, and in view of the manner in which his complaints had been dealt with by the authorities, the Court concluded that there had been a violation of Article 3 in respect of the applicant.[179]

In *Chahal v. the United Kingdom*, which concerned Mr Chahal's proposed deportation to India, his wife and children also joined the case as applicants and argued that Mr Chahal's deportation would violate their right to respect for family life under Article 8 of the Convention.[180]

---

179   *İpek v. Turkey*, cited above, §§ 178-183.
180   *Chahal v. the United Kingdom*, no. 22414/93, 15 November 1996.

d) Adoption of Applications of Deceased Applicants

Under certain circumstances, the Court may allow a family member to "adopt" the application of an applicant who dies during the pendency of proceedings. Such a situation arose in the case of *Aksoy v. Turkey*; while the the Court was considering Mr. Aksoy's application – in which he complained of having been tortured in police custody – he was shot and killed by unknown assailants. The Court subsequently allowed the applicant's father to pursue the case.[181]

In cases where no close relative wishes to pursue the application subsequent to the applicant's death, the Court may decide to strike the application out of its list of cases, considering that the demise of the applicant constitutes a fact "of a kind to provide a solution of the matter".[182] However, where the subject matter of the case raises issues of general importance, the Court may continue to examine the case despite the absence of a family member or an heir to adopt the case.[183]

2.3 Compatibility of the Application (Article 35 § 3)

2.3.1 Summary

Under Article 35 § 3 of the Convention, the Court will declare a complaint inadmissible if it is not compatible with the provisions of the Convention or its Protocols. A complaint may be incompatible for one or more of the following four reasons: *ratione temporis* (time), *ratione loci* (place), *ratione personae* (person) or *ratione materiae* (subject matter). In essence, these requirements mean that a complaint must concern events which took place at the right point in "time" and in the right "place" and must be filed by, and relate to, the right "person" and involve the right "subject matter". Thus, complaints relating to events which took place before entry into force of the Convention in the Contracting Party are inadmissible *ratione temporis*; complaints relating to events over which the Contracting Party has no jurisdiction, such as those occurring outside its territory are inadmissible *ratione loci*; complaints by persons who are not victims or which relate to the acts of entities over which the Contracting Party has no jurisdiction, or against States that are not Contracting Parties are inadmissible *ratione personae*; com-

---

181   *Aksoy v. Turkey*, cited above, § 7.
182   *Scherer v. Switzerland*, no. 17116/90, 25 March 1994, § 32. See also Section 8.2. below.
183   See *Karner v. Austria*, no. 40016/98, 24 July 2003.

plaints relating to infringement of rights that are not protected by the Convention will be dismissed *ratione materiae*. There are a number of important exceptions to these general rules particularly concerning continuing violations[184] and the liability of Contracting Parties for extraterritorial acts.[185] They are explained below.

2.3.2 Discussion

a) Incompatibility *Ratione Temporis*

By virtue of a generally recognised rule of international law, a Contracting Party can only be required to answer to facts and events which occurred subsequent to the entry into force of the Convention and Protocols with regard to the Party in question.[186] Accordingly, the Court cannot examine a complaint relating to events that occurred before the ratification of the Convention and Protocols by the respondent State. The case of *Kalashnikov v. Russia*[187] may serve as an example. The applicant complained about his ill-treatment by Russian special forces in July 1996 while in detention on remand. Considering that the Convention entered into force with respect to Russia on 5 May 1998, the Court observed that the applicant's complaint related to a period prior to that date. It therefore declared this complaint inadmissible as being incompatible *ratione temporis* with the provisions of the Convention within the meaning of Article 35 § 3.

Although the Convention can have no retroactive effect, there is an important exception to this general rule. If a complaint relates to a continuing situation, that is to say, a violation of the Convention caused by an act which was committed prior to the entry into force of the Convention in respect of a Contracting Party, but which continues after the entry into force of the Convention owing to the consequences of the original act,[188] then the Court will have jurisdiction to examine the complaint provided that it also complies with the other admissibility criteria. The case of *Loizidou v. Turkey*[189] illustrates the Court's approach to continuing situations. This case concerned the

---

184 See, for example, *Loizidou v. Turkey* (preliminary objections), no.15318/89, 23 March 1995, which concerned the applicant's inability to use her property in Cyprus since 1974. For dates of entry into force of the Convention and Protocols in Contracting Parties, see *Textbox i*.

185 See, for example, *Issa v. Turkey*, cited above, which concerned the killing of a number of persons in Iraq, allegedly by members of the Turkish security forces.

186 *Nielsen v. Denmark*, judgment of 2 September 1959, Yearbook II (1958-1959), p. 412 (454).

187 *Kalashnikov v. Russia* (dec.), no. 47095/99, 18 September 2001.

188 P. van Dijk and G.J.H. van Hoof, *Theory and Practice of the European Convention on Human Rights*, Kluwer Law International, 1998 (hereinafter referred to as "Van Dijk & van Hoof"), p. 11.

189 *Loizidou v. Turkey* (preliminary objections), cited above.

applicant's inability to access her property in Turkish controlled northern Cyprus since 1974. Upon ratification of the European Convention, the Turkish Government had accepted the jurisdiction of the Court only in relation to facts and events subsequent to 22 January 1990 and objected to the Court's jurisdiction to examine the application for this reason. But the Court decided that the continuous denial of access to the applicant's property in northern Cyprus and the ensuing loss of all control over it amounted to a continuous violation of the Convention. Therefore, the Turkish Government's objection was rejected.

Similarly, in the case of *Moldovan and Others v. Romania* the Court observed that police officers had been involved in the destruction of houses and belongings of the applicants who were Romanian citizens of Roma ethnic origin. The destruction had taken place before Romania ratified the Convention and for that reason the Court could not examine the applicants' allegations concerning the destruction of their property. However, the Court also noted that:

> "following this incident, having been hounded from their village and homes, the applicants had to live, and some of them still live, in crowded and improper conditions – cellars, hen-houses, stables, etc. – and frequently changed address, moving in with friends or family in extremely overcrowded conditions".[190]

Having regard to the direct repercussions of the acts of State agents on the applicants' rights, and the fact that these repercussions continued after the Convention went into effect in respect of Romania, the Court considered that the Government's responsibility was engaged and found a violation of Article 3 of the Convention.[191]

In *Blečić v. Croatia*, which concerned the applicant's right to respect for her home and to peaceful enjoyment of her possessions under Article 8 of the Convention and Article 1 of Protocol No. 1, a majority of the Grand Chamber (11 judges of the 17) considered that it had no jurisdiction (*ratione temporis*) to examine the case as the termination of the applicant's lease had been finalised when the Supreme Court rejected the applicant's appeal on 15 February 1996, before Croatia ratified the Convention. The applicant's appeal to the Constitutional Court had been rejected on 8 November 1999, after the ratification of the Convention by Croatia. However, the Court held that the interference giving rise to the application was the Supreme Court's judgment of 15 February 1996, and not the Constitutional Court's decision of

---

190   *Moldovan and Others v. Romania*, nos. 41138/98, 64320/01, 12 July 2005, § 103.
191   *Ibid.*, §§ 104-114.

8 November 1999. In forceful dissenting opinions the minority judges (i.e. six of the seventeen judges) argued, *inter alia*, that:

> "[a] judgment becomes *res judicata* i.e. a final, unappealable judgment, when it is legally irreversible under the domestic law. This result in the present case was brought about by the above decision of the Constitutional Court... In the present case the interference was the result of a series of judicial proceedings ending with the decision of the Constitutional Court, which was the only final, irreversible judicial decision in these proceedings. [I]t is the final Constitutional Court decision which followed that made the relevant civil action irreversible thus terminating the applicant's tenancy and bringing the problem of the interference complained of by the applicant within the competence of our Court".[192]

and

> "For the sake of argument, we can also imagine the reverse order of the events. The decision of the Supreme Court could have been in favour of the applicant – say on purely non-Conventional grounds – only for the Constitutional Court to reverse it. In that case, presumably, the violation *would* have occurred after the critical date and the Convention would be applicable *ratione temporis*. The Grand Chamber would then delve into the merits of this case and perhaps find that there was a violation. Before that, however, one would have to explain why such a reverse order of events would bring the case within the temporal limits of the Convention...Will the import of this precedent be that the last decision of the national court, which does not reverse the penultimate decision – but merely permits it to "subsist" – may count as a required domestic remedy, but does not count as a real decision bringing the case within the temporal limits of the Convention?"[193]

As will be seen below when examining the issue of exhaustion of domestic remedies, applicants are required to exhaust all relevant domestic remedies before they introduce their applications. For this reason, it is difficult to reconcile the Grand Chamber's judgment in *Blečić* with the Court's established case-law concerning exhaustion of domestic remedies,[194] unless, of course, this judgment amounts to a finding that the constitutional remedy in Croatia is, from now on, to be regarded as an ineffective remedy, and therefore one which applicants do not need to pursue.

---

192 *Blečić v. Croatia* [GC], no. 59532/00, 8 March 2006, dissenting opinion of Judge Loucaides joined by Judges Rozakis, Zupančič, Cabral Barreto, Pavlovschi, and David Thòr Björgvinssson.
193 Separate opinion of Judge Zupančič joined by Judge Cabral Barreto.
194 See Section 2.4 below for issues concerning exhaustion of domestic remedies.

b) Incompatibility *Ratione Loci*

According to Article 1 of the Convention:

> "the High Contracting Parties shall secure to everyone within their jurisdiction the rights and freedoms defined in Section 1 of this Convention".

Although this Article talks of the "Convention", if a Contracting Party has ratified any of the Protocols Nos. 1, 4, 6, 7, 12, or 13, the obligation mentioned in Article 1 of the Convention also applies to the rights and freedoms laid down in that Protocol. Protocols are considered supplementary Articles of the Convention, to which all the provisions of the Convention apply in a similar manner.[195]

Article 1 is of the utmost importance because it defines the scope of the Convention and of the obligations of the Contracting Parties. These obligations apply, however, only to those within the jurisdiction of the Contracting Party. Accordingly, a person claiming to be the victim of a violation of the Convention must first demonstrate that he or she was within the jurisdiction of the respondent State at the time of the alleged violation of the Convention. It follows that the issue of jurisdiction is a threshold requirement in the Convention; the question of State responsibility or imputability will arise only after the Court is satisfied that the matters complained of are within the jurisdiction of the respondent State.[196]

However, the term "jurisdiction" should not be interpreted as strictly coextensive with the Contracting Parties' "territory". Rather, it is well established in the jurisprudence of the Convention organs that Contracting Parties may be held accountable for certain types of extraterritorial conduct. In the aforementioned *Loizidou* case,[197] the Court ruled that when a State exercises effective control of an area – lawfully or unlawfully – outside its national territory and regardless of whether such control was exercised directly, through its armed forces, or through a subordinate local administration, that State may be considered to be exercising jurisdiction in that area, and its obligation under Article 1 extends to securing the entire range of substantive rights set out in the Convention and those additional Protocols which it has ratified, to that area.

Similarly, a Contracting Party is considered to exercise Article 1 jurisdiction wherever its agents – military or civilian – exercise power and authority over

---

195 See van Dijk and van Hoof, p. 3.
196 M. O'Boyle, "Comment on Life after Bankovic", in F. Coomans and M.T. Kamminga (eds) *Extraterritorial Application of Human Rights Treaties* (Intersentia Antwerp-Oxford 2004).
197 *Loizidou v. Turkey* (preliminary objections), cited above, § 62.

persons on foreign territory. In the case of *Illich Sanchez Ramirez v. France*,[198] the Commission examined the French authorities' arrest and detention of the applicant in Sudan. The Commission ruled that from the moment the applicant was handed over to the French authorities in Sudan, he was effectively under their authority and therefore within the jurisdiction of France.[199]

In the case of *Issa v. Turkey*, which concerned the killing of a number of persons in Iraq allegedly by members of the Turkish security forces, the Court held that a State may be held:

> "accountable for violation of the Convention rights and freedoms of persons who are in the territory of another State but who are found to be under the former State's authority and control through its agents operating – whether lawfully or unlawfully – in the latter State... Accountability in such situations stems from the fact that Article 1 of the Convention cannot be interpreted so as to allow a State party to perpetrate violations of the Convention on the territory of another State, which it could not perpetrate on its own territory".[200]

In *Issa* the Court did not exclude the possibility that, as a consequence of a military action, a respondent State could be considered to have exercised temporarily, effective overall control of a particular portion of the territory of northern Iraq:

> "Accordingly, if there is a sufficient factual basis for holding that, at the relevant time, the victims were within that specific area, it would follow logically that they were within the jurisdiction of Turkey".[201]

However, the Court concluded on the basis of all the material before it that it had not been established to the required standard of proof that the Turkish armed forces had conducted operations in the area in question.[202]

---

198   *Ramirez Sanchez v. France*, no. 28780/95, Commission decision of 24 June 1996.
199   *Ibid.*
200   *Issa v. Turkey*, cited above, § 71 (with references omitted).
201   *Ibid.*, § 74.
202   In its examination of a case concerning the killing of six persons whose deaths had occurred as a result of the UK military operations in Iraq, the Divisional Court in the United Kingdom considered that the conclusion of the Court in *Issa v. Turkey* was *obiter*, i.e. it was not binding as a precedent; see *R. Secretary of State for Defence Ex p. Al Skeini*, 14 December 2004, unreported. However, it must be pointed out that a request for the referral of the *Issa* case to the Grand Chamber was rejected, and the judgment became final on 30 March 2005. This is to be understood as meaning, in effect, that the Panel of the Grand Chamber did not consider that the case raised a serious question affecting the interpretation or application of the Convention and that the Chamber's conclusion was in line with the Court's established case-law. In any event the doctrine of *obiter* is unknown in Convention proceedings. See Nuala Mole, "*Issa v. Turkey*: Delineating the Extra-territorial Effect of the European Convention on Human Rights" (2005) E.H.R.L.R. Issue 1, Sweet & Maxwell, pp. 86-91.

Finally, mention must be made of the decision in the case of *Saddam Hussein v. Albania, Bulgaria, Croatia, the Czech Republic, Denmark, Estonia, Hungary, Iceland, Ireland, Italy, Latvia, Lithuania, the Netherlands, Poland, Portugal, Romania, Slovakia, Slovenia, Turkey, Ukraine and the United Kingdom*, in which the applicant complained about his arrest, detention and transfer to the Iraqi authorities and about his ongoing trial and its outcome. According to the applicant, he was within the respondent States' jurisdiction following his transfer to the Iraqi authorities in June 2004 because the respondent States remained in *de facto* control in Iraq. The Court held, however, that the applicant had not addressed each respondent State's role and responsibilities or the division of labour/power between them and the U.S. For the Court, there was:

> "no basis in the Convention's jurisprudence and the applicant had not invoked any established principle of international law which would mean that he fell within the respondent States' jurisdiction on the sole basis that those States allegedly formed part (at varying unspecified levels) of a coalition with the US, when the impugned actions were carried out by the US, when security in the zone in which those actions took place was assigned to the US and when the overall command of the coalition was vested in the US.

> Accordingly, the Court does not consider it to be established that there was or is any jurisdictional link between the applicant and the respondent States or therefore that the applicant was capable of falling within the jurisdiction of those States, within the meaning of Article 1 of the Convention".[203]

c) Incompatibility *Ratione Personae*

Article 35 § 3 of the Convention requires the Court to reject as inadmissible an application that is not compatible *ratione personae* with the provisions of the Convention or its Protocols. This requirement implies that the Court cannot examine an application against a State that is not a party to the Convention or the relevant Protocol. In the case of *Ataman v. Turkey*, the applicant complained under Article 5 of Protocol No. 7 (equality between spouses) that the authorities had refused her and her husband the right to adopt her maiden name as their family name. The Court considered that the applicant's complaint was incompatible *ratione personae* because Turkey was not a party to Protocol No. 7 and it thus rejected this complaint pursuant to Article 35 §§ 3 and 4 of the Convention.[204]

---

203 *Saddam Hussein v. Albania, Bulgaria, Croatia, the Czech Republic, Denmark, Estonia, Hungary, Iceland, Ireland, Italy, Latvia, Lithuania, the Netherlands, Poland, Portugal, Romania, Slovakia, Slovenia, Turkey, Ukraine and the United Kingdom* (dec.), no. 23276/04, 14 March 2006.

204 *Ataman v. Turkey* (dec.), no. 47738/99, 1 June 2004.

It should be pointed out in this connection that applications brought against States not parties to the Convention, such as the United States, are not even registered by the Court and that the applicants are merely informed by a letter that the Court has no competence to examine their application.

The Court has further declared inadmissible numerous complaints directed against persons for whom the respondent State was not responsible. In the case of *Papon v. France*, the applicant complained of the hostile media campaign to which he had been subjected and the attitude of the civil parties before and during his trial.[205] The Court rejected this complaint as incompatible *ratione personae* holding that the State authorities could not be held responsible for the actions of private persons.

Moreover, according to Article 34 of the Convention, the Court may receive applications

> "from any person ... claiming to be the victim of a violation ... of the rights set forth in the Convention ....".

Pursuant to this provision, the Court dismisses applications as incompatible *ratione personae* where the applicant is not a victim of the events or measures in question. It has done so in a case where one of the applicants complained of the length of proceedings to which she was not a party.[206]

d) Incompatibility *Ratione Materiae*

The Court is only empowered to examine complaints falling within the scope of the Convention and its Protocols. If a person complains of a violation of a right not guaranteed by the Convention or Protocols, the complaint will be rejected as incompatible *ratione materiae*.

The case of *Maaouia v. France* may illustrate this. The applicant complained under Article 6 of the Convention of unfairness of expulsion proceedings. The Court ruled that decisions regarding the entry, stay, and deportation of aliens do not concern the determination of an applicant's civil rights or obligations or of a criminal charge against him within the meaning of Article 6 § 1 of the Convention, and that, therefore Article 6 did not apply.[207] This finding of the Court does not mean, however, that a person who is subject to expulsion from the territory of a Contracting Party cannot benefit from the protection provided for in Articles 2 and 3 of the Convention. Although domestic proceedings relating to the removal of a person from the territory of a

---

205 *Papon v. France* (no. 2) (dec.), no. 54210/00, 15 November 2001.
206 *Santos Lda and Fachatas v. Portugal* (dec.), no. 49020/99, 19 September 2000.
207 *Maaouia v. France* [GC], no. 39652/98, 5 October 2000, §§ 40-41.

Contracting Party cannot attract Article 6 guarantees, they are relevant from the standpoint of Articles 2 and 3 of the Convention. Namely, the Court will scrutinise the domestic decision making process with a view to establishing whether the national authorities have adequately assessed the risks of ill-treatment or inhuman or degrading punishment in the receiving country if the applicant has raised such claims.[208]

The Court would also reject complaints which fall outside the scope of a particular provision. As an example, in the case of *Kaplan v. Turkey*, the applicant complained under Article 8 of the Convention that his personal reputation had been damaged on account of his being prosecuted as an alleged terrorist.[209] The Commission observed that Article 8 did not guarantee a right to honour and good reputation and therefore dismissed this complaint for want of subject matter jurisdiction (*ratione materiae*).

2.4 Exhaustion of Domestic Remedies (Article 35 § 1)

2.4.1 Summary

Applicants must exhaust domestic remedies before they can complain before the Strasbourg Court. This means that applicants must avail themselves of the normal avenues of judicial relief that exist in the national system and they must have appealed their case to the highest instance possible within that system.[210] Applicants cannot raise claims before the Court which were not previously raised with the national authorities during the exhaustion process.[211] In the context of Article 3 violations, the normal remedy consists of an effective official investigation into the allegations of ill-treatment followed by the prosecution and punishment of the perpetrators.[212] Therefore, in order to comply with the exhaustion requirement, applicants in Article 3 cases must have taken all reasonable steps to ensure that their complaints reached the appropriate national authorities, and must have shared relevant evidence with the authorities on a timely basis and diligently pursued their cases at all stages of the national proceedings.

---

208 See, *mutatis mutandis, Said v. the Netherlands*, cited above, §§ 48-49. See also Judge Thomassen's concurring opinion in the same judgment where she argued that the lack of rigorous scrutiny of the applicant's allegations by the domestic courts justified the Strasbourg Court's decision not to follow their assessment.

209 *Kaplan v. Turkey*, no. 31830/96, Commission decision of 20 May 1998.

210 See *Akdıvar and Others v. Turkey*, 21893/93, 16 September 1996, § 66.

211 See *Cardot v. France*, no. 11069/84, 19 March 1991, § 34.

212 See *Assenov v. Bulgaria*, no. 24760/94, 28 September 1998, § 102.

A mere doubt as to the effectiveness of domestic remedies, even in circumstances where the national authorities systematically fail to act on complaints of ill-treatment, does not absolve the applicant of the requirement of exhausting remedies.[213] Generally, civil or administrative remedies which are only aimed at monetary compensation of the victim but which are not capable of identifying the perpetrator or establishing individual criminal responsibility are not considered "effective" for purposes of Article 3 and do not need to be exhausted.[214]

As a procedural matter, the applicant has the initial burden of proving exhaustion. If the Court is satisfied that an applicant has made out a *prima facie* case showing that he or she has complied with the exhaustion requirement, then the burden shifts to the Contracting Party to show that an effective remedy was available and not exhausted by the applicant.[215] The applicant will then have an opportunity to comment further on the respondent Government's submission. After this point the Government is estopped from making further arguments on exhaustion or any other admissibility issues.[216] The Court can, however, declare a case inadmissible at any stage of the proceedings.

There are several important exceptions to the exhaustion rule, such as the fact that applicants do not need to exhaust remedies that are unavailable or extraordinary.[217] There may also exist special circumstances absolving the applicant from the exhaustion requirement.[218] Finally, the rule of exhaustion interacts in important ways with the six-month rule, which is discussed in Section 2.5 below.

2.4.2 Discussion

According to Article 35 § 1 of the Convention:

> "[t]he Court may only deal with the matter after all domestic remedies have been exhausted, according to the generally recognised rules of international law...".

The rationale behind this rule lies in the subsidiary character of the Convention machinery: the Contracting Party ought first to be given an opportunity to put matters right through its own legal system before being

---

213 See *Epözdemir v. Turkey* (dec.), no. 57039/00, 31 January 2002.
214 See *Tepe v. Turkey* (dec.), no. 31247/96, 22 January 2002.
215 See *Akdıvar and Others v. Turkey*, cited above, § 68.
216 See *Savitchi v. Moldova*, no. 11039/02, 11 October 2005, § 28.
217 See *Moyá Alvarez v. Spain* (dec.), no. 44677/98, 23 November 1999.
218 See *Akdıvar and Others v. Turkey*, cited above, § 68.

called to account before the Court in Strasbourg. For example, an applicant who wishes to bring an application against a Contracting Party concerning ill-treatment will be expected to have approached the relevant national authorities and complained about the ill-treatment before lodging an application in Strasbourg. If the applicant receives adequate redress at the national level, for example, when those responsible for the ill-treatment are prosecuted and punished by the domestic authorities, he or she will no longer be able to claim to be a victim within the meaning of Article 34. If, on the other hand, the applicant is unable to obtain adequate redress from the national authorities, for example when those authorities have remained passive in the face of the applicant's allegations, he or she will be deemed to have exhausted domestic remedies as required by Article 35. The foregoing description is an over-simplification of a complex Convention requirement, and as will be seen below, there are a number of other issues that must be taken into account.

The rule of exhaustion of domestic remedies was explained in great detail by the Court in its judgment in the case of *Akdıvar and Others v. Turkey:*[219]

> "The Court recalls that the rule of exhaustion of domestic remedies ... obliges those seeking to bring their case against the State before an international judicial or arbitral organ to use first the remedies provided by the national legal system. Consequently, States are dispensed from answering before an international body for their acts before they have had an opportunity to put matters right through their own legal system. The rule is based on the assumption, reflected in Article 13 of the Convention – with which it has close affinity – that there is an effective remedy available in respect of the alleged breach in the domestic system whether or not the provisions of the Convention are incorporated in national law. In this way, it is an important aspect of the principle that the machinery of protection established by the Convention is subsidiary to the national systems safeguarding human rights...".

The Court further explained in the same judgment that:

> "[i]n the area of the exhaustion of domestic remedies there is a distribution of the burden of proof. It is incumbent on the Government claiming non-exhaustion to satisfy the Court that the remedy was an effective one available in theory and in practice at the relevant time, that is to say, that it was accessible, was one which was capable of providing redress in respect of the applicant's complaints and offered reasonable prospects of success. However, once this burden of proof has been satisfied it falls to the applicant to establish that the remedy advanced by the Government was in fact exhausted or was for some reason inadequate and ineffective in the particular circumstances of the case or that there existed special circumstances absolving him or her from the requirement...".[220]

---

219 *Akdıvar and Others v. Turkey*, cited above, § 65.
220 *Ibid.*, § 68.

As pointed out above, after the burden of proof shifts, respondent Government is expected to prove the existence in practice of a particular remedy as well as its effectiveness. For example, in a case which concerned the deliberate destruction of the applicants' home and possessions by members of the security forces in south-east Turkey, the Turkish Government had submitted to the Court a number of decisions of the Turkish Administrative Courts. In these decisions, the plaintiffs had been awarded compensation for the destruction of their homes and possessions in a non-fault based procedure under Article 125 of the Constitution that did not require them to establish that their property had been destroyed deliberately. Having examined the decisions, the Court found that,

> "...despite the extent of the problem of village destruction, there appears to be no example of compensation being awarded in respect of allegations that property has been purposely destroyed by members of the security forces or of prosecutions having been brought against them in respect of such allegations".[221]

The Court, concluding that the remedy in question was not effective for the purposes of the Convention because it did not establish culpability and therefore it did not lead to the prosecution and punishment of those responsible for the destruction, proceeded to dismiss the Government's objection to the admissibility of the application.

The initial burden of showing that relevant domestic remedies have been exhausted rests with the applicant. In fact, the Court will examine the issue of exhaustion *ex officio* in its first examination of the complaint as contained in the application form. It is therefore imperative that the applicant demonstrate clearly, in the application form, that he or she has exhausted the relevant domestic remedies in relation to the complaints made. Failure to show exhaustion, or to explain why a nominally available remedy was not pursued – for example by providing arguments to the effect that the remedy was ineffective because it was inaccessible, or incapable of providing adequate redress, or that there existed special circumstances which absolved the applicant from exhausting domestic remedies – will most likely result in the complaint being declared inadmissible by a Committee. It must be recalled here that complaints declared inadmissible by Committees never reach the stage of communication to the respondent Government. They are final and cannot be challenged in any way by the applicant as referral to the Grand Chamber is not possible. Moreover, letters informing applicants of the decision of the Committee contain only skeletal reasoning (providing only that the Court has decided the case is inadmissible "because it did not comply

---

221 *Menteş and Others v. Turkey*, no. 23186/94, 28 November 1997, § 59.

with the requirements set out in Articles 34 and 35 of the Convention", see *Textbox x*) which may leave the applicant wondering about the specific reasons for the inadmissibility finding, unlike inadmissibility decisions taken by the Chambers in which the reasoning of the Court is laid out in greater detail.[222]

The Court has already developed a body of case-law in respect of most Contracting Parties which discusses the domestic remedies that are generally available in those countries. It is important for applicants to refer to this case-law when arguing exhaustion in their application forms. While taking this case-law into account, the Court will nevertheless have regard to the particular circumstances of each case in its findings on whether remedies have been exhausted. Satisfying the Court that relevant domestic remedies have been exhausted will result in the communication of the application to the respondent Contracting Party, provided of course that other grounds of admissibility have also been satisfied and the application is not manifestly ill-founded. The burden will then shift to the respondent Contracting Party to show why remedies were not exhausted.[223]

If the application is communicated and the respondent Government in its observations on the admissibility of the case does not claim that the applicant has failed to exhaust domestic remedies, the Court will not subsequently raise any exhaustion problems of its own motion. Furthermore, a respondent Government that fails to object to the admissibility of an application in its observations on admissibility will be estopped from doing so at subsequent stages of the proceedings.[224]

In *Akdıvar*, the Court further emphasised that:

> "the application of the rule [of exhaustion of domestic remedies] must make due allowance for the fact that it is being applied in the context of machinery for the protection of human rights that the Contracting Parties have agreed to set up. Accordingly, it has recognised that Article 35 must be applied with some degree of flexibility and without excessive formalism.... It has further recognised that the rule of exhaustion is neither absolute nor capable of being applied automatically; in reviewing whether it has been observed it is essential to have regard to the particular circumstances of each individual case".[225]

---

222 See Section 1.7 above.
223 See Harris, O'Boyle and Warbrick, p. 615 *et seq.*
224 See, *Savitchi v. Moldova*, cited above, § 28. See also Rule 55 of the Rules of Court which states that any plea of inadmissibility must be raised by the respondent Contracting Party in its written or oral observations on the admissibility of the application.
225 *Akdivar and Others v. Turkey*, cited above, § 69.

a) Only "Available" and "Effective" Remedies Need to be Exhausted

According to the *Akdıvar* judgment:

> "...normal recourse should be had by an applicant to remedies which are available and sufficient to afford redress in respect of the breaches alleged...".[226]

For a remedy to be "available", it must exist at the time the application is lodged and must be directly accessible to individuals. If a new and relevant remedy is introduced in the Contracting Party after the application has been lodged, applicants will not normally be required to exhaust that new remedy.[227] Furthermore, "...[t]he existence of the remedies in question must be sufficiently certain not only in theory but in practice, failing which they will lack the requisite accessibility and effectiveness...".[228]

The answer to the question whether a particular remedy is "effective", or, in the words of the *Akdıvar* judgment, "sufficient to afford redress" – and therefore requires exhausting – is a more complex one. In the context of complaints concerning ill-treatment the general rule is that "an official investigation capable of leading to the identification and punishment of those responsible"[229] will be regarded by the Court to be an appropriate form of redress. It must be stressed at this juncture that a remedy does not mean "a remedy bound to succeed but simply an accessible remedy before an authority competent to examine the merits of a complaint".[230] The issue of "effectiveness" of a remedy in the Article 3 context is examined below in subsections d(i)-(ii) in more detail.

---

226 *Akdivar and Others v. Turkey*, cited above, § 66.

227 However, there have been exceptions, notably in Article 6 cases concerning the alleged unfairness of domestic proceedings due to their excessive length. For example, in the case of *Charzyński v. Poland* ((dec.), no. 15212/03, 1 March 2005), which had been lodged in 2003, the Court held that the possibility of filing a complaint, which had been introduced in Polish legislation in 2004, provided the applicant with an effective remedy in respect of his complaint. It therefore declared the application inadmissible for the applicant's failure to exhaust the remedy created in 2004. Similarly, in the case of *İçyer v. Turkey* (dec.), no. 18888/02, 12 January 2006), which concerned the inability of the applicant to return to his house in his village after having been evicted from there for security reasons, the Court observed that a new remedy had been introduced since the applicant lodged his application and declared the case inadmissible for the applicant's failure to exhaust that new remedy. The new remedy, in the Court's opinion, was capable of providing redress for the applicant as it would compensate for the damage suffered as a result of his inability to gain access to his property. In this connection the Court stressed that the most appropriate strategy to be followed in situations where it identified structural or general deficiencies in national law or practice was to ask the respondent Government to review, and where necessary, set up effective remedies, in order to avoid repetitive cases being brought before the Court. However, it is unlikely that the Court would declare an Article 3 complaint inadmissible for an applicant's failure to exhaust a remedy newly created at the national level after the application was lodged with the Court.

228 *Akdivar and Others v. Turkey*, cited above, § 66.

229 *Assenov v. Bulgaria*, cited above, § 102. See also Section 10.3 below.

230 See *Lorsé v. the Netherlands*, no. 52750/99, 4 February 2003, § 96.

b) Extraordinary Remedies do Not Need to be Exhausted

If the remedy is not directly accessible to individuals, it will normally be regarded as an "extraordinary remedy". According to the Court, extraordinary remedies do not satisfy the requirements of "accessibility" and "effectiveness" and therefore do not require exhaustion for purposes of Article 35 § 1 of the Convention.[231] For example, if access to a particular domestic remedy is dependent on the discretionary power of a public authority, it will not be considered an accessible remedy.[232] Examples include applications to the constitutional court in Italy for purposes of challenging a law's constitutionality, because only other courts, and not individuals, are able to refer a case to the Constitutional Court. Therefore, this particular remedy was not directly accessible to individuals.[233] Similarly, applications to the Ministry of Justice in Turkey for requests to issue written orders to public prosecutors requiring them to ask the Court of Cassation to set aside judgments[234] and applications for rectification of decisions of the Turkish Court of Cassation which can only be lodged by public prosecutors but not by individual complainants directly were also held by the Court to be extraordinary remedies.

c) Special Circumstances

The Court acknowledged in *Akdıvar and Others* that the existence of "special circumstances" may absolve an applicant from the requirement of exhaustion of domestic remedies. Such circumstances may exist, for example, in situations where the national authorities have remained totally passive in the face of serious allegations of misconduct by State agents, for instance where State agents have failed to undertake investigations or offer assistance[235] or where they have failed to execute a court order.[236] Furthermore, in a case which concerned the destruction of the applicants' property by the Turkish security forces, the Court found that the indifference displayed by the investigating authorities to the applicants' complaints, coupled with the applicants' feelings of upheaval and insecurity following the destruction of their homes, constituted special circumstances which absolved them from the obligation to exhaust domestic remedies.[237]

---

231   *Moyá Alvarez v. Spain* (dec.), cited above.
232   *Kutcherenko v. Ukraine* (dec.), no. 41974/98, 4 May 1999.
233   *Immobiliare Saffi v. Italy* [GC], no. 22774/93, 28 July 1999, § 42; see also Leach p. 137.
234   *Zarakolu v. Turkey* (dec.), no. 37061/97, 5 December 2002.
235   See *Selmouni v. France*, cited above, § 76.
236   *A.B. v. the Netherlands*, no. 37328/97, 29 January 2002, §§ 69 and 73.
237   *Selçuk and Asker v. Turkey*, nos. 23184/94 and 23185/94, 24 September 1998, §§ 70-71.

In *Ayder and Others v. Turkey* the Government argued that the applicants' failure to apply for compensation before the domestic authorities in respect of the destruction of their property by members of the security forces constituted non-exhaustion. The Court, however, observed that a public assurance had been given by the Provincial Governor that all damage sustained would be compensated by the State. In the light of that unqualified undertaking by a senior public official, the Court found that property owners could have legitimately expected that compensation would be paid without the necessity of their commencing administrative proceedings. Thus, the Court concluded that special circumstances existed, absolving the applicants from the requirement of exhausting domestic remedies.[238]

In *Sejdovic v. Italy*, which concerned the conviction *in absentia* of the applicant – a national of the then Federal Republic of Yugoslavia – without providing him the opportunity to present his defence before the Italian courts, the Court found that the fact that the applicant had not been informed of the possibility of reopening the time allowed for appealing against his conviction and of the short time available for attempting such a remedy, constituted "objective obstacles" to the use of that remedy by the applicant. Taking into account "the difficulties which a person detained in a foreign country would probably have encountered in rapidly contacting a lawyer familiar with Italian law in order to enquire about the legal procedure for obtaining the reopening of his trial, while at the same time giving his counsel a precise account of the facts and detailed instructions", the Court concluded that there were special circumstances releasing the applicant from the obligation to avail himself of the remedy in question.[239]

In several cases where the Court has found that the existence of special circumstances absolved the applicants from the exhaustion requirement, it has also stressed that its ruling was confined to the particular circumstances of those cases and was not to be interpreted as a general statement that remedies were ineffective in the respondent Contracting Party or that applicants were absolved from the obligation under Article 35 to have normal recourse to the

---

238 *Ayder v. Turkey*, no. 23656/94, 8 January 2004, §§ 101-102.
239 *Sejdovic v. Italy* [GC], no. 56581/00, 1 March 2006, §§ 54 -55. This case can be contrasted with the case of *Bahaddar v. the Netherlands* (no. 25894/94, 19 February 1998), which concerned the applicant's proposed expulsion to Bangladesh where, according to the applicant, he would be exposed to a serious risk of being killed or ill-treated. In its admissibility decision the Commission found that the merits of the applicant's case had not been considered by any Netherlands authority in the light of new documentary evidence. Although this evidence had been submitted out of time, the national authorities were not prevented from taking cognisance of it. There were accordingly, in the Commission's view, special circumstances absolving the applicant from exhausting domestic remedies according to the established procedures. However the Court, noting in particular the failure of the applicant's lawyer to ask for an extension of the time limit from the domestic courts to submit the documentary evidence, upheld the Government's preliminary objection and held that, as domestic remedies had not been exhausted, it could not consider the merits of the case.

system of remedies.[240] Furthermore, according to the Court, it is only in exceptional circumstances that it could accept that applicants seek relief before the Court without first having made any attempt to seek redress before the local courts.[241]

Indeed, although the Court has acknowledged in a number of judgments that the application of the rule of exhaustion must make due allowance for the fact that it is being applied in the context of machinery for the protection of human rights that the Contracting Parties have agreed to establish and that the rule must be applied with some degree of flexibility and without excessive formalism,[242] the fact remains that a mere doubt as to the effectiveness of domestic remedies does not absolve the applicant of the requirement of exhausting remedies.

d) "Effective" Remedies in the Context of Article 3 Violations

The issue of the "effectiveness" of domestic remedies is examined below under separate headings for criminal, civil, and administrative remedies.

i. Criminal Remedies

As the Court expressly stated in its *Akdıvar and Others* judgment, the rule of exhaustion of domestic remedies is based on the assumption reflected in Article 13 of the Convention, that effective remedies are in fact available in the domestic systems of Contracting Parties in respect of alleged breaches of Convention rights and that this is the case regardless of the specific manner in which the provisions of the Convention have been incorporated into national law. Thus, the issue of effectiveness of criminal remedies in respect of complaints of ill-treatment is closely linked to the Contracting Parties' positive obligation under Article 3 and their obligation under Article 13 to provide an effective remedy.[243] As pointed out earlier, in the context of Article 3 violations adequate redress will include an effective official investigation capable of leading to the identification and punishment of those responsible. Whereas certain rights and freedoms guaranteed in the Convention may not have been incorporated into the national laws of all Contracting Parties, most types of ill-treatment nevertheless constitute criminal offences in all Contracting Parties. Furthermore, in most Contracting

---

240 See, *inter alia, Selçuk and Asker v. Turkey*, cited above, § 71 and *Akdıvar and Others v. Turkey*, cited above, § 77.
241 *Akdıvar and Others v. Turkey*, cited above, § 77.
242 See, *inter alia, Ayder v. Turkey*, cited above, § 92.
243 See Sections 6.2 and 10 below; see also *Buldan v. Turkey* (dec.) no. 28298/95, 4 June 2002.

Parties, ill-treatment inflicted by State agents is either classified as a criminal offence separate from the offence of ill-treatment inflicted by private persons, or is considered an aggravating element of ill-treatment offences.

At first sight it would therefore appear that the national laws of the Contracting Parties themselves provide for an effective remedy – as required by Article 13 of the Convention – in respect of complaints of ill-treatment. However, the mere existence of national legislation criminalising acts of ill-treatment is not sufficient in and of itself to guarantee a remedy for victims, and problems often arise in the context of the enforcement of those national laws. One of the most common problems is the reluctance of investigating authorities to investigate allegations of ill-treatment by State agents.[244] In such circumstances, an applicant who has brought his or her complaint of ill-treatment before the relevant investigating authority, which remains passive in the face of those allegations, will be expected to submit his or her application to the Court as soon as he or she becomes aware of the ineffectiveness of the remedy. Failure to do so may result in the application being declared inadmissible for non-compliance with the six-month rule.[245]

The Court has also dealt with applications introduced when criminal investigations continued for long periods of time without yielding any tangible results. In such cases, the respondent Government, who will in all likelihood object to the admissibility of the application on the basis of the applicant's failure to await the conclusion of the proceedings, will be expected to prove that the proceedings in question are being conducted diligently and that they are capable of providing redress to the applicant. For example, in the case of *Bati and others v. Turkey*, the applicants introduced their application with the Court while the criminal proceedings against the police officers suspected of having inflicted ill-treatment on them were still pending. Observing that the proceedings in question – a criminal trial – had continued for eight years during which time the judicial authorities had failed to take a number of important steps such as summoning and questioning the defendants directly and ensuring that the injuries of the applicants were medically examined, the Court held that the applicants had satisfied the obligation to exhaust the relevant remedies and were not required to await the conclusion of the criminal trial.[246]

---

244 See for example, *Khashiyev and Akayeva v. Russia*, nos. 57942/00 and 57045/00, 24 February 2005, § 145, in which the Court observed that although the domestic courts had found that the killings of the first applicant's relatives had been perpetrated by servicemen and awarded the first applicant damages against the State, they did not prosecute those servicemen. In the same judgment the Court also found a violation of Article 3 of the Convention on account of a lack of thorough and effective investigation into the applicants' allegations of ill-treatment, see § 180.

245 For further information, see Section 2.5.2 (c) below.

246 *Bati and Others v. Turkey*, nos. 33097/96 and 57834/00, 3 June 2004, § 148. On the basis of those failures the Court also found a violation of Article 13 of the Convention.

According to the Court's established case-law, a mere doubt as to the prospect of success of a particular remedy is not sufficient to exempt an applicant from the requirement of exhausting that remedy.[247] The Court's decision on admissibility in *Epözdemir v. Turkey*[248] provides a good example of this point. The *Epözdemir* case concerned the killing of the applicant's husband by a group of four village guards. An autopsy was carried out and the body was buried. The family of the deceased were not informed of the death of Mr Epözdemir – despite the fact that the applicant had already informed the relevant prosecutor that her husband was missing – and no action was taken by the investigating authorities to investigate the circumstances of the killing notwithstanding an *ex officio* obligation under domestic law to do so. The applicant subsequently – by pure coincidence – found out that her husband had been killed by the village guards and asked the prosecutor to mount a prosecution. Her request was rejected, the prosecutor stating that although it was established that her husband had been killed by the village guards, it was not possible to establish which one of the four village guards had fired the fatal shot. The applicant did not avail herself of the opportunity to appeal the prosecutor's decision and instead applied directly to the Court in Strasbourg. In its decision declaring the application inadmissible, the Court held by a majority, that although the decision not to prosecute the four named village guards suggested that the clear wording of domestic legislation on joint enterprises in the commission of the offence of homicide had been disregarded by the prosecutor, the applicant could have brought this issue to the attention of the appeal judge and thus could have substantially increased her prospects of success. The applicant had not shown, therefore, that an appeal would have been devoid of any chance of success.[249]

In jurisdictions where the commission of the offence of ill-treatment gives rise to an *ex officio* duty of the investigating authorities to investigate the incident without waiting for the victim to lodge a formal complaint, the victim may be required to co-operate with the authorities by assisting them, for example, in identifying and locating eye-witnesses. The conduct of the applicant in exhausting domestic remedies may therefore also play a role in the Court's examination of the question as to whether those remedies have been exhausted.

---

247 *Whiteside v. the United Kingdom*, no. 20357/92, Commission decision of 7 March 1994.
248 See *Epözdemir v. Turkey* (dec.), cited above.
249 Compare to *İlhan v. Turkey* [GC], cited above, § 63, where the investigating authorities had remained totally passive in investigating the circumstances of the severe ill-treatment to which soldiers had subjected the applicant's brother. The Grand Chamber, in rejecting the Government's objection to the admissibility of the case, held that the matter had been sufficiently brought to the attention of the relevant domestic authority, which had an *ex officio* obligation to investigate the circumstances of the ill-treatment without waiting for a formal complaint from the applicant.

ii. Civil and Administrative Remedies

In its judgment in the case of *Assenov and Others v. Bulgaria* the Court found that the applicant had exhausted all the possibilities available to him within the criminal justice system, as he had made numerous appeals to the prosecuting authorities at all levels, requesting a full criminal investigation into the allegations of ill-treatment carried out by police and requesting that the officers concerned be prosecuted. In the absence of a criminal prosecution in connection with his complaints, the applicant was therefore not required to embark upon another attempt to obtain redress by bringing a civil action for damages.[250] In reaching this conclusion, the Court also considered the fact that under Bulgarian law it was not possible for a complainant to initiate a criminal prosecution in respect of offences allegedly committed by agents of the State in the performance of their duties. The Court went on to state in paragraph 102 of its judgment that:

> "where an individual raises an arguable claim that he has been seriously ill-treated by the police or other such agents of the State unlawfully and in breach of Article 3, that provision, read in conjunction with the State's general duty under Article 1 of the Convention to "secure to everyone within their jurisdiction the rights and freedoms defined in ... [the] Convention", requires by implication that there should be an effective official investigation. This investigation, as with that under Article 2, should be capable of leading to the identification and punishment of those responsible... If this were not the case, the general legal prohibition of torture and inhuman and degrading treatment and punishment, despite its fundamental importance, would be ineffective in practice and it would be possible in some cases for agents of the State to abuse the rights of those within their control with virtual impunity".

It follows, therefore, that in the context of Article 3 complaints, a civil or an administrative action in respect of illegal acts attributable to a State or its agents may only be regarded as an effective remedy where that remedy is capable of establishing the circumstances of the ill-treatment and of leading to the identification and punishment of those responsible. Civil or administrative proceedings aimed solely at awarding damages rather than identifying and punishing those responsible will not be regarded as effective remedies in the context of Article 3 complaints.[251]

e) Compliance With Rules of Domestic Procedure

When exhausting domestic remedies, applicants are expected to comply with the relevant procedural rules in their domestic jurisdiction. Thus, when an

---

250   See, *Assenov and Others v. Bulgaria*, cited above, § 86.
251   See *Tepe v. Turkey* (dec.), cited above.

appeal is dismissed without the national court having examined the substance of the appeal because, for example, the applicant failed to lodge it within the applicable time limit, that applicant will be deemed by the Court not to have complied with the rule of exhaustion of domestic remedies.

The Court further requires that in order for an application to be admissible, complaints made therein must have been raised, at least in substance, before the domestic courts.[252] It is not strictly necessary to refer to the Convention Article(s) in domestic proceedings, provided that the substance of the Convention complaint is adequately brought to the attention of the relevant national authorities.[253]

2.4.3 Concluding Remarks

As described above, applicants are expected to show in their application forms that they have exhausted relevant domestic remedies and that in doing so they have complied with the relevant domestic rules of procedure and invoked the substance of the Convention complaint in the course of the domestic proceedings. Readers are referred to the *Model Article 3 Application* in Appendix No. 6 for an example of how this can be done.

In the context of Article 3, identifying the relevant domestic remedy is perhaps easier than is the case with other Articles of the Convention. As pointed out above, the most appropriate domestic remedy for allegations of ill-treatment will be a criminal investigation since such an investigation will be the best means to establish the accuracy of the allegations as well as being potentially capable of leading to the identification and punishment of those responsible. Furthermore, any decision which is not favourable to the applicant, such as a decision to discontinue the investigation or to acquit those responsible for the ill-treatment must be appealed against if and when the national legislation provides for such a course of action. It must be reiterated that according to the Court's established case-law, a mere doubt as to the prospect of success of a particular remedy is not sufficient to exempt an applicant from the requirement of exhausting that remedy.

If the applicant has not exhausted a particular remedy, he or she must explain in the application form the reasons for his or her decision not to do so. Such explanations may include, for example, the fact that the particular remedy has

---

252 *Cardot v. France*, cited above, § 34.
253 See, for example, *Hudson v. former Yugoslav Republic of Macedonia* (dec.), no. 67128/01, 24 March 2005, in which the applicant's complaint under Article 3 of the Convention arising from the conditions of his detention in prison was declared inadmissible by the Court because of the applicant's failure to bring those complaints to the attention of the national authorities.

already been examined by the Court itself in another case which concerned similar facts and the Court has concluded that the remedy is indeed ineffective. If the remedy in question has not yet been examined by the Court, on the other hand, and if it is the applicant's belief that the particular remedy is not capable of providing redress, he or she should consider providing examples of domestic court decisions demonstrating the ineffectiveness of that remedy. This may be done by showing that the remedy in question has been tried in the past under similar circumstances and provided no relief.

In case of any doubts about the effectiveness of a particular domestic remedy, the applicant should consider exhausting the remedy in question while at the same time introducing his or her application with the Court.[254] Finally, it should be noted that the rule of exhaustion interacts in important ways with the six-month rule. Therefore, applicants are advised to read this section on exhaustion together with the following section describing the six-month rule.

2.5 The Six-Month Rule (Article 35 §1)

2.5.1 Summary

A complaint must be filed with the Court within six months of the date on which the final domestic decision was taken in the case. The six-month period starts running from 1) the date the domestic judgment is rendered orally in public,[255] 2) the date of service of the written decision if the applicant is entitled to such service[256], or 3) the date when the decision was finalised and signed in situations where judgments are not rendered orally or served.[257] If no domestic remedies are available, the six-month period starts running from the date of the incident or act of which the applicant complains.[258] Where domestic remedies turn out to be ineffective, the period starts running from the moment the applicant became aware, or should have become aware, that remedies were ineffective.[259] For continuing situations the six-month period does not start to run until after the situation ends, but a complaint can be filed prior to the end of the situation.

---

254 See the Concluding Remarks in Section 2.5.3 below.
255 See *Loveridge v. the United Kingdom* (dec.), no. 39641/98, 23 October 2001.
256 *Worm v. Austria*, no. 2714/93, 29 August 1997, §§ 32-33.
257 *Papachelas v. Greece* [GC], no. 31423/96, 25 March 1999, § 30.
258 See, *inter alia, Vayiç v. Turkey* (dec.), no. 18078/02, 28 June 2005.
259 See, *inter alia, Bulut and Yavuz v. Turkey* (dec.), no. 73065/01, 28 May 2002.

The date of introduction of an application with the Court is the date on the letter introducing the application or on the application form itself, unless there is a difference of more than one day between the date of the letter or application form and the date of the postal stamp on the envelope.[260] If there is a risk of missing the six-month deadline, applicants should fax the introductory letter to the registry. Such faxes must be followed up with a signed original within five days.

2.5.2 Discussion

a) The General Rule

An application must be lodged with the Court within a period of six months from the date on which the final domestic decision was taken in the case concerned (Article 35 § 1 of the Convention). A survey of the Court's case-law reveals a number of reasons for this rule. For instance:

> "[t]he object of the six-month time limit under Article 35 § 1 is to promote legal certainty, by ensuring that cases raising issues under the Convention are dealt with in a reasonable time and that past decisions are not continually open to challenge. The rule also affords the prospective applicant time to consider whether to lodge an application and, if so, to decide on the specific complaints and arguments to be raised".[261]

The Court has also explained that the rule is:

> "designed to facilitate establishment of the facts of the case; otherwise, with the passage of time, this would become more and more difficult, and a fair examination of the issue raised under the Convention would thus become problematic".[262]

Finally,

> "in reflecting the wish of the Contracting Parties to prevent past decisions being called into question after an indefinite lapse of time, the rule marks out the temporal limits of supervision carried out by the organs of the Convention and signals to both individuals and State authorities the period beyond which such supervision is no longer possible".[263]

The six-month period includes weekends and national holidays; e.g. if the starting date of the six-month period is 1 January 2005 the application must

---

260 *Arslan v. Turkey* (dec.), no. 36747/02, 21 November 2002.
261 *Finucane v. the United Kingdom* (dec.), no. 29178/95, 2 July 2002; see also *Worm v. Austria*, cited above, §§ 32-33.
262 *Alzery v. Sweden* (dec.), no. 10786/04, 26 October 2004.
263 *Walker v. the United Kingdom*, (dec.), no. 34979/97, 25 January 2000.

be introduced by 1 July 2005. If there is a risk of running out of time, an application can be introduced by letter or by fax message[264] provided that certain criteria are complied with in such communications.[265]

b) The Date of Introduction

The date of introduction of an application will be the date on the letter introducing the application or the application form, unless it differs by more than one day from the date of the postal stamp on the envelope. In the case of *Arslan v. Turkey*, the application form was dated 12 April 2002, however, it had not been posted until 19 April 2002.[266] The Court stated that, assuming that the applicant had completed the form on 12 April, he should have posted it at the latest on the following day, i.e. 13 April 2002. Noting that the applicant had not provided an explanation for the six-day interval between the date on the application form and the date on which it was posted, the Court declared the application inadmissible for failure to observe the six-month time limit which had started to run on 13 October 2001. This case illustrates that the rule is applied strictly by the Court and makes clear that where there is a difference of more than one day between the date on the letter by which the application is introduced and the date of the postal stamp, the date of the postal stamp will be taken as the date of introduction.

If the letter or the application form is not dated, the date of the introduction will in any event be taken as the date of the postal stamp; if that stamp is illegible, the date of receipt at the Court will be considered to be the date of introduction.

It must also be stressed that the six-month rule, together with the rule of exhaustion of domestic remedies, is probably the most frequently used formal ground of inadmissibility; the Court applies it of its own motion[267] and a respondent Government cannot waive it.[268]

---

264   If sent by fax message a signed original should also be sent to the Court within 5 days by surface mail. See Article 5 of the Practice Direction on the Institution of Proceedings.
265   See Section 4.1 below. Also, the sample letter drafted on the basis of hypothetical facts, which can be found in *Textbox vii*, may be taken as a starting point.
266   *Arslan v. Turkey* (dec.), cited above.
267   *Soto Sanchez v. Spain* (dec.), no. 66990/01, 20 May 2003.
268   *Walker v. the United Kingdom* (dec), cited above; see also Jacobs & White, p. 411.

c) The Starting Point of the Six-Month Period

The six-month rule is closely connected with the rule of exhaustion of domestic remedies, and the moment on which the six-month period starts to run depends on the existence, or the lack thereof, of domestic remedies. As a general rule, a complaint must be submitted to the Court within six months from the day following the final domestic court decision rendered in relation to that complaint.[269] However, different practices of the domestic courts in the Contracting Parties – and, indeed, varying practices between different courts within the same Contracting Party – have made it impossible to apply a uniform rule in every case and have led the Commission and the Court to devise the following rules in relation to each scenario with which they have been confronted.

i. Where Domestic Remedies Exist

The Commission's view,[270] which was also adopted by the Court,[271] was that the six-month period starts to run from the day on which the judgment was rendered orally in public, meaning that the following day is the first day of the six-month period. However, where an applicant is entitled to be served *ex officio* with a written copy of the final domestic decision, the six-month period starts to run on the date of service of the written judgment,[272] irrespective of whether the judgment concerned, or parts thereof, were previously pronounced orally.[273] As seen above, one of the principles underlying the rule is to allow a prospective applicant to refer to the full reasoning set out in the domestic court decision when formulating the complaints he or she wishes to lodge with the Court in Strasbourg. An applicant will obviously be better able to do so when he or she has been provided with the written copy of the judgment.

If domestic law does not provide for oral pronouncement or service – or if it is not the practice of the domestic courts to serve their decisions notwithstanding legislation to the contrary[274] – the Court will take as the starting point the date on which the decision was finalised and signed, that being the

---

269 In calculating the six-month time limit, regard must also be had to the explanations in Section 2.4.2 above; the time spent on exhausting an ineffective remedy may result in the six-month time limit being missed.

270 *K.C.M. v. the Netherlands*, no. 21034/92, Commission decision of 9 January 1995.

271 *Loveridge v. the United Kingdom* (dec.), cited above.

272 *Worm v. Austria*, cited above, §§ 32-33.

273 *Worm v. Austria*, no. 22714/93, Commission decision of 27 November 1995.

274 As is the situation in Turkey where decisions of the Criminal Division of the Court of Cassation are not served on defendants despite the clear wording of the domestic legislation requiring the Court of Cassation to serve them; see *Caralan v. Turkey* (dec.), no. 27529/95, 14 November 2002.

date when the parties or their legal representatives were definitely able to discover its content.[275]

ii. Where There are no Domestic Remedies

In cases where there are no domestic remedies, an applicant will be expected to introduce his or her application within six months from the date of the incident or act of which the applicant complains. For example, an applicant who complains about the excessive length of his or her pre-trial detention which is lawful under domestic legislation, will be expected to lodge an application, at the latest, within six months from the date of release, since he or she cannot challenge the lawfulness of the detention before the domestic authorities.[276] Obviously, it is open to an applicant in such a situation to bring the application before he or she is released.

Similarly, where an applicant argues that existing domestic remedies are ineffective or that there are special circumstances which absolve him or her from the obligation to exhaust those remedies, he or she will be expected to introduce the application within six months of the date of the incident complained of, or of the date when he or she first became aware of the ineffectiveness of the remedy or the special circumstances in question.

iii. Where Domestic Remedies Turn Out to be Ineffective

Difficulties arise in the determination of the starting point of the six-month period in cases where domestic authorities remain inactive in the face of complaints of ill-treatment or where domestic criminal investigations continue for long periods of time without yielding any tangible results. According to the Court, if the domestic remedy invoked by the applicant is adequate in theory, but in the course of time proved to be ineffective, the applicant is no longer obliged to exhaust it.[277] The challenge for the applicant is to determine the point in time when it becomes apparent that the remedy is "ineffective" for purposes of the Convention. As described below, the Court imposes a high burden of due diligence on the applicant in this respect: the Court will declare a case inadmissible for non-respect of the six-month rule if it finds that the applicant continued to pursue a domestic remedy for more than six months when it should have been clear to him or her that the remedy was ineffective.

---

275   *Papachelas v. Greece* [GC], cited above, § 30.
276   See, *inter alia, Vayiç v. Turkey* (dec.), cited above. See also "Continuing Situations" in Section 2.5.2 (c) (iv) below.
277   See *Mikheyev v. Russia*, cited above, § 86.

The Commission addressed the issue of the starting point of the six-month period in such circumstances in the case of *Laçin v. Turkey* where it held the following:[278]

> "[s]pecial considerations could apply in exceptional cases where an applicant first avails himself of a domestic remedy and only at a later stage becomes aware, or should have become aware, of the circumstances which make that remedy ineffective. In such a situation, the six-month period might be calculated from the time when the applicant becomes aware, or should have become aware, of these circumstances".[279]

The Court has followed the Commission's approach in a number of cases[280] and further added in *Bayram and Yıldırım v. Turkey* that if the applicants did not become aware of the ineffectiveness of the domestic remedies for a long period, this "was due to their own negligence".[281]

According to the Court, "the six-month rule is autonomous and must be construed and applied according to the facts of each individual case, so as to ensure the effective exercise of the right to individual application".[282] Nevertheless, the cases in which the Court has expected applicants to have "become aware" of the ineffectiveness of an ongoing domestic remedy at an earlier stage than they did, do not provide uniform guidance from which a potential applicant, in the midst of exhausting a doubtful remedy, may benefit.

It appears from a number of cases introduced against Turkey, for example, that the applicants should not have awaited the outcome of criminal investigations that were marked by long periods of inactivity on the part of the investigating authorities. Thus, in the case of *Bulut and Yavuz v. Turkey*, concerning the killing on 29 July 1994 of the applicants' husband and father allegedly by persons acting with the connivance of the State, the applicants claimed in their application form – submitted to the Court on 1 March 2001 – that they had applied to the office of the public prosecutor in order to obtain information on numerous occasions. On each occasion they had been told that no one had yet been prosecuted for the killing. The final time they checked with the investigating authorities was on 26 October 2000, when they were once again informed that no one had yet been prosecuted for the

---

278   *Laçin v. Turkey*, no. 23654/94, Commission decision of 15 May 1995.
279   See also *Çelik v. Turkey*, no. 23655/94, Commission decision of 15 May 1995.
280   See, *inter alia*, *Ekinci v. Turkey* (dec.), no. 27602/95, 8 June 1999; *Gündüz v. Turkey* (dec.), no. 36212/97, 12 October 1999; *Hazar and Others v. Turkey* (dec.), nos. 62566/00-62577/00 and 62579-62581/00, 10 January 2002; *Camberrow MM5 AD v. Bulgaria* (dec.), no. 50357/99, 1 April 2004 and *Gongadze v. Ukraine* (dec.), no. 34056/02, 22 March 2005.
281   See *Bayram and Yıldırım v. Turkey*, (dec.) no. 38587/97, 29 January 2002.
282   *Fernandez-Molina and Others v. Spain* (dec.), no. 64359/01, 8 October 2002.

killing. The applicants argued that the domestic authorities were, nominally at least, still investigating the killing and this investigation would, pursuant to Article 102 of the Turkish Criminal Code, continue until 20 years had elapsed from the date of the killing. They submitted that the six-month time limit did not apply in their case given that there had as yet not been a domestic decision to discontinue the investigation. The Court rejected these arguments holding that the applicants should have displayed greater diligence and initiative in staying abreast of the progress of the investigation, and if, as they alleged, they had not become aware of the ineffectiveness of the investigation until October 2000, that was due to their own negligence.[283]

Reference can similarly be made to the case of *Şükran Aydın and Others v. Turkey*,[284] which concerned the ill-treatment and killing of the first applicant's husband Vedat Aydın following his abduction allegedly by undercover agents of the State in July 1991. The applicants had joined the criminal investigation as an intervening party. On 23 February 1998 they alerted the investigating prosecutor to the conclusion, published in a report,[285] that agents of the State had killed Vedat Aydın. They asked the prosecutor to investigate this fresh information and to inform the family of the results of that investigation. Following a reminder sent to the prosecutor in October 1998, the applicants received a reply in which the prosecutor simply stated that the investigation into the killing was still pending. In their application to the Court, which was introduced on 3 November 1998, the applicants claimed that they had become aware of the ineffectiveness of the domestic remedies following the unsatisfactory reply of the prosecutor. Nevertheless, the Court declared the application inadmissible for non-respect of the six-month rule and held that the applicants must be considered to have been aware of the lack of any effective criminal investigation long before they petitioned the public prosecutor on 23 February 1998. In its decision the Court made no reference to the evidence which had only been made public a month before the applicants brought it to the attention of the investigating authorities. This case illustrates that a long period of inactivity may result in an inadmissibility finding, despite an applicant's demonstrated diligence in assisting the investigating authorities by means of alerting them to fresh evidence.

---

283 *Bulut and Yavuz v. Turkey* (dec.), cited above.
284 *Şükran Aydın and Others v. Turkey* (dec.), no. 46231/99, 26 May 2005.
285 The Susurluk Report. In another case (*Buldan v. Turkey*, no. 28298/95, 20 April 2004, § 80), the Court considered that that Report, which was drawn up at the request of the Turkish Prime Minister in January 1998 and which he decided should be made public, could not be solely relied upon to meet the required standard of proof that State officials were implicated in any particular incident but that it had to be regarded as a serious attempt to provide information on, and analyse problems associated with, the fight against terrorism from a general perspective and to recommend preventive and investigative measures.

By contrast to the cases discussed above, in the case of *Paul and Audrey Edwards v. the United Kingdom*,[286] the Court held that it was reasonable for the applicants to have awaited for a long period for the outcome of a non-statutory inquiry set up to investigate the circumstances of the death on 29 November 1994 of their son in prison. Although in this case the applicants had waited for a period of over four years before introducing their application they were found by the Court to have been justified in doing so. Had the applicants chosen to introduce their application prior to the publication of the Inquiry Report, there would have been a strong argument for finding that their complaints concerning the substantive and procedural aspects of Article 2 of the Convention were premature. The Court further considered that:

> "the findings reached by the Inquiry could have potentially affected the existence of remedies whether by providing the basis for a criminal prosecution or disclosing facts supporting an action for damages in the civil courts. In those circumstances, it may be considered that the non-availability of any effective remedies finally became apparent on publication of the Inquiry Report on 15 June 1998 and that this date must be regarded as the final decision for the purposes of Article 35 § 1 of the Convention. The application, introduced on 14 December 1998, was therefore introduced within the requisite six months and cannot be rejected pursuant to Article 35 § 4 of the Convention".[287]

Time spent on exhausting a remedy which, according to the Court's case-law, is considered an extraordinary remedy and which therefore need not be exhausted, may result in the application being declared inadmissible for non-respect of the six-month rule. The Court stated in the case of *Berdzenishvili v. Russia* that applications for a retrial made to domestic courts or authorities, or similar extraordinary remedies, cannot, as a general rule, be taken into account for the purposes of Article 35 of the Convention. The proceedings which were held to be extraordinary in *Berdzenishvili* were supervisory reviews of judgments which could be brought at any time after a judgment became enforceable, even years later. The Court considered that if the supervisory-review procedure was considered a remedy to be exhausted, the uncertainty thereby created would have rendered nugatory the six-month rule. In the light of the above, the Court held that the applicant, who had sought a supervisory review of the Supreme Court's judgment convicting him, should have introduced his application with the Court within six months of the Supreme Court judgment.[288]

---

286 *Paul and Audrey Edwards v. the United Kingdom* (dec.), no. 46477/99, 21 February 2002.
287 *Ibid.*
288 *Berdzenishvili v. Russia* (dec.), no. 31697/03, 29 January 2004. See also Leach pp. 148-151.

iv. Continuing Situations

The six-month time limit does not start to run if the Convention complaint stems from a continuing situation. Examples of continuing situations include complaints concerning length of domestic court proceedings, detention, and an inability to enjoy possessions.[289] Such situations are continuing because of the absence of a domestic remedy capable of putting an end to them or because of the ineffectiveness of existing remedies. It follows, therefore, that the six-month time limit will not start running until the end of the situation. As pointed out earlier, this does not mean that an application cannot be lodged before the situation comes to an end. For example, the case of *Assanidze v. Georgia*,[290] concerning the continuing detention of the applicant despite his acquittal by the Supreme Court of Georgia on 29 January 2001 and the order issued by that court for his immediate release, illustrates how absurd it would be if the Court expected a person to continue to suffer indefinitely before he or she is allowed to introduce an application. In *Assanidze*, the Grand Chamber of the Court explained that:

> "to detain a person for an indefinite and unforeseeable period, without such detention being based on a specific statutory provision or judicial decision, is incompatible with the principle of legal certainty … and arbitrary, and runs counter to the fundamental aspects of the rule of law".

Having regard to the fact that the applicant was still in prison when the Court adopted its judgment on 24 March 2004 and "having regard to the particular circumstances of the case and the urgent need to put an end to the violation"[291] the Court considered that the respondent State must secure the applicant's release at the earliest possible date.

2.5.3 Concluding Remarks

It is for the applicant to provide the Court with information that enables it to establish whether he or she has complied with the six-month rule. Failure to provide such information may result in the application being declared inadmissible. For this reason, it is recommended that applicants enclose with the application a photocopy of the envelope – with a legible postal stamp – in which the final domestic court decision was sent to them or any other document showing the date of service of the final domestic court decision.

In case of doubt about the effectiveness of a particular remedy, the decisions and the judgments of the Commission and the Court should be consulted to

---

289 *Loizidou v. Turkey* (preliminary objections), cited above.
290 *Assanidze v. Georgia* [GC], cited above, § 175.
291 *Ibid.,* § 203.

check whether the remedy in question has been examined before. Another possible course of action is to introduce the application while at the same time exhausting the doubtful remedy and keeping the Court informed of developments. Obviously, if the remedy in question has been exhausted before the Court examines the application, it should be informed about the outcome in order to eliminate the risk of the application being declared inadmissible for non-exhaustion.[292] If, on the other hand, the Court examines the application before the remedy is exhausted and declares the case inadmissible for non-exhaustion of that remedy, the applicant may bring a new application once he or she has exhausted the remedy, since the domestic decision obtained will be regarded as relevant new information within the meaning of Article 35 § 2 (b) of the Convention. If an applicant waits to lodge the application until a doubtful remedy has been exhausted, and if the Court subsequently rules that the remedy was in fact an ineffective one which did not require exhaustion, the application may well be declared inadmissible for non-respect of the six-month rule, with no possibility for the applicant to lodge a new application based on the same facts. Proceeding to exhaust the domestic remedy, doubtful though its effectiveness may be, at the same time as introducing an application with the Court will also eliminate the risk that the domestic time limit in respect of that remedy will have expired should the Court consider that the remedy at issue does require exhaustion.

2.6 "Well-Foundedness" of the Application (Article 35 § 3)

2.6.1 Summary

An application is "well-founded" if the Court is satisfied that there is a case to answer. If the application on its face does not disclose a violation of the Convention, either because 1) the allegations are not sufficiently substantiated by the evidence, or 2) because the complaint, even if substantiated, does not fall within the scope of Convention rights because, for instance, the ill-treatment complained of is not sufficiently severe to constitute a violation of Article 3, then the application will be dismissed as "manifestly ill-founded".

Applications relating to Article 3 violations should be 1) supported by evidence of the ill-treatment such as medical reports, eye-witness affidavits,

---

292   Obviously, if appropriate redress is obtained from the "doubtful remedy", the applicant can inform the Court of his or her intention to withdraw the application. See Section 8.2 below for further information.

custody records, court transcripts, domestic complaints, and any other documents showing that the ill-treatment occurred *and* that the complaints and relevant evidence were brought to the attention of the national authorities, and
2) applicants must show that the alleged ill-treatment was severe enough to
cross the threshold of the Article 3 prohibition. Regarding the latter, the
applicant should consult the Court's considerable jurisprudence on the definition of torture and inhuman or degrading treatment or punishment outlined in
this section and discussed in more detail in Appendix No. 10.

2.6.2 Discussion I: Evidentiary Requirements

According to Article 35 § 3 of the Convention, the Court may declare any
individual application inadmissible if it considers it to be "manifestly ill-
founded". Applications can be declared inadmissible on this ground both by
Committees – i.e. without the application being communicated to the respondent Government – or by Chambers. A Chamber may do so either before or
after communication of the case to the respondent Government. This ground
of admissibility constitutes an important means for the Court to weed out
unmeritorious – indeed also frivolous – applications.

If an application is declared inadmissible by a Committee of three judges[293]
as being manifestly ill-founded, the applicant will be informed in a letter
which states only that "in the light of all the material in its possession, and in
so far as the matters complained of were within its competence, the Court
found that they did not establish a violation of the rights and freedoms set out
in the Convention or its Protocols".[294]

There are numerous and diverse grounds on which an application may be
declared inadmissible as being manifestly ill-founded, but for purposes of the
present *Handbook* two of them are of particular relevance: failure to substantiate allegations, and situations where the ill-treatment complained of is not
sufficiently severe to amount to a breach of Article 3.

a) Substantiation of Allegations[295]

Before the Court can establish whether there has been a violation of the
Convention, it must first establish the facts at issue. According to the Court,

---

293 If the case is declared inadmissible on this ground by a Chamber, on the other hand, a copy of the
   Chamber's decision, which sets out the reasons for inadmissibility, will be sent to the applicant.
294 See *Textbox x*. The applicant will receive a letter with the same wording if the application has been
   declared inadmissible on more than one ground; e.g. if the applicant has neither complied with the six-
   month rule nor exhausted the relevant domestic remedies.
295 See also Section 11 below for evidential issues and for establishment of facts.

Convention proceedings do not in all cases lend themselves to rigorous application of the principle of *affirmanti incumbit probatio* (he who alleges something must prove that allegation).[296] In the cases referred to it, the Court will
examine all the material before it, whether originating from the parties or
other sources, and if necessary, will obtain material *proprio motu*.[297]
Nevertheless, according to the established case-law of the Court, an applicant
does bear the initial burden of producing evidence in support of his or her
complaints at the time the application is lodged. Once this burden has been
discharged and the Court is satisfied that there is a case to answer, the Court
will communicate the application – provided, of course, that the other
requirements of admissibility are also met. The Court's attitude towards the
distribution of the burden of proof is a corollary of the fact that Convention
proceedings are distinct from criminal proceedings where the principle of
affirmanti incumbit probatio does apply and where, therefore, the prosecution
bears the legal burden of proving the guilt of the accused party.

The required standard of proof to convince the Court that there is a case to
answer – i.e. that the allegations are not manifestly ill-founded – depends on
the nature of the allegation. In cases concerning ill-treatment for example, it
appears from the case-law of the Court that an applicant is required to make
out a *prima facie* case at the time of introduction of the application in order to
discharge this initial burden.[298] In the context of Article 3 of the Convention,
a *prima facie* case may be loosely defined as an arguable case or a case in
which there is some evidence in support of the allegations. Such evidence
may include medical records and other medical documents such as x-rays,
photographs, eye-witness accounts, custody records and any documents
showing that the complaints have been brought to the attention of the national
authorities.

In order to avoid any risk of an inadmissibility finding at the initial stages, it
is imperative that allegations of ill-treatment be adequately supported by documents and argumentation at the time the application is lodged.[299] Where an
applicant is not in a position to provide such documentation, for example
because the documents are in the possession of the national authorities or
because the applicant is unable to obtain the evidence without the assistance
of the national authorities, the Court should be informed of this. Depending
on the persuasiveness of the explanations and other material submitted by the
applicant, the Court may seek to obtain the documents from the national

---

296 See, *inter alia, Timurtaş v. Turkey*, cited above, § 66.
297 *Ireland v. the United Kingdom*, no. 5310/71, 18 January 1978, § 160.
298 See, *inter alia, Birutis and Others v. Lithuania* (dec.), nos. 47698/99, 48115/99, 7 November 2000; see
     also *Artico v. Italy*, no. 6694/74, 13 May 1980, § 30; Harris, O'Boyle and Warbrick, pp. 627-628.
299 See also Leach, p. 35.

authorities with the help of the respondent Government. It may do so either by communicating the application to the respondent Government or by requesting the Government, pursuant to Rule 54 § 2 (a) of the Rules of Court, to submit the documents in question.[300]

b) Special Evidential Considerations in Expulsion Cases

According to the well established case-law of the Court, expulsion by a Contracting Party may give rise to an issue under Articles 2 or 3, or both, and hence engage the responsibility of that State where substantial grounds have been shown for believing that the person, if expelled, would face a real risk of being subjected to treatment contrary to Article 3 or would be deprived of his or her life in violation of Article 2 in the receiving country (for example, by falling victim to an extrajudicial killing). In these circumstances, Articles 2 and 3 imply the obligation not to expel the applicant to that country.[301]

The Court has developed the following standard in expulsion cases: the applicant must show that "substantial grounds" exist for believing that, if expelled, he or she would face "a real risk of being subject to treatment contrary to Article 3".[302] It is evident from this language that the applicant must show more than a *mère possibility* of ill-treatment.[303]

Applicants may face particular evidential challenges in expulsion cases. Although the general conditions in the country of destination constitute a relevant factor in the Court's risk assessment, it is insufficient to show that the general situation in the country of destination is dangerous; rather, an applicant must also establish that he or she personally runs a real risk of being subjected to treatment contrary to Articles 2 and 3 of the Convention, for example by showing that he or she has previously been subjected to ill-treatment, or that he or she is a member of a group which is known to be targeted by the authorities of the country of destination,[304] or that he or she is actively being sought by the authorities.[305]

---

300 See Section 5 below.
301 See, *inter alia*, *Soering v. the United Kingdom*, no. 14038/88, 7 July 1989, §§ 90-91; *Cruz Varas and Others v. Sweden*, no. 15576/89, 20 March 1991, §§ 69-70; and, *Chahal v. the United Kingdom*, cited above, §§ 73-74.
302 See, *inter alia*, *Chahal v. the United Kingdom,* cited above, § 74.
303 See *Vilvarajah and Others v. the United Kingdom*, nos. 13163/87, 13164/87, 13165/87, 13447/87, and 13448/87, 30 October 1991, §§ 107 and 111; *H.L.R. v. France*, no. 24573/94, 29 April 1997, § 37; *Hilal v. the United Kingdom*, no. 45276/99, 6 March 2001, § 60.
304 See, *mutatis mutandis, N. v. Finland*, no. 38885/02, 26 July 2005, §§ 161-167.
305 See "Short Survey of Cases Examined by the Court in 2004" at http://www.echr.coe.int/NR/rdonlyres/94484030-2547-4FFC-9F91-8E96A87C7D74/0/2004analysisof-caselaw.pdf

In assessing whether "substantial grounds" exist, the Court will examine all the circumstances of the case.[306] The types of evidence that may be adduced to prove such substantial grounds can vary from one case to another; they will be examined in more detail in Section 11 below. However, it suffices to say here that the Court acknowledges the difficulties that applicants in this type of case will face in submitting evidence. It should be noted that if the receiving country is not a Contracting Party to the Convention,[307] the Court has no powers to ask that receiving country to submit any material that may be in the possession of that country's national authorities and which supports the applicant's allegations.

Aware of the difficulties of proving the existence of a real risk of ill-treatment in receiving countries, the Court has expressed its readiness to lower the high standard of proof in such cases. In its decision in the case of *Mawajedi Shikpokht and Mahkamat Shole v. the Netherlands*, the Court noted the following:

> "the case hinges on whether there is a real risk that the applicants will suffer treatment contrary to Article 3 if forced to return to Iran. Neither applicant has submitted any direct documentary evidence proving that they themselves are wanted for any reason by the Iranian authorities. That, however, cannot be decisive *per se*: the Court has recognised that in cases of this nature such evidence may well be difficult to obtain (*Bahaddar v. the Netherlands*, judgment of 19 February 1998, *Reports of Judgments and Decisions* 1998-I, p. 263, § 45). To demand proof to such a high standard may well present even an applicant whose fears are well-founded with a *probatio diabolica*".[308]

It then added:

> "[e]ven so, as regards Ms Mahkamat Sholeh, it would have been helpful had the Court been provided with, for example, the written threat that caused her to go into hiding – or at least, plausible information which would enable the Court to assess *prima facie* the nature and seriousness of the threat which it represented to Ms Mahkamat Sholeh herself".[309]

Whether the Court will follow this reasoning in similar cases is an open question. For a discussion of the standard and burden of proof in expulsion cases, applicants may find it useful to look at the *amicus* brief in the case of *Ramzy v. The Netherlands* (no. 25424/05) in Appendix No. 9. This *amicus*, submitted by a coalition of NGOs, contains a comparative examination of the

---

306 See *D. v. the United Kingdom*, no. 30240/96, 2 May 1997, § 49.

307 If the receiving country is a Contracting Party, on the other hand, the Court may, pursuant to Rule 44A of the Rules of Court, ask that Party to cooperate fully in the proceedings and to take such action within its power as the Court considers necessary for the proper administration of justice. This duty applies also to a Contracting Party not party to the proceedings where such cooperation is necessary.

308 See *Mawajedi Shikpokht and Mahkamat Shole v. the Netherlands* (dec.), no. 39349/03, 27 January 2005.

309 *Ibid.*

standard and burden of proof on applicants in expulsion cases in the jurisprudence of international bodies, primarily the European Court and the United Nations Committee against Torture.

Another challenge applicants might face in the expulsion context is the use of so-called "diplomatic assurances" (variously referred to as "diplomatic guarantees", "diplomatic contacts", "memoranda of understanding"). These concern assurances that the country of destination provides to the expelling respondent Government that the applicant will not be subjected to ill-treatment if expelled. The use of such assurances to expel persons in the face of a risk of torture or other ill-treatment has become increasingly common albeit also increasingly controversial. In numerous instances since September 11, States have relied on diplomatic assurances asserting that they effectively mitigated the risk of torture and ill-treatment to the expelled person. However, applicants faced with this issue should note that a growing number of international authorities have explicitly rejected the use of diplomatic assurances including, in particular, the Parliamentary Assembly of the Council of Europe,[309bis] the Council of Europe Commissioner for Human Rights,[310] United Nations Special Rapporteur on Torture,[311] and the United Nations High Commissioner for Human Rights.[312]

The UN Committee against Torture has also explicitly rejected the use of diplomatic assurances in its case-law. Specifically, in *Agiza v. Sweden* the Committee against Torture considered the issue in relation to the expulsion by Sweden of an Egyptian national and found that "... the State party's expulsion of the complainant was in breach of Article 3 of the Convention. The procurement of diplomatic assurances, which, moreover, provided no mechanism for their enforcement, did not suffice to protect against this manifest risk."[313] Indeed, in *Chahal v. the United Kingdom*, the European Court itself found that the diplomatic assurances provided by the Government of India were not sufficient to mitigate the risk of ill-treatment to the applicant and that his expulsion would therefore put the UK in breach of its obligations under Article 3.

309bis   Relevant parts of Article 20 of the Parliamentary Assembly Resolution, adopted on 27 June 2006, provides as follows: "The Assembly also calls on the United States of America, which is an Observer State to the Council of Europe and Europe's long-standing ally in resisting tyranny and defending human rights and the rule of law, to prohibit the extralegal transfer of persons suspected of involvement in terrorism and all forcible transfers of persons from any country to countries that practise torture or that fail to guarantee the right to a fair trial, regardless of any assurances received"

310   Report of Mr. Alvaro Gil-Robles, Council of Europe Commissioner for Human Rights, on his visit to Sweden, 21-23 April 2004, Strasbourg, 8 July 2004, CommDH(2004) 13, para.19.

311   Report of the Special Rapporteur on torture and other cruel, inhuman or degrading treatment or punishment, A/60/316, 30 August 2005.

312   Protection of human rights and fundamental freedoms while countering terrorism, Report of the High Commissioner for Human Rights, E/CN.4/2006/94, 16 February 2006.

313   *Agiza v. Sweden*, CAT/C/34/D/233/2003, para. 13.4.

Regarding diplomatic assurances, the United Nations Special Rapporteur on Torture has stated the following:

> "[D]iplomatic assurances are unreliable and ineffective in the protection against torture and ill-treatment: such assurances are sought usually from States where the practice of torture is systematic; post-return monitoring mechanisms have proven to be no guarantee against torture; diplomatic assurances are not legally binding, therefore they carry no legal effect and no accountability if breached; and the person whom the assurances aim to protect has no recourse if the assurances are violated. The Special Rapporteur is therefore of the opinion that States cannot resort to diplomatic assurances as a safeguard against torture and cruel, inhuman or degrading treatment or punishment where there are substantial grounds for believing that a person would be in danger of being subjected to torture or cruel, inhuman or degrading treatment or punishment upon return."[314]

NGOs have also argued that reliance on diplomatic assurances is incompatible with States' obligations to prevent torture,[315] and that there is a growing body of evidence that such assurances are ineffective in practice, are not capable of being monitored adequately, and have actually resulted in the torture and ill-treatment of persons subject to expulsion.[316]

c) Concluding Remarks on Substantiation

The Court uses the following standard text when declaring an application admissible:

> "The Court considers, in the light of the parties' submissions, that this complaint raises complex issues of law and of fact under the Convention, the determination of which should depend on an examination of the merits of the application. The Court concludes, therefore, that [the application] or [this part of the application] is not manifestly ill-founded, within the meaning of Article 35 § 3 of the Convention. No other grounds for declaring it inadmissible have been established".

However, although an admissible complaint implies that the applicant has proved his or her allegations with adequate evidence to the extent necessary to show that his or her complaint is not manifestly ill-founded, it does not necessarily follow that the same evidence will be sufficient to establish a violation of the Convention. This is because of the different standards of proof

---

314 A/60/316, para. 51.

315 See for instance, *Reject rather then regulate: Call on Council of Europe member states not to establish minimum standards for the use of diplomatic assurances in transfers to risk of torture and other ill-treatment*. Amnesty International, Human Rights Watch and the International Commission of Jurists, 2 December 2005.

316 See Human Rights Watch, *Still at Risk: Diplomatic Assurances No Safeguard against Torture*, April 2005; *Empty Promises: Diplomatic Assurances No Safeguard against Torture*, April 2004; See also, Amnesty International, *Memorandums of Understanding and NGO Monitoring: a challenge to fundamental human rights*, 19 February 2006.

required by the Court at different stages of the proceedings. For example, the Court unanimously concluded in its decision on admissibility in the case of *Bensaid v. the United Kingdom* that the applicant's complaint under Article 3 of the Convention was not manifestly ill-founded. However, in its judgment in the same case the Court was also unanimous in deciding that there had not been a violation of Article 3.[317]

An admissible Article 3 complaint which is not manifestly ill-founded but which ultimately does not lead to a finding of a violation of that Article, is not necessarily devoid of substance. It may still, if the applicant is held to have had an arguable claim[318] of a violation of that provision, give rise to a breach of Article 13 of the Convention[319] if the applicant was not afforded an effective remedy at the national level in respect of that complaint. Support for this can be found in the judgment in the case of *D.P. and J.C. v. the United Kingdom* in which the Court held the following:

> "The Court has not found it established in this case that there has been a violation of Article 3, or Article 8, of the Convention in respect of the applicants' claims that the authorities failed in a positive obligation to protect them from the abuse of their stepfather, N.C. This does not however mean, for the purposes of Article 13, that their complaints fall outside the scope of its protection. These complaints were not declared inadmissible as manifestly ill-founded and necessitated an examination on the merits".[320]

2.6.3 Discussion II: Severity of Ill-Treatment

Substantiation of the accuracy and veracity of allegations of ill-treatment is not on its own sufficient for the Court to conclude that the complaint is "well founded" (or, if the complaint gets beyond the admissibility stage, that there has been a violation of Article 3). This is because Article 3 does not prohibit every form of ill-treatment but only ill-treatment that crosses a minimum level of severity. In its judgment in the inter-state case of *Ireland v. the United Kingdom*, adopted in 1978, the Court established a test to determine whether a particular form of ill-treatment violated Article 3. According to this test:

> "ill-treatment must attain a minimum level of severity if it is to fall within the scope of Article 3. The assessment of this minimum is, in the nature of

---

317 *Bensaid v. the United Kingdom* (dec.), no. 44599/98, 25 January 2000, and *Bensaid v. the United Kingdom*, no. 44599/98, 6 February 2001.

318 See *Boyle and Rice v. the United Kingdom*, nos. 9659/82 and 9658/82, 27 April 1998, §§ 54-55.

319 And sometimes to a procedural violation of Article 3 of the Convention; see Section 10.2.2 (a) below.

320 *D.P. and J.C. v. the United Kingdom*, no. 38719/97, 10 October 2002, § 136; see also *Çelik and İmret v. Turkey*, 44093/98, 26 October 2004, § 57.

things, relative; it depends on all the circumstances of the case such as the duration of the treatment, its physical and mental effects and, in some cases, the sex, age and state of health of the victim".[321]

This threshold, which was set by the Court in 1978, is a difficult one to attain and was perhaps set high because of a "sentiment that to find a State in violation of [Article 3 of the Convention] was particularly serious and not to be taken lightly".[322] Nevertheless, since the Convention is a living instrument which must be interpreted in the light of present-day conditions, certain acts previously falling outside the scope of Article 3 might today (or in future) attain the required level of severity to be considered a violation of the article.[323] The Court explained in *Selmouni* that:

> "the increasingly high standard being required in the area of the protection of human rights and fundamental liberties correspondingly and inevitably requires greater firmness in assessing breaches of the fundamental values of democratic societies".[324]

Some examples are given below to illustrate the Court's examination of, and its approach to, the question of what minimum level of severity is required in order for the Court to find a violation of Article 3. The examples given below are drawn from a series of situations which have been examined by the Court and which involve typical "severity threshold" questions. It should be noted, however, that this list of categories is not exhaustive but merely illustrative. For a more extensive discussion of the Court's jurisprudence, readers are referred to Appendix No. 10.

a) Inhuman or Degrading Treatment or Punishment

The Convention prohibits both inhuman or degrading *treatment* and inhuman or degrading *punishment*. As regards the latter, the Court has held that in order for a judicially sanctioned punishment to violate Article 3, it must be a type of punishment which causes suffering and humiliation which *go beyond* the inevitable element of suffering and humiliation which is inherent in any form of legitimate criminal punishment. Examples of punishment which violate this prong of the prohibition include flogging, stoning, etc. For instance, Article 3 has been invoked in the *non-refoulement* context where the applicant faces *Sharia* punishment in his or her country of origin. In *Jabari v. Turkey*, the applicant had committed adultery in Iran, a crime under Iranian law for which she was liable to be sentenced to death by stoning. The Court

---

321   *Ireland v. the United Kingdom*, cited above, § 162.
322   See Reid p. 518.
323   See *Henaf v. France*, no. 65436/01, 27 November 2003, § 55.
324   *Selmouni v. France*, cited above, § 100.

found that type of punishment to be clearly contrary to Article 3 and found that her return would therefore constitute a violation of that article.[325]

In addition to the severity and proportionality of the punishment, the Court will also consider the purpose of the punishment and whether such a purpose involves the gratuitous humiliation or debasement of the victim. This was a factor in *Tyrer v. the United Kingdom* where the Court found that the judicial corporal punishment which the applicant complained of (in this case, birching) amounted to inhuman and degrading punishment.[326] In its judgment, the Court stated in relevant part that:

> "... although the applicant did not suffer any severe or long-lasting physical effects, his punishment – whereby he was treated as an object in the power of the authorities – constituted an assault on precisely that which it is one of the main purposes of Article 3 to protect, namely a person's dignity and physical integrity".[327]

The Court will also look to the purpose of the acts complained of in determining whether there is a violation of the prohibition of inhuman or degrading *treatment*.[328] *T. v. the United Kingdom* affords an illustration in this regard. This case concerned an applicant who, at the age of ten, was convicted of the killing of a two year old boy. The applicant argued that the cumulative effect of a number of factors associated with his criminal trial amounted to inhuman and degrading treatment contrary to Article 3, including the following: the low age of criminal responsibility, the accusatorial nature of the trial, the adult proceedings in a public court, the length of the trial, the jury of twelve adult strangers, the physical layout of the courtroom, the overwhelming presence of the media and public, the attacks by the public on the prison van which brought him to court, and the disclosure of his identity, together with a number of other factors linked to his sentence. The Court found, however, that the criminal proceedings against the applicant had not been motivated by any intention on the part of the State authorities to humiliate him or cause him suffering.[329] Furthermore, while the public nature of the proceedings may have exacerbated to a certain extent the applicant's feelings of guilt, distress, anguish and fear, the Court was not convinced that the particular features of the trial process as applied to the applicant caused, to a significant degree, suffering beyond that which would inevitably have been engendered by any attempt by the authorities to deal with the applicant following his commission of the offence in question.[330]

---

325 *Jabari v. Turkey*, no. 40035/98, 11 July 2000, §§ 33 - 42
326 *Tyrer v. the United Kingdom*, no. 5856/72, 25 April 1978.
327 *Ibid.*, § 33.
328 See, for example, *Raninen v. Finland*, no. 20972/92, 16 December 1997, § 55.
329 *T. v. the United Kingdom* [GC], 24724/94, 16 December 1999, § 69.
330 *Ibid.*, § 77.

However, it must be stressed that although the question whether the purpose of the treatment or punishment was to humiliate or debase the victim is a factor to be taken into account, the absence of such a purpose cannot conclusively rule out a finding that Article 3 was violated.[331]

b) Prison Conditions

Virtually any form of lawful detention (arrest, pre-trial detention, imprisonment, administrative custody, etc.) involves an inevitable element of suffering or humiliation. According to the Court, the imposition of a sentence of detention in itself does not raise issues under Article 3 of the Convention. Furthermore, Article 3 cannot be interpreted as laying down a general obligation to release a detainee on health grounds or to place him or her in a civil hospital to enable the detainee to obtain a particular kind of medical treatment.[332] Nevertheless, the Court requires the State to ensure that any person who is detained is held under conditions that are compatible with respect for human dignity, that the manner and method of the detention do not subject the detainee to distress or hardship of an intensity exceeding the unavoidable level of suffering inherent in detention, and that given the practical demands of imprisonment, the detainee's health and well-being are adequately secured by, among other things, providing him or her with the requisite medical assistance.[333]

When examining complaints of prison conditions that are alleged to constitute ill-treatment, the Court refers to reports published by the CPT. Furthermore, the Court will take into account the cumulative effects of those conditions, as well as the specific allegations made by the applicant.[334] For example, in the case of *Labzov v. Russia*, the Court observed that the applicant was detained at a remand facility where he was afforded less than 1 square metre of personal space and shared a sleeping place with other inmates, taking turns with them to rest. Except for one hour of daily outside exercise, the applicant was confined to his cell for 23 hours a day. The Court considered that the conditions in the prison cell were:

> "sufficient to cause distress or hardship of an intensity exceeding the unavoidable level of suffering inherent in detention, and arouse in [the applicant] the feelings of fear, anguish and inferiority capable of humiliating and debasing him".[335]

---

331 See, for example, *Van der Ven v. the Netherlands*, cited above, § 48.
332 *Kudła v. Poland* [GC], no. 30210/96, 26 October 2000, § 93.
333 *Ibid.*, § 94 and the cases cited therein.
334 *Dougoz v. Greece*, no. 40907/98, 6 March 2001, § 46.
335 *Labzov v. Russia*, no. 62208/00, 28 February 2002, § 46.

By contrast, in its judgment in the case of *Valašinas v. Lithuania*,[336] in which the applicant complained of the conditions in the two prison cells where he was detained and which measured between 2.7 and 3.2 square metres, the Court found that the conditions of the applicant's detention did not attain the minimum level of severity because the restricted space in the sleeping facilities was compensated for by the freedom of movement enjoyed by the detainees during the daytime.

Therefore, applicants arguing a violation of Article 3 based on conditions of detention are advised to consult the Court's extensive case-law on this issue, and in particular, to distinguish the applicant's situation from the facts of cases where the Court has found no violation.

c) Solitary Confinement

Prohibiting contact with other prisoners for security, disciplinary, or other protective reasons does not in itself amount to inhuman treatment or punishment.[337] However, the Court has found that complete sensory deprivation coupled with total social isolation can destroy the personality of a detainee and may constitute a form of inhuman treatment contrary to Article 3.[338] One factor that the Court will examine in these cases is whether the special regime imposed on the detainee is reasonably tailored to, and proportionate with, the legitimate interest – security, disciplinary, etc. – which the State is seeking to advance through the particular measure.

In the case of *Mathew v. the Netherlands* the detention in solitary confinement for a period of approximately 19 months of an applicant with health problems was considered excessive and in violation of Article 3.[339] Firstly, the applicant was detained for at least seven of those months in a cell in which there was a large opening in the roof exposing him to rain and extreme heat. Further, the location of his cell on the second floor prevented his access to outdoor exercise: because of his serious spinal condition and the absence of an elevator in the building, the applicant could only gain access to outdoor exercise at the expense of unnecessary and avoidable physical suffering. On the other hand, in *Rohde v. Denmark* the Court found that the applicant's pre-trial solitary confinement for a period in excess of eleven months did not in itself amount to treatment contrary to Article 3 of the

---

336 *Valašinas v. Lithuania*, no. 44558/98, 24 July 2001, §§ 103-111.
337 See *Öcalan v. Turkey* [GC], no. 46221/99, 12 May 2005, § 191.
338 See *Van der Ven v. the Netherlands*, cited above, § 51.
339 *Mathew v. the Netherlands*, no. 24919/03, 29 September 2005, § 217.

Convention.[340] In reaching this conclusion the Court examined the conditions of detention including the extent of the social isolation. The Court observed that:

> "[t]he applicant was detained in a cell which had an area of about eight square metres and in which there was a television. Also, he had access to newspapers. He was totally excluded from association with other inmates, but during the day he had regular contact with prison staff, e.g. when food was delivered; when he made use of the outdoor exercise option or the fitness room; when he borrowed books in the library or bought goods in the shop. In addition, every week he received lessons in English and French from the prison teacher and he visited the prison chaplain. Also, every week he received a visit from his counsel. Furthermore, during the segregation period in solitary confinement the applicant had contact twelve times with a welfare worker; and he was attended to thirty-two times by a physiotherapist, twenty-seven times by a doctor; and forty-three times by a nurse. Visits from the applicant's family and friends were allowed under supervision. The applicant's mother visited the applicant approximately one hour every week. In the beginning friends came along with her, up to five persons at a time, but the police eventually limited the visits to two persons at a time in order to be able to check that the conversations did not concern the charge against the applicant. Also, the applicant's father along with a cousin visited the applicant every two weeks".[341]

In the case of *Ramirez Sanchez v. France*, in which the applicant – better known as "Carlos the Jackal" – had been detained in solitary confinement for over eight years in a cell measuring 6.84 square metres, the Court found that

> "the general and very special conditions in which the applicant was being held in solitary confinement and the length of that confinement had not reached the minimum level of severity necessary to constitute inhuman or degrading treatment within the meaning of Article 3 of the Convention, having regard to his character and the unprecedented danger he poses".[342]

The three cases referred to above illustrate that the period of solitary confinement is not on its own dispositive for purposes of Article 3. Other factors such as the identity of the victim, his or her health, the threat he or she poses, the conditions of the detention and whether the regime imposed by the Contracting Party is reasonably tailored to legitimate security interests will also be taken into account.

---

340 *Rohde v. Denmark*, no. 69332/01, 21 July 2005, § 98. See also the dissenting opinion of Judges Rozakis, Loucaides and Tulkens in which they argued that "a distinction needs to be made between, on the one hand, social isolation or a special regime imposed after a conviction by a court and, on the other, pre-trial detention in solitary confinement, as in the present case".

341 § 97.

342 *Ramirez Sanchez v. France*, no. 59450/00, 27 January 2005, § 120. It must be noted that on 15 June 2005 the case was referred to the Grand Chamber at the applicant's request, and the Grand Chamber had not yet decided the case at the time of writing.

d) Strip Searches

Other conditions of detention which the Court has had occasion to examine include strip searches of applicants. The Court considers that while strip searches may be necessary on occasion to ensure prison security or prevent disorder or crime, they must be conducted in an appropriate manner. It found that no such appropriateness was present in a case in which the (male) applicant was obliged to strip naked in the presence of a woman, and his sexual organs and the food he had received from a visitor were examined by guards who were not wearing gloves. This, in the words of the Court, showed "a clear lack of respect for the applicant, and diminished in effect his human dignity".[343] Furthermore, in the case of *Van der Ven v. the Netherlands*, the Court considered that the practice of weekly strip searches applied to the applicant over a period of approximately three and a half years, in the absence of convincing security needs and on top of a great number of surveillance measures to which he was already subjected, diminished his human dignity and must have given rise to feelings of anguish and inferiority capable of humiliating and debasing him.[344]

In another case, the Court appreciated that the fact that the applicant was permanently observed by a camera for a period of about four and a half months in his prison cell may have caused him feelings of distress on account of being deprived of any form of privacy. However:

> "it did not find it sufficiently established on the basis of objective and concrete elements that the application of this measure had in fact subjected the applicant to mental pain and suffering of a level which could be regarded as attaining the minimum level of severity which constitutes inhuman or degrading treatment within the meaning of Article 3 of the Convention".[345]

e) Prisoner Transport

In a number of cases, the Court has considered complaints concerning the manner in which detainees are transported to and from places of detention. As with prison conditions, the Court will look to whether the conditions under which the detainee is being transported are consistent with respect for human dignity, and if additional restraint measures are imposed during the transportation process such as blindfolding, handcuffing, etc., the Court will assess these complaints in relation to whether such measures are reasonably

---

343 *Valašinas v. Lithuania*, cited above, § 117.
344 *Van der Ven v. the Netherlands*, cited above, § 62; see also *Lorsé v. the Netherlands*, cited above, § 74. The respondent Government's observations in the case of *Van der Ven* are found in Appendix No.14.
345 *Van der Graaf v. the Netherlands* (dec.), no. 8704/03, 1 June 2004.

necessary under the circumstances. In situations where the impugned treatment is not made necessary by the applicant's own conduct or "dangerousness" and where it consequently results in the humiliation of the detainee in a manner which exceeds the normal level of humiliation inherent in any lawful detention or arrest, the Court will find that the minimum level of severity will have been reached in violation of Article 3.

In *Khudoyorov v. Russia*, the applicant claimed that the conditions of his transportation between his detention facility and the court where he was being tried were inhuman and degrading. In particular, he complained that to attend court hearings he was transported to the courthouse in a prison van in which he shared a 1 m^2 individual compartment with another prisoner, forcing the two of them to take turns sitting on each other's lap. He received no food during the entire day and was deprived of outdoor exercise and even, on occasion, the chance to take a shower. The Court observed that the applicant had to endure these crammed conditions twice a day, on the way to and from the courthouse, and that he had been transported in that van no fewer than 200 times in four years of detention. Also, the Court noted that he was subjected to this treatment precisely on the occasions when he most needed his powers of concentration and mental alertness, i.e. during his trial and during the hearings on his detention status. Concluding that the treatment to which the applicant was subjected during his transport to and from the trial court exceeded the minimum level of severity, the Court found a violation of Article 3 of the Convention.[346] In reaching its conclusion the Court also examined the CPT's observations on transport facilities in various Council of Europe Member States.[347]

In *Raninen v. Finland*, the applicant complained of being handcuffed when transported between a prison and a hospital and argued that such measures constituted "degrading treatment" in violation of Article 3. The applicant stressed that the handcuffing occurred in the context of unlawful deprivation of liberty and thus possessed an element of arbitrariness causing him particular distress. He further argued that there had been nothing in his conduct when arrested and detained nor in the past suggesting that he might resist the authorities' measures, nor were any reasons given to him at the time of the handcuffing. According to him, the sole purpose of the handcuffing was to degrade, humiliate, and frighten him in order to discourage him from objecting to military service and substitute service. The two hours' duration of the treatment was significant because a few months after the event, he was diagnosed with an undefined psychosocial problem and was declared unfit for

---

346　*Khudoyorov v. Russia*, cited above, §§ 110-120.
347　*Ibid.*, § 117.

military service. According to the applicant, this clearly indicated that the unlawful detention and handcuffing had had adverse mental effects on him. In the opinion of the Commission, the Contracting Party's recourse to physical force by handcuffing the applicant for some two hours had not been made strictly necessary by his own conduct or by any other legitimate consideration and had been imposed while the applicant could be seen in public, including by his own supporters. In sum, the measure had diminished his human dignity and amounted to "degrading treatment" in violation of Article 3.[348]

The Court, however, disagreed. Unlike the Commission, it was not convinced that the applicant's handcuffing had adversely affected his mental state. There was nothing in the evidence to suggest a causal link between the impugned treatment and his "undefined psychosocial problem" which in any event had been diagnosed only several months later. Nor had the applicant substantiated his allegation that the handcuffing had been aimed at debasing or humiliating him. Finally, it had not been contended that the handcuffing had affected the applicant physically. In the light of these considerations, the Court concluded that the treatment in issue had not attained the minimum level of severity required by Article 3 of the Convention.[349]

In *Öcalan v. Turkey*, the Grand Chamber of the Court examined the applicant's allegations that his being handcuffed and blindfolded from the moment of his arrest in Kenya until his arrival at the prison on the island of İmralı in Turkey amounted to a violation of Article 3. The Grand Chamber held that artificially depriving prisoners of their sight by blindfolding them for lengthy periods spread over several days may, when combined with other ill-treatment, subject them to strong psychological and physical pressure and raise an issue under Article 3. However, it endorsed the findings of the Chamber and held that the applicant, who was suspected of being the leader of an armed separatist movement that was engaged in an armed struggle against the Turkish security forces, was considered dangerous. It accepted the Government's submission that the sole purpose of requiring the applicant to wear handcuffs was to prevent him from attempting to abscond or cause injury or damage to himself or others. As regards to the blindfolding of the applicant during his journey from Kenya to Turkey, the Court observed that this was a measure taken by the members of the security forces in order to avoid being recognised by the applicant. They also considered that it was a means of preventing the applicant from attempting to escape or injuring himself or others. The Court accepted the Government's explanation that the

---

348   *Raninen v. Finland*, no. 20972/92, Commission Report of 24 October 1996, § 59.
349   *Raninen v. Finland*, cited above, §§ 52-59.

purpose of that precaution was not to humiliate or debase the applicant but to ensure that the transfer proceeded smoothly; in view of the applicant's character and the reactions to his arrest, considerable care and proper precautions were necessary if the operation was to be a success. The Court concluded that it had not been established beyond reasonable doubt that the applicant's arrest and the conditions under which he was transferred from Kenya to Turkey exceeded the usual degree of humiliation inherent in every arrest and detention or attained the minimum level of severity required for Article 3 to apply.[350]

f) Force-Feeding

The case of *Nevmerzhitsky v. Ukraine* concerned the force-feeding of an applicant who was on hunger strike. In order to force-feed him, the authorities used handcuffs, a mouth-widener, and a special rubber tube inserted into the mouth. The Court held that:

> "the force-feeding of the applicant, without any medical justification having been shown by the Government, using the equipment foreseen in the decree, but resisted by the applicant, constituted treatment of such a severe character warranting the characterisation of torture within the meaning of Article 3 of the Convention".[351]

It must be stressed that this conclusion does not necessarily mean that a Contracting Party will breach its obligations under Article 3 of the Convention each time its agents force-feed persons on hunger strike. As the Court noted in the same judgment,

> "a measure which is of therapeutic necessity from the point of view of established principles of medicine cannot in principle be regarded as inhuman and degrading. The same can be said about force-feeding that is aimed at saving the life of a particular detainee who consciously refuses to take food. The Convention organs must nevertheless satisfy themselves that the medical necessity has been convincingly shown to exist... Furthermore, the Court must ascertain that the procedural guarantees for the decision to force-feed are complied with. Moreover, the manner in which the applicant is subjected to force-feeding during the hunger strike shall not trespass the threshold of a minimum level of severity envisaged by the Court's case-law under Article 3 of the Convention".[352]

---

350 *Öcalan v. Turkey* [GC], cited above, §§ 176-185.
351 *Nevmerzhitsky v. Ukraine*, no. 54825/00, 5 April 2005, § 98.
352 *Ibid.*, § 94.

g) Racial Discrimination

According to the Commission, discrimination based on race can in itself amount to degrading treatment within the meaning of Article 3.[353] The Commission's view was adopted by the Court in *Cyprus v. Turkey*, in which it found:

> "it is an inescapable conclusion that the interferences at issue were directed at the Karpas Greek-Cypriot community for the very reason that they belonged to this class of persons. The treatment to which they were subjected during the period under consideration can only be explained in terms of the features which distinguish them from the Turkish-Cypriot population, namely their ethnic origin, race and religion. The Court would further note that it is the policy of the respondent State to pursue discussions within the framework of the inter-communal talks on the basis of bi-zonal and bi-communal principles... The respondent State's attachment to these principles must be considered to be reflected in the situation in which the Karpas Greek Cypriots live and are compelled to live: isolated, restricted in their movements, controlled and with no prospect of renewing or developing their community. The conditions under which that population is condemned to live are debasing and violate the very notion of respect for the human dignity of its members... In the Court's opinion, and with reference to the period under consideration, the discriminatory treatment attained a level of severity which amounted to degrading treatment".[354]

More recently, and with reference to the *East African Asians* case, the Court has held in *Moldovan and Others v. Romania* that discrimination based on race can in itself amount to degrading treatment within the meaning of Article 3 and that racist remarks should therefore be taken into account as an aggravating factor in the examination of applicants' complaints under this Article. On the basis of the circumstances of the case, the Court found that the racial discrimination to which the applicants had been publicly subjected and the way in which their grievances were dealt with by the various authorities constituted interference with their human dignity which, in the special circumstances of this case, amounted to "degrading treatment" within the meaning of Article 3 of the Convention.[355]

In the vast majority of cases, allegations of racial discrimination have been examined from the standpoint of Article 14 of the Convention which prohibits discriminatory treatment. In a landmark judgment the Court considered that

> "any evidence of racist verbal abuse being uttered by law enforcement agents in connection with an operation involving the use of force against

---

353 See *East African Asians v. the United Kingdom*, nos. 4403/70 et seq., Commission Report of 14 December 1973.

354 *Cyprus v. Turkey*, cited above, §§ 309-311.

355 *Moldovan and Others v. Romania*, cited above, § 113.

persons from an ethnic or other minority is highly relevant to the question whether or not unlawful, hatred-induced violence has taken place. Where such evidence comes to light in the investigation, it must be verified and – if confirmed – a thorough examination of all the facts should be undertaken in order to uncover any possible racist motives".[356]

It follows from this judgment that the Contracting Parties are now under an obligation to carry out investigations into allegations of use of force triggered by racial motives. Although in the facts of the *Nachova* case the issue of racial discrimination was examined from the standpoint of Article 2 as it concerned the killing of a person, it can by no means be ruled out that the Contracting Parties' positive obligation in this area extends to ensuring that allegations of ill-treatment triggered by racial motives are also properly investigated.

h) Expulsion of Persons with Health Problems

The Court has further dealt with a number of cases in which applicants with health problems complained that their expulsion to a particular country, where there was a lack of health care and/or support, would exacerbate their health problems to such an extent as to amount to ill-treatment within the meaning of Article 3 of the Convention. The fact that an applicant's circumstances in the receiving country will be less favourable than those enjoyed by him or her in the host country cannot be regarded as decisive from the point of view of Article 3.[357] According to the Court's established case-law:

"aliens who are subject to expulsion cannot in principle claim any entitlement to remain in the territory of a Contracting State in order to continue to benefit from medical, social or other forms of assistance provided by the expelling State".[358]

According to the Court's judgment in the case of *D. v. the United Kingdom*, it is only in exceptional circumstances, and owing to compelling humanitarian considerations, that the implementation of a decision to remove an alien may result in a violation of Article 3. This case concerned the impending removal from the United Kingdom to the Caribbean island of St Kitts of the applicant who was in the advanced stages of a terminal and incurable illness (AIDS). The Court noted that the removal of the applicant and the resulting abrupt loss of access to a number of health and comforting facilities afforded to him in the United Kingdom would hasten his death. The Court held that

"in view of these exceptional circumstances and bearing in mind the critical stage now reached in the applicant's fatal illness, the implementation

---

356 *Nachova v. Bulgaria* [GC], cited above, §§ 162-168.
357 *Bensaid v. the United Kingdom*, cited above, § 38.
358 See, *inter alia, Salkic and Others v. Sweden* (dec.), no. 7702/04, 29 June 2004.

of the decision to remove him to St Kitts would amount to inhuman treatment by the respondent State in violation of Article 3".[359]

The *D. v. the United Kingdom* judgment remains, however, the only case in which the Court has accepted that "exceptional circumstances" existed such that a State should refrain from removing an alien from its territory. The case of *Bensaid v. the United Kingdom*, for instance, concerned the removal of the applicant – a long-term sufferer of schizophrenia – from the United Kingdom to Algeria where he would not be able to continue taking, as an outpatient and free of charge, a particular course of medication. While the Court accepted the seriousness of the applicant's medical condition, it did not find that there was a sufficiently real risk that the applicant's removal, under the circumstances of the case, would be contrary to the standards of Article 3, noting the high threshold set by Article 3 and particularly the fact that the case did not concern the direct responsibility of the Contracting Party for the infliction of harm.[360]

The case of *Ndangoya v. Sweden* concerned the removal of the applicant back to his native Tanzania. He was infected with HIV, but while in Sweden had been receiving treatment such that the HIV levels in his blood were no longer detectable. The doctor who had treated the applicant estimated that he would develop AIDS within 1 to 2 years if the treatment were discontinued. The Court observed that adequate treatment was available in Tanzania, albeit at a considerable cost and difficult to come by in the countryside where the applicant apparently would prefer to live upon return. Noting that it had not appeared that the applicant's illness had attained an advanced or terminal stage, or that he had no prospect of medical care or family support in his country of origin, the Court found that the circumstances of his situation were not of such an exceptional nature that his expulsion would amount to treatment proscribed by Article 3 of the Convention.[361]

---

359 *D. v. the United Kingdom*, cited above, § 53.

360 *Bensaid v. the United Kingdom*, cited above, § 40. See also the separate opinion of Judge Sir Nicolas Bratza, the national judge in the case, joined by judges Costa and Greve, in which he stated that "...the present case does not disclose exceptional circumstances similar to those of *D. v. the United Kingdom...* Nevertheless, on the evidence before the Court, there exist in my view powerful and compelling humanitarian considerations in the present case which would justify and merit reconsideration by the national authorities of the decision to remove the applicant to Algeria".

361 *Ndangoya v. Sweden* (dec.), no. 17868/03, 22 June 2004. See also *Nasimi v. Sweden* (dec.), no. 38865/02, 16 March 2004 in which the considerable stress caused to the applicant by the national authorities' decision to expel him was not sufficient to attract the protection under Article 3 of the Convention.

2.6.4 Concluding Remarks

If the Court concludes that the applicant has failed to support his or her case with adequate evidence and has failed, therefore, to make out a *prima facie* case, the application will be declared inadmissible as being manifestly ill-founded. Similarly, if the Court concludes that the treatment of which the applicant complains has not reached the minimum level of severity to constitute a breach of Article 3, the application will be declared inadmissible as being manifestly ill-founded.

In order to avoid having an application fail for lack of substantiation, the applicant should make out the strongest possible case from the beginning by submitting all relevant evidence which can support the allegations with the completed application form. If the evidence submitted by the applicant is rebutted or challenged by the respondent Government, the applicant will have the opportunity to counter the Government's allegations[362] by adducing further evidence and/or arguments. Such additional evidence may take the form of additional medical reports confirming the applicants' earlier medical submissions or challenging the submissions of the Government.[363]

Similarly, persuading the Court that the treatment in question has reached the required minimum level of severity may also be achieved by resorting to medical reports. In order to tip the scales, applicants should consider obtaining detailed medical reports describing the physical and mental effects of the ill-treatment to which they were subjected. If the applicant is suffering from psychological disturbances as a result of the ill-treatment, it is particularly important that these effects be documented since the finding of such effects requires the Court to make an assessment of a number of subjective elements. A psychological assessment, carried out by a trained specialist, preferably a psychiatrist, "linking" the applicant's psychological problems to his or her allegations will assist the Court in its examination and is strongly recommended.

The Court's assessment of the severity of the treatment will take into account all the circumstances of the case such as the duration of the treatment, its physical and mental effects and, in some cases, the sex, age, and state of health of the victim. Consequently, in some cases the Court might consider a particular form of treatment severe enough to cross the severity threshold, where the applicant can show characteristics which make him or her particularly vulnerable to such treatment. Thus in some cases, ill-treatment of a

---

362 See Section 11 for a discussion of the evidential issues in the Court's proceedings.
363 See, as an example, the applicant's observations in the case of *Kişmir v. Turkey*, cited above, (in Appendix No. 13) in which the applicant enclosed a report prepared by a consultant pathologist.

child, pregnant woman, or elderly or infirm person might constitute a breach of Article 3 while the same treatment, when meted out to a healthy adult, might not be sufficient to constitute prohibited ill-treatment.[364] If relevant to the case, applicants are therefore advised to call to the attention of the Court, through argument and evidence, any particular characteristic which exacerbates their suffering.

Applicants whose health condition has deteriorated because of the ill-treatment should prove this by submitting medical evidence showing their state of health before and after the ill-treatment.

Finally, applicants should support their arguments that the treatment in question reaches the required minimum by referring to the Court's case-law in which similar allegations have been examined. This is particularly appropriate for complaints relating to prison conditions and other circumstances where the threshold level of severity might be an issue. For example, an applicant who has been detained in a prison in conditions similar to that of the applicant in the above mentioned case of *Labzov v. Russia*, may parallel the facts of that case or other similar cases.

2.7 Abuse of the Right of Application (Article 35 § 3)

According to Article 35 § 3 of the Convention, the Court will declare inadmissible an application if it considers the application to be an abuse of the right of application. What constitutes an abuse within the meaning of this Article has not been defined by the Convention institutions, which preferred, as the Court continues to do, to deal with the issue on a case-by-case basis.

This ground of inadmissibility has been used by the Court as a tool to weed out vexatious applications which hinder it in carrying out its duty under Article 19 of the Convention to ensure observance of the obligations undertaken by the Contracting Parties in the Convention.

It must be stressed at the outset that any attempt to mislead the Court in its examination of the application, for example by forging documents or by deliberately concealing relevant facts, may result in the Court's conclusion that there has been an abuse of the right of application.

---

364 See, for example, *Mathew v. the Netherlands*, cited above, § 203, where the Court observed that the applicant with health problems was not a person fit to be detained in the conditions of which he complained.

The Court – as did the Commission – receives a considerable number of applications that concern frivolous and repeated complaints by vexatious applicants. In the case of *Philis v. Greece* the Commission observed that the applicant had already introduced five applications with the Commission concerning the same complaint, all of which had been declared inadmissible. Apart from finding that the latest application constituted an abuse of the right of application, the Commission added:

> "[i]t cannot be the task of the Commission, a body set up under the Convention to ensure the observance of the engagements undertaken by the High Contracting Parties in the present Convention, to deal with a succession of ill-founded and querulous complaints, creating unnecessary work which is incompatible with its real functions, and which hinders it in carrying them out".[365]

The Court has adopted the same approach. Applicants receive prior warning that if the new application is rejected for amounting to an abuse of the right of application, no further correspondence will be entertained with them regarding future similar complaints.

Furthermore, in a number of cases the Court has examined whether the use of offensive language in proceedings before the Court – language that was directed either against the respondent Government or its agents,[366] the regime in the respondent Contracting Party,[367] or the Court and its Registry,[368] constituted an abuse of the right of application.[369] Finding that the use of offensive language in proceedings is undoubtedly inappropriate, the Court also held that, except in extraordinary cases, an application may only be rejected as abusive if it was knowingly based on untrue facts.[370]

Finally, in a number of cases the Commission and the Court have rejected claims made by respondent Governments that applications constituted an abuse of the right of application because they had been made for political purposes. For example, in the case of *Aslan v. Turkey* the respondent Government argued that the application, being devoid of any sound legal basis, had been lodged for purposes of political propaganda against the Turkish Government. The Commission concluded that the Government's

---

365 *Philis v. Greece*, no. 28970/95, Commission decision of 17 October 1996.
366 See *Manoussos v. the Czech Republic and Germany* (dec.), no. 46468/99, 9 July 2002.
367 See *Iordachi and Others v. Moldova* (dec.) no. 25198/02, 5 April 2005.
368 See *Řehák v. the Czech Republic* (dec.), no. 67208/01, 18 May 2004.
369 See also Rule 44D according to which, "[i]f the representative of a party makes abusive, frivolous, vexatious, misleading or prolix submissions, the President of the Chamber may exclude that representative from the proceedings, refuse to accept all or part of the submissions or make any other order which he or she considers it appropriate to make, without prejudice to Article 35 § 3 of the Convention".
370 See *Varbanov v. Bulgaria*, no. 31365/96, 5 October 2000, § 36.

argument could only be accepted if it was clear that the application was based on untrue facts. However, as this was far from clear at that stage of the proceedings, the Commission found it impossible to reject the application on this ground.[371]

2.8 Anonymous Applications (Article 35 § 2 (a))

The Court will not accept anonymous applications.[372] Rule 47 § 1 (a) of the Rules of Court requires that the name, date of birth, nationality, sex, occupation, and address of the applicant be set out in the application form.

The public nature of the Convention proceedings entails that the Court's decisions and judgments list the name, the year of birth, and the place of residence of the applicants. However, some applicants do not wish that their identity be disclosed to the public. In such circumstances, they may ask the Court to refer to them in public documents by their initials or by a single letter such as "X", "Y", "Z", etc.[373] Any such requests, however, must be supported by a statement of the reasons justifying such a departure from the rule of public access to information in proceedings before the Court. The President of the Chamber may authorise anonymity in exceptional and duly justified cases.[374]

Applicants should note that even where the Court grants a request for anonymity, their identities will always be disclosed to the concerned Contracting Party because the Contracting Party cannot, for obvious reasons, be expected to respond to anonymous complaints. In other words, an applicant can be anonymous *vis-à-vis* the general public but not *vis-à-vis* the other party to the complaint.

---

371 *Aslan v. Turkey*, no. 22497/93, Commission decision of 20 February 1995.
372 Article 35 § 2 (a) of the Convention.
373 See paragraph 17 of the Practice Direction on the "Institution of Proceedings" which can be found in Appendix No. 3.
374 Rule 47 § 3 of the Rules of Court.

2.9 Applications Substantially the Same (Article 35 § 2 (b))

A complaint which has already been examined either by the Court itself or which has already been submitted to another procedure of international investigation or settlement, and which contains no new information, will be declared inadmissible.[375] According to the Court:

> "this provision is intended to avoid the situation where several international bodies would be simultaneously dealing with applications which are substantially the same. A situation of this type would be incompatible with the spirit and the letter of the Convention, which seeks to avoid a plurality of international proceedings relating to the same cases".[376]

Two of the terms mentioned in this provision, namely "another international investigation or settlement" and "new information", necessitate further examination. The Commission has held that the word "another" suggests that that provision is concerned with a procedure similar to that provided by the Commission".[377] Both the Commission[378] and the United Nations' Human Rights Committee[379] have been held by the Court to be capable of providing "international investigations or settlements" within the meaning of this provision. Examination of an allegation of ill-treatment by the CPT, on the other hand, will not prevent the Court from examining the same allegation.[380] Furthermore, in its admissibility decision in the case of *Jeličić v. Bosnia and Herzegovina*, the Court also found that the Human Rights Chamber of Bosnia and Herzegovina was not an international tribunal within the meaning of Article 35 § 2 (b) of the Convention. In reaching its conclusion the Court observed, *inter alia*, that the Human Rights Chamber's mandate did not concern obligations between States but strictly those undertaken by Bosnia and Herzegovina and its constituent entities.[381]

Secondly, the Court will not declare a complaint inadmissible on this ground if it is based on facts which have been examined by one of the above mentioned international organisations or by the Court itself, if the complaint

---

375 Article 35 § 2 (b) of the Convention.
376 See *Smirnova and Smirnova v. Russia* (dec.), nos. 46133/99 and 48183/99, 3 October 2002.
377 *Council of Civil Service Unions and Others v. the United Kingdom*, no. 11603/85, Commission decision of 20 January 1987.
378 See, *inter alia*, *Vogl and Vogl v. Austria* (dec.), no. 50171/99, 23 October 2001.
379 *Pauger v. Austria*, no. 24872/94, Commission decision of 9 January 1995.
380 Paragraph 92 of the Explanatory Report to the European Convention for the Prevention of Torture and Inhuman or Degrading Treatment or Punishment expressly addresses this issue. According to this paragraph, "it is not envisaged that a person whose case has been examined by the committee would be met with a plea based on Article [35 § 2 (b) of the Convention] if he subsequently lodges a petition with the European [Court] of Human Rights alleging that he has been the victim of a violation of that Convention".
381 See *Jeličić v. Bosnia and Herzegovina* (dec.), no. 41183/02, 15 November 2005.

raised in relation to those facts is a different one. It thus appears that the Court interprets the concept of "substantially the same application" very restrictively.[382]

Unless the new application contains "relevant new information", it will be declared inadmissible by the Court. "Relevant new information" within the meaning of this provision may include a domestic court decision obtained by an applicant whose previous application was declared inadmissible by the Court for non-exhaustion of that particular remedy. However, this happens rarely in practice because, as pointed out elsewhere in this section, it is very likely that by the time the Court declares an application inadmissible for non-exhaustion of a particular domestic remedy, the applicant will have missed the time limit in national system to make use of that remedy. A domestic court decision in which the applicant's appeal was rejected for non-respect of the time limit under the national legislation will not constitute a "relevant new fact".

2.10 The New Admissibility Criterion in Protocol No. 14

Following the entry into force of Protocol No. 14, Article 35 § 3 of the Convention will include a new admissibility criterion according to which an application will be declared inadmissible if:

> "the applicant has not suffered a significant disadvantage, unless respect for human rights as defined in the Convention and the Protocols thereto requires an examination of the application on the merits and provided that no case maybe rejected on this ground which has not been duly considered by a domestic tribunal".[383]

According to the Explanatory Report to Protocol No. 14:

> "the purpose of this amendment is to provide the Court with an additional tool which should assist it in its filtering work and allow it to devote more time to cases which warrant examination on the merits, whether seen from the perspective of the legal interest of the individual applicant or considered from the broader perspective of the law of the Convention and the European public order to which it contributes. The introduction of this criterion was considered necessary in view of the ever increasing case load of the Court".

---

382 See *Kovačić and Others v. Slovenia* (dec.), nos. 44574/98, 45133/98, and 48316/99, 9 October 2003.
383 Article 12 of Protocol No. 14.

As acknowledged in the Explanatory Report, it is intended that the new admissibility criterion lead to the rejection of complaints in respect of which, under the current practice, violations of the Convention would be found.[384] It is for the Court to interpret the rather ambiguous term "significant disadvantage", and in the two years following the entry into force of Protocol No. 14, the new admissibility criterion will only be applied by Chambers and the Grand Chamber and not by Committees, in order that reasoned and publicly accessible case-law is created.

The new criterion allows the Court to exercise its discretion when deciding whether "respect for human rights" requires an examination of the application on the merits.[385] Furthermore, the new criterion aims to ensure that all Convention complaints are examined either at the national level or by the Court.

It must be stressed, however, that even before Protocol No. 14 has been ratified by the Contracting Parties to the Convention, serious doubts are already being expressed as to the capacity of this new criterion to reduce the case load of the Court.[386]

---

384 See paragraph 79 of the Explanatory Report in Appendix No.18.
385 This 'safeguard clause' was adopted from Article 37 § 1 of the Convention which allows the Court to continue the examination of a case even if the applicant does not intend to pursue his or her application or even if the parties want to settle the case; see Section 8 below for further information.
386 See Leach p. 8 *et seq.* and the references cited therein.

PART III

PROCEEDINGS BEFORE THE COURT

INTERIM MEASURES AND CASE PRIORITY

3.1 Interim Measures (Rule 39 of the Rules of Court)

3.1.1 Summary

3.1.2 Discussion

3.1.3 Application Procedure for Interim Measures

3.2 Case Priority and Urgent Notification of Applications (Rules 40-41)

3.1 Interim Measures (Rule 39)

3.1.1 Summary

Interim measures are issued by the Court to a respondent Contracting Party indicating that it should refrain from carrying out an act which could be detrimental to the Court's examination of an applicant's case. Interim measures under Rule 39 of the Rules of Court are predominantly granted in expulsion and extradition cases in order to prevent the removal of the applicant to a country where he or she may be subjected to treatment in violation of Articles 2 and/or 3 of the Convention. According to the Court's established case-law, Contracting Parties have a duty to comply with any interim measures indicated to them, failing which, issues will arise under Article 34 as regards the applicant's enjoyment of his or her right to an individual petition.[387]

Interim measures are often sought but rarely granted. For an interim measure to be granted, the applicant must demonstrate an imminent risk of irreparable damage to life or limb.[388]

This section includes practical information for filing interim measure requests. Furthermore, the reader may refer to the sample application for an interim measure and the Practice Direction on Interim Measures in Appendices Nos. 15 and 3, respectively.

3.1.2 Discussion

As pointed out above, Rule 39 of the Rules of Court authorizes interim measures and provides as follows:

> "1. The Chamber or, where appropriate, its President may, at the request of a party or of any other person concerned, or of its own motion, indicate to the parties any interim measure which it considers should be adopted in the interests of the parties or of the proper conduct of the proceedings before it.
>
> 2. Notice of these measures shall be given to the Committee of Ministers.
>
> 3. The Chamber may request information from the parties on any matter connected with the implementation of any interim measure it has indicated".

---

387   *Mamatkulov and Askarov v. Turkey* [GC], cited above, § 127.
388   *Ibid.*, § 104.

One of the most noteworthy cases concerning the indication of interim measures is that of *Soering v. the United Kingdom*,[389] which concerned the extradition by the British authorities of a German national to the United States where the authorities wanted to put him on trial for murder. If convicted, the applicant was liable to be sentenced to death. Mr. Soering argued that his surrender to the authorities of the United States of America might, if implemented, give rise to a breach by the United Kingdom of Article 3 of the Convention because he would be exposed to the so-called "death row phenomenon", which he alleged constituted treatment contrary to that Article. His application to the Commission for the interim measure under Rule 36 of the Commission's Rules of Procedure (now Rule 39 of the Rules of Court) was accepted, and the Commission indicated to the United Kingdom Government that it would be advisable not to extradite the applicant to the United States while the proceedings were pending in Strasbourg.[390] The United Kingdom Government complied with the interim measure and the Court subsequently held that the United Kingdom would be in breach of Article 3 if it were to extradite the applicant to the United States because the circumstances of death row would represent treatment prohibited by that Article.[391] Without the interim measure, Mr. Soering might have been extradited before the Convention institutions had had a chance to examine the application, and the risk of ill-treatment as alleged by the applicant might have materialised.

According to the Court, indications of interim measures given by the Court:

> "permit it not only to carry out an effective examination of the application but also to ensure that the protection afforded to the applicant by the Convention is effective; such indications also subsequently allow the Committee of Ministers to supervise execution of the final judgment. Such measures thus enable the State concerned to discharge its obligation to comply with the final judgment of the Court, which is legally binding by virtue of Article 46 of the Convention".[392]

The Court approaches Rule 39, therefore, from the perspective of the effective exercise of the right of individual application, which is guaranteed under Article 34 of the Convention. In the case of *Mamatkulov and Askarov v. Turkey*, in which the Turkish Government failed to comply with the Court's indication under Rule 39 and extradited the applicants to Uzbekistan anyway, the Grand Chamber of the Court found that the Turkish Government had not complied with its obligation under Article 34 of the Convention. It held:

---

389   *Soering v. the United Kingdom,* cited above.
390   *Ibid.,* § 4.
391   *Ibid.,* § 111. See also Appendix No. 10 below.
392   *Mamatkulov and Askarov v. Turkey* [GC], cited above, § 125.

"[t]he facts of the case, as set out above, clearly show that the Court was prevented by the applicants' extradition to Uzbekistan from conducting a proper examination of their complaints in accordance with its settled practice in similar cases and ultimately from protecting them, if need be, against potential violations of the Convention as alleged. As a result, the applicants were hindered in the effective exercise of their right of individual application guaranteed by Article 34 of the Convention, which the applicants' extradition rendered nugatory".[393]

The Grand Chamber further held that:

"The Court reiterates that by virtue of Article 34 of the Convention Contracting States undertake to refrain from any act or omission that may hinder the effective exercise of an individual applicant's right of application. A failure by a Contracting State to comply with interim measures is to be regarded as preventing the Court from effectively examining the applicant's complaint and as hindering the effective exercise of his or her right and, accordingly, as a violation of Article 34 of the Convention".[394]

The Grand Chamber of the Court has thus established that indications under Rule 39 impose binding obligations on the Contracting Parties.

Most interim measures indicated by the Commission and the Court have been complied with[395] by the Contracting Parties notwithstanding the fact that until the adoption of the judgment in the case of *Mamatkulov and Askarov,* indications under Rule 39 were not regarded by the Court as binding.

The Grand Chamber further set out in *Mamatkulov and Askarov v. Turkey* that:

"[i]nterim measures have been indicated only in limited spheres. Although it does receive a number of requests for interim measures, in practice the Court applies Rule 39 only if there is an imminent risk of irreparable damage. While there is no specific provision in the Convention concerning the domains in which Rule 39 will apply, requests for its application usually concern the right to life (Article 2), the right not to be subjected to torture or inhuman treatment (Article 3) and, exceptionally, the right to respect for private and family life (Article 8) or other rights guaranteed by the Convention. The vast majority of cases in which interim measures have

---

393 *Ibid.*, § 127.
394 *Ibid.*, § 128. In this case the Court, while acknowledging that Turkey's failure to comply with the indication given under Rule 39 had prevented it from assessing whether a real risk existed, nevertheless concluded by a majority of 14 to 3 that it was unable to find that substantial grounds existed for believing that the applicants faced a real risk of treatment proscribed by Article 3 (§ 77). See also the partly dissenting opinion of Judges Bratza, Bonello, and Hedigan in which they stated, *inter alia*, the following: "It is unclear to us what further corroborative evidence could reasonably be expected of the applicants, particularly in a case such as the present, where it was Turkey's failure to comply with the interim measures indicated by the Court which has prevented the Court from carrying out a full and effective examination of the application in accordance with its normal procedures. In such a situation, we consider that the Court should be slow to reject a complaint under Article 3 in the absence of compelling evidence to dispel the fears which formed the basis of the application of Rule 39".
395 *Ibid.*, § 105: "…Cases of States failing to comply with indicated measures remain very rare."

been indicated concern deportation and extradition proceedings".[396]

It follows from this quote that an interim measure under Rule 39 will generally only be granted if the applicant can show that there is an imminent risk of irreparable damage to life or limb.[397] For example, interim measures were applied in the case of *Shamayev and 12 Others v. Georgia and Russia*, which concerned the extradition by Georgia of a number of Chechens to Russia. The Court concluded that in the light of the extremely alarming phenomenon of persecution – in the form of threats, harassment, detention, enforced disappearances, and killings – of persons of Chechen origin who had lodged applications with the Court, the extradition to Russia of the one applicant still remaining in Georgia would constitute a violation of Article 3 of the Convention.[398]

Interim measures were also applied in the case of *D. v. the United Kingdom*, which concerned the removal of a person suffering from AIDS from the United Kingdom. As mentioned earlier, the Court held in that case that the United Kingdom would be in breach of Article 3 of the Convention if it were to proceed with the removal of the applicant.

In an application for an interim measure which concerned somewhat more extraordinary circumstances, the Court rejected Saddam Hussein's request:

> "to permanently prohibit the United Kingdom from facilitating, allowing for, acquiescing in, or in any other form whatsoever effectively participating, through an act or omission, in the transfer of the applicant to the custody of the Iraqi Interim Government unless and until the Iraqi Interim Government has provided adequate assurances that the applicant will not be subject to the death penalty".[399]

Interim measures, by their nature, will usually be indicated to a Contracting Party, but there have been exceptions. In the case of *Ilaşcu and Others v. Moldova and Russia*, for instance, the President of the Grand Chamber decided on 12 January 2004 to invite the respondent Governments, under Rule 39, to take all necessary steps to ensure that one of the applicants who had been on hunger strike since 28 December 2003 "was detained in conditions which were consistent with respect for his rights under the Convention".[400] An interim measure to that effect was thus indicated to the Contracting Parties concerned. In addition, however, the President decided on 15 January 2004 to urge the applicant himself, under Rule 39, to call off his hunger strike, a

---

396 *Ibid.*, § 104.
397 See also Leach, p. 38 *et seq.*
398 *Shamayev and 12 Others v. Georgia and Russia*, no. 36378/02, 12 April 2005.
399 See the press release of 30 June 2004 at
      http://www.echr.coe.int/Eng/Press/2004/June/RequestforInterimmeasure-SaddamHussein.htm
400 *Ilaşcu and Others v. Moldova and Russia*, cited above, § 10.

request which the applicant complied with on the same day.[401]

Perhaps the most far-reaching interim measure indicated by the Court was the one issued in the case of *Öcalan v. Turkey*, which concerned the arrest and subsequent trial, by a State Security Court, of the leader of the PKK (Kurdistan Workers' Party) for offences that were punishable by death under the Turkish legislation in force at the time. The Court requested the Turkish Government to take:

> "interim measures within the meaning of Rule 39 of the Rules of Court, notably to ensure that the requirements of Article 6 were complied with in proceedings which had been instituted against the applicant in the State Security Court and that the applicant was able to exercise his right of individual application to the Court effectively through lawyers of his own choosing".[402]

The Government, which was subsequently invited to clarify specific points concerning the measures that had been taken pursuant to Rule 39 to ensure that the applicant had a fair trial, informed the Court that it was "not prepared to reply to the Court's questions, as they went far beyond the scope of interim measures within the meaning of Rule 39".[403] However, the Government did comply with another interim measure indicated by the Court pursuant to which it was asked "to take all necessary steps to ensure that the death penalty is not carried out so as to enable the Court to proceed effectively with the examination of the admissibility and merits of the applicant's complaints under the Convention".[404]

Providing the Court with adequate evidence, showing that there is a real risk of irreparable harm to life or limb, may lead the Court to grant an interim measure but it does not necessarily mean that the same evidence is sufficient for the Court subsequently to find a violation of Articles 2 or 3. For example, although the evidence submitted by the applicant in the case of *Thampibillai v. the Netherlands* was sufficient for the Court to indicate to the respondent Government "that it was desirable in the interests of the parties and the proper conduct of the proceedings that the applicant should not be expelled to Sri Lanka pending the Court's decision", it was not sufficient for the Court to conclude in its judgment that substantial grounds had been established "for believing that the applicant, if expelled, would be exposed to a real risk of being subjected to torture or inhuman or degrading treatment within the meaning of Article 3 of the Convention".[405]

---

401 *Ibid.*, § 11.
402 *Öcalan v. Turkey* [GC], cited above, § 5.
403 *Ibid.*
404 *Ibid.*
405 *Thampibillai v. the Netherlands*, no. 61350/00, 17 February 2004, § 68.

Conversely, a rejection by the Court of a request for an interim measure does not prevent the applicant from pursuing the application, provided obviously that he or she is able to do so. For example, in *Mamatkulov and Askarov v. Turkey* the Court continued its examination of the application despite the fact that the lawyers representing the applicants had been unable to contact them following their extradition to Uzbekistan by the Turkish authorities in violation of the interim measure indicated under Rule 39.[406]

The Court will be much less inclined to issue an interim measure if the country of destination in an expulsion case is another Contracting Party. This is because there is a presumption that the receiving State will comply with its Convention obligations and also because of the fact that the Court will be able to scrutinise any alleged failures by that state to uphold its Convention obligations.[407] Nevertheless, and as was shown in the case of *Shamayev and 12 Others v. Georgia and Russia*,[408] the fact that the receiving country is a Contracting Party will not necessarily prevent the Court from indicating interim measures if it perceives that the risk to an applicant is serious.

In expulsion cases, respondent Governments are increasingly seeking to counter applicants' claims by proffering so called "diplomatic assurances," which the country of destination provides the expelling respondent Government and in which the country of destination promises that the applicant will not be subjected to the treatment he or she complains of. However, in the ill-treatment context, it must be stressed that the Court will approach diplomatic assurances with caution if it perceives that there is a real risk of ill-treatment in the receiving country. For example, in its judgment in the case of *Chahal v. the United Kingdom* the Court observed that the British authorities had sought and received assurances from the Indian authorities to the effect that the applicant, if returned to India, would not be subjected to ill-treatment. The Court, while not doubting the good faith of the Indian Government in providing the assurances, observed that despite the efforts of that Government, the Indian National Human Rights Commission, and the Indian courts to bring about reform, the violation of human rights by members of the security forces in Punjab and elsewhere in India was a recalcitrant and enduring problem. Against this background, the Court was not persuaded that the above assurances would provide Mr Chahal with an adequate guarantee of safety.[409] For more on diplomatic assurances, see Section 2.6.2(b).

---

406   See, by contrast, *Nehru v. the Netherlands* (dec.), no. 52676/99, 27 August 2002, examined in Section 8.2 below.
407   See *A.G. v. Sweden*, no. 27776/95, Commission decision of 26 October 1995. See also Leach at p. 39.
408   *Shamayev and 12 Others v. Georgia and Russia*, cited above.
409   See *Chahal v. the United Kingdom*, cited above, §§ 92 and 105.

On the other hand, in the extradition context, if the applicant has complained about conditions on "death row" the Court may reject the request of an interim measure if the Contracting Party has received an assurance from the concerned government that the applicant will not be subject to the death penalty. Thus, in the case of *Einhorn v. France*,[410] where the applicant was wanted for the murder of his former girlfriend, the Court concluded that the assurances obtained by the French Government from the United States authorities were such as to remove the danger of the applicant's being sentenced to death in Pennsylvania. Consequently, there was no risk of him being put on death row.[411]

3.1.3 Application Procedure for Interim Measures

Requests for interim measures should comply with the requirements set out in the Practice Direction issued by the President of the Court on 5 March 2003.[412] It states in relevant part that:

> "[s]uch requests should normally be received as soon as possible after the final domestic decision has been taken to enable the Court and its Registry to have sufficient time to examine the matter. However, in extradition or deportation cases, where immediate steps may be taken to enforce removal soon after the final domestic decision has been given, it is advisable to make submissions and submit any relevant material concerning the request before the final decision is given".[413]

Thus, to enable the Court to examine such requests in good time, they should in so far as possible be submitted during working hours and by a swift means of communication such as facsimile, e-mail, or courier. In cases where time is of the essence, it is important that the communication be clearly marked "Urgent" and that it be written in English or French. Furthermore, it is advisable to contact the Court by telephone and inform its Registry that the request is being made. Indeed, many requests for interim measures are made only hours before the scheduled departure. During holiday periods (i.e. around Christmas and the New Year) the Court's Registry maintains a skeletal staff to deal with any urgent requests for application of Rule 39.

Where it is expected that the final deportation order or a negative outcome of a final domestic remedy will be very swiftly followed by the removal of the person concerned, without there being time to contact the Court or for a

---

410 *Einhorn v. France* (dec.), no. 71555/01, 16 October 2001.
411 See *Soering v. the United Kingdom*, cited above, § 111.
412 See Appendix No. 3.
413 *Ibid.*

request for an interim measure to be examined, a potential applicant or his or her representative may consider lodging a "provisional" request for an interim measure. The Court can then beforehand be provided with the relevant documents – apart from the very last domestic decision – and, should the removal be approved at the domestic level, be informed by telephone or fax that the request for an interim measure has now become "definite".

A request for an interim measure should normally be accompanied by a completed application form, but in circumstances where time does not permit the preparation of that form, as much information as possible should be provided in the communication in which the request is made. Such information should include the steps taken by the applicant to exhaust domestic remedies and copies of relevant decisions. In any event, a request should, to the greatest extent possible, be supported by adequate and relevant evidence to show the extent of the risk involved in the country of destination.[414]

If the request for an interim measure is accepted, the Court will inform the respondent Government and the Committee of Ministers and will generally grant priority to the application over other pending cases.

3.2 Case Priority and Urgent Notification of Applications (Rules 40-41)

Where possible, the Court deals with applications in the order they are submitted, that is, chronologically. Because of its very heavy workload, proceedings before the Court frequently last for some years. However, in urgent circumstances, the Chamber or its President may decide at any stage of the proceedings to give priority to the examination of a particular application pursuant to Rule 41 of the Rules of Court. Furthermore, pursuant to Rule 40, the Registrar of the Court, with the authorisation of the President of the Chamber, may, in any case of urgency, inform the Contracting Party concerned of the introduction of the application and provide a summary of its contents. If it rejects a request for an interim measure under Rule 39, the Court may still resort to this "urgent notification" procedure under Rule 40 and inform the expelling Contracting Party of the application lodged with the Court. Although it is by no means obliged to do so, the Contracting Party may then decide to postpone the removal of the applicant from its territory until the Court has had an opportunity to examine the application.

---

414   See Section 11 below. See also Leach p. 40 *et seq.*

The Court may thus expedite its examination of a case of its own motion, but it may also be requested to do so by an applicant. Requests for a case to be granted priority must be duly reasoned. In particular, such reasons must be capable of leading the Court to depart from its practice of examining the case in chronological order. The cases referred to below illustrating the wide range of reasons may be taken as a starting point. The Court has discretion to decide whether to accept such requests and it will do so only in exceptional cases. Thus, the Court may grant case priority to a case if delays would render the examination of the merits of that case more difficult. For example, the Court granted priority to the case of *Sıddık Aslan and Others v. Turkey*,[415] which concerned the alleged killing of the applicants' relatives by members of the security forces, in view of the risk that important evidence would otherwise be destroyed with the passage of time due to the decomposition of the bodies.

The Court may also grant priority to cases in which the issue at stake needs to be resolved urgently because, for example, the applicant is seriously ill or old. In the case of *Pretty v. the United Kingdom*, for instance, which concerned the claim made by the terminally ill applicant to a right to assisted suicide,[416] priority was granted and a judgment was adopted in the record time of less than four months after the case was lodged. Similarly, in *Mouisel v. France*, which concerned the detention in prison of the applicant – a cancer sufferer – allegedly in violation of Article 3 of the Convention, the Court granted the case priority and it was concluded by a judgment in just over two years.[417] Priority was also granted to the case of *Lebedev v. Russia* in which the seriously ill applicant argued that his detention subjected him to inhuman and degrading treatment within the meaning of Article 3 of the Convention.[418] In the case of *Poltorachenko v. Ukraine*, concerning the applicant's right to a fair trial and the protection of his property, priority was granted on account of his advanced age.[419]

Priority has on occasion also been granted to cases concerning the right to respect for family life within the meaning of Article 8 of the Convention. For example, in *Tuquabo-Tekle and Others v. the Netherlands*, which concerned the refusal of the Netherlands authorities to grant permission to the applicants' (step-)daughter and (step-)sister – who were living in Eritrea – to join the rest of the family in the Netherlands.[420]

---

415 *Sıddık Aslan and Others v. Turkey*, no. 75307/01, 18 October 2005.
416 *Pretty v. the United Kingdom*, no. 2346/02, 29 April 2002.
417 *Mouisel v. France*, no. 67263/01, 14 November 2002.
418 *Lebedev v. Russia* (dec.), no. 4493/04, 25 November 2004.
419 *Poltorachenko v. Ukraine*, no. 77317/01, 18 January 2005, § 3.
420 *Tuquabo-Tekle and Others v. the Netherlands* (dec.), no. 60665/00, 19 October 2004.

Other than the cases referred to above, applications which have been granted priority under Rule 41 include the following: *Luluyev and Others v. Russia*, concerning the alleged killing by federal forces of the applicant's relative, whose body was found in a mass grave;[421] *Jørgensen v. Denmark*, concerning the Danish authorities' refusal to issue the applicant's wife of Philippine nationality with a residence permit in Denmark;[422] *I.I.N. v. the Netherlands*, concerning the intended expulsion of the applicant to Iran where, he claimed, he risked being subjected to treatment in breach of Article 3 of the Convention on account of his homosexuality;[423] and *Ilaşcu and Others v. Moldova and Russia*, concerning, *inter alia*, the lawfulness and the conditions of the applicants' detention.[424]

---

421 *Luluyev and Others v. Russia* (dec.), no. 69480/01, 30 June 2005.
422 *Jørgensen v. Denmark* (dec.), no. 31260/03, 9 June 2005.
423 *I.I.N. v. the Netherlands* (dec.), no. 2035/04, 9 December 2004.
424 *Ilaşcu and Others v. Moldova and Russia* (dec.), no. 48787/99, 4 July 2001

LODGING THE APPLICATION

Textbox vi   Contact Details of the Court

4.1 The First Communication to the Court: the Introductory Letter

Textbox vii   Model Introductory Letter

Textbox viii   Registry's response to Introductory Letter requesting that applicant submit a completed application form

4.2 The Application Form

4.3 The Court's Processing of the New Application

Textbox ix   Registration Letter

4.4 Inadmissibility Decided by Committees

Textbox x   Letter informing the Applicant of the Decision of the Committee

Textbox vi   *Contact Details of the European Court of Human Rights*

The Registrar
European Court of Human Rights
Council of Europe
F-67075 Strasbourg Cedex
France

Telephone: **+33 (0)3 88 41 20 18**
Fax: **+33 (0)3 88 41 27 30**
www.echr.coe.int

4.1 The First Communication to the Court: the Introductory Letter

As pointed out above, if there is a risk that the applicant will not be able to complete the full-blown application form before the end of the six-month period, it is important to note that an application may also be introduced by letter or by fax. There are many reasons why the preparation of a complete application form might take a significant amount of time, including the fact that the necessary documentation (domestic judgments, decisions, medical records, witness statements, etc.) might not be immediately available to the applicant.

If the introductory letter is sent by fax, a signed original must be sent to the Court within 5 days by post. If the applicant is represented by a lawyer, a *Form of Authority* signed by the representative and the applicant must accompany the letter.

Many applications are introduced by means of an introductory letter because such letters represent a very important and relatively easy way for applicants to stop the six-month clock. Nevertheless, as explained below, certain critical formalities must be observed when submitting the introductory letter in order for it to have the desired effect of preserving the applicant's complaints.

Rule 47 § 5 of the Rules of Court provides that

> "[t]he date of introduction of the application shall as a general rule be considered to be the date of the first communication from the applicant setting out, even summarily, the object of the application. The Court may for good cause nevertheless decide that a different date shall be considered to be the date of introduction".

As the rule specifies, such letters will interrupt the running of the six-month period provided that there is no "good cause" to do otherwise. In this connection, several considerations must be observed. The first concerns the substance of introductory letters: the subject matter of the application and a brief summary of the relevant facts and complaints must be set out clearly in the introductory letter. Secondly, the introductory letter should set out the Articles of the Convention which the applicant intends to rely on in the subsequent application. Thirdly, the letter should include information on exhaustion of domestic remedies.

Applicants must exercise care when listing the Convention Articles in the introductory letter. Merely invoking the Convention Articles is not on its own sufficient to make out a complaint. The Court also requires that "some indication of the nature of the alleged violation under the Convention" is given before a complaint is considered to have been introduced for purposes of interrupting the running of the six-month period.[425] For this reason, the applicant will be expected to "link" his or her allegations with the Articles referred to in the letter. Applicants should further note that if they invoke a Convention Article in the application form that was not previously mentioned in the introductory letter, the Court may declare that particular complaint inadmissible for non-respect of the time limit. Also, when a specific Article is mentioned in the introductory letter but not subsequently in the application form, the complaint in the introductory letter relating to that Article will not be examined since the application form constitutes the basis for the Court's examination of the case.

The importance of the contents of the introductory letter cannot be overemphasised. For example, in *Schälchli v. the Switzerland* the applicant's introductory letter mentioned only the Articles of the Convention which had allegedly been violated, and provided only skeletal information to the effect that the applicant was serving a prison sentence as a result of a judgment of the Federal Court but without describing the relevant details of the said judgment. The Court held that this was not sufficient to set out, even summarily, the object of the application and therefore did not stop the clock.[426]

The following example of an Introductory Letter – based on hypothetical facts – may provide guidance as to the form and content of the initial communication to the Court in an Article 3 case.

---

425 See *Bozinovski v. the former Yugoslav Republic of Macedonia* (dec.), no. 68368/01, 1 February 2005.
426 *Schälchli v. Switzerland* (dec.), no. 54908/00, 25 November 2003.

Textbox vii   **Model Introductory Letter**

The Registrar
European Court of Human Rights
Council of Europe
F-67075 Strasbourg Cedex
FRANCE

1 May 2006

Dear Sir/ Madam,

On behalf of my client [name] I am writing to introduce an application under Article 34 of the European Convention on Human Rights.

On 10 January 2005 my client was arrested in [city] by officers from the Anti-Terrorist Branch on suspicion of involvement in terrorist activities. He was taken to the City Hospital for a medical examination. According to the medical report drawn up at the end of the examination, there were no signs of any injuries on his body. My client was then placed in the detention facility of the police station. During his detention my client was questioned by police officers on three occasions. When he denied the allegations against him, the police officers became agitated and subjected him to serious ill-treatment which included being stripped naked, hosed down with pressurised cold water, suspended from his arms, and being beaten up with a truncheon on his chest. Also, electric shocks were administered to his toes.

On 14 January 2005 the police officers took him back to the City Hospital where they remained in the room while my client was being examined by a doctor. When the doctor asked my client to remove his clothes, the police officers told him not to do so. As a result, the doctor stated in a medical report that there were no signs of any ill-treatment on the applicant. My client was then brought before the judge where he informed the judge of his ordeal. The judge ordered his release on account of lack of sufficient evidence to charge him.

On his release my client was met outside the court building by his father, who took him to their family doctor. The doctor recorded in his report that there were extensive bruises under his armpits consistent with the client's account that he was suspended by his arms, and the marks on his chest were consistent with having been beaten up with an object. Furthermore, the doctor also observed that the client's toes bore signs of electric burns.

On the same day my client went back to the court building where he submitted a petition to the prosecutor containing the details of the ill-treatment to which he had been subjected. With his petition he also enclosed copies of the three medical reports. He asked the prosecutor to investigate his allegations and prosecute the police officers involved.

On 1 April 2005 my client received the decision of the prosecutor not to prosecute the police officers. The prosecutor's decision was based on a report prepared by the police chief of the police station where my client had been detained and ill-treated. According to the police chief's report, the police officers involved had been questioned by their commanding officer and had vehemently denied any wrongdoing. The prosecutor's decision also stated that according to the medical report of the City Hospital, there were no signs of any injury on my client's body. As to the medical report obtained from my client's family doctor, the prosecutor decided to exclude it because it was drawn up by a private practitioner, as opposed to a doctor employed by the State. The decision also stated that it would become final if no appeal was lodged against it within the statutory period of two weeks.

On 4 April 2005 my client appealed the prosecutor's decision not to prosecute the police officers. The appeal, which is the final remedy under domestic law, was dismissed on 1 November 2005. The decision was served on my client on 2 November 2005.

My client submits that the ill-treatment to which he was subjected whilst in the custody of the police officers amounted to torture within the meaning of Article 3 of the Convention. He further submits that the investigating authorities failed to carry out an effective investigation into his allegations of ill-treatment in violation of the positive obligation inherent in Article 3 and that they have thus deprived him of an effective remedy in violation of Article 13 of the Convention.

As my client has instructed me only this morning to lodge this application, it has not been possible to prepare a full application form and to compile the relevant supporting documents. I therefore ask the Court to accept this letter, which is being posted within the six-month time limit specified in Article 35 of the Convention, as an introductory letter. A completed application form, together with photocopies of the relevant documents, will be submitted shortly.

Yours faithfully,

Enc: Form of authority signed by my client and myself.

Following the submission of the introductory letter, it is important to comply strictly with any time limits indicated by the Registry relating to further submissions. When the Registry receives the application, it will be given a number[427] and the applicant will be given six weeks to submit the full application form with the supporting documents. If the applicant fails to comply with the six-week time limit, the Court may decide to regard the date of introduction as the date of the submission of the full application form, rather than the date of the introductory letter. This in turn, may result in the application being declared inadmissible for non compliance with the six-month rule. Therefore, applicants are advised to observe the six-week time limit notwithstanding Article 11 of the Practice Direction on the Institution of Proceedings, which provides that "where within a year, an applicant has not returned an application form or has not answered any letter sent to him by the Registry, the file will be destroyed". Applicants finding the six-week period insufficient to compile the necessary documents and to prepare the application form should inform the Court of the difficulties and request an extension of the time limit. The Court will normally grant the first such request provided that it is duly reasoned.

The Court is eager to eliminate unnecessary delays in the processing of complaints. Consequently, it has stated that "delays in the pursuit of an application are acceptable only in so far as they are explained by duly justified reasons connected to the subject matter of the application or the applicant personally".[428] In the case of *Nee v. Ireland*,[429] the final domestic court decision had been adopted in January 1998, and the applicant's lawyer informed the Commission in an introductory letter on 17 July 1998 that her client wished to introduce an application. The lawyer was urged by the Commission to send the full application form as soon as possible.[430] The lawyer, who acknowledged receipt of the Commission's letter in September 1998 and indicated to the Commission that the application form would be submitted within six weeks, did not submit it until 22 September 1999. In its decision – adopted more than three years after receipt of the application form – the Court considered 22 September 1999 to be the date of introduction of the application and declared it inadmissible for failure to comply with the six-month rule. Given the lack of any contact with the Commission or the Court for a period of more than one year, the Court was not convinced by the lawyer's explanations for the delay, which included her lack of familiarity with the Convention system, the complexity of the domestic proceedings and the difficulties she experienced in contacting her client who lived in England.

---

427 The application number must be mentioned in all subsequent correspondence.

428 *Quaresma Afonso Palma v. Portugal* (dec.), no. 72496/01, 13 February 2003.

429 *Nee v. Ireland* (dec.), no. 52787/99, 30 January 2003.

430 The practice of the Commission to ask applicants to submit their applications forms "as soon as possible" led to a number of difficulties and is now replaced by the Court's practice of requiring the full application form "within six weeks".

Textbox viii   *Registry's response to Introductory Letter requesting that applicant submit completed application form*[431]

ECHR-PE0   DATE

Our Ref.
v.
Your Ref.

The Registry of the European Court of Human Rights has received your communication of [DATE], from which it appears that you intend to lodge an application with the Court on behalf of your client. **It has been given the above file-number, to which you must refer in any further correspondence relating to this case.**

You will find enclosed a copy of the Convention and its Protocols, the text of Rules 45 and 47 of the Rules of Court, a notice for prospective applicants and the official application form, with an explanatory note.

If, after a careful study of the foregoing documents you are satisfied that your case meets all the appropriate criteria, you should fill in the application form carefully, legibly and completely as it will provide the basis for the Court's examination. It should be accompanied by **copies of all relevant documents**, *in particular any decisions of national courts or authorities which you wish to challenge before the Court.* **Please do not send originals as they will not be returned to you by the Court.**

You must return the application form and any necessary supplementary documents to the Court **without undue delay, and at the latest within six weeks after receipt of the present letter.** *Otherwise you run the risk that the Court will not accept the date of your first letter as the date on which the application was lodged and may consequently conclude that the six-month time limit for the submission of applications under Article 35 § 1 of the Convention has not been complied with.*

IMPORTANT

If the Registry receives no response from you, your complaints will be taken to have been withdrawn and the file opened in respect of the application will be destroyed – **without further warning** – one year after dispatch of this letter.

Encs: Convention and Protocols
        Notice to applicants
        Application form and explanatory note
        Authority form (for legal representation)

---

431   Source: Council of Europe

4.2 The Application Form

Rule 47 of the Rules of Court requires that all applications be made using the standard application form provided by the Registry unless the President of the Section concerned decides otherwise.[432] When completing the application form, applicants should also have regard to the "Notes for the guidance of persons wishing to apply to the ECHR" and the "Explanatory note for persons completing the Application Form" which are prepared by the Registry and figure in Appendices Nos. 17 and 4, respectively. Further reference must be made to the "Practice Direction on the Institution of Proceedings" in Appendix No. 3. Using the standard application form and completing it in compliance with the instructions in these documents will help the Court to examine the application and will ensure that all relevant information and documents required by Rule 47 of the Rules of Court are included in the application. The applicant may also find it useful to look at the Model Article 3 Application in Appendix No. 6, prepared on the basis of hypothetical facts.

The application form may be completed in one of the official languages of the Contracting Parties.[433] The form must be completed legibly, preferably typed. Applicants may also consider appending a short cover letter to their application form along the following lines:

> *Please find enclosed my [client's] application form and supporting documents. The application concerns the ill-treatment to which I [my client] was subjected while in the custody of the police, as well as the authorities' failure to investigate the circumstances of the ill-treatment and to punish those responsible....*

Such a cover letter is helpful to the Registry in the attribution of cases to lawyers and may speed up the processing of the application.

It is imperative that the facts, complaints, and steps taken when exhausting domestic remedies are set out clearly and concisely and, as far as possible, in chronological order. If the space reserved in the application form is not sufficient, applicants may continue on separate sheets. Where the length of the application (excluding annexes) exceeds 10 pages, a short summary should also be enclosed with the application form, for example in the cover letter.

When completing Part III of the application form, which is entitled "Statement of Alleged Violation(s) of the Convention and/or Protocols and of Relevant Arguments", the Convention and the relevant Protocols should be

---

432 Application forms exist in the official languages of all of the Contracting Parties and can be accessed at http://www.echr.coe.int/ECHR/EN/Header/Applicants/Information+for+applicants/Application+form/.

433 See Rule 34; see also Section 1.10 above

consulted and their terminology must be observed. If the applicant wishes to invoke a provision of a Protocol to the Convention, the document setting out the "Dates of ratification of the European Convention on Human Rights and Additional Protocols"[434] should be consulted to ensure that the respondent Contracting Party has ratified the relevant Protocol and that it was in force at the relevant point in time. See *Textbox i, Dates of Entry into Force of Convention and Protocols.*

In Part V of the application form, applicants are required to set out briefly what they want to achieve through their application. It is common practice for applicants to set out their claims under Article 41 of the Convention for just satisfaction and costs and expenses in this part of the application form. However, this is not strictly necessary since – as described in Section 7 on "Just Satisfaction" – the Court does not require claims for just satisfaction at this early stage.

As noted above in Section 1.15 on the effects of the Court's judgments, the Court has recently begun to provide certain guidelines to respondent States on how the consequences of a particular violation of the Convention may be remedied. For example, an applicant who has been convicted on the basis of a confession extracted under ill-treatment may argue in this part of the application form that the most appropriate form of relief would be to grant him or her a retrial. An applicant whose allegations of ill-treatment have not been adequately examined at the national level may claim that the most appropriate form of redress would be the re-opening of the investigation into his or her allegations. Similarly, an applicant who is complaining about the lawfulness of his or her detention may argue that the most appropriate form of relief would be to release him or her from detention. An applicant in an expulsion case may claim, for example, that the most appropriate form of relief would be not to expel him or her.

In Part VII of the application form, applicants are required to list supporting documents, e.g. the applicants' complaints to domestic authorities, decisions of the domestic courts, and other documentary evidence such as medical records, witness statements, etc. Only copies – not originals – of these documents should be submitted to the Court. For practical reasons, it is advisable to number each document so that easy reference can be made to them in the application form and in subsequent submissions.

Finally, applicants must ensure that they date and sign the application form.

---

434   For an updated list of ratifications, the following website should be consulted:
http://www.echr.coe.int/ECHR/EN/Header/Basic+Texts/Basic+Texts/Dates+of+ratification+of+the+
European+Convention+on+Human+Rights+and+Additional+Protocols/

If an applicant is represented by a lawyer or other representative, the signature of the representative is required and not that of the applicant.[435] In such cases the applicant must complete and sign the form of authority authorising the representative to represent him or her in the proceedings before the Court.[436] The form of authority should also be signed by the representative to indicate his or her acceptance.

4.3 The Court's Processing of the New Application

Upon receipt by the Court, the completed application form and the supporting documents will be forwarded to the relevant legal division of the Registry. The application will be given a number and assigned to one of the Registry's lawyers who will work as the case lawyer for that application. The Applicant will receive a letter from the Registry, confirming that the application has been registered and indicating a case number to which the applicant must refer in all future correspondence with the Court. The standard Registration Letter is reproduced in *Textbox ix* below.

The case lawyer will carry out an examination of the file and at this stage he or she may ask the applicant to submit further documents, information, or clarifications. Any time limits indicated by the Registry for submission of additional information must be complied with and if there are difficulties in obtaining the requested information, the Registry should be informed and an extension of the time limit should be sought.

When the file is complete, the application will be assigned to a decision body in one of the five Sections. In cases where the material submitted by the applicant on its own is sufficient to disclose that the application is inadmissible or should be struck out of the list,[438] and also where such action can be taken "without further examination",[439] it will be assigned to a Committee. Otherwise the application will be assigned to a Chamber and a judge rapporteur will be appointed. The classification of the application as a Committee or as a Chamber case is confidential and is not disclosed to applicants at this stage of the proceedings. The Registry will inform the applicant that it is his

---

435   See also Section 1.8 above.
436   Form of authority is included in *Textbox iii*. It may be downloaded at:
      http://www.echr.coe.int/NR/rdonlyres/001F1ADA-0F5A-4975-8B10-25D0C239865B/0/English.pdf
438   Rule 49 § 1 of the Rules of Court.
439   Article 28 of the Convention.

Textbox ix   *Registration Letter*[437]

FIRST/SECOND/THIRD/FOURTH/FIFTH SECTION

ECHR-LE1.1R   DATE

Application no.

v.

Dear Sir,

I acknowledge receipt of your letter of [DATE], with enclosures, including a completed application form.

The Court will deal with the case as soon as practicable. It will do so on the basis of the information and documents submitted by you. The proceedings are primarily in writing and you will only be required to appear in person if the Court invites you to do so. You will be informed of any decision taken by the Court.

You should inform me of any change in your address or that of your client. Furthermore, you should, of your own motion, inform the Court about any major developments regarding the above case, and submit any further relevant decisions of the domestic authorities.

Please note that no acknowledgment will be made as to the receipt of subsequent correspondence. No telephone enquiries either please. If you wish to be assured that your letter is actually received by the Court then you should send it by recorded delivery with a prepaid acknowledgment of receipt form.

Yours faithfully,

For the Registrar

xxx

Legal Secretary

---

437   Source: Council of Europe

or her duty to inform the Court of any subsequent developments relating to the case.[440]

4.4 Inadmissibility Decided by Committees

An application assigned to a Committee will generally be concluded within 12 months of its introduction but it may take shorter or longer depending on the case load of the legal division involved. Decisions of inadmissibility are final.[441] The majority of applications routed to Committees are declared inadmissible. However, Committee decisions need to be unanimous. If there is no unanimity amongst the 3 judges of the Committee, then the application will be referred to a Chamber of 7 judges.

If the application is declared inadmissible by a Committee, the applicant will be informed of the decision by means of a form letter which contains only the briefest of indications of the reasons for the decision.[442] As mentioned above, these decisions are nevertheless final, and there will be no further opportunity for the applicant to enquire into the specific reasons for the decision. By contrast, Chamber decisions on admissibility contain an individualised analysis of the case and reasons for the decision as described in Section 5 below.

---

440 See *Textbox ix*.
441 A total of 26,360 applications had been declared inadmissible by Committees of three judges in 2005; this figure represents almost 94% of the cases which were disposed of judicially – as opposed to administratively - by the Court in 2005.
442 See *Textbox x* for a sample letter.

Textbox x   ***Letter Informing the Applicant of the Decision of the Committee[443]***

FIRST/SECOND/THIRD/FOURTH/FIFTH SECTION

ECHR-LE11.0R(CD1)

<u>Application no.</u>

v.

Dear Sir,

I write to inform you that on [DATE] the European Court of Human Rights, sitting as a Committee of three judges (xxx, President, xxx and xxx) pursuant to Article 27 of the Convention, decided under Article 28 of the Convention to declare the above application inadmissible because it did not comply with the requirements set out in Articles 34 and 35 of the Convention.

In the light of all the material in its possession, and in so far as the matters complained of were within its competence, the Court found that they did not disclose any appearance of a violation of the rights and freedoms set out in the Convention or its Protocols.

This decision is final and not subject to any appeal to either the Court, including its Grand Chamber, or any other body. You will therefore appreciate that the Registry will be unable to provide any further details about the Committee's deliberations or to conduct further correspondence relating to its decision in this case. You will receive no further documents from the Court concerning this case and, in accordance with the Court's instructions, the file will be destroyed one year after the date of the decision.

The present communication is made pursuant to Rule 53 § 2 of the Rules of Court.

Yours faithfully,

For the Committee
xxx
Section Registrar

---

443   Source: Council of Europe

COMMUNICATION OF THE APPLICATION

5.1 General

5.2 Observations on Admissibility and Merits of the Application

5.1 General

If the application is assigned to a Chamber or referred to the Chamber from a Committee, it will either be declared inadmissible or notification of it will be given to the respondent Government. The notification of respondent Governments is referred to as "communication" of the application. Pursuant to Article 30 of the Convention, the Chamber may also refer the case to the Grand Chamber. However, such a course of action is extremely rare at this stage of the proceedings.

Both the Chamber and its President may decide to communicate an application. This decision is made on the basis of a report provided by the judge rapporteur.[444] If the Chamber or its President agrees with the judge rapporteur's proposal, the case will be communicated to the government of the respondent Contracting Party[445] which will be invited to respond to the applicant's allegations and submit its observations on the admissibility and merits of the case pursuant to Rule 54 § 2 (c). It is also possible that at this stage one or more of the complaints will be declared inadmissible and the remainder of the application is communicated. Such a decision can only be taken by the Chamber, the President not being authorised to reject complaints.

In certain circumstances, prior to or instead of the case being communicated, the Chamber, its President, or the judge rapporteur may ask both or one of the parties to submit any factual information, documents and other material which they consider to be relevant.[446] Such a course of action will usually occur in cases in which the Court needs to refer to documents, information or clarifications which the applicant him or herself is unable to obtain and submit to the Court without the respondent Government's assistance. Upon receipt of the documentation and/or information, the case will either be communicated or declared inadmissible.

When a case is communicated, the respondent Government will be asked to respond to a number of issues in its observations, which it is required to submit within twelve weeks of the notification (in urgent cases, a shorter time limit may be fixed). It is not uncommon for Governments – nor, indeed, for applicants – to request an extension of the deadline. The first such request will generally be granted.

The nature of the questions with which the respondent Government will be asked to deal in its observations will depend on the applicant's allegations

---

444   Rule 49 § 3 (c).
445   Rule 54 § 2 (b).
446   Rule 54 § 2 (a).

and the circumstances of the case, but in an application concerning ill-treatment in police custody, questions along the following lines may be expected:

> "Did the applicant comply with the admissibility requirements set out in Article 35 of the Convention?"

> "Was the applicant subjected to treatment in police custody in breach of Article 3 of the Convention?"

> "Did the authorities carry out an effective official investigation into the applicant's complaints of ill-treatment in compliance with the requirements of Articles 3 and 13 of the Convention?"

When the case is communicated, applicants who were until then unrepresented will be required, pursuant to Rule 36 § 2, to be represented by an advocate authorised to practice in any of the Contracting Parties and resident in the territory of one of them, or any other person approved by the President of the Chamber.[447]

If, at the time of communication, the Chamber or its President decides to apply the joint procedure, the parties will be informed accordingly. As set out above, this procedure has become the rule rather than the exception.[448] This means at this stage of the proceedings that, in addition to observations on admissibility and merits, the respondent Government is also invited to inform the Court of its position regarding a friendly settlement of the case and of any proposals it might wish to make in that connection.[449]

5.2 Observations on Admissibility and Merits of the Application

The respondent Government will in most cases submit its observations in one of the official languages of the Court, i.e. English or French. However, the President of the Chamber may invite the respondent Contracting Party to provide a translation into an official language of that Party in order to facilitate the applicant's understanding of those submissions.[450] An applicant may make a request to that effect. Furthermore, the President of the Chamber may also ask the respondent Contracting Party to provide a translation into, or a

---

447 Rule 36 § 4; see also Section 1.8 above.
448 Article 9 of Protocol No. 14 provides that " ..., a Chamber shall decide on the admissibility and merits of individual applications submitted under Article 34. The decision on admissibility may be taken separately."
449 See Section 8 below for friendly settlement related issues.
450 Rule 34 § 5.

summary in, English or French of all or certain annexes to its written submissions or of any other relevant documents.[451] In the alternative, the applicant can arrange for the translation of the respondent Contracting Party's observations and of any documents and subsequently claim the costs under Article 41 of the Convention.[452]

The observations and any documents submitted to the Court by the respondent Contracting Party will be forwarded to the applicant, who must respond to them within a certain time limit (usually six weeks). It is possible to request an extension of the time limit, but any such request must be reasoned and made within the time limit. Failure to submit the observations – or to request an extension – within the given time limit, may result in the exclusion of those observations from the case file unless the President of the Chamber decides otherwise.[453] For purposes of observing the time limit, the material date is the certified date of dispatch of the document or, if there is none, the actual date of receipt by the Registry. Applicants must send three copies of the observations by surface post and, if possible, a copy by facsimile.

In principle, the applicant's observations should be drafted in one of the official languages of the Court. However, the applicant may seek leave from the President of the relevant Chamber for the continued use of the official language of a Contracting Party.[454]

In preparing observations, applicants should refer to the "Practice Direction on Written Pleadings".[455] The form which should be followed in preparing the observations and the contents required are set out in Part II of the Practice Direction. It is imperative that the observations be legible; it is recommended that they be typed.

The fact that the applicant has the opportunity to respond to the observations of the Contracting Party is a consequence of the adversarial nature of the Court's proceedings. In certain circumstances, the applicant may also be requested by the Court to address in his or her observations specific issues identified by the Court or answer specific questions posed by the Court.

In their observations, applicants should respond to any objections raised by the respondent Government to the admissibility of the application. For example, if the Government contends that the applicant has failed to comply with

---

451   Rule 34 § 4 (c).
452   See Section 7.
453   Rule 38 § 1.
454   Rule 34 § 3 (a).
455   Issued by the President of the Court on 1 November 2003. See Appendix No. 3.

the requirement of exhaustion of domestic remedies, it is the applicant who, at this stage of the proceedings, bears the burden of establishing that:

> "the remedy advanced by the Government was in fact exhausted or was for some reason inadequate and ineffective in the particular circumstances of the case or that there existed special circumstances absolving him or her from the requirement…".[456]

A failure by the applicant to counter the Government's objections to the admissibility of the application may result in the application being declared inadmissible for non-exhaustion of domestic remedies. In their observations applicants should also describe any developments which might have taken place since the introduction of the application.[457]

---

456 See *Akdıvar and Others v. Turkey*, cited above, § 68.

457 Relevant parts of observations submitted by the Netherlands Government in the case of *Van der Ven v. the Netherlands*, cited above, and observations submitted by the applicants' representatives in the cases of *Akkum and Others v. Turkey* and *Kişmir v. Turkey*, both cited above, are included in Appendices Nos. 14, 12 and 13, respectively, and may be consulted as to the form and content of observations in cases concerning allegations of ill-treatment.

ADMISSIBILITY DECISIONS

6.1 The Decision on Admissibility

6.2 Admissibility with the Government's Objections Joined to the Merits of the Case

6.3 Inadmissibility and its Consequences

6.4 Admissibility and its Consequences

6.1 The Decision on Admissibility

As discussed in Section 1.7.3 and in Part II of this *Handbook*, the Court, prior to communicating an application to the respondent Government, examines whether it is not clearly in admissible. An application (or parts thereof) deemed admissible at this early stage may then be communicated to the respondent Government. The Government may then submit its arguments against the application's admissibility. This section addresses the admissibility evaluation that takes place following the application's communication to the respondent Government.

Following the receipt of the respondent Government's observations on the admissibility and merits of the case and the applicant's observations in reply, and if no friendly settlement has been reached, the Court will again address the application's admissibility. In some cases the Chamber may decide to hold a hearing on admissibility of the application.[458] When the Court determines admissibility in a separate decision (i.e. when the joint procedure has not been applied or has been discontinued) such a decision will typically contain the following components:

- Name of the case and of the Section, application number and names of the judges of the Chamber,

- Date of introduction of the application and date of adoption of the decision,

- THE FACTS, consisting of THE CIRCUMSTANCES OF THE CASE: the details of the applicant, together with the facts as submitted by the parties, and, if deemed necessary, RELEVANT DOMESTIC LAW AND PRACTICE,

- COMPLAINTS,

- THE LAW,

- Conclusion(s) reached by the Chamber.

The facts as submitted by the parties will be summarised in the "Facts" part of the decision. If the facts of the case are in dispute, they will be set out separately. Furthermore, documents submitted to the Court by the parties together with their observations, in so far as they are relevant, may also be summarised in this part of the decision. Relevant domestic law and practice may be summarised before describing the applicant's complaints under the Convention.

---

458   See Section 1.14 above.

In the "Law" part of the decision, the respondent Contracting Party's objections to the admissibility of the complaints(s) and the applicant's responses thereto will be examined. If the Chamber concludes that the applicant has complied with the formal requirements of admissibility within the meaning of Convention Articles 34 and 35, most notably that he or she has exhausted the relevant domestic remedies and has lodged the application within the required six-month time limit, the Chamber will proceed to examine the merits of the case to establish whether (any of) the complaints are manifestly ill-founded. If the case is deemed not to be manifestly ill-founded, it will be declared admissible. As was the case at the communication stage, it is possible that some of the complaints are declared inadmissible and the remainder of the application admissible.

It must be pointed out here that a failure by the Government to object to the admissibility of an application may result in the Court declaring the application admissible. The reason for this is that communication of an application means, in effect, that the application was deemed not to be *prima facie* inadmissible. For example, in the case of *İpek v. Turkey* the Court observed that the respondent Government, beyond arguing in its observations that the "application should be declared inadmissible as being premature, imaginary and ill-founded" had not raised any other objections to its admissibility[459]. The Court, in concluding that the application was not manifestly ill-founded within the meaning of Article 35 § 3 of the Convention, stated that "[n]o other grounds for declaring it inadmissible have been raised by the Government and the Court sees no reason to do so of its own motion".[460]

6.2 Admissibility with the Government's Objections Joined to the Merits of the Case

As described elsewhere in this *Handbook*, Contracting Parties are under an obligation – referred to as a positive obligation – to carry out effective investigations into allegations of ill-treatment and killings.[461] They are also under an obligation under Article 13 to provide effective remedies to those whose Convention rights and freedoms have been violated. Criminal investigations which continue for long periods of time without any tangible results may be deemed by the Court to be ineffective investigations in

---

459 *İpek v. Turkey*, (dec.) no. 25760/94, 14 May 2002.
460 *Ibid.*
461 See in particular Section 10 below.

violation of the Contracting Party's positive obligations under Articles 2 and 3 of the Convention and/or of their obligations under Article 13 of the Convention to provide effective remedies. It follows, therefore, that the issue of exhaustion of remedies may be closely linked both to the issue of positive obligations and the issue of effective remedies within the meaning of Article 13 of the Convention.

The examination of the question of whether an applicant has exhausted domestic remedies (i.e. an admissibility issue) requires the Court in some cases – most notably cases in which complaints are made under Articles 2, 3, and/or 13 – to determine the effectiveness of investigations which have been continuing for long periods of time without yielding any results and the outcome of which the applicant has not awaited before lodging an application to the Court. In such circumstances, the Chamber will abstain from examining the issue in its admissibility decision, since it will want to avoid making a ruling at the admissibility stage about the ineffectiveness of an investigation which would in effect amount to a declaration of a violation of the positive obligation under Articles 2 or 3 and/or of the obligation under Article 13 to provide an effective remedy. Therefore, where the examination of the Government's objection based on non-exhaustion of a particular remedy is inextricably linked to the substance of the applicant's complaint, the Court will join that issue to the merits of the case and will deal with it in its judgment.[462]

A survey of the Court's case law illustrates that, in the great majority of applications in which the Court joined to the merits the Government's objection based on exhaustion of domestic remedies, the Contracting Parties involved were subsequently found to have breached their positive obligation to carry out an effective investigation. In its admissibility decision in the case of *Kişmir v. Turkey*, for example, the Court, noting that "the Government's preliminary objection as to the criminal procedure raised issues that are closely linked to those raised by the applicant's complaints under Articles 2 and 13 of the Convention", decided to join that preliminary objection to the merits.[463] When the Court subsequently concluded in its judgment that the authorities had failed to carry out an effective investigation into the applicant's complaints as required by Article 2, it logically rejected the Government's preliminary objection regarding exhaustion of domestic remedies, based on the finding that there were no effective domestic remedies for the applicant to exhaust.[464]

---

462   See, for example, *Khashiyev and Akayeva v. Russia*, cited above, § 115.
463   *Kişmir v. Turkey* (dec.), no. 27306/95, 14 December 1999.
464   *Kişmir v. Turkey*, cited above.

6.3 Inadmissibility and its Consequences

Inadmissibility decisions – whether adopted by a Chamber or a Committee – are final. The parties cannot request that the case be referred to the Grand Chamber pursuant to Article 43 of the Convention. Furthermore, a new application lodged by the applicant based on the same facts will be declared inadmissible pursuant to Article 35 § 2 (b) as being "substantially the same as a matter that has already been examined by the Court".[465] There are, however, two circumstances in which the Court may re-examine an application based on the same facts.

Firstly, and as mentioned earlier, if the application is declared inadmissible for non-exhaustion of a domestic remedy, after exhausting that particular domestic remedy, the applicant may submit a new application based on the same complaints. Exhaustion of the domestic remedy will result in a new domestic decision, which is regarded as "relevant new information" within the meaning of Article 35 § 2 (b). In any event, this will not amount to a re-examination of the complaints by the Court; in its inadmissibility decision it will have limited its finding to the exhaustion of domestic remedies, without addressing the merits of the case. However, this happens rarely in practice because by the time the Court examines the application and declares it inadmissible, the applicant will most likely have missed the time limit prescribed in national legislation within which to make use of the relevant remedy. As explained above, applicants are expected to comply with domestic rules of procedure when exhausting domestic remedies. Where an action instituted by an applicant, be it an appeal or otherwise, is dismissed because of his or her non-compliance with a procedural requirement, for instance the time limit within which to file the appeal, this will be regarded by the Court as a failure to exhaust the domestic remedy. The rationale for this is that, as a result of the applicant's non-compliance, he or she has not afforded the national authorities an opportunity to deal with the substance of the complaints.

The second possibility for the Court to re-examine an application occurs pursuant to the operation of Article 37 § 2 of the Convention. According to that provision,

> "[t]he Court may decide to restore an application to its list of cases if it considers that the circumstances justify such a course".

However, this possibility should by no means be perceived as an opportunity to appeal against a decision of inadmissibility. The Court will only restore an

---

465   See also Section 2.9 above.

inadmissible case to its list of cases if its decision on the admissibility was based on a factual error which is relevant to the conclusion or where new circumstances have arisen justifying the Court's resumption of the examination of the case. Such factual errors may include overlooking a letter introducing the application which affected the calculation of the six-month time limit or where the Court relied on a fact that was not correct[466].

6.4 Admissibility and its Consequences

If the case is declared (partially) admissible in a separate decision, the Court may ask the parties to respond to specific questions, to submit observations on a particular issue, or to submit additional evidence.[467] Additionally, the Court might instead inform the parties that it requires no further information or observations but that the parties may nevertheless submit any additional evidence or observations that they wish. Any material thus submitted by a party will be transmitted to the other party for information or for comment, but only if the Court deems it necessary. At this stage of the proceedings it is thus not automatic that an applicant will be allowed to respond to observations submitted by the respondent Government.

The information and explanations concerning observations, set out above in the section on communication of the application (Section 5), are also applicable to observations which the applicant may submit at this stage of the proceedings. However, applicants should take particular note of paragraph 13 of the "Practice Direction on Written Pleadings"[468] which stipulates that the parties' pleadings following the admission (admissibility) of the application should include:

i. a short statement confirming a party's position on the facts of the case as established in the decision on admissibility;

ii. legal arguments relating to the merits of the case;

iii. a reply to any specific questions on a factual or legal points put by the Court.

At this stage of the proceedings the scope of the case will have been determined by the Court's admissibility decision; that is to say, if only some of the

---

466 See Reid, p. 36.
467 *Khashiyev and Akayeva v. Russia*, cited above, § 11.
468 See Appendix No. 3.

complaints have been declared admissible, the applicant should not address the complaints declared inadmissible in his or her observations on the merits. Further observations on the merits give the applicant a final opportunity to support his or her case with adequate evidence and argumentation, and for this reason applicants are advised to avail themselves of this opportunity even if the Court does not specifically require further observations at this stage.[469]

---

469   See also Leach p. 81 *et seq.*

JUST SATISFACTION (Article 41)

7.1 Summary

7.2 Discussion

7.2.1 Criteria for Adjudicating Just Satisfaction

a) Pecuniary Damage

b) Non-pecuniary Damage

c) Costs and Expenses

7.3 Concluding Remarks

7.1 Summary

If it finds a violation of the Convention, the Court may in its judgment order the respondent Contracting Party to pay the applicant a sum of money – just satisfaction – under Article 41 of the Convention. As pointed out elsewhere in this *Handbook*, the Court may also conclude that the most appropriate form of redress is for the respondent Contracting Party to take a specific action, such as to grant the applicant a re-trial,[470] to release him or her from prison,[471] or to stop his or her removal from the territory of the Contracting Party.[472] For purposes of the Convention proceedings, the term "just satisfaction" includes monetary awards to compensate an applicant's 1) pecuniary damage, i.e. financial losses which have actually been sustained by the applicant as a direct consequence of the violation; 2) non-pecuniary damage, i.e. those based on the applicant's mental suffering and distress stemming from the actions that violated the Convention; and finally, 3) the costs and expenses associated with bringing the Convention complaints to the attention of the national authorities and the Court in Strasbourg.

Just satisfaction is a major subject in its own right and, as such, the scope of the present *Handbook* does not allow for a comprehensive analysis of the issue. However, the general requirements and strategic considerations it entails will be examined below in so far as they are relevant for Article 3 claimants.[473]

7.2 Discussion

According to Article 41 of the Convention,

> "[i]f the Court finds that there has been a violation of the Convention or the protocols thereto, and if the internal law of the High Contracting Party concerned allows only partial reparation to be made, the Court shall, if necessary, afford just satisfaction to the injured party".

---

470 See *Ükünç and Güneş v. Turkey*, cited above, § 32.
471 See, for example, *Assanidze v. Georgia* [GC], cited above, § 203.
472 See, *mutatis mutandis*, *N. v. Finland*, cited above, § 177.
473 For just satisfaction related issues, see Leach p. 397 *et seq.* and Reid p. 542 *et seq.* As an example of just satisfaction claims, see Appendix No. 12 for the applicants' observations in the case of *Akkum and Others v. Turkey*.

SECTION 7: JUST SATISFACTION

It must be stressed at the outset that awards for just satisfaction are an equitable remedy and that they are made in discretion of the Court.[474] That is to say that, although the Court will undoubtedly have regard to the claims made by the applicant, it will make an award that it considers equitable or reasonable under the circumstances.

The issue of just satisfaction is also dealt with in Rule 60 of the Rules of Court, which provides as follows:

> "1. An applicant who wishes to obtain an award of just satisfaction under Article 41 of the Convention in the event of the Court finding a violation of his or her Convention rights must make a specific claim to that effect.
>
> 2. The applicant must submit itemised particulars of all claims, together with any relevant supporting documents, within the time-limit fixed for the submission of the applicant's observations on the merits unless the President of the Chamber directs otherwise.
>
> 3. If the applicant fails to comply with the requirements set out in the preceding paragraphs the Chamber may reject the claims in whole or in part.
>
> 4. The applicant's claims shall be transmitted to the respondent Government for comment".[475]

If the Court has decided to examine the admissibility and merits of the case simultaneously in accordance with Article 29 § 3 of the Convention and Rule 54A of the Rules of Court (the joint procedure), the applicant will be required to submit his or her claims under Article 41 of the Convention at the same time as submitting observations in reply to those of the Government. Presumably, the Court will adopt a similar course of action following the entry into force of Protocol No. 14, pursuant to which separate admissibility decisions will become the exception. As long as Protocol No. 14 has not yet entered into force, and if the Court has not applied the joint procedure in a particular case, the applicant will be required to submit his or her just satisfaction claims following the admissibility determination. In any event, the Court will always let the applicant know when he or she is supposed to submit just satisfaction claims, and will provide him or her with more information on the matter along the following lines:

> "... according to the Court's established case-law, failure to submit quantified claims within the time allowed for the purpose under Rule 60 § 1, together with the required supporting documents, entails the consequence that the Chamber will either make no award of just satisfaction or else reject the claim in part. This applies even if the applicant has indicated his wishes concerning just satisfaction at an earlier stage of the proceedings. No extension of the time allowed will be granted.

---

474 See Leach, p. 397.

475 It is expected that the President of the Court will issue a practice direction on filing just satisfaction claims; see paragraph 13 (b) of the "Practice Direction on Written Pleadings" at Appendix No. 3.

The criteria established by the Court's case-law when it rules on the question of just satisfaction (Article 41 of the Convention) are: (1) pecuniary damage, that is to say losses actually sustained as a direct consequence of the alleged violation; (2) non-pecuniary damage, meaning compensation for suffering and distress occasioned by the violation; and (3) the costs and expenses incurred in order to prevent or obtain redress for the alleged violation of the Convention, both within the domestic legal system and through the Strasbourg proceedings. These costs must be itemised, and it must be established that they are reasonable and have been actually and necessarily incurred.

You must attach to your claims the necessary vouchers, such as bills of costs. The Government will then be invited to submit their comments on the matter".

The Court thus requires applicants to submit their claims for just satisfaction regardless of whether they have already claimed them in the application form.[476] Furthermore, applicants should also include the details of their bank account in their claims for just satisfaction.

7.2.1 Criteria for Adjudicating Just Satisfaction

a) Pecuniary Damage

In claims for pecuniary damage – referred to in some jurisdictions as "material" or "financial" damage – applicants may claim compensation for financial losses they have actually sustained as a direct consequence of the violation. In the context of Article 3, such claims may include loss of income for the period during which the applicant was prevented from working as a result of the ill-treatment and the costs of medical care. For example, in the case of *Dizman v. Turkey* the applicant claimed:

"after being assaulted by the police officers, he had been given medical treatment in a hospital for a period of 90 days. During that time, and a further period of three months, he had been unable to work. His six months' loss of income amounted to 1,571 pounds sterling (GBP). He had a wife and three children, aged between 6 and 9 years old, for whom he was financially responsible. He also claimed that his hospital expenses amounted to GBP 3,492.84".

In finding an Article 3 violation, the Court observed a "direct causal link" between on the one hand, the injuries inflicted on the applicant and, on the other hand, the applicant's medical expenses and loss of earnings. It held the following:

---

476   See Section 4.2 above.

> "... the applicant needed an operation and was unable, according to the Forensic Medicine Directorate's report of 7 October 1994, to work for a period of 25 days... The Court, deciding on an equitable basis in the absence of any hospital bills, awards the applicant the sum of 5,000 euros (EUR) in respect of his pecuniary damage".[477]

Thus, in upholding the applicant's claim for pecuniary damage, the Court referred to the "direct causal link" between the injuries which it found to have been inflicted on the applicant in violation of Article 3 of the Convention on the one hand, and the medical expenses and a certain loss of earnings on the other.[478] Had the applicant submitted his hospital bills, the Court might have awarded him the full amount claimed.

By contrast, in the case of *Mathew v. the Netherlands*[479] the Court held that no "causal link" had been established between the pecuniary damage claimed by the applicant in respect of his medical treatment and the violations the Court found on account of an extended period of solitary confinement:

> "[The Court's] findings of violation of Article 3 of the Convention relate only to certain aspects of the conditions in which the applicant was detained. They do not impute responsibility for the applicant's medical condition to the respondent Party, from which it follows that the costs thereby caused cannot be recovered from the respondent Party under Article 41 of the Convention".

It is noteworthy that in this case the respondent Government had not objected to an award being made for medical expenses.

Claims for pecuniary damage must be supported by adequate evidence, e.g. by submitting hospital bills, documents showing the costs of medicines, etc. In a claim for loss of earnings, documents showing the income of the applicant must be submitted to support the claim, together with medical documents showing the period during which the applicant was unable to work. A failure to substantiate claims for pecuniary damage is very likely to lead the Court to reject the claim or to accept only part of it. The Court may, however, consider any inability on the part of the applicant to provide evidence due to circumstances beyond his or her control, and compensate the applicant when awarding non-pecuniary damage.[480]

Pursuant to Rule 60 § 4 of the Rules of Court, the applicant's claims will be transmitted to the respondent Government for comment. Where – even

---

477 *Dizman v. Turkey*, no. 27309/95, 20 September 2005, §§ 105-107.
478 See also *Messegué and Jabardo v. Spain* (Article 50), nos. 10588/83, 10589/83, 10590/83, 13 June 1994, §§ 16-20.
479 *Mathew v. the Netherlands*, cited above, §§ 220-224.
480 See *Hasan and Chaush v. Bulgaria* [GC], no. 30985/96, 26 October 2000, § 118.

though extremely unlikely – the respondent Government does not comment on the applicant's claims or does not dispute the amount claimed or the factual basis for the claim, the Court may award the applicant the full amount claimed. For example, in the case of *Aktaş v. Turkey*, the respondent Government did not comment on the applicant's detailed claims for pecuniary damage in respect of the loss of earnings of his brother who had been killed in custody, apart from its argument that the sums claimed by him were excessive. The Court, having found the respondent State responsible for the death of the applicant's brother, concluded that the loss of his future earnings was also imputable to the respondent State and awarded the applicant the full amount claimed, i.e. 226,065 EUR.[481]

The Court's review of its case-law in paragraphs 352-353 of the *Aktaş* judgment illustrates its approach when calculating damages and explains to a certain extent the reasons behind the greatly varying amounts awarded by the Court, even in cases involving similar facts:

> "352. The Court reiterates that there must be a clear causal connection between the damage claimed by the applicant and the violation of the Convention and that this may, in the appropriate case, include compensation in respect of loss of earnings...
>
> 353.   In addition, it is recalled that a precise calculation of the sums necessary to make complete reparation *(restitutio in integrum)* in respect of the pecuniary losses suffered by an applicant may be prevented by the inherently uncertain character of the damage flowing from the violation *(Young, James and Webster v. the United Kingdom*, judgment of 18 October 1982 (former Article 50), Series A no. 55, § 11). An award may still be made notwithstanding the large number of imponderables involved in the assessment of future losses, though the greater the lapse of time involved the more uncertain the link between the breach and the damage becomes. The question to be decided in such cases is the level of just satisfaction, in respect of either past and future pecuniary loss, which it is necessary to award an applicant, the matter to be determined by the Court at its discretion, having regard to what is equitable *(Sunday Times v. the United Kingdom*, judgment of 6 November 1989 (former Article 50), Series A no. 38, p. 9, § 15; *Lustig-Prean and Beckett v. the United Kingdom* (just satisfaction), nos. 31417/96 and 32377/96, §§ 22-23; ...'"

b) Non-pecuniary Damage

Non-pecuniary damage – also referred to as "moral" damage – may be loosely defined as an award to help alleviate an applicant's mental suffering and distress stemming from the actions which led to a violation of the

---

481   *Aktaş v. Turkey*, no. 24351/94, 24 April 2003, §§ 349-355.

Convention. The following judgments give an idea of the amounts awarded by the Court for non-pecuniary damage in cases in which there have been violations of Article 3.

- *Mathew v. the Netherlands*: violation of Article 3 on account of the length and circumstances of solitary confinement: 10,000 EUR[482]

- *Dizman v. Turkey*: violation of Article 3 on account of the applicant's chin having been broken by police officers: 15,000 EUR[483]

- *Ostrovar v. Moldova*: violation of Article 3 on account of the "frustration, uncertainty and anxiety" suffered by the applicant due to the conditions of his detention in prison: 3,000 EUR[484]

- *Labzov v. Russia*: violation of Article 3 for the distress and hardship suffered by the applicant on account of prison conditions: 2,000 EUR[485]

- *Balogh v. Hungary*: violation of Article 3 on account of the "distress and suffering resulting from [the applicant's] ill-treatment by the police": 10,000 EUR[486]

- *M.C. v. Bulgaria*: violation of Article 3 on account of the "distress and psychological trauma resulting at least partly from the shortcomings in the authorities' approach" in investigating the applicant's allegations of rape: 8,000 EUR[487]

- *McGlinchey and Others v. the United Kingdom*: violation of Article 3 on account of the prison authorities' treatment of Ms McGlinchey – the applicants' daughter and mother. Because Ms McGlinchey died in prison, her two daughters and mother were awarded a total sum of 22,900 EUR[488]

- *Nazarenko v. Ukraine*: violation of Article 3 on account of conditions of detention: 2,000 EUR[489]

- *Mouisel v. France*: violation of Article 3 on account of the continued detention of the applicant – a cancer sufferer – which "undermined his dignity and entailed particularly acute hardship that caused suffering

482   *Mathew v. the Netherlands*, cited above, § 229.
483   *Dizman v. Turkey*, cited above, § 110.
484   *Ostrovar v. Moldova*, no. 35207/03, 13 September 2005, § 118.
485   *Labzov v. Russia*, cited above, § 59.
486   *Balogh v. Hungary*, no. 47940/99, 20 July 2004, § 85.
487   *M.C. v. Bulgaria*, no. 39272/98, 4 December 2003, § 194.
488   *McGlinchey and Others v. the United Kingdom*, no. 50390/99, 29 April 2003, § 71.
489   *Nazarenko v. Ukraine*, no. 39483/98, 29 April 2003, § 172.

beyond that inevitably associated with a prison sentence and treatment for cancer": 15,000 EUR[490]

- *Peers v. Greece*: violation of Article 3 on account of the prison conditions which "diminished the applicant's human dignity and aroused in him feelings of anguish and inferiority capable of humiliating and debasing him and possibly breaking his physical or moral resistance": 5,000,000 drachmas[491]

- *Egmez v. Cyprus*: violation of Article 3 on account of the intentional ill-treatment to which the applicant was subjected by police officers at the time of his arrest and in the immediate aftermath but "over a short period of heightened tension and emotions": 10,000 GBP[492]

The Court has awarded higher sums in cases where the violation was particularly serious. For example, in *Selmouni v. France*, the Court found that the applicant had been tortured while in police custody and it found that he had suffered non-pecuniary damage for which the findings of violations alone did not afford sufficient satisfaction. It therefore awarded him 500,000 French francs.[493] Similarly, in the case of *Tomasi v. France*, in which the applicant's body:

> "had borne marks which had only one origin, the ill-treatment inflicted on him for a period of forty odd hours by some of the police-officers responsible for his interrogation: he had been slapped, kicked, punched and given forearm blows, made to stand for long periods and without support, hands handcuffed behind the back; he had been spat upon, made to stand naked in front of an open window, deprived of food, threatened with a firearm and so on,"[494]

the Court awarded the applicant 700,000 French francs.

In its judgment in the case of *Aydın v. Turkey*, the Court,

> "having regard to the seriousness of the violation of the Convention suffered by the applicant while in custody and the enduring psychological harm which she may be considered to have suffered on account of being raped,"

decided to award a sum of GBP 25,000 by way of compensation for non-pecuniary damage.[495] Reference may also be made to the more recent case of

---

490 *Mouisel v. France*, cited above, § 48.
491 *Peers v. Greece*, no. 28524/95, 19 April 2001, §§ 75 and 88.
492 *Egmez v. Cyprus*, no. 30873/96, 21 December 2001, §§ 78 and 106.
493 *Selmouni v. France*, cited above, § 123.
494 *Tomasi v. France*, no. 12850/87, 27 August 1992, § 108.
495 *Aydın v. Turkey*, no. 23178/94, 25 September 1997, § 131.

Ilaşcu and Others v. Moldova and Russia, which was brought by four applicants. The Court found it established that two of the applicants had been subjected to treatment amounting to torture and the remaining two applicants to inhuman and degrading treatment. The ill-treatment in question consisted of the time spent on death row (seven and a half years in the case of one of the applicants), having been "savagely" beaten by prison wardens, withholding of food, protracted periods of time spent in solitary confinement, and unacceptable conditions of detention. On account of these allegations the Court found violations of Articles 3, 5, and 34 of the Convention. The Court awarded 190,000 EUR to each of the applicants on account of the "extreme seriousness of the violations of the Convention of which the applicants were victims".[496]

In cases which concern expulsion or extradition of applicants to a country where they would run a real risk of being subjected to treatment in violation of Article 3 of the Convention, the Court will not usually make any awards for pecuniary or non-pecuniary damage but only for costs and expenses incurred by the applicant in having the application examined by the Court, e.g. lawyer's fees and costs, etc. The Court's logic is that if the applicant has not yet been physically removed from the territory of the respondent Contracting Party, no violation will have occurred. For example, in its judgment in the case of *N. v. Finland* the Court held the following:

> "Having regard to all the elements before it, the Court considers that the finding that the applicant's expulsion to the Democratic Republic of Congo at this moment in time would amount to a violation of Article 3, constitutes in itself sufficient just satisfaction in respect of any non-pecuniary damage suffered by the applicant"[497]

Because of the wide spectrum of circumstances in which mental suffering may occur, the variation in the amounts awarded by the Court for non-pecuniary damage is even greater than that among awards made for pecuniary damage. Nevertheless, awards made by the Court for non-pecuniary damage are the only source of information on which an applicant may rely when claiming non-pecuniary damage. It must be stressed that the Court will not look favourably upon six-digit claims. For this reason, parity of the sum claimed by an applicant with the sums awarded by the Court in its judgments in previous cases against the same Contracting Party, concerning similar facts and complaints, may increase the chances of success of obtaining the claimed sum.

---

496 *Ilaşcu and Others v. Moldova and Russia,* cited above, § 489.
497 *N. v. Finland,* cited above, § 177.

c) Costs and Expenses

The Court will award a successful applicant all or part of the costs and expenses incurred by him or her in order to prevent or obtain redress for the alleged violation of the Convention, both within the domestic legal system and in the Strasbourg proceedings.

The claims for costs and expenses must be itemised, and it must be established that they are reasonable and have been actually and necessarily incurred. For this reason, at the time of introducing the application, practitioners must start recording their costs and expenses and the time spent by them on the case in the course of the proceedings, such as the preparation of the application form and the drafting of the observations and other submissions. Costs of any translation, postage, telephone and fax, stationeries, etc., must be itemised with as much detail as possible. In calculating their fees practitioners may have regard to the domestic fee scales issued, for example, by their own bar association. It must be stressed, however, that such fee scales, although relevant, are not binding. A survey of the Court's judgments reveals that when making awards for legal fees, the Court takes into account the earnings of legal practitioners in the respondent Contracting Party. For this reason practitioners should consult the Court's jurisprudence concerning the relevant Contracting Party when making claims for fees, just as they would when calculating damages. Furthermore, when awarding legal fees, the Court will take into account the complexity of the case and the extent to which the applicant has succeeded in his or her application. Needless to say, if the Court finds no violation of any of the Articles invoked by the applicant, it will not make an award for costs and expenses. Any money already received from the Council of Europe in legal aid will be deducted from the sum awarded for costs and expenses, but if the Court does not find a violation, the applicant will not be asked to repay the sum received in legal aid.

Applicants may also make a claim in respect of costs incurred in efforts made at the national level to prevent the violation from occurring or, when it has already occurred, in obtaining redress from the national authorities for that violation. As the Court held in its judgment in the case of *Société Colas Est and Others v. France*:

> "...if it finds that there has been a violation of the Convention, it may award the applicant the costs and expenses incurred before the national courts for the prevention or redress of the violation... In the instant case the Court notes that the point at which the applicant companies first relied on their right to respect for their home – the right which it has found to have been violated – was when the case was remitted by the Court of Cassation to the Paris Court of Appeal".[498]

---

498   *Société Colas Est and Others v. France*, 37971/97, 16 April 2002, § 56.

7.3 Concluding Remarks

Awards for just satisfaction will be in euros, but the judgment will stipulate that the sums awarded are to be converted into the official currency of the respondent Contracting Party at the rate applicable at the date of payment and that they are to be paid into the applicant's bank account. If the applicant is not living in the territory of the respondent Contracting Party, the Court may, on the applicant's request, stipulate that the sum is to be paid into the national currency of the country in which the applicant is living and into the applicant's bank account in that country.[499]

Any sums awarded by the Court are to be paid within three months from the date on which the judgment becomes final according to Article 44 § 2 of the Convention.[500] The judgment will also stipulate that:

> "from the expiry of the above-mentioned three months until settlement simple interest shall be payable on the above amounts at a rate equal to the marginal lending rate of the European Central Bank during the default period plus three percentage points".

Finally, when making an award for costs and expenses, the Court will often stipulate that the sum awarded is to be paid together with any value added tax (VAT) that may be chargeable.

Should any problems arise as to the payment of the awards by the respondent Government – such as non-payment, late payments, and part payments – applicants are advised to contact the Committee of Ministers as it is not the Court's duty to supervise the execution of judgments.[501]

If a legal representative encounters problems in recovering his or her legal fees from the applicant, as per the award in the judgment, this is a matter for domestic courts and not for the Committee of Ministers or the Court. When making the claim for just satisfaction, legal representatives may request the Court to stipulate in its judgment that sums awarded in respect of legal fees are to be paid into the representative's bank account and not that of the applicant's.

499　See *Süheyla Aydın v. Turkey*, cited above, § 228 where the applicant was living in Switzerland and where the Court stated that the sums awarded were to be converted into Swiss francs.
500　See Section 9.2 below.
501　See Section 9.3 below.

FRIENDLY SETTLEMENT AND STRIKE OUT (Articles 37-38)

8.1 Friendly Settlement

8.1.1 Introduction

8.1.2 Friendly Settlement Declaration

Textbox xi Example of Friendly Settlement Declaration

8.1.3 Enforcement of Undertakings Expressed in a Friendly Settlement Declaration

8.2 Strike Out

8.2.1 Absence of Intention to Pursue the Application (Article 37 § 1 (a))

8.2.2 Resolution of the Matter (Article 37 § 1 (b))

8.2.3 Strike Out "for any other reason" (Article 37 § 1 (c))

8.3 Concluding Remarks

8.1 Friendly Settlement

8.1.1 Introduction

The friendly settlement procedure under the Convention – very much like an out of court settlement in national legislation – affords the parties an opportunity to resolve an issue, usually on payment to the applicant by the respondent Contracting Party of a specified sum of money or on the basis of an undertaking by the respondent Contracting Party to provide appropriate resolution of the issue, or both. The basis for friendly settlements is found in Article 38 of the Convention,[502] the relevant parts of which provide as follows:

> "1. If the Court declares the application admissible, it shall
>
> ...
>
> (b) place itself at the disposal of the parties concerned with a view to securing a friendly settlement of the matter on the basis of respect for human rights as defined in the Convention and the protocols thereto.
>
> 2. Proceedings conducted under paragraph 1 b. shall be confidential."

Furthermore, Article 39 provides that if a friendly settlement is effected, the Court shall strike the case out of its list by means of a decision which shall be confined to a brief statement of the facts and of the solution reached.

It must be stressed at this juncture that, although Article 38 speaks of the Court placing itself at the disposal of the parties to secure a friendly settlement only after the application is declared admissible, it does not prevent the parties from making proposals at earlier stages of the Court's proceedings.[503] Indeed, according to Article 37 § 1, the Court may at any stage of the proceedings strike an application out of its list of cases on the basis of a friendly settlement. Moreover, and as described above, when the joint procedure is applied, parties are asked to state their positions on the subject of friendly settlement at the communication stage of the proceedings. The parties will be informed that, regarding the requirement of strict confidentiality under Rule 62 § 2, any submissions made in this respect should be set out in a separate document, the contents of which must not be referred to in any submissions made in the context of the contentious proceedings. If the parties let it be known that they are interested in reaching a settlement, the Registry will be prepared to make a suggestion for an appropriate arrangement.

---

502 See also Rule 62 of the Rules of Court.
503 Obviously not before the application has been communicated to the respondent Contracting Party.

If a settlement is reached before the application has been declared admissible, the Court will strike the case out in a decision. Otherwise, it will do so in a judgment.

If the Court decides to examine the admissibility and merits of a case at the same time, in accordance with Article 29 § 3 of the Convention and Rule 54A, the Registrar of the relevant Chamber, at the time of communication the case[504] will ask the respondent Government to inform the Court in its observations on admissibility and merits of its position regarding friendly settlement of the case and any proposals it may wish to make. If the respondent Government has made no proposal for friendly settlement by the time it submits its observations, when forwarding the Government's observations to the applicant, the Registrar will ask the applicant to indicate his or her position regarding a friendly settlement of the case.

8.1.2 Friendly Settlement Declaration

The terms of a friendly settlement will be set out in a declaration which will be signed by the parties and submitted to the Court. The parties' declarations in the case of *Sakı v. Turkey* are reproduced in the *Textbox* below and may serve as an illustration of the form and contents of friendly settlement declarations in a case which concerns complaints under Article 3 of the Convention.

On receipt of the declarations, the Court will examine the terms with a view to establishing whether respect for human rights as defined in the Convention and the protocols is upheld in the declaration; pursuant to Article 37 § 1 (c), the Court may continue the examination of the application if, as mentioned above, respect for human rights so requires and in spite of the parties' intention to settle the case.

A friendly settlement declaration signed by a Government may include the Government's expression of regret for the actions which have led to the bringing of the application. For example, in the case of *Sakı v. Turkey*, the respondent Turkish Government submitted in its declaration that it

> "...regret[ted] the occurrence, as in the present case, of individual cases of ill-treatment by the authorities of persons detained in custody notwithstanding existing Turkish legislation and the resolve of the Government to prevent such occurrences."

---

504   If no decision has been taken by the Court to examine the case in a joint procedure, at the time of forwarding the admissibility decision.

Furthermore, the Turkish Government also accepted in the same declaration that:

> "recourse to ill-treatment of detainees constitutes a violation of Article 3 of the Convention"

and undertook:

> "to issue appropriate instructions and adopt all necessary measures to ensure that the prohibition of such forms of ill-treatment – including the obligation to carry out effective investigations – is respected in the future."[505]

Governments may be willing to settle cases for a number of reasons. For example, they may wish to settle a case in which complaints are based on national legislation which the Court has previously identified as incompatible with the Convention or which the respondent Contracting Party has itself acknowledged is incompatible with the Convention. For example, in the case of *Zarakolu v. Turkey*, the applicant, owner of a publishing company, was convicted under the Prevention of Terrorism Act for having disseminated propaganda in support of a terrorist organisation in a book published by her company. The application lodged by the applicant was struck out of the Court's list of cases as the parties subsequently reached a settlement on the basis of a declaration made by the Turkish Government which included, *inter alia*, the following acknowledgement:

> "The Government note that the Court's rulings against Turkey in cases involving prosecutions under the provisions of the Prevention of Terrorism Act relating to freedom of expression show that Turkish law and practice urgently need to be brought into line with the Convention's requirements under Article 10 of the Convention. This is also reflected in the interference underlying the facts of the present case. The Government undertake to this end to implement all necessary reform of domestic law and practice in this area, as already outlined in the National Programme of 24 March 2001".[506]

As pointed out above, friendly settlement declarations may include terms pursuant to which a respondent Government may undertake to take specific action to resolve the issue. For example, the case of *K.K.C. v. the Netherlands*, which concerned the intended expulsion of the applicant – a Russian national of Chechen origin – to Russia, where the applicant argued there was a real risk he would be subjected to treatment contrary to Article 3 of the Convention, was struck out on the basis of the settlement reached between the parties. Pursuant to the terms of the declaration, the respondent

---

505 *Sakı v. Turkey*, cited above, § 12.1
506 *Zarakolu v. Turkey*, no. 32455/96, 27 May 2003, § 19.

Government undertook to issue the applicant a residence permit without restrictions.[507]

Parties are expected to stipulate in their respective declarations that the settlement will constitute the final resolution of the case and that they will not request the referral of the case to the Grand Chamber under Article 43 § 1 of the Convention.[508]

Textbox xi   *Example of Friendly Settlement Declaration*

THE PARTIES' DECLARATIONS IN THE CASE OF *SAKI v. TURKEY* (No. 29359/95)

THE GOVERNMENT'S DECLARATION

I declare that the Government of the Republic of Turkey offer to pay *ex gratia* to Ms Özgül Saki the amount of 55,000 French francs with a view to securing a friendly settlement of the application registered under no. 29359/95. This sum, which also covers legal expenses connected with the case, shall be paid, free of any taxes that may be applicable, to a bank account named by the applicant. The sum shall be payable within three months from the date of delivery of the judgment by the Court pursuant to Article 39 of the European Convention on Human Rights. This payment will constitute the final resolution of the case.

The Government regret the occurrence, as in the present case, of individual cases of ill-treatment by the authorities of persons detained in custody notwithstanding existing Turkish legislation and the resolve of the Government to prevent such occurrences.

It is accepted that the recourse to ill-treatment of detainees constitutes a violation of Article 3 of the Convention and the Government undertake to issue appropriate instructions and adopt all necessary measures to ensure that the prohibition of such forms of ill-treatment – including the obligation to carry out effective investigations – is respected in the future. The Government refer in this connection to the commitments which they undertook in the Declaration agreed on in Application no. 34382/97 and reiterate their resolve to give effect to those commitments. They note that new legal and administrative measures have been adopted which have resulted in a reduction in the occurrence of ill-treatment in circumstances similar to those of the instant application as well as more effective investigations.

---

507   *K.K.C. v. the Netherlands*, no. 58964/00, 21 December 2001, § 26.
508   See Section 9.2 below.

The Government consider that the supervision by the Committee of Ministers of the execution of Court judgments concerning Turkey in this and similar cases is an appropriate mechanism for ensuring that improvements will continue to be made in this context. To this end, necessary co-operation in this process will continue to take place.

Finally, the Government undertake not to request the reference of the case to the Grand Chamber under Article 43 § 1 of the Convention after the delivery of the Court's judgment.

THE APPLICANT'S DECLARATION

I note that the Government of Turkey are prepared to pay *ex gratia* the sum of 55,000 French francs covering both pecuniary and non-pecuniary damage and costs to the applicant, Ms Özgül Saki, with a view to securing a friendly settlement of application no. 29359/95 pending before the Court. I have also taken note of the declaration made by the Government.

I accept the proposal and waive any further claims in respect of Turkey relating to the facts of this application. I declare that the case is definitely settled.

This declaration is made in the context of a friendly settlement which the Government and the applicant have reached.

I further undertake not to request the reference of the case to the Grand Chamber under Article 43 § 1 of the Convention after the delivery of the Court's judgment.

8.1.3 Enforcement of Undertakings Expressed in a Friendly Settlement Declaration

According to Article 46 § 1 of the Convention, Contracting Parties undertake to abide by the final judgment of the Court in any case to which they are parties. Furthermore, paragraph 2 of the same provision stipulates that final judgments of the Court shall be transmitted to the Committee of Ministers which will supervise their execution.[509] It follows, therefore, that the Committee of Ministers is responsible for the supervision of a judgment in which the case was struck out on the basis of a friendly settlement. In case of a failure by the respondent Government to uphold the terms of its friendly settlement declaration, applicants may seek assistance from the Committee of Ministers.

When a friendly settlement is concluded before the case is declared admissible, the case will be struck out in a decision rather than a judgment. In such cases problems may arise since Article 46 of the Convention speaks only of the Contracting Parties' obligation to abide by judgments, and does not mention decisions. However, this "loophole" will be eliminated following the entry into force of Protocol No. 14, which amends Article 39 such that the Court will be able to place itself at the disposal of the parties with a view to securing a friendly settlement at any stage of the proceedings. Furthermore, if a friendly settlement is concluded, the Court will strike the case out by means of a decision and not a judgment, regardless of whether that settlement was reached before or after the case was declared admissible. Such decisions will be transmitted to the Committee of Ministers, which will supervise the execution of the terms of the friendly settlement as set out in the decision.

8.2 Strike Out

Article 37 of the Convention provides as follows:

> "1. The Court may at any stage of the proceedings decide to strike an application out of its list of cases where the circumstances lead to the conclusion that
>
> a. the applicant does not intend to pursue his application; or
>
> b. the matter has been resolved; or
>
> c. for any other reason established by the Court, it is no longer justified to continue the examination of the application.

---

509   See Section 9.3 below.

However, the Court shall continue the examination of the application if respect for human rights as defined in the Convention and the protocols thereto so requires.

2. The Court may decide to restore an application to its list of cases if it considers that the circumstances justify such a course".

An application may be struck out of the Court's list of cases by a Committee[510] or by a Chamber.

8.2.1 Absence of Intention to Pursue the Application (Article 37 § 1 (a))

Article 37 § 1 of the Convention provides for an applicant's withdrawal of his or her case. However, in dealing with a request for withdrawal, the Court must first examine whether respect for human rights as defined in the Convention and the Protocols nevertheless requires that the Court continue the examination of the application. For example, the case of *Tyrer v. the United Kingdom* concerned the applicant's complaint regarding corporal punishment under Article 3 of the Convention. The applicant informed the Commission that he wished to withdraw his application. However, the Commission decided it could not accede to this request, "since the case raised questions of a general character affecting the observance of the Convention which necessitated a further examination of the issues involved".[511] The applicant took no further part in the proceedings but the Court examined the complaints *ex officio* and concluded that the applicant had been subjected to degrading treatment in violation of Article 3.[512]

The Court will also strike an application out if the applicant fails to respond to letters and/or fails to submit his or her observations and any other documents requested by the Court. The applicant's inactivity is interpreted as a lack of intention on his or her part to pursue the case. Before striking the case out in such a situation, the Court will give the applicant adequate opportunities to reply and will warn him or her in a letter – sent by registered post – of the possibility that the case might be struck out of the Court's list.[513]

The case of *Nehru v. the Netherlands* illustrates the fact that in situations where an applicant is unable to contact the Court over an extended period of time – in this case almost 3 years – the Court is likely to consider the application to have been abandoned. In *Nehru*, the applicant, a Sri Lankan national

---

510   Article 28 of the Convention.
511   *Tyrer v. the United Kingdom*, no. 5856/72, 25 April 1978, § 21.
512   *Ibid.*, § 35.
513   See, *inter alia, Starodub v. Ukraine* (dec.), no. 5483/02, 7 June 2005, in which the applicant failed to respond to the Court's letter for more than a year and a half.

whose request for an interim measure under Rule 39 of the Rules of Court to suspend his expulsion had been rejected by the Court on 10 November 1999, was deported to Canada by the Netherlands authorities on 18 November 1999. A day later, on 19 November 1999, the applicant was deported from Canada to Sri Lanka. Nothing further was heard from him either by his lawyer or by the Court. In its decision of 27 August 2002, the Court noted that it could neither find it established that the applicant no longer wished to pursue his application nor that the matter had been resolved. It went on to state the following:

> "Although the Court would not exclude that an expulsion carried out speedily might frustrate an applicant's attempts to obtain the protection to which he or she is entitled under the Convention, the Court notes that there is no indication that the applicant, during the period that has elapsed since his expulsion from the Netherlands, has sought in one way or another to contact his lawyer in the Netherlands in relation to his application. In these circumstances, the Court cannot but conclude that there is no indication whatsoever that the applicant intends to pursue his application. In reaching this conclusion, the Court has taken into account its competence under Article 37 § 2 of the Convention to restore the case to its list of cases if it considers that the circumstances justify such a course".[514]

8.2.2 Resolution of the Matter (Article 37 § 1 (b))

In its judgment in the case of *Ohlen v. Denmark*, the Court stated that:

> "[i]n order to conclude that the matter has been resolved within the meaning of Article 37 § 1 (b) or that for any other reason established by the Court, it is no longer justified to continue the examination of the application within the meaning of Article 37 § 1 (c), and that there is therefore no longer any objective justification for the applicant to pursue his application, the Court considers that it must examine whether the circumstances complained of directly by the applicant still obtain and, secondly, whether the effects of a possible violation of the Convention on account of those circumstances have also been redressed".[515]

Thus, in a case where the applicant complains of his or her impending expulsion to a country where he or she runs a real risk of being subjected to ill-treatment in violation of Article 3, the Court will conclude that the matter at issue has been resolved if the respondent Contracting Party subsequently issues the applicant a residence permit thereby eliminating the possibility of deportation. After all, in such a situation, where the applicant no longer faces expulsion, the risk of ill-treatment also no longer exists.[516]

---

514 *Nehru v. the Netherlands* (dec.), cited above.
515 See *Ohlen v. Denmark*, no. 63214/00, 24 February 2005, § 26.
516 See, for example, *Sokratian v. the Netherlands* (dec.), no. 41/03, 8 September 2005.

8.2.3 Strike Out "for any other reason" (Article 37 § 1 (c))

This provision gives the Court a large measure of discretion and may, for example, be used in a situation where the applicant wishes to pursue his or her application even though in the view of the Court this is no longer necessary. Thus, the Court struck out three cases introduced by Iranian nationals and their families in which they complained that their expulsion to Iran by the Turkish Government would expose them to treatment contrary to Articles 2, 3, and 8 of the Convention. However, after submitting their applications they moved to and settled in Finland, Norway, and Canada respectively. They nevertheless informed the Court that they wished to pursue their applications and maintained that, notwithstanding their resettlement in third countries, the Court should still examine their complaints on the merits. However, given that they no longer faced forced return to Iran, the Court found that the applicants could no longer claim to be victims within the meaning of Article 34 of the Convention and decided that it was no longer justified to continue the examination of the applications.[517]

The Court has also used its powers to strike an application out on the basis of so-called 'unilateral declarations' submitted by respondent Governments, usually following the applicants' rejection of a respondent Government's offer of friendly settlement. For example, in the case of *Akman v. Turkey*, which concerned the killing of the applicant's son allegedly by members of the security forces, the parties had been unable to reach a friendly settlement. Five days before the Court was to hold a fact-finding hearing in Turkey to establish the disputed facts of the case,[518] the respondent Government submitted to the Court a declaration on the basis of which it invited the Court to strike the application out of its list of cases. In the declaration, the Turkish Government expressed its regret for the deaths which resulted from excessive use of force, as was the case with the death of the applicant's son, and offered to pay the applicant 85,000 GBP. The applicant, for his part, asked the Court to reject the Government's initiative and stressed, *inter alia*, that the proposed declaration omitted any reference to the unlawful nature of the killing of his son. In upholding the respondent Government's request, the Court stated in its judgment that it had:

> "carefully examined the terms of the Government's declaration. Having regard to the nature of the admissions contained in the declaration as well as the scope and extent of the various undertakings referred to therein, together with the amount of compensation proposed, the Court considers

---

517   See, respectively, *M.T. v. Turkey* (dec.), no. 46765/99, 30 May 2002; *A.E. v. Turkey* (dec.), no. 45279/99, 30 May 2002; *A.Sh. v. Turkey* (dec.), no. 41396/98, 28 May 2002.

518   See Section 11.3 below for information on fact-finding missions.

that it is no longer justified to continue the examination of the application (Article 37 § 1 (c)) ... The Court notes in this regard that it has [previously] specified the nature and extent of the obligations which arise for the respondent State in cases of alleged unlawful killings by members of the security forces under Articles 2 and 13 of the Convention...".[519]

This same reasoning was subsequently applied by the Court in striking out the cases of, *inter alia*, *Haran v. Turkey*, *Toğcu v. Turkey*, and *T.A. v. Turkey*. These three cases concerned allegations that close relatives of the applicants' had been disappeared by security forces, and in each case the applicants asked the Court to reject the Government's unilateral declaration.[520] However, in *T.A. v. Turkey* the Grand Chamber subsequently decided that the application should not have been struck out because, in view of the gravity of the violation at issue, the Government's declaration offered an insufficient basis for holding that it was no longer justified to continue the examination of the application. In reaching that conclusion the Court considered the following:

> "The Court accepts that a full admission of liability in respect of an applicant's allegations under the Convention cannot be regarded as a condition *sine qua non* for the Court's being prepared to strike an application out on the basis of a unilateral declaration by a respondent Government. However in cases concerning persons who have disappeared or have been killed by unknown perpetrators and where there is prima facie evidence in the case-file supporting allegations that the domestic investigation fell short of what is necessary under the Convention, a unilateral declaration should at the very least contain an admission to that effect, combined with an undertaking by the respondent Government to conduct, under the supervision of the Committee of Ministers in the context of the latter's duties under Article 46 § 2 of the Convention, an investigation that is in full compliance with the requirements of the Convention as defined by the Court in previous similar cases... As the unilateral declaration made by the Government in the present case contains neither any such admission nor any such undertaking, respect for human rights requires that the examination of the case be pursued pursuant to the final sentence of Article 37 § 1 of the Convention...".[521]

---

519 *Akman v. Turkey*, no. 37453/97, 26 June 2001.

520 *Haran v. Turkey*, no. 25754/94, 26 March 2002; *Toğcu v. Turkey* (strike out), no. 27601/95, 9 April 2002; *T.A. v. Turkey*, no. 26308/95, 9 April 2002. The judgments in these cases have led to intense criticism of the Court; see Leach p. 79 *et seq.*

521 See *Tahsin Acar v. Turkey* (preliminary objection) [GC], no. 26308/95, 6 May 2003, §§ 84-85. The Grand Chamber subsequently examined the merits of the case and adopted its judgment on the merits on 8 April 2004. Also, on 1 March 2005 the Court decided, pursuant to Article 37 § 2 of the Convention, to restore the above mentioned *Toğcu v. Turkey* case to its list of cases and adopted its judgment on the merits of the case on 31 May 2005; see §§ 8-14 of the Court's judgment of 31 May 2005. A request made by the Turkish Government in another case which also concerned the disappearance of the applicant's son, to strike the case out on the basis of a unilateral declaration, was rejected by the Court in the light of the principles laid down in the Grand Chamber's judgment in the case of *Tahsin Acar v. Turkey*; see *Akdeniz v. Turkey*, no. 25165/94, 31 May 2005, § 8.

Cases raising less serious issues may nevertheless still be struck out on the basis of a unilateral declaration submitted by a respondent Government despite the applicant's opposition.[522]

8.3 Concluding Remarks

Given the very heavy workload of the Court, the friendly settlement procedure affords the Court an opportunity to clear up its docket in order to focus on cases which justify merits decisions. Nevertheless, as pointed out above, the Court has powers to review the undertakings in friendly settlement declarations and may refuse to strike a case out if it considers that respect for human rights as defined in the Convention and the Protocols requires an examination on the merits.

The importance and the time-saving potential of friendly settlements has been identified in a report drawn up by Lord Woolf, former Lord Chief Justice of England and Wales and member of the Group of Wise Persons established by the Council of Europe's Third Summit in Warsaw in May 2005. The purpose of the report was to draft a comprehensive strategy to secure the long-term effectiveness of the European Convention on Human Rights and its control mechanism. Lord Woolf's report recommends that the Court establish a specialist "Friendly Settlement Unit" in the Registry, to initiate and pursue proactively a greater number of friendly settlements.[523] The report invites the Court to consider whether it would be desirable or appropriate to strike out an application under Article 37 § 1 (c) on the grounds that the applicant has unreasonably refused to agree to what the Court considers to be a satisfactory friendly settlement offer. According to Lord Woolf, given the safeguards provided by Article 37, this would be an appropriate use of the Court's powers to strike out applications and would give greater weight to friendly settlement negotiations, and would ensure that friendly settlement offers were only rejected for good reason.

In cases concerning allegations of ill-treatment within the meaning of Article 3 of the Convention, applicants may negotiate with respondent Governments to obtain specific undertakings, such as an undertaking to carry out an effective investigation into his or her allegations of ill-treatment. If the respondent Government refuses to carry out such an investigation as part of the friendly

---

522   See *Van Houten v. the Netherlands*, no. 25149/03, 29 September 2005.
523   The report may be accessed at www.echr.coe.int

settlement agreement, the applicant may argue that striking the case out solely on the basis of monetary payment represents insufficient redress and request that the Court continue to examine the merits of the case.[524] In this context it must be reiterated that civil or administrative proceedings which are aimed solely at awarding damages rather than identifying and punishing those responsible are not regarded as effective remedies in the context of Article 3 complaints.[525]

---

524 The same argument would also be relevant if the Court decides to strike the case out on the basis of a unilateral declaration submitted by the respondent Government and despite the applicant's rejection of the settlement offer.

525 See *Tepe v. Turkey* (dec.), cited above in Section 2.4.2 (d) (i).

THE JUDGMENT AND THE SUBSEQUENT PROCEDURE

9.1 Finding of a Violation

9.2 Referral to the Grand Chamber

9.3 Execution of Judgments

9.1 Finding of a Violation

As explained earlier,[526] if the Chamber deems the application admissible, under the joint procedure it will immediately move on to the judgment stage. It will receive a draft judgment prepared under the instructions of the judge rapporteur, declaring the application admissible and concluding whether there has been a violation of any of the Articles of the Convention invoked by the applicant. A typical judgment concerning an Article 3 complaint will consist of the following components:

Name of the case and of the Section, application number, names of judges of the Chamber and name of the Section Registrar, date(s) of deliberations;

PROCEDURE: A summary of the proceedings, containing the name of the applicant and that of the respondent Contracting Party;

THE FACTS, consisting of

I. THE CIRCUMSTANCES OF THE CASE: other details of the applicant, together with the facts as submitted by the parties. If the facts are disputed between the parties they will be set out separately. Documents submitted by the parties, in so far as they are relevant, may also be summarised under this heading; and

II. RELEVANT DOMESTIC LAW AND PRACTICE;

THE LAW, consisting of

I. The applicant's complaints; the parties' arguments; any objections by the Government to the admissibility of the case; the Court's conclusion on the admissibility; establishment of facts and the Court's conclusion on the merits; and

II. APPLICATION OF ARTICLE 41 OF THE CONVENTION: The applicant's claims for pecuniary and non-pecuniary damage and for costs and expenses; the Government's response to the applicant's claims and the Court's conclusion on just satisfaction;

OPERATIVE PART: A recapitulation of the conclusions reached and any violations found; and, finally,

SEPARATE OPINIONS[527]

---

526   See Section 1.7.3 above.
527   See also Rules 74-75 of the Rules of Court.

With the exception of "establishment of facts", these components have already been dealt with in the preceding sections of this *handbook*.[528] The Court's judgments will be given in one of the official languages of the Court, i.e. English and French. In some cases, the judgment may be translated into the other official language.[529] In exceptional cases, the judgment may be pronounced, i.e. read aloud, at a public hearing. The judgment will be transmitted to the Committee of Ministers for its execution. Certified copies of the judgment will be transmitted to the parties, the Secretary General of the Council of Europe, to any third party, and to any other person directly concerned.[530]

Rule 79 of the Rules of Court provides that parties may request the interpretation of a judgment within one year of the delivery of that judgment. Furthermore, Rule 80 of the Rules of Court provides for situations in which a new fact is discovered; if the fact by its nature might have a decisive influence on the Court's deliberations, if it was unknown to the Court at the time of delivery of its judgment, and if it could not reasonably have been known to the party, that party may ask the Court to revise the judgment. Requests of this nature must be made within a period of six months after that party learned of the fact. They are, however, quite rare.

Finally, the Court may, of its own motion or at the request of a party made within one month of the delivery of a decision or a judgment, rectify clerical errors, errors in calculation, or obvious mistakes.[531]

9.2 Referral to the Grand Chamber

Pursuant to Article 43 of the Convention, any party to the case may, in exceptional cases and within a period of three months from the date of the judgment of the Chamber, request that the case be referred to the Grand Chamber. It must be pointed out that the judgments adopted by the Grand Chamber are final and cannot be referred back to the Grand Chamber.

A request for referral to the Grand Chamber will be examined by a panel of five judges of the Grand Chamber, who will only accept the request in the following circumstances:

---

528 The issue of establishment of facts will be dealt with in Section 11 below.
529 Rule 76 of the Rules of Court.
530 Rule 77 § 3 of the Rules of Court.
531 Rule 81 of the Rules of Court.

"if the case raises a serious issue affecting the interpretation or application of the Convention or the protocols thereto, or a serious issue of general importance".[532]

The panel of the Grand Chamber will be composed of the President of the Court, two Presidents of Sections designated by rotation (to be replaced by the Vice-Presidents of their Section if they are prevented from sitting), two judges, and two substitute judges. The substitute judges are designated by rotation from among the judges elected by the remaining Sections to sit on the panel for a period of six months (Rule 24 § 5 (a) of the Rules of Court). The panel shall include neither any judge who took part in the consideration of the admissibility or merits of the case in question nor the judge elected in respect of, or who is a national of, a Contracting Party concerned by a referral request (Rule 24 § 5 (b-c)). Any member of the panel unable to sit for these reasons shall be replaced by one of the substitute judges (Rule 24 § 5 (d)).

Decisions of the Panel are final. Since the Panel does not provide reasons for referral decisions, it is difficult to determine exactly what considerations are decisive in any particular case. In any event, it appears from Article 43 that the referral procedure should not be regarded as an appeal on points of fact. It is not surprising, therefore, that the nature and the number of the cases referred to the Grand Chamber illustrate that the Panel will only accept requests for referral in exceptional cases. Indeed, in 2005 the Panel examined a total of 183 requests for referrals and accepted only 20.[533]

If the request is accepted by the Panel, the case referred to the Grand Chamber will embrace in principle all aspects of the application previously examined by the Chamber in its judgment. The scope of its jurisdiction is limited only by the Chamber's decision on admissibility. This means that the Grand Chamber is precluded from examining complaints which have been declared inadmissible by the Chamber. However, as regards the complaints declared admissible by the Chamber, the Grand Chamber may also examine, where appropriate, issues relating to their admissibility in the same manner as this is possible in normal Chamber proceedings: for example by virtue of Article 35 § 4 *in fine* of the Convention (which empowers the Court to "reject any application which it considers inadmissible ... at any stage of the proceedings"), or where such issues have been joined to the merits or where they are otherwise relevant at the merits stage.[534] The Grand Chamber will generally hold a hearing in Strasbourg before adopting its judgment.

---

532 Article 43 § 2 of the Convention.
533 Fifty-six of the 121 requests were made by Governments and five by both parties. See for further information the Annual Activity Report 2005 of the Grand Chamber at http://www.echr.coe.int/NR/rdonlyres/AF356FA8-1861-4A6B-95E9-28ED53787710/0/2005GrandChamberactivityreport.pdf.
534 *K. and T. v. Finland* [GC], no. 25702/94, 12 July 2001, §§ 140-141.

9.3 Execution of Judgments

It was mentioned earlier that the Committee of Ministers, which consists of the Ministers of Foreign Affairs of the Member States of the Council of Europe, is the decision-making body of the Council of Europe. Amongst its functions is the supervision of the execution of judgments of the European Court of Human Rights. Under Article 44, a judgment becomes final at the time of its delivery by the Grand Chamber. A judgment delivered by a Chamber, on the other hand, becomes final if no request for referral to the Grand Chamber is made within three months of delivery or, when such a request has been made, when it is rejected by the Panel of the Grand Chamber.

Under Article 46 § 1, Contracting Parties undertake to abide by the final judgment of the Court in any case in which they are parties. The final judgment will be transmitted to the Committee of Ministers for supervision of its execution. The respondent Government will be expected to pay the applicant any sums awarded for just satisfaction in the judgment within three months of the date the judgment becomes final according to Article 44 § 2 of the Convention.

Judgments referred to the Committee of Ministers are placed on the agenda of Committee meetings without requiring any action on the part of the applicant. However, it is up to the applicant to ensure that the respondent Government is in possession of the necessary bank account details to allow for the payment of just satisfaction awarded by the Court.[535] An applicant will facilitate the Committee's work by informing it of any specific difficulties encountered, e.g. just satisfaction paid after the due date, interest for overdue payments not paid, refusal to reopen proceedings, etc.

"The Committee of Ministers is a political organ and as such it can bring its weight to bear on the State concerned in order to persuade it to execute the Court's judgment, including through the use of serious political sanctions provided for in the Statute of the Council of Europe".[536] It will ensure that respondent Contracting Parties pay applicants any awards made by the Court and take any individual measures indicated in the Court's judgment. It will

---

535 As pointed out in Section 7 above, applicants should include their bank account details in their claims for just satisfaction when sending those claims to the Court.

536 The ultimate sanction is the expulsion of a Member State from the Council of Europe if that Member State is deemed to have seriously violated Article 3 of the Statute of the Council of Europe, which provides as follows: "Every member of the Council of Europe must accept the principles of the rule of law and of the enjoyment by all persons within its jurisdiction of human rights and fundamental freedoms, and collaborate sincerely and effectively in the realisation of the aim of the Council as specified in Chapter I". See also Article 8 of the same Statute.

also oversee the implementation of more general measures by Contracting Parties so that similar violations are prevented in the future.[537] For example, this may occur where the violation is due to a clear incompatibility between domestic legislation and the Convention, or if it is the result of a structural problem of judicial practice at national level. After establishing that the Contracting Party concerned has taken all the necessary measures to abide by the judgment, the Committee of Ministers adopts a resolution concluding that its functions under Article 46 § 2 of the Convention have been completed.[538] Resolutions adopted by the Committee of Ministers may be searched through the above mentioned HUDOC search engine of the Court.[539]

Protocol No. 14 will enhance the powers of the Committee of Ministers in the area of execution of judgments by adding the following three new sub-paragraphs to Article 46 of the Convention, the second of which is probably the most far-reaching:[540]

> "If the Committee of Ministers considers that the supervision of the execution of a final judgment is hindered by a problem of interpretation of the judgment, it may refer the matter to the Court for a ruling on the question of interpretation. A referral decision shall require a majority vote of two thirds of the representatives entitled to sit on the Committee.
>
> If the Committee of Ministers considers that a High Contracting Party refuses to abide by a final judgment in a case to which it is a party, it may, after serving formal notice on that Party and by decision adopted by a majority vote of two thirds of the representatives entitled to sit on the Committee, refer to the Court the question whether that Party has failed to fulfil its obligation under paragraph 1.
>
> If the Court finds a violation of paragraph 1, it shall refer the case to the Committee of Ministers for consideration of the measures to be taken. If the Court finds no violation of paragraph 1, it shall refer the case to the Committee of Ministers, which shall close its examination of the case".

---

537 In this connection, it must be noted that according to Article 9 § 2 of the Rules of the Committee of Ministers for the supervision of the execution of judgments and of the terms of friendly settlements which were adopted on 10 May 2006, "The Committee of Ministers shall be entitled to consider any communication from non-governmental organisations, as well as national institutions for the promotion and protection of human rights, with regard to the execution of judgments under Article 46, paragraph 2, of the Convention".

538 See the Committee of Ministers' webpage devoted to "Execution of Judgments of the European Court of Human Rights" for further information: http://www.coe.int/T/E/Human_Rights/execution/.

539 Which may be accessed at http://cmiskp.echr.coe.int/tkp197/search.asp?skin=hudoc-en

540 See Article 16 of Protocol No. 14. See also the paragraphs 16 and 95-100 of the Explanatory Report to that Protocol in Appendix No.18.

PART IV

THE ABSOLUTE NATURE
OF THE PROHIBITION AND THE INHERENT
OBLIGATIONS OF ARTICLE 3

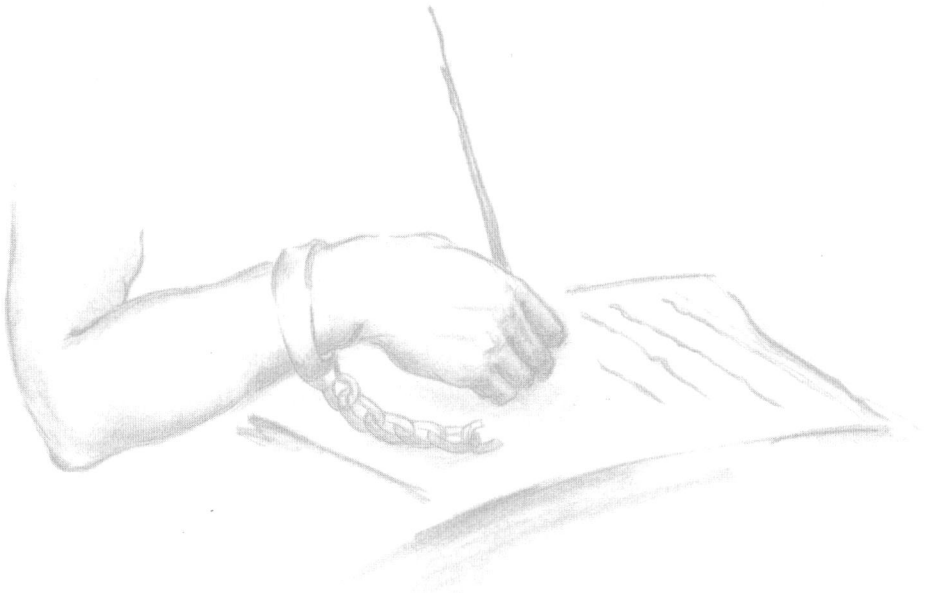

THE ABSOLUTE NATURE OF THE PROHIBITION AND THE INHERENT OBLIGATIONS OF ARTICLE 3

10.1 Summary

10.2 Discussion

10.2.1 The Negative Obligation

10.2.2 The Positive Obligation

a) The Obligation to Investigate Allegations of Ill-treatment

i. Concluding Remarks

b) The Obligation to Protect Against Ill-treatment by Private Individuals

i. Concluding Remarks

10.1 Summary

Article 3 of the Convention simply states that

"[n]o one shall be subjected to torture or to inhuman or degrading treatment or punishment".

At first sight, Article 3 appears to impose only a negative obligation on Contracting Parties, i.e. an obligation only to refrain from inflicting ill-treatment on individuals within their jurisdiction. However, such a restrictive approach to Article 3 would not provide individuals with adequate protection against ill-treatment for two primary reasons. Firstly, if the right guaranteed by Article 3 did not also impose an obligation on the Contracting Party to conduct effective investigations into allegations of ill-treatment which are capable of leading to the prosecution and punishment of the perpetrators, the obligations of Article 3 would in practice not deter agents of the State from abusing the rights of those within their control. Secondly, if the obligation of Article 3 were only negative, it would in theory allow a Contracting Party to sit by as a passive spectator to ill-treatment by *private actors* without engaging its responsibilities under the Convention.

According to the Court's case-law, it is now well established that in addition to the negative obligation, Article 3 also imposes two separate positive obligations (sometimes referred to as procedural obligations). Thus, under Article 3, Contracting Parties have a positive obligation to conduct effective investigations into allegations of ill-treatment (regardless of whether the perpetrator is alleged to be an official of the State or a private party) capable of leading to the identification and punishment of those responsible for the ill-treatment.[541] There arises a separate positive obligation to take effective measures to ensure that individuals within their jurisdiction are not subjected to ill-treatment by officials or by private parties.[542] This second positive obligation requires that effective criminal law provisions be in force in order to afford maximum protection from ill-treatment. It also requires that the relevant officials of the Contracting Parties take pre-emptive steps to protect vulnerable individuals from ill-treatment.[543] Indeed, similar positive obligations are inherent in various Articles of the Convention to ensure that the rights guaranteed under the Convention are not theoretical or illusory but practical and effective.[544]

---

541   See *Assenov v. Bulgaria*, cited above, § 102.
542   See *A. v. the United Kingdom*, no. 25599/94, 23 September 1998, § 22.
543   See *Z. v. the United* Kingdom, no. 29392/95, 10 May 2001, §§ 73-74.
544   See *İlhan v. Turkey*, cited above, § 91.

10.2 Discussion

Article 3, together with Article 2 (right to life), is regarded by the Court as:

> "one of the most fundamental provisions of the Convention and as enshrining core values of the democratic societies making up the Council of Europe. In contrast to the other provisions in the Convention, it is cast in absolute terms, without exception or proviso, or the possibility of derogation under Article 15 of the Convention".[545]

Article 3 of the Convention prohibits torture and inhuman or degrading treatment or punishment in absolute terms and irrespective of the circumstances or the victim's conduct.[546] The Court has recognised this to be the case even when Contracting Parties are confronted with difficult challenges such as the fight against terrorism and organised crime.[547] Indeed, the Court has recognized that the prohibition of torture constitutes a *jus cogens* norm, that is, a peremptory norm of international law. In *Al-Adsani v. UK*, the Court stated the following:

> "Other areas of public international law bear witness to a growing recognition of the overriding importance of the prohibition of torture. Thus, torture is forbidden by Article 5 of the Universal Declaration of Human Rights and Article 7 of the International Covenant on Civil and Political Rights. The United Nations Convention against Torture and Other Cruel, Inhuman and Degrading Treatment or Punishment requires, by Article 2, that each State Party should take effective legislative, administrative, judicial or other measures to prevent torture in any territory under its jurisdiction, and, by Article 4, that all acts of torture should be made offences under the State Party's criminal law (see paragraphs 25-29 above). In addition, there have been a number of judicial statements to the effect that the prohibition of torture has attained the status of a peremptory norm or jus cogens [reference is made to Furundzija and Pinochet (No. 3)] ...
>
> ... the Court accepts, on the basis of these authorities, that the prohibition of torture has achieved the status of a peremptory norm in international law ...".[548]

Because of the absolute nature of the prohibition, the Court's vigilance is heightened when dealing with Article 3 complaints. Unlike some of the qualified Articles of the Convention, such as Articles 8-11, Article 3 makes no provision for exceptions. It follows, therefore, that although the Court may allow a Contracting Party's national authorities a certain margin of

---

545   See, *inter alia, Pretty v. the United Kingdom*, cited above, § 49.
546   See, *inter alia, Lorsé v. the Netherlands*, cited above, § 58.
547   See, *inter alia, Elçi and Others v. Turkey*, nos. 23145/93 and 25091/94, 13 November 2003, § 632; *Chahal v. the United Kingdom*, cited above, § 79.
548   *Al-Adsani v. the United Kingdom*, no. 35763/97, 21 November 2001.

appreciation when dealing with issues concerning the rights guaranteed in Articles 8-11 (in particular when striking a fair balance between the competing interests of the individual and of the community as a whole), it will not accord Contracting Parties the same latitude in their examination of allegations of ill-treatment. For example, any attempt by the national authorities to balance the dangers of terrorism or organised crime against an individual's rights under Article 3 will fall foul of the standard of the protection guaranteed in that Article.[549]

The absolute nature of the prohibition of torture and other forms of ill-treatment is examined in detail in the *amicus* briefs submitted by third party interveners in the case of *Ramzy v. The Netherlands*, at Appendix No. 9, and in the *Written Submission to the UK House of Lords by Third Party Interveners in the case of A and Others v. Secretary of State for the Home Department and A and Others (FC) and another v. Secretary of State for the Home Department*, at Appendix No. 16.

10.2.1 The Negative Obligation

Despite the absolute nature of the prohibition of ill-treatment, there are situations which permit Contracting Parties to use force against individuals in the exercise of legitimate State functions, as in the context of making arrests. In these situations however, the Court has clarified that:

> "in respect of a person deprived of liberty, any recourse to physical force which has not been made strictly necessary by his own conduct, diminishes human dignity and is in principle an infringement of the right set forth in Article 3"[550]

The phrase "strictly necessary by the victim's own conduct" must be construed in a restrictive manner. For example, law enforcement officers sometimes must use force when effecting an arrest if the arrestee resists the arrest by violent or forceful means. In such a situation, an injury caused to the arrested person may fall outside the protection afforded by Article 3 provided that the use of force by the authorities was strictly necessary under the circumstances. In *Klaas v. Germany*, for instance, force used by police officers in the course of the arrest of the applicant who tried to run away resulted in a

---

549 The absolute nature of the prohibition has also been emphasised by the European Committee for the Prevention of Torture (CPT): "Like the prohibition of slavery, the prohibition of torture and inhuman or degrading treatment is one of those few human rights which admit of no derogations. Talk of 'striking the right balance' is misguided when such human rights are at stake. Of course, resolute action is required to counter terrorism; but that action cannot be allowed to degenerate into exposing people to torture or inhuman or degrading treatment. Democratic societies must remain true to the values that distinguish them from others".

550 *Ribitsch v. Austria*, no. 18896/91, 4 December 1995, § 38.

number of injuries. The Court found, as the domestic German courts had, that the injuries were caused during the applicant's struggle and that the force used by the police officers was not excessive.[551]

Perhaps one of the most extreme examples of the legitimate use of force is found in the case of *Douglas-Williams v. the United Kingdom*. In this case, the applicant's brother threatened the arresting police officers with a knife. The officers then hit him with their truncheons and pinned him face down on the ground, restrained his hands behind his back, handcuffed him, and transferred him in this position to the police station in a police car. He died of positional asphyxia within one hour and ten minutes of his arrest. The Court did not find a violation in this case because it concluded that the use of restraint techniques was justified by the applicant's own violence.[552] By contrast, in the case of *Rehbock v. Slovenia*, where the use of force against an unarmed person who did not resist caused a double fracture of the jaw, the Court found that such use of force was excessive and therefore amounted to inhuman treatment within the meaning of Article 3.[553]

As the Court held in its judgment in *Pretty v. the United Kingdom*, mentioned above,

> "[a]n examination of the Court's case-law indicates that Article 3 has been most commonly applied in contexts in which the risk to the individual of being subjected to any of the proscribed forms of treatment emanated from intentionally inflicted acts of State agents or public authorities... It may be described in general terms as imposing a primarily negative obligation on States to refrain from inflicting serious harm on persons within their jurisdiction".[554]

If the Court finds that a Contracting Party has failed in its negative obligation, it will find a violation of Article 3 in its substantive aspect.[555]

Cases in which the Court has found a substantive violation of Article 3 may be categorized under three headings: 1) ill-treatment intentionally inflicted by law enforcement officers, such as police and other security forces; 2) ill-treatment resulting from a lawful or unlawful act carried out by State agents; and finally, 3) ill-treatment emanating from State agents' omissions.[556]

---

551 *Klaas v. Germany*, no. 15473/89, 22 September 1993, §§ 30-31.
552 *Douglas-Williams v. the United Kingdom* (dec.), no. 56413/00, 8 January 2002.
553 *Rehbock v. Slovenia*, no. 29462/95, 20 May 1998, §§ 68-78.
554 *Pretty v. the United Kingdom*, cited above, § 50.
555 See, for example, *Elçi and Others v. Turkey*, nos. 23145/93 and 25091/94, 13 November 2003, § 2 of the operative part of the judgment.
556 556 See also Appendix No. 10 for the section in which the Court's judgments in Article 3 cases are examined in different contexts.

Notable examples of the first category include, *inter alia*, ill-treatment by police officers at the time of arrest and immediately afterwards;[557] ill-treatment during interrogation in police custody;[558] physical and mental violence in police custody;[559] rape in a gendarmerie station;[560] the force-feeding of an applicant on hunger strike;[561] and interrogation techniques employed by law enforcement officers.[562]

The second group of cases concerns actions of State agents which constitute ill-treatment indirectly. It must be noted that such actions need not be carried out with an intention to subject a person to ill-treatment; in fact, in most cases they are not. This group of cases can be divided into two sub-groups: ill-treatment stemming from lawful actions of State agents and ill-treatment stemming from unlawful actions of State agents. Cases in which lawful actions of State agents have led to violations of Article 3 include expulsions or extraditions of applicants to countries where they would be subjected to ill-treatment;[563] prison conditions[564] and corporal punishment.[565] Unlawful actions that subject applicants to indirect ill-treatment have included the intentional destruction of applicants' homes and possessions by soldiers in the course of military operations in southeast Turkey,[566] and the disappearances of the applicants' close relatives after having been taken into unacknowledged detention.[567]

The third group of cases concerns situations where national authorities have failed to assist persons in need of medical assistance. It appears from the Court's case-law that Contracting Parties owe a duty to provide medical care

---

557 *Egmez v. Cyprus*, cited above, §§ 74-79.

558 *Salman v. Turkey* cited above, §§ 103 and 115.

559 *Selmouni v. France*, cited above, § 105.

560 *Aydın v. Turkey*, cited above, §§ 86-87

561 *Nevmerzhitsky v. Ukraine*, cited above, §§ 98-99.

562 *Ireland v. the United Kingdom*, cited above, § 96. The five interrogation techniques which the Court found to be degrading and inhuman included wall-standing, hooding, subjection to noise, sleep deprivation, and deprivation of food and drink.

563 See *Soering v. the United Kingdom*, cited above, which concerned the applicant's intended extradition to the United States where there was the possibility that he would be placed on death row; see also *Said v. the Netherlands*, cited above, § 55, in which the Netherlands authorities intended to expel the applicant to Eritrea.

564 See Section 2.6.3 (b) above.

565 *Tyrer v. the United Kingdom*, cited above, § 35.

566 See, *inter alia, Ayder and Others v. Turkey*, cited above, § 110, in which the Court found that "the destruction of the applicants' homes and possessions, as well as the anguish and distress suffered by members of their family, must have caused them suffering of sufficient severity for the acts of the security forces to be categorised as inhuman treatment within the meaning of Article 3".

567 See, *Kurt v. Turkey*, no. 24276/94, 25 May 1998, § 134; see also, more recently, *Akdeniz v. Turkey*, cited above, § 124, in which the Court found that "the applicant suffered, and continues to suffer, distress and anguish as a result of the disappearance of her son and of her inability to find out what has happened to him. The manner in which her complaints have been dealt with by the authorities must be considered to constitute inhuman treatment contrary to Article 3".

to detainees and also to persons whose health problems are caused by Government actions. In its judgment in *McGlinchey and Others v. the United Kingdom*, the Court found a violation of Article 3 on account of the prison authorities' failure to provide adequate medical assistance to a detainee suffering from heroin withdrawal as well as asthma.[568] Similarly, in the case of *Keenan v. the United Kingdom* concerning the suicide in prison of the applicant's son who was an identifiable suicide risk, the Court, in finding a violation, stated:

> "[t]he lack of effective monitoring of Mark Keenan's condition and the lack of informed psychiatric input into his assessment and treatment disclose significant defects in the medical care provided to a mentally ill person known to be a suicide risk"[569]

In its judgment in the case of *İlhan v. Turkey*, the Court's finding of a violation of Article 3 was influenced by the authorities' failure to provide the applicant's brother, who had been badly beaten up by soldiers and who suffered brain damage and long-term impairment of function as a result of the beating, with medical care until 36 hours after the incident.[570]

Finally, it must be noted that the scope of the duty of care owed by Contracting Parties under the substantive aspect of Article 3 was extended in the case of *Moldovan and Others v. Romania*. In this case, the Court found that police officers had been involved in the destruction of houses and belongings of the applicants, who were Romanian citizens of Roma origin. The destruction took place before Romania ratified the Convention, and for that reason the Court could not examine it. However, the Court pointed out that:

> "following this incident, having been hounded from their village and homes, the applicants had to live, and some of them still live, in crowded and improper conditions – cellars, hen-houses, stables, etc. – and frequently changed address, moving in with friends or family in extremely over-crowded conditions".[571]

Noting "the direct repercussions of the acts of State agents on the applicants' rights", the Court found that the Government had a responsibility as regards the applicants' subsequent living conditions. The Court concluded that the destitute conditions in which the applicants had to live following the destruction of their houses and belongings, coupled with "the racial discrimination to which they have been publicly subjected by the way in which their grievances were dealt with by the various authorities" constituted interference with

---

568 *McGlinchey and Others v. the United Kingdom*, cited above.
569 *Keenan v. the United Kingdom*, no. 27229/95, 3 April 2001, § 116.
570 *İlhan v. Turkey* [GC], cited above, §§ 86-88.
571 *Moldovan and Others v. Romania*, cited above, § 103.

their human dignity which, in the special circumstances of the case, amounted to "degrading treatment" within the meaning of Article 3.[572]

10.2.2 The Positive Obligation

According to the Court's established case-law, Contracting Parties have, in addition to the negative obligation examined above, a positive obligation under Article 3 to carry out effective investigations into allegations of ill-treatment and to take measures designed to ensure that individuals within their jurisdictions are not subjected to ill-treatment, including ill-treatment administered by private individuals. As explained below, the Court examines the obligation to carry out an effective investigation either from the standpoint of the positive obligation inherent in Article 3 or from the standpoint of the right to an effective remedy under Article 13. In some cases it has even examined the obligation under both Articles 3 and 13.[573] Before the Court resolves this somewhat inconsistent practice, applicants are strongly advised to invoke both Articles in their applications to the Court.

The issue of positive obligation is examined below under two sub-headings: a) The Obligation to Investigate and b) The Obligation to Protect Against Ill-Treatment by Private Individuals.

a) The Obligation to Investigate Allegations of Ill-treatment

In its judgment in the case of *McCann and Others v. the United Kingdom* concerning the killing of the applicants' relatives by members of the British special forces in Gibraltar, the Court held:

> "[A] general legal prohibition of arbitrary killing by the agents of the State would be ineffective, in practice, if there existed no procedure for reviewing the lawfulness of the use of lethal force by State authorities. The obligation to protect the right to life under [Article 2 of the Convention], read in conjunction with the State's general duty under Article 1 of the Convention to 'secure to everyone within their jurisdiction the rights and freedoms defined in [the] Convention', requires by implication that there should be some form of effective official investigation when individuals have been killed as a result of the use of force by, *inter alios*, agents of the State".[574]

---

572   *Ibid.*, § 113.
573   See, *inter alia, Menesheva v. Russia*, no. 59261/00, 9 March 2006, §§ 61-74.
574   *McCann and Others v. the United Kingdom*, no. 18984/91, 27 September 1995, § 161.

This approach was adopted by the Court in its judgment in the case of *Assenov v. Bulgaria* and was applied, *mutatis mutandis*, to investigations into allegations of ill-treatment. In *Assenov*, the Court stated the following:

> "...where an individual raises an arguable claim that he has been seriously ill-treated by the police or other such agents of the State unlawfully and in breach of Article 3, that provision, read in conjunction with the State's general duty under Article 1 of the Convention to 'secure to everyone within their jurisdiction the rights and freedoms defined in [the] Convention', requires by implication that there should be an effective official investigation. This investigation, as with that under Article 2, should be capable of leading to the identification and punishment of those responsible... If this were not the case, the general legal prohibition of torture and inhuman and degrading treatment and punishment, despite its fundamental importance... would be ineffective in practice and it would be possible in some cases for agents of the State to abuse the rights of those within their control with virtual impunity".[575]

The obligation to carry out an effective investigation into allegations of ill-treatment was later "described as a 'procedural obligation' which devolves on Contracting Parties under Article 3".[576] Violations of Article 3 of the Convention based on failures to comply with the positive obligation are referred to as "procedural violations" of Article 3.[577]

It must be noted that the Contracting Parties' obligation to carry out effective investigations into allegations of ill-treatment existed prior to the adoption of the judgment in the case of *Assenov* and was examined from the standpoint of the obligation to provide adequate remedies under Article 13 of the Convention. The Court stated in its judgment in the case of *Aksoy v. Turkey* that:

> "[t]he nature of the right safeguarded under Article 3 of the Convention has implications for Article 13. Given the fundamental importance of the prohibition of torture and the especially vulnerable position of torture victims, Article 13 imposes, without prejudice to any other remedy available under the domestic system, an obligation on States to carry out a thorough and effective investigation of incidents of torture. Accordingly, as regards Article 13, where an individual has an arguable claim that he has been tortured by agents of the State, the notion of an 'effective remedy' entails, in addition to the payment of compensation where appropriate, a thorough and effective investigation capable of leading to the identification and punishment of those responsible and including effective access for the complainant to the investigatory procedure".[578]

---

575   *Assenov v. Bulgaria*, cited above, § 102.
576   *Sevtap Veznedaroğlu v. Turkey*, no. 32357/96, 11 April 2000, § 35. See also Jacobs & White, pp. 66-68 for a review of the evaluation of the positive obligation.
577   See, *inter alia*, *Elçi and Others v. Turkey*, cited above, § 2 of the operative part of the judgment.
578   *Aksoy v. Turkey*, cited above, § 98.

In its judgment in the case of *İlhan v. Turkey* the Court preferred to examine the applicant's allegations concerning the effectiveness of the investigation into his allegations of ill-treatment under Article 13 because it found, *inter alia*, that:

> "[p]rocedural obligations have been implied in varying contexts under the Convention, where this has been perceived as necessary to ensure that the rights guaranteed under the Convention are not theoretical or illusory but practical and effective. The obligation to provide an effective investigation into the death caused by, *inter alios*, the security forces of the State was for this reason implied under Article 2 which guarantees the right to life (see the McCann and Others judgment cited above, pp. 47-49, §§ 157-64). This provision does, however, include the requirement that the right to life be "protected by law". It may also concern situations where the initiative must rest on the State for the practical reason that the victim is deceased and the circumstances of the death may be largely confined within the knowledge of State officials... Article 3, however, is phrased in substantive terms. Furthermore, although the victim of an alleged breach of this provision may be in a vulnerable position, the practical exigencies of the situation will often differ from cases of use of lethal force or suspicious deaths. The Court considers that the requirement under Article 13 of the Convention that a person with an arguable claim of a violation of Article 3 be provided with an effective remedy will generally provide both redress to the applicant and the necessary procedural safeguards against abuses by State officials...".[579]

However, since the adoption of the judgment in *İlhan*, the Court has continued to examine the obligation to carry out investigations both from the standpoint of Article 13 and from the standpoint of Article 3.[580] Recent judgments adopted by the Court highlight the Court's somewhat inconsistent practice in this area. For example, in *Bekos and Koutropoulos v. Greece* the Court, having found a procedural violation of Article 3 on account of the lack of an effective investigation, did not deem it necessary to examine separately the same allegation under Article 13.[581] On the other hand, in *Murat Demir v. Turkey*, the Court considered it more appropriate to examine the allegation of the lack of an effective investigation solely from the standpoint of Article 13.[582] Finally, in a number of cases, including the recent case of *Corsacov v. Moldova*, the Court examined the allegations of a lack of an effective investigation under both Articles 3 and 13 and found a violation of both Articles.[583]

---

579 *İlhan v. Turkey* [GC], cited above, §§ 91-92.
580 See, *inter alia*, *Poltoratskiy v. Ukraine*, no. 38812/97, 29 April 2003, §§ 127-128 and *Elçi and Others v. Turkey*, cited above, § 649; see also the separate opinions of judge Sir Nicolas Bratza in both judgments.
581 *Bekos and Koutropoulos v. Greece*, no. 15250/02, 13 December 2005, §§ 53-57.
582 *Murat Demir v. Turkey*, no. 879/02, 2 March 2006, §§ 43-45.
583 See *Corsacov v. Moldova*, no. 18944/02, 4 April 2006, §§ 68-82.

Applicants should note that it is not necessary for the Court to find a substantive violation of Article 3 before it can examine whether the respondent Contracting Party has complied with its procedural obligations under the article. In fact, sometimes the Court is unable to find a substantive violation *precisely because* the respondent Government has violated its procedural obligations by not conducting an effective investigation. In particular, where the authorities fail to take basic investigative steps (for example by performing medical examinations, autopsies, taking statements from key witnesses, etc.) the substantive violation might be very difficult or impossible for the applicant to prove. This was the case in *Khashiev and Akayeva v. Russia*, which concerned the ill-treatment and killing of Chechen civilians by Russian forces in the vicinity of Grozny in January 2000. The Court found a procedural and substantive violation of Article 2 (right to life). However, because the Russian authorities had failed to conduct autopsies or prepare other forensic reports, it was not possible for the Court to conclude that the victims were tortured before they were killed, and it therefore could not find a substantive violation of Article 3. However, in finding a procedural violation of Article 3, it stated the following:

> "[t]he procedural limb of Article 3 is invoked, in particular, where the Court is unable to reach any conclusions as to whether there has been treatment prohibited by Article 3 of the Convention, *deriving at least in part, from the failure of the authorities to react effectively to such complaints* at the relevant time …".[584]

The kind of investigation that will satisfy a Contracting Party's obligation under the procedural limb of Article 3 may vary according to the circumstances of the case and nature of the allegations. However, minimum standards identified by the Court in its case-law must be observed. The following paragraphs from the judgment in the case of *Batı and Others v. Turkey*, in which the Court reviewed its case-law on the subject, illustrate the required standards.[585] An investigation into allegations of ill-treatment lacking the following steps will fall foul of the requirement and result in a procedural violation of Article 3 or a violation of Article 13:

> "133. … whatever the method of investigation, the authorities must act as soon as an official complaint has been lodged. Even when strictly speaking no complaint has been made, an investigation must be started if there are sufficiently clear indications that torture or ill-treatment has been used (see, among other authorities, *Özbey v. Turkey* (dec.), no. 31883/96, 8

---

584 *Khashiyev and Akayeva v. Russia*, nos. 57942/00 and 57945/00, § 178 (emphasis supplied).
585 It must be noted that in *Batı and Others v. Turkey* the Court examined the allegation of a lack of an effective investigation from the standpoint of Article 13 of the Convention only.

March 2001; see also the Istanbul Protocol, paragraph 100 above[586]). The authorities must take into account the particularly vulnerable situation of victims of torture and the fact that people who have been subjected to serious ill-treatment will often be less ready or willing to make a complaint (see *Aksoy*, cited above, pp. 2286-87, §§ 97-98).

134.   The investigation must be 'effective' in practice as well as in law, and not be unjustifiably hindered by the acts or omissions of the authorities of the respondent State (see *Aksoy*, cited above, p. 2286, § 95, and *Aydın*, cited above, pp. 1895-96, § 103). It should be capable of leading to the identification and punishment of those responsible (see *Aksoy*, cited above, p. 2287, § 98). Otherwise, the general legal prohibition of torture and inhuman or degrading treatment or punishment would, despite its fundamental importance, be ineffective in practice and it would be possible in some cases for agents of the State to abuse the rights of those within their control with virtual impunity (see *Labita v. Italy* [GC], no. 26772/95, § 131, ECHR 2000-IV).

Admittedly, this is a qualified, not an absolute, obligation. The Court takes note of the fact that allegations of torture in police custody are extremely difficult for the victim to substantiate if he has been isolated from the outside world, without access to doctors, lawyers, family or friends who could provide support and assemble the necessary evidence (see *Aksoy*, cited above, p. 2286, § 97). The authorities must take whatever reasonable steps they can to secure the evidence concerning the incident, including, *inter alia*, a detailed statement concerning the allegations from the alleged victim, eyewitness testimony, forensic evidence and, where appropriate, additional medical certificates apt to provide a full and accurate record of the injuries and an objective analysis of the medical findings, in particular as regards the cause of the injuries. Any deficiency in the investigation which undermines its ability to establish the cause of injury or the person responsible will risk falling foul of this standard.

135.   For an investigation into torture or ill-treatment by agents of the State to be regarded as effective, the general rule is that the persons responsible for the inquiries and those conducting the investigation should be independent of anyone implicated in the events (see, *mutatis mutandis, Güleç v. Turkey*, judgment of 27 July 1998, *Reports* 1998-IV, p. 1733, §§ 81-82, and *Oğur v. Turkey* [GC], no. 21594/93, §§ 91-92, ECHR 1999-III). This means not only that there should be no hierarchical or institutional connection but also that the investigators should be independent in

---

586   The Istanbul Protocol referred to by the Court in this judgment is the *Manual on the Effective Investigation and Documentation of Torture and Other Cruel, Inhuman or Degrading Treatment or Punishment*, which was submitted to the United Nations High Commissioner for Human Rights on 9 August 1999. The "Istanbul Principles" subsequently received the support of the United Nations through resolutions of the United Nations Commission on Human Rights and the General Assembly. It is the first set of guidelines to have been produced for the investigation of torture. The Protocol contains full practical instructions for assessing persons who claim to have been the victims of torture or ill-treatment, for investigating suspected cases of torture and for reporting the investigation's findings to the relevant authorities. The principles applicable to the effective investigation and documentation of torture and other cruel, inhuman or degrading treatment or punishment are to be found in Annex 1 of the Manual, reprinted in Appendix No. 7 of the present *Handbook*. See also Conor Foley, *Combating Torture Handbook: A Manual for Judges and Prosecutors*, published by the Human Rights Centre of the University of Essex, United Kingdom, 2003. An online version of the *Handbook* may be consulted at http://www2.essex.ac.uk/human_rights_centre/publications/index.shtm.

practice (see, *mutatis mutandis*, *Ergi v. Turkey*, judgment of 28 July 1998, *Reports* 1998-IV, pp. 1778-79, §§ 83-84, and *Hugh Jordan v. the United Kingdom*, no. 24746/94, § 120, 4 May 2001).

136.   It is beyond doubt that a requirement of promptness and reasonable expedition is implicit in this context. A prompt response by the authorities in investigating allegations of ill-treatment may generally be regarded as essential in maintaining public confidence in their adherence to the rule of law and in preventing any appearance of collusion in or tolerance of unlawful acts (see, among other authorities, *Indelicato v. Italy*, no. 31143/96, § 37, 18 October 2001, and *Özgür Kılıç v. Turkey* (dec.), no. 42591/98, 24 September 2002). While there may be obstacles or difficulties which prevent progress in an investigation in a particular situation, it may generally be regarded as essential for the authorities to launch an investigation promptly in order to maintain public confidence in their adherence to the rule of law and prevent any appearance of collusion in or tolerance of unlawful acts (see, *mutatis mutandis*, *Paul and Audrey Edwards v. the United Kingdom*, no. 46477/99, § 72, ECHR 2002-II).

137.   For the same reasons, there must be a sufficient element of public scrutiny of the investigation or its results to secure accountability in practice as well as in theory. The degree of public scrutiny required may well vary from case to case. In all cases, however, the complainant must be afforded effective access to the investigatory procedure (see *Aksoy*, cited above, p. 2287, § 98, and *Büyükdağ*, cited above, § 67)".[587]

In its judgment in the case of *Abdülsamet Yaman v. Turkey* the Court added the following:

"...where a State agent has been charged with crimes involving torture or ill-treatment, it is of the utmost importance for the purposes of an 'effective remedy' that criminal proceedings and sentencing are not time-barred and that the granting of an amnesty or pardon should not be permissible. The Court also underlines the importance of the suspension from duty of the agent under investigation or on trial as well as his dismissal if he is convicted (see Conclusions and Recommendations of the United Nations Committee against Torture: Turkey, 27 May 2003, CAT/C/CR/30/5)".[588]

Finally, it should be noted that the obligation to investigate "is not an obligation of result, but of means".[589] Naturally, the Court does not require that every criminal investigation result in a conviction. In *Mikheyev v. Russia* the Court stated the following:

"Not every investigation should necessarily be successful or come to a conclusion which coincides with the claimant's account of events; however, it should in principle be capable of leading to the establishment of the

---

587   *Batı and Others v. Turkey*, cited above. See also Leach pp. 191-198 for a review of the Court's case-law on the requirement of effective investigations into killings under Article 2 of the Convention, which are also applicable, *mutatis mutandis*, in the context of Article 3 of the Convention.
588   *Abdülsamet Yaman v. Turkey*, cited above, § 55.
589   *Paul and Audrey Edwards v. the United Kingdom*, no. 46477/99, § 71.

facts of the case and, if the facts prove to be true, to the identification and punishment of those responsible (see, *mutatis mutandis, Mahmut Kaya v. Turkey*, no. 22535/93, § 124, DCHR 2000-III)".[590]

i. Concluding Remarks

It must be stressed once more that the positive obligation examined above is not limited solely to cases of ill-treatment by State agents;[591] investigating authorities of the Contracting Parties are under an obligation to investigate allegations of ill-treatment regardless of the identity of the alleged perpetrator.

The types and methods of domestic criminal investigations and criminal trials in the Contracting Parties vary considerably, and neither the Convention nor the Court's case-law require uniformity in these respects. However, the Court's paramount consideration is that whatever methods are employed, criminal investigations should be capable of establishing the accuracy of allegations of ill-treatment and lead to the identification and punishment of those responsible. The requirements of an effective investigation set out in the above mentioned judgments have been identified by the Court on a case-by-case basis, and the list is by no means exhaustive. When distilling these requirements the Court has sometimes identified defects in the national legislation of the Contracting Parties while observing in some other instances that the shortcomings were due to negligence – or reluctance – of the authorities to investigate the allegations. Defects identified in a national criminal justice system obviously need to be remedied by the national law-making bodies to ensure compliance with the Convention system. Furthermore, the Contracting Parties need to ensure that their investigating authorities conduct their business properly and in accordance with applicable law and procedure. Mention must once more be made of the close relationship between effective remedies and the requirement of exhaustion of domestic remedies. As pointed out earlier, there is no obligation to exhaust a remedy that is ineffective.[592] Furthermore, if an applicant succeeds in demonstrating that a particular remedy is ineffective, this will not only absolve the applicant from the requirement of exhausting that remedy but may also lead the Court to find a procedural violation of Article 3 or a violation of Article 13.

When arguing that the national authorities have failed to investigate their allegations of ill-treatment, applicants should refer to the criteria described in

---

590   *Mikheyev v. Russia*, no. 77617/01, 26 January 2006, § 107.
591   See, *mutatis mutandis, Calvelli and Ciglio v. Italy* [GC], no. 32967/96, 17 January 2002.
592   See Section 2.4.2 above.

the Court's case-law, using these criteria as a "check list" and should refer to the relevant judgments in which they figure.

Finally, because of the Court's present practice of examining allegations of ineffective investigations both under Articles 3 and 13, and until the Court resolves the issue, applicants should consider invoking both Article 3 and Article 13 in relation to complaints concerning the effectiveness of investigations.

b) The Obligation to Protect Against Ill-treatment by Private Individuals

According to the Court's case-law, Article 3 protects individuals not only from ill-treatment emanating directly from State agents but also, in certain circumstances, from ill-treatment at the hands of private individuals. This is a positive obligation, sometimes referred to as the third-party effect, or *drittwirkung*, of the Convention under Article 3 which is conferred upon Contracting Parties by the Court's case-law. Under this obligation, States are not only required to enact legislation criminalising ill-treatment but also to enforce their legislation in a way that affords real and effective protection for individuals.

This obligation was described in the judgment in the case of *A. v. the United Kingdom* where the Court held that the obligation on the Contracting Parties:

> "under Article 1 of the Convention to secure to everyone within their jurisdiction the rights and freedoms defined in the Convention, taken together with Article 3, requires States to take measures designed to ensure that individuals within their jurisdiction are not subjected to torture or inhuman or degrading treatment or punishment, including such ill-treatment administered by private individuals".[593]

Such protection requires the existence of effective domestic law provisions criminalising ill-treatment by private individuals and adequate application of those provisions by the judiciary.

The *A. v. the United Kingdom* case concerned an applicant who at the age of nine was regularly beaten by his stepfather. The Court found that this treatment rose to the level of severity prohibited by Article 3. The stepfather did not deny having beaten A. and was charged with and tried for assault occasioning actual bodily harm. However, he was found not guilty of assault occasioning actual bodily harm as he successfully invoked the defence of "reasonable chastisement" provided for parents and other persons *in loco parentis* in domestic law. The Court in Strasbourg, in agreement with the

---

593 *A. v. the United Kingdom*, cited above, § 22.

respondent Government, found that the law did not provide adequate protection to the applicant against treatment or punishment contrary to Article 3.[594]

When the victim is a vulnerable individual, the scope of the obligation to protect individuals from harm at the hands of private individuals is broader. In such circumstances the Contracting Parties will be under an obligation to take reasonable steps to prevent harm if their authorities knew or had reason to know of that maltreatment.[595]

For example in *Z. v. the United Kingdom* the Court stated that the measures referred to in its judgment in the case of *A. v. the United Kingdom* "should provide effective protection, in particular, of children and other vulnerable persons and include reasonable steps to prevent ill-treatment of which the authorities had or ought to have had knowledge".

In the *Z. v. the United Kingdom* case, the failure of social services to protect the applicants – four siblings – from serious abuse at the hands of their parents for a period of four and a half years, notwithstanding their awareness of the abuse, left "no doubt as to the failure of the system to protect these applicant children from serious, long-term neglect and abuse" in violation of Article 3 of the Convention.[596]

The scope of the positive obligation to provide effective protection was further extended by the Court in its decision in the case of *M.C. v. Bulgaria*, where the Court considered that States also "have a positive obligation inherent in Articles 3 and 8 of the Convention to enact criminal-law provisions effectively punishing rape and to apply them in practice through effective investigation and prosecution".[597] In this case, the investigating authorities discontinued the investigation into the applicant's allegations that she had been raped by two men on a date. The absence of direct proof of rape, such as traces of violence and resistance or calls for help, formed the basis for the authorities' decision to discontinue the investigation. The Court held:

> "the investigation of the applicant's case and, in particular, the approach taken by the investigator and the prosecutors in the case fell short of the requirements inherent in the States' positive obligations – viewed in the light of the relevant modern standards in comparative and international law – to establish and apply effectively a criminal-law system punishing all forms of rape and sexual abuse."[598]

---

594   *Ibid.*, §§ 18 and 24.
595   See also Alastair R. Mowbray, *The development of positive obligations under the European Convention on Human Rights by the European Court of Human Rights*, Oxford, 2004, pp. 43-65.
596   *Z. v. the United Kingdom*, cited above, §§ 73-74.
597   *M.C. v. Bulgaria*, cited above, § 153.
598   *Ibid.*, § 185.

The Court went on to find a violation of Article 3.

i. Concluding Remarks

It follows from the jurisprudence discussed above that the positive obligation to take steps to protect individuals from harm at the hands of other private individuals exists primarily when the victim is a "vulnerable" individual, such as a child. On the other hand, the positive obligation to enact domestic law provisions criminalising ill-treatment by private individuals and adequate application of those provisions by the judiciary exists regardless of the identity of the victim. In this connection, parallels may be drawn between the positive obligations under Article 3 and those that exist under Article 2. According to the Court's established case-law concerning the right to life, the first sentence of Article 2 § 1 requires the Contracting Parties not only to refrain from the intentional and unlawful taking of life, but also to take appropriate steps to safeguard the lives of those within their jurisdiction.[599] As with the obligation inherent in Article 3, Article 2 also imposes an obligation to put in place effective criminal law provisions to deter the commission of offences against the person. Furthermore, the State's obligation in this respect includes "in certain well-defined circumstances a positive obligation on the authorities to take preventive operational measures to protect an individual whose life is at risk from the criminal acts of another individual".[600]

However, not every claimed risk to life entails for the authorities a Convention requirement to take operational measures to prevent that risk from materialising. It must be established to the Court's satisfaction that the authorities knew or should have known of the existence of a real and immediate risk to the life of the individual(s) from the criminal acts of a third party and that they failed to take measures within the scope of their powers which reasonably might have prevented the harm.[601] It follows, therefore, that the obligation to take pre-emptive steps to protect an individual from being killed depends on the identity or the circumstances of the victim. In an Article 3 case, on the other hand, the applicant will be expected to show that he or she belongs to a category of persons who are vulnerable for reasons of, for example, age, mental or physical health and that the authorities therefore were under an obligation to exercise a heightened standard of vigilance to protect them from harm.

---

599 See, *inter alia*, *L.C.B. v. the United Kingdom*, no. 23413/94, 9 June 1998, § 36.
600 See *Osman v. the United Kingdom*, no. 23452/94, 28 October 1998, § 115.
601 *Ibid.*, § 116.

PART V

ESTABLISHMENT OF FACTS

THE ESTABLISHMENT OF FACTS

11.1 Summary

11.2 The Court's Powers in the Establishment of Facts

11.3 Fact-finding Hearings

11.4 Admissibility of Evidence

11.4.1 Medical Evidence

11.4.2 Witnesses

11.4.3 Other Evidence

11.4.4 Reports Compiled by International Organisations

11.5 Burden of Proof

11.5.1 Obligation to Account for Injuries Caused During Custody

11.5.2 Obligation to Assist the Court in Establishing Facts

11.5.3 Concluding Remarks

11.6 Standard of Proof

11.1 Summary

In the preceding section's discussion of the negative obligation, Article 3 cases were examined as belonging to three groups, namely those in which 1) ill-treatment was intentionally inflicted by law enforcement officers, 2) ill-treatment was caused as a consequence of a lawful or unlawful act carried out by State agents, and finally, 3) ill-treatment emanated from State agents' omissions. It is particularly in the first type of cases that the facts will most often be in dispute and where they will need to be established by the Court. In the second and third categories of cases, facts will not usually be disputed but the applicants will need to satisfy the Court that the ill-treatment they allege reached the minimum threshold and that the use of force by State agents was not warranted in the circumstances of the case. The second and third category cases have already been discussed above (see Section 2.2.4, on the "well-foundedness" of the application) and further regard may be had to Appendix No. 10 where the Court's Article 3 jurisprudence is examined in detail in all three categories of cases. For purposes of examining the way in which the Court establishes the facts in an Article 3 case, the present section will predominantly deal with the first category of cases, i.e. where ill-treatment is intentionally inflicted by State officials. Reference will be made to judgments which concerned not only ill-treatment but also violations of Article 2 (violations of the right to life) since considerations pertaining to the establishment of facts are generally applicable in both types of cases.

Before the Court can reach a finding under Article 3 on an allegation of ill-treatment, it must first establish the facts of the case, i.e. the accuracy of the applicant's allegations and the circumstances surrounding those allegations. In establishing the facts, the Court has adopted a system of free evaluation of evidence whereby no evidence is inadmissible and no witness is incompetent to testify.[602] Furthermore, although the Court will expect the applicant to adduce evidence in support of his or her allegations, in circumstances where the applicant is unable to do so, the Court may obtain such evidence of its own motion, either by asking the respondent Government to provide it or by taking evidence *in situ*.

The types of evidence which may be adduced in order to substantiate allegations of ill-treatment include – but are not limited to – medical and forensic reports, x-rays and other similar medical records, witness statements, photographs, custody records, reports compiled by inter-governmental and non-governmental organisations, and documents showing that the applicant's

---

602 See *Nachova and Others v. Bulgaria*, cited above, § 147.

allegations of ill-treatment have been brought to the attention of the domestic authorities.

The Court, in assessing the evidence before it, employs a very high standard of proof, i.e. the "beyond reasonable doubt" standard.[603] Nevertheless, it should be noted that this high standard is to a certain extent mitigated by the Court's reliance on inferences[604] and the fact that the Court will under certain circumstances shift the burden of proof to the respondent Government.[605]

In cases involving allegations of ill-treatment, the burden to disprove the applicant's allegations will shift to the Government in two circumstances. Firstly, if the applicant has been detained in good health but is found to be injured upon release, the respondent Government must explain those injuries.[606] Secondly, if the Government withholds evidence that the Court believes has a bearing on the applicant's case, the Government will be required to show that the documents do not corroborate the applicant's allegations.[607]

11.2 The Court's Powers in the Establishment of Facts

In most instances, the facts of a case will already have been established by national courts. The duty of the Strasbourg Court will then usually be limited to examining whether or not those factual findings "entail a result compatible with the requirements of the Convention".[608] The Court has often made it clear that it is:

> "sensitive to the subsidiary nature of its role and must be cautious in taking on the role of a first-instance tribunal of fact, where this is not rendered unavoidable by the circumstances of a particular case. Where domestic proceedings have taken place, it is not the Court's task to substitute its own assessment of the facts for that of the domestic courts and as a general rule it is for those courts to assess the evidence before them. Though the Court is not bound by the findings of domestic courts, in nor-

---

603 See *Ireland v. the United Kingdom*, cited above, § 161.
604 See Section 11.5.2 below.
605 See Section 11.5 below.
606 See *Selmouni v. France*, cited above, § 87.
607 See *Akkum and Others v. Turkey*, cited above, § 211. As will be seen below, the Court may, instead of shifting the burden to the Government, prefer to draw inferences from the Government's failure to cooperate with the Court; see *Timurtaş v. Turkey*, cited above, § 66.
608 See P. Mahoney, "Determination and Evaluation of Facts in Proceedings Before the Present and Future European Court of Human Rights" in Salvino Busutil, ed., *Mainly Human Rights: Studies in Honour of J. J. Cremona*, (Fondation Internationale Malte, 1999) pp. 119-134.

mal circumstances it requires cogent elements to lead it to depart from the findings of fact reached by those courts. The same principles apply *mutatis mutandis* where no domestic court proceedings have taken place because the prosecuting authorities have not found sufficient evidence to initiate such proceedings. Nonetheless, where allegations are made under Articles 2 and 3 of the Convention the Court must apply a particularly thorough scrutiny even if certain domestic proceedings and investigations have already taken place".[609]

It follows that under certain circumstances, particularly in the context of Article 2 and 3 violations, the Court will not hesitate to take on the role of a first instance tribunal and establish the disputed facts. Such circumstances may include situations where domestic authorities have failed to carry out effective investigations into allegations of ill-treatment or where they have failed to punish those responsible. The *Adalı v. Turkey* judgment cited above illustrates the point that a purported lack of evidence, which might have prevented domestic authorities from bringing criminal proceedings against persons implicated in ill-treatment, will not deter the Court from investigating the allegations of its own motion if such a course of action appears justified under the circumstances. Furthermore, whatever the outcome of the domestic proceedings, the conviction or acquittal of those implicated in ill-treatment does not absolve the respondent State from its responsibility under the Convention to account for any injuries found on a person at the time of his or her release from detention.[610] For example, in the case of *Ribitsch v. Austria*, the Court observed that the police officers allegedly responsible for the ill-treatment had been acquitted because of the high standard of proof required in the domestic legislation. In this connection the Court observed that significant weight had been given by the domestic court to the explanation that the injuries were caused by a fall against a car door. The Court, finding this explanation unconvincing, considered that even if Mr Ribitsch had fallen while he was being moved under escort, this could only have provided a very incomplete, and therefore insufficient, explanation of the injuries he sustained.[611]

The following sub-sections will deal with the evidential issues and the methods employed by the Court in establishing facts.

---

609   See, *inter alia, Adalı v. Turkey*, no. 38187/97, 31 March 2005, § 213.
610   *Selmouni v. France*, cited above, § 87.
611   *Ribitsch v. Austria*, cited above, § 34.

11.3 Fact-finding Hearings

Before the entry into force of Protocol No. 11, it was the Commission that established the facts of a case and reached a conclusion as to whether those facts revealed a breach of the Convention. While the Court was not bound by the Commission's findings and remained free to make its own assessment of the facts in light of all the material before it, it was only in exceptional circumstances that it exercised such powers in this area.[612] Following the entry into force of Protocol No. 11, however, the Court has assumed this role as the Commission no longer exists.

During its time, the Commission carried out a number of fact-finding hearings in the territory of the respondent Contracting Party in cases where the facts were disputed between the parties. The majority of such hearings were held in Turkey. To carry out these fact-finding hearings, the Commission appointed delegations comprised of Commission and Registry members. The Commission delegates questioned the applicants, eye-witnesses, and expert witnesses, such as doctors. Representatives of the parties were also entitled to cross-examine the applicants and witnesses. Despite a number of difficulties associated with such hearings, including language and cultural differences and the fact that witnesses could not be compelled to attend, these fact-finding hearings enabled the Commission to carry out its task of establishment of facts satisfactorily.

Following the entry into force of Protocol No. 11, the Court has continued to hold fact-finding hearings. However, because of its very heavy case load, it has done so in only a small number of cases. These fact-finding missions are carried out pursuant to Article 38 § 1 (a) of the Convention, which provides:

> "If the Court declares the application admissible,[613] it shall pursue the examination of the case, together with the representatives of the parties, and if need be, undertake an investigation, for the effective conduct of which the States concerned shall furnish all necessary facilities".

Furthermore, the Annex to the Rules of Court[614] sets out the procedure to be followed in such hearings and regulates the conduct of those participating in them. According to Rule 1 § 3 of the Annex to the Rules of Court,

> "[a]fter a case has been declared admissible or, exceptionally, before the decision on admissibility, the Chamber may appoint one or more of its

---

612 *Akdıvar and Others v. Turkey,* cited above, § 78.

613 Following the entry into force of Protocol No. 14, Contracting Parties will have the obligation under this Article to cooperate with the Court not only after admissibility of the application, but at all stages of the proceedings. See Article 14 of Protocol No. 14.

614 The Annex to the Rules of Court entered into force on 7 July 2003.

members or of the other judges of the Court, as its delegate or delegates, to conduct an inquiry, carry out an on-site investigation or take evidence in some other manner. The Chamber may also appoint any person or institution of its choice to assist the delegation in such manner as it sees fit."

The Court may decide to hold a fact-finding hearing of its own motion, but applicants can also invite the Court to do so. Any such request must be reasoned, and the applicant should explain how a fact-finding hearing would help establish the facts. The applicant should also submit a list of the proposed witnesses together with information about their relevance to the events in question. In the context of Article 3 complaints, such witnesses may include the perpetrators of the ill-treatment, doctors who carried out medical examinations of the applicant, investigating authorities to whose attention the allegations of ill-treatment were brought, and eye-witnesses. As an example of such a request, Appendix No. 13 can be consulted for the applicant's observations in the case of *Kişmir v. Turkey*, in which the applicant invited the Court to hold a fact-finding hearing to question a number of witnesses identified by her in her observations.

If the Court decides to hold a fact-finding hearing, it is imperative for an applicant to be represented by a lawyer who is capable of asking pertinent questions and adequately cross-examining witnesses. It is not uncommon for previously undisclosed documents to be produced during a fact-finding hearing and the representative must be able to study such documents on very short notice and formulate new questions in light of them.

Simultaneous interpretation will be arranged by the Court's Registry, and the costs associated with fact-finding hearings will be borne by the Council of Europe. Following the hearing, the parties will receive the verbatim records of the hearing and will usually be able to submit further observations on the basis of the information obtained in the hearing.

11.4 Admissibility of Evidence

The Court has a very liberal attitude towards the admissibility of evidence; it has adopted a system of free evaluation of evidence[615] whereby no evidence is inadmissible and no witness is incompetent to testify.

---

615 *Nachova and Others v. Bulgaria* [GC], cited above, § 147.

The Court made it clear in its judgment in the case of *Ireland v. the United Kingdom* that it is:

> "not bound, under the Convention or under the general principles applicable to international tribunals, by strict rules of evidence. In order to satisfy itself, the Court is entitled to rely on evidence of every kind, including, insofar as it deems them relevant, documents or statements emanating from governments, be they respondent or applicant, or from their institutions or officials".[616]

Furthermore:

> "the Court being master of its own procedure and of its own rules ... has complete freedom in assessing not only the admissibility and the relevance but also the probative value of each item of evidence before it".[617]

This liberal approach of the Court to the admissibility of evidence is unavoidable because in many human rights cases there is an understandable lack of direct evidence. Furthermore, for an international court which in most cases is located far from the location where the incident has occurred, there will be inevitable difficulties in accessing first-hand evidence, and therefore decisions will have to be made largely on the basis of the evidence submitted by the parties. What follows is a review of the Convention institutions' case-law with regard to the types of evidence which have been found to be particularly important in cases concerning complaints of ill-treatment.

11.4.1 Medical Evidence

Where allegations of ill-treatment are contested, medical findings constitute the most objective and convincing type of evidence.[618] In this regard, the applicant should note that the *most* probative kind of medical evidence is evidence that is obtained *immediately upon*, or *very shortly after*, the applicant's ill-treatment and which is consistent with the applicant's allegations. In practical terms, this usually means that medical evidence should be obtained upon the applicant's release from State custody, since ill-treatment most often occurs in the custodial setting. This is in line with the fact that in order to prevail in an Article 3 case, the applicant must establish a direct causal link between his or her injuries and the fact of having been in the control of the State. Therefore, the longer the applicant waits before seeking medical assistance, the more difficult it is going to be for him or her to prove that the

---

616 *Ireland v. the United Kingdom*, cited above, § 209.
617 *Ibid.*, § 210.
618 See D. R. Jones and S. V. Smith, "Medical Evidence in Asylum and Human Rights Appeals," in *International Journal of Refugee Law*, (2004) Vol. 16 No. 3, pp. 381-410 and the references cited therein.

injuries were sustained during, or were connected with, his or her custody. If the applicant succeeds in establishing that his or her injuries occurred while in the custody of the State, then the burden of proof shifts to the respondent State to disprove the allegations, or to prove that the use of force which caused the injuries was warranted and proportionate under the circumstances. Moreover, for purposes of showing exhaustion of domestic remedies, it is equally important that the applicant has shared such evidence with the relevant domestic authorities in the context of a complaint as soon as possible after the occurrence of the ill-treatment. These issues are discussed further below in the context of the Court's case-law.

As mentioned above, by far the strongest medical evidence is a medical report drawn up immediately after the period of detention during which the person was ill-treated. However, in some cases the applicant might not have been medically examined at the time of release. Furthermore, there may be problems associated with medical reports drawn up while the person is still in the custody of the State. For example, the applicant's medical examination might have been carried out in the presence of police officers, in which case the applicant may conceivably have been too frightened to inform the doctor of the extent or cause of his or her injuries. The medical examinations and reports drawn up in the course of those examinations themselves may sometimes be very short and therefore not capable of proving or disproving the applicant's allegations of ill-treatment.[619] For example, in the case of *Elçi and Others v. Turkey* the Court observed that "[t]he collective medical examination of the applicants prior to being brought before the Public Prosecutor can only be described as superficial and cursory... The Court does not therefore attach great weight to it".[620]

In this context, it may be useful to consult the CPT Standards on Police Custody, the relevant parts of which provide as follows:

> "As regards the medical examination of persons in police custody, all such examinations should be conducted out of the hearing, and preferably out of the sight, of police officers. Further, the results of every examination as well as relevant statements by the detainee and the doctor's conclusions should be formally recorded by the doctor and made available to the detainee and his lawyer".[621]

---

619 See Camille Giffard, *The Torture Reporting Handbook: How to document and respond to allegations of torture within the international system for the protection of human rights*, published by the Human Rights Centre of the University of Essex, United Kingdom, 2000. An online version of the Handbook may be consulted at http://www2.essex.ac.uk/human_rights_centre/publications/index.shtm.

620 *Elçi and Others v. Turkey*, cited above, § 642.

621 CPT Standards may be consulted at http://www.cpt.coe.int/en/documents/eng-standards.doc

When examining allegations of ill-treatment, the Court takes these standards into account. For example, in the case of *Akkoç v. Turkey* the applicant alleged that she had been subjected to ill-treatment in police custody which included being doused with hot and cold water and subjected to electric shocks and blows to the face. Upon release she was brought together with sixteen other detainees before a doctor who stated in a "medical report" that they had not suffered any physical blows. A few days after her release, she was medically examined at a university where x-rays of her head were taken showing that her chin had been broken. The Commission, after holding a fact-finding hearing in Turkey and hearing a number of persons who had witnessed the applicant's state of health following her release from police custody, concluded that she had indeed been subjected to the treatment described in her application form. This conclusion was subsequently upheld by the Court, which found a violation of Article 3. In its judgment the Court stated the following:

> "The Court further endorses the comments expressed by the Commission concerning the importance of independent and thorough examinations of persons on release from detention. The European Committee for the Prevention of Torture (CPT) has also emphasised that proper medical examinations are an essential safeguard against ill-treatment of persons in custody. Such examinations must be carried out by a properly qualified doctor, without any police officer being present and the report of the examination must include not only the detail of any injuries found, but the explanations given by the patient as to how they occurred and the opinion of the doctor as to whether the injuries are consistent with those explanations. The practices of cursory and collective examinations illustrated by the present case undermines [*sic*] the effectiveness and reliability of this safeguard".[622]

The lack of medical evidence in an ill-treatment case will not necessarily mean that the applicant will be unable to prove his or her allegations of ill-treatment. As the Commission stated in *Çakıcı v. Turkey*, in cases of unacknowledged detention and disappearance, independent, objective medical evidence or eyewitness testimony is unlikely to be forthcoming and to require either as a prerequisite of a finding of a violation of Article 3 would undermine the protection afforded by that provision.[623] Similarly, in the case of *Tekin v. Turkey* the Court observed that:

> "[i]t is true that, as the Government have pointed out, the applicant was unable to provide any independent evidence, for example medical reports, to substantiate his allegations of ill-treatment. However, in this respect the Court notes that the State authorities took no steps to ensure that Mr Tekin was seen by a doctor during his time in detention or upon his release,

---

622   *Akkoç v. Turkey*, nos. 22947/93 and 22948/93, 10 October 2000, § 118.
623   *Çakıcı v. Turkey*, no. 23657/94, Commission Report of 12 March 1998.

despite the fact that he had complained of ill-treatment to the public prosecutor ... who was under a duty under Turkish law to investigate this complaint".[624]

In both cases the Court found the applicants' allegations of ill-treatment to be
substantiated but it based its decision on evidence obtained by the
Commission which had held fact-finding missions in Turkey during which
members of the Commission questioned the applicants and a number of eye-
witnesses.[625] The lack of medical evidence obtained immediately after the
period of detention may therefore be compensated by obtaining evidence *in
situ*. However, and as pointed out earlier, the Court holds fact-finding hearings in only a small number of cases and for this reason applicants should
consider obtaining independent medical reports as soon as possible after their
release from custody.

The probative value of independent medical reports is increased if those
reports have been brought to the attention of the national authorities.
Bringing the evidence to the attention of the national authorities is also criti-
cally important for the requirement of exhaustion of domestic remedies. For
example, in the case of *Dizman v. Turkey*, the applicant had been taken away
from a café by plain-clothes police officers who ill-treated him in a deserted
field. He was then released and taken to a hospital by his relatives the same
day. The medical examination and x-rays taken in the course of that examination revealed that his jaw had been broken and required surgery. The following day the applicant submitted the x-rays to the attention of the prosecutor
and made an official complaint about the ill-treatment. In response, the prosecutor sent the applicant to the Forensic Medicine Directorate where he
obtained another medical report, confirming that his jaw had been broken.
The police officers were subsequently tried but acquitted for lack of sufficient
evidence, in particular, due to the fact that the medical report in question had
been obtained two days after the alleged event. The Strasbourg Court accepted the accuracy of the applicant's allegations of ill-treatment and noted that
neither the respondent Government nor any other domestic authority had con-
tacted the hospital where the applicant claimed to have been examined and
where x-rays were taken immediately after his release in order to verify the
accuracy of the applicant's statement.[626]

---

624 *Tekin v. Turkey*, no. 22496/93, 9 June 1998, § 41.
625 For a review of the issue of the role of medical evidence in international human rights tribunals, see
   Camille Giffard and Nigel Rodley, "The Approach of International Tribunals to Medical Evidence in
   Cases Involving Allegations of Torture" in Michael Peel and Vincent Iacopino (eds.), *The Medical
   Documentation of Torture*, Greenwich Medical Media Limited, 2002, pp. 19-43.
626 *Dizman v. Turkey*, cited above, §§ 75-76.

Similarly, in the case of *Balogh v. Hungary*, the applicant alleged that he had been beaten in the course of his interrogation by police. However, the applicant did not obtain a medical examination until two days after his release. He claimed that:

> "he had had no experience with the police or with any other authorities before the incident. He was not therefore aware of the importance of contacting officials at once about his injuries. Although his injuries required immediate medical attention, he felt humiliated and ashamed because of the incident. Being unfamiliar with the towns which he subsequently passed through on his way home, he did not seek medical help until he returned to his home town. However, he was in constant pain throughout this period on account of the severity of his injuries".[627]

The respondent Government submitted, for its part, that "[d]ue to the applicant's belatedness in seeking medical help ... the medical expert ... could not determine with certainty whether the applicant's injuries had been inflicted before, during or after his interrogation".[628] The Court rejected the Government's submissions and held that:

> "... the applicant, having been interrogated in police custody on 9 August 1995, was said by his four companions to have left the police station with a red and swollen face. All these witnesses deposed, in consistent terms, that he must have been beaten ... It is true that the applicant did not seek medical help in the evening of the alleged incident or on the next day, but waited until 11 August 1995 before doing so. However, in view of the fact that the applicant immediately sought medical assistance on his arrival in his home town, the Court is reluctant to attribute any decisive importance to this delay, which, in any event, cannot be considered so significant as to undermine his case under Article 3".[629]

This case illustrates that independent medical reports that are corroborated by witness statements will have an even higher evidential value than medical reports standing on their own.

Moreover, before relying on a medical report obtained some time after the release, the Court will take into account the degree of consistency of the applicant's allegations and will expect the applicant to describe with a certain amount of precision the causal link between the medical report and the ill-treatment. This is illustrated in the case of *Gurepka v. Ukraine* in which the applicant submitted to the Court a medical report, drawn up six days after his release from detention, showing that the conditions of detention had had a negative effect on his health. The Court rejected the allegation as being manifestly ill-founded, holding in relevant part:

---

627   *Balogh v. Hungary*, cited above, § 37.

628   *Ibid.*, § 40.

629   *Ibid.*, §§ 48-49.

"[i]n so far as the applicant complains of his detention in a cold cell and his ensuing health problems allegedly caused by it, the Court finds that the applicant has failed to demonstrate that the impugned treatment, formulated by the applicant in very general terms, attained the minimum level of severity proscribed by Article 3 of the Convention, particularly in the absence of any medical or other evidence ... The sick leave certificate presented by the applicant as to his illness from 7 December 1998, that is 6 days after his release, does not constitute sufficient proof of a causal link with the alleged ill-treatment".[630]

Where possible, medical evidence obtained from institutions specialising in identifying and treating ill-treatment should also be submitted to the Court in support of allegations of ill-treatment.[631]

However, and as pointed out above, the Court requires that such evidence is first brought to the attention of the national authorities to give them the opportunity to investigate allegations of ill-treatment. Failure to do so may result in the complaint being declared inadmissible for non-exhaustion of domestic remedies. This is illustrated in the case of *Saraç v. Turkey* in which the applicant argued that she had been taken into police custody where she was hung from her arms and hit repeatedly on the head with truncheons until she lost consciousness. While unconscious, her feet were burnt by cigarettes. Following this, she was raped with a truncheon on two occasions. She was then taken by car to an isolated place and abandoned. Thirteen days after the event in question the applicant went to the Human Rights Foundation of Turkey and sought medical assistance. Following medical examinations carried out over a period of three days in two different hospitals and the Nuclear Medical Centre in Istanbul, including gynaecological and neurological tests, x-rays, thorax graphics, scintigraphic imaging, and examinations by an ear, nose and throat consultant as well as a psychiatrist, the doctors concluded in a medical report that the applicant's allegations of ill-treatment, such as post-traumatic stress, depression, marks on her feet caused by cigarette burns, and a pelvic complaint were compatible with the medical findings. The Strasbourg Court, observing that neither this report nor any relevant evidence in support of the allegations of ill-treatment had ever been conveyed to the public prosecutor, concluded that the applicant had failed to exhaust domestic remedies as required by Article 35 § 1 of the Convention.[632]

---

630 *Gurepka v. Ukraine*, no. 61406/00, 6 September 2005, § 35.

631 For a review of the medical techniques in documenting ill-treatment, see Michael Peel and Vincent Iacopino (eds.), *The Medical Documentation of Torture*, Greenwich Medical Media Limited, 2002. See also Appendix No. 8 for "Diagnostic Tests", published in the Istanbul Protocol, for a review of advanced medical techniques used in the diagnoses of ill-treatment.

632 *Saraç v. Turkey* (dec.), no. 35841/97, 2 September 2004.

241

11.4.2 Witnesses

According to Rule 1 of the Annex to the Rules of Court:

> "...[t]he Chamber may, *inter alia*, invite the parties to produce documentary evidence and decide to hear as a witness or expert or in any other capacity any person whose evidence or statements seem likely to assist it in carrying out its tasks".

Other than hearing witnesses directly, the Court also accepts statements taken from any eye-witnesses or other persons whose testimonies may help it establish the facts of cases. Naturally, statements taken from such witnesses by domestic authorities will have a higher evidential value. For example, in the case of *Akdeniz v. Turkey*, the Court accepted the applicant's allegation that her son had been detained and ill-treated by soldiers solely on the basis of statements taken by the investigating prosecutor from a number of eye-witnesses to the events. In fact, the prosecutor himself had concluded, on the basis of the same eye-witness evidence, that the applicant's allegations were true but had failed to prosecute those responsible.[633]

The Court also takes into account eye-witness statements taken by an applicant him or herself or by his or her lawyer or an NGO. However, such statements need to be corroborated by other evidence. Furthermore, as both parties to a case will be given the opportunity to comment on any documents submitted in Convention proceedings, the Court may attach greater evidential value to an unauthenticated document if its accuracy and veracity is not contested by the parties. For instance, in the case of *Koku v. Turkey* the applicant submitted to the Court a chronology of events in which attacks against, and killings of, members of a pro-Kurdish political party were detailed. He argued that his brother, who had been a member of that party, was kidnapped and his disappearance was not investigated by the authorities. The body of his brother was found some months after the kidnapping. The Court, noting that the respondent Government had not contested the accuracy of the document submitted by the applicant, and noting further that the alleged kidnapping and disappearance happened at a time when dozens of other politicians of the same political party were being kidnapped, injured, and killed, accepted that the authorities had failed to protect the right to life of the applicant's brother and found a violation of Article 2 of the Convention.[634]

---

633   *Akdeniz v. Turkey*, cited above, §§ 81-82.
634   *Koku v. Turkey*, cited above, § 131.

11.4.3 Other Evidence

In cases concerning allegations of ill-treatment, the Court has examined a wide variety of evidence submitted to it by the parties or obtained by the Court itself. Such evidence has included, *inter alia*, custody records showing that a particular person had or had not been detained at a particular detention facility, photographs of the applicant's body,[635] video footage of the prison cell in which the applicant was allegedly detained,[636] plans of the detention facility where the applicant was detained and raped and which she described in her application form,[637] a piece of cloth used to blindfold the applicant in police custody while he was being ill-treated,[638] autopsy reports showing that the person had been subjected to ill-treatment prior to his killing,[639] and photographs showing that a body had been mutilated.[640] It must be stressed that such objects, individually, do not constitute conclusive evidence and in most cases they will be regarded as circumstantial evidence. However, sufficient circumstantial evidence may persuade the Court, in the absence of any direct evidence – which can be very difficult to obtain in human rights cases – to find an applicant's allegations established.

11.4.4 Reports Compiled by International Organisations

Reports compiled by governmental and non-governmental organisations are regularly relied on as evidence by the Court. For example, in examining allegations relating to prison conditions, the Court frequently relies on the reports of the Committee for the Prevention of Torture and Inhuman or Degrading Treatment or Punishment (CPT) based on that organisation's visits to prisons in the territory of the respondent Contracting Party.[641]

Furthermore, reports prepared by such organisations enable the Court to take into account the general human rights situation in a Contracting Party when examining allegations of ill-treatment against that Party. For example, in its judgment in the case of *Elçi and Others v. Turkey* the Court relied on the CPT's reports on Turkey when examining the testimony of the Government's witnesses during the fact-finding hearing. The Court observed that:

"In its second public statement, issued on 6 December 1996, the CPT

---

635   *Mathew v. the Netherlands*, cited above, §§ 158-165.
636   *Ostrovar v. Moldova*, cited above, § 72.
637   *Aydın v. Turkey*, cited above, § 39.
638   *Tekin v. Turkey*, no. 22496/93, Commission Report of 17 April 1997, § 190.
639   *Süheyla Aydın v. Turkey*, cited above, § 188.
640   *Akkum and Others v., Turkey*, cited above, §§ 51-52.
641   See, *inter alia*, *Van der Ven v. the Netherlands*, cited above, §§ 32-33. For further details on the mandate and working methods of the CPT, see Appendix No. 11.

noted that some progress had been made over the intervening four years. However, its findings after its visit in 1994 demonstrated that torture and other forms of ill-treatment were still important characteristics of police custody. In the course of visits in 1996, CPT delegations once again found clear evidence of the practice of torture and other forms of severe ill-treatment by the police. It referred to its most recent visit in September 1996 to police establishments. It noted the cases of seven persons who had been very recently detained at the headquarters of the anti-terrorism branch of the Istanbul Security Directorate and which ranked among the most flagrant examples of torture encountered by CPT delegations in Turkey. It concluded that resort to torture and other forms of severe ill-treatment remained a common occurrence in police establishments in Turkey".[642]

In reference to this information, the Court stated that the Government witnesses before the Commission Delegates had "constantly denied the applicants' allegations, but in such a strident manner as to cast doubt on their testimony in the light of the accepted background knowledge for the period".[643] Similarly, in its judgment in the case of *Khashiyev and Akayeva v. Russia* the Court, in concluding that the applicants' version of the events was accurate, consulted reports prepared by human rights groups and documents prepared by international organisations which supported their version of events.[644]

Furthermore, in expulsion and extradition cases the Court may consult the Guidelines, Position Papers, and Country Reports published by the United Nations High Commissioner for Refugees (UNHCR).[645] The Court also has regard to information and reports compiled by non-governmental organisations. For example, in the case of *Kalantari v. Germany* the Court examined evidence submitted to it by the World Organisation Against Torture (OMCT) showing that the applicant would be at risk of persecution if expelled to Iran.[646] In *Said v. the Netherlands*, the Court concluded that the expulsion of the applicant to Eritrea would expose him to a real risk of being subjected to treatment contrary to Article 3 relying in part on material compiled by Amnesty International showing the existence of such a risk.[647]

Applicants are therefore advised to append any such reports or information to their application or to their observations. Applicants should avoid submitting such information separately, and in order to avoid the risk of rejection by the Court, all supporting evidence should be submitted within the applicable time limits for submission of written pleadings (see Rule 38 § 1).

---

642 *Elçi and Others v. Turkey*, cited above, § 599.
643 *Ibid.*, § 643.
644 *Khashiyev and Akayeva v. Russia*, cited above, § 144.
645 See, *inter alia*, *N. v. Finland*, cited above, §§ 119-121.
646 *Kalantari v. Germany*, no. 51342/99, 11 October 2001, §§ 35-36.
647 *Said v. the Netherlands*, cited above, §§ 31-35.

11.5 Burden of Proof

As pointed out above, Convention proceedings do not always lend themselves to a rigorous application of the principle *affirmanti incumbit probatio* (he who alleges something must prove that allegation).[648] In this connection, reference may be made to the Court's judgment in *Ireland v. the United Kingdom*:

> "[i]n order to satisfy itself as to the existence or not in Northern Ireland of practices contrary to Article 3, the Court will not rely on the concept that the burden of proof is borne by one or other of the two Governments concerned. In the cases referred to it, the Court examines all the material before it, whether originating from the Commission, the Parties or other sources, and, if necessary, obtains material *proprio motu*".[649]

Nevertheless, according to the Court's established case-law, an applicant bears the initial burden of producing evidence in support of his or her complaints at the time the application is introduced. Once the applicant satisfies this burden and the Court decides that the complaint is not manifestly ill-founded within the meaning of Article 35 § 3,[650] the burden may shift to the Government to disprove the applicant's allegations. The Court's case-law provides for such a shift in two circumstances. They are examined below.

11.5.1 Obligation to Account for Injuries Caused During Custody

The difficulties associated with proving ill-treatment have perhaps best been described by Judge Bonello in his dissenting opinion in the case of *Sevtap Veznedaroğlu v. Turkey*, in which he stated the following:

> "[e]xpecting those who claim to be victims of torture to prove their allegations 'beyond reasonable doubt' places on them a burden that is as impossible to meet as it is unfair to request. Independent observers are not, to my knowledge, usually invited to witness the rack, nor is a transcript of proceedings in triplicate handed over at the end of each session of torture; its victims cower alone in oppressive and painful solitude, while the team of interrogators has almost unlimited means at its disposal to deny the happening of, or their participation in, the gruesome pageant. The solitary victim's complaint is almost invariably confronted with the negation 'corroborated' by many".[651]

---

648   See Section 2.6.2.above.
649   *Ireland v. the United Kingdom*, cited above, § 160.
650   See Section 2.6 above.
651   *Sevtap Veznedaroğlu v. Turkey*, cited above. As regards the issue of standard of proof beyond reasonable doubt, see Section 11.6 below.

Indeed, in most cases of ill-treatment, the only evidence the victim will be able to produce is his or her own testimony. However, the Court is aware of this difficulty and has created its own unique set of rules to mitigate it. Thus, according to the Court's established case-law, if the victim of ill-treatment is able to show that he or she suffered injuries while in the custody of the State, the Court will shift the burden onto the Government to explain those injuries.

Ribitsch v. Austria was the first case in which the burden was expressly shifted onto the respondent Government to explain injuries caused during police custody.[652] In this case, it was not disputed that the applicant had suffered injuries in custody. However, the respondent Government submitted that because of the required high standard of proof in the proceedings before the national courts, it had not been possible to establish that the policemen had been responsible for the applicant's injuries. The Government also argued that in order for a violation of the Convention to be found, it was necessary for the ill-treatment to be proved beyond reasonable doubt. The Commission rejected the Government's argument and found that where a person sustains injuries in police custody, it is for the Government to produce evidence establishing facts which cast doubt on the allegations of the victim, particularly if the victim's account is supported by medical certificates. In this case, the explanations put forward by the Government were not sufficient to cast a reasonable doubt on the applicant's allegations concerning ill-treatment.[653] The Commission's approach was adopted by the Court, which found in its subsequent judgment that Article 3 had been violated.[654]

This approach was followed by the Court in its judgment in the case of *Selmouni v. France*; the Court stated that

> "... where an individual is taken into police custody in good health but is found to be injured at the time of release, it is incumbent on the State to provide a plausible explanation of how those injuries were caused, failing which a clear issue arises under Article 3 of the Convention".[655]

In its judgment in the case of *Salman v. Turkey*, the Court added that "[t]he obligation on the authorities to account for the treatment of an individual in custody is particularly stringent where that individual dies".[656]

Three aspects of the Court's finding in *Selmouni* require further exploration. They are: 1) the question of *when* the obligation to account for a detainee's

652 For a review of the issue of burden of proof in Convention proceedings, see U. Erdal, "Burden and Standard of Proof in Proceedings under the European Convention" (2001) *26 EL Rev. Human Rights Survey*, 81 et seq., (hereinafter referred to as "Erdal").

653 *Ribitsch v. Austria*, cited above, § 31.

654 Ibid., § 40.

655 *Selmouni v. France*, cited above, § 87.

656 *Salman v. Turkey*, cited above, § 99.

fate starts, 2) the *duration* of the period during which the obligation is in force, and 3) the meaning of the term "plausible explanation".

As regards the first question, it must be stressed that the term "police custody" in *Selmouni*, or "custody" in *Salman*, does not necessarily imply that the person has been placed in a detention facility.[657] In its judgment in the case of *Yasin Ateş v. Turkey*, which concerned the killing of the applicant's son during a military operation following his arrest, the Court held that a lack of evidence in support of the applicant's allegation that his son had been killed by agents of the State did not:

> "mean that the respondent Government are absolved from their responsibility to account for Kadri Ateş's death, which occurred while he was under arrest. In this connection the Court reiterates that persons in custody are in a vulnerable position and that the authorities are under a duty to protect them".[658]

Referring to its earlier case-law, the Court went on to hold:

> "... States are under an obligation to account for the injuries or deaths which occurred, not only in custody, but also in areas within the exclusive control of the authorities of the State because, in both situations, the events in issue lie wholly, or in large part, within the exclusive knowledge of the authorities (see *Akkum and Others v. Turkey*, no. 21894/93, § 211, 24 March 2005)".[659]

It follows, therefore, that a Contracting Party's obligation will begin as soon as its agents detain a person, regardless of whether that person is subsequently placed in a detention facility.

As regards the second aspect – the duration of the obligation to account for a detainee's fate – the Contracting Parties' obligation to protect a detained person continues until that person is released. It appears from the Court's case-law that it is incumbent on the Contracting Party to show that the person is released. This issue is well illustrated by the judgment in the case of *Süheyla Aydın v. Turkey*, in which the applicant's husband was arrested and detained at a police station. He was then brought before a judge at the court house who ordered his release on 4 April 1994. However, he never emerged from that court house and on 9 April 1994 his body was found in a field some 40 kilometres away. The Government argued that the applicant's husband had been released on 4 April 1994 and responsibility for his subsequent death could not be attributed to agents of the State. The Commission held a fact-finding

---

657 See, *mutatis mutandis*, *H.L. v. the United Kingdom*, no. 45508/99, 5 October 2004, § 91.
658 *Yasin Ateş v. Turkey,* no. 30949/96, 31 May 2005, § 93.
659 *Ibid.,* § 94.

hearing in Turkey to hear a number of witnesses, but the respondent Government failed to identify and summon police officers who had accompanied the applicant's husband to the court house on 4 April 1994. Furthermore, the Government failed to produce any documents to prove that the applicant's husband had indeed been released. The Court concluded in its judgment of 24 May 2005 that:

> "[i]n the light of the above-mentioned failure of the Government to identify and summon the police officers who accompanied Necati Aydın to the Diyarbakır Court on 4 April 1994, coupled with the absence of a release document, the Court concludes that the Government have failed to discharge their burden of proving that Necati Aydın was indeed released from the Diyarbakır Court building on 4 April 1994. The Court finds it established that Necati Aydın remained in the custody of the State. It follows that the Government's obligation is engaged to explain how Necati Aydın was killed while still in the hands of State agents. Given that no such explanation has been put forward by the Government, the Court concludes that the Government have failed to account for the killing of Necati Aydın".[660]

In this judgment the Court also referred to Article 11 of the Declaration on the Protection of all Persons from Enforced Disappearance (United Nations General Assembly resolution 47/133 of 18 December 1992). This Article provides that

> "[a]ll persons deprived of liberty must be released in a manner permitting reliable verification that they have actually been released and, further, have been released in conditions in which their physical integrity and ability fully to exercise their rights are assured".[661]

Finally, as regards the third aspect, i.e. the nature of the "plausible explanation" for the injuries caused during custody, the Commission has held that in cases where injuries occurred in the course of police custody, it is "not sufficient for the Government to point at other possible causes of injuries, but it is incumbent on the Government to produce evidence showing facts which cast doubt on the account given by the victim and supported by medical evidence".[662] Similarly, in the above mentioned case of *Ribitsch v. Austria* the respondent Government's explanations "were not sufficient to cast a reasonable doubt on the applicant's allegations concerning ill-treatment he had allegedly undergone while in police custody".[663]

In establishing whether a respondent Government has accounted for injuries caused in custody, the Court refers to investigations – in particular forensic

---

660 *Süheyla Aydın v. Turkey*, cited above, § 154.
661 *Ibid.*, § 153.
662 See *Klaas v. Germany*, cited above, § 103.
663 *Ribitsch v. Austria*, cited above, § 31.

and medical examinations – carried out at the national level. For example, in the case of *Salman v. Turkey*, in which the detained person died in police custody, the Court observed that no plausible explanation had been provided by the respondent Government:

> "for the injuries to the left ankle, bruising and swelling of the left foot, the bruise to the chest and the broken sternum. The evidence does not support the Government's contention that the injuries might have been caused during the arrest, or that the broken sternum was caused by cardiac massage".[664]

In reaching that conclusion, the Court noted a number of medical reports prepared by international forensic experts on the basis of the post-mortem reports prepared following the death of the detained person. Thus, it concluded that the opinion expressed in the post-mortem report which found that the bruising of the chest pre-dated the arrest and that the detained person died of a heart attack brought on by the stress of his detention alone and after a prolonged period of breathlessness, "was rebutted by the evidence of Professors Pounder and Cordner".[665]

In the case of *Kişmir v. Turkey*, the respondent Government submitted, as a possible explanation for the death of the applicant's son in police custody, that the death could have been due to a childhood illness. However, the Court observed that the Government had failed to put forward any evidence in support of that submission. There was no indication in the documents submitted by the Government that the deceased person had any previous health problems.[666] The Court further observed that the Government had not specifically dealt in its observations with the cause of the oedema in the lungs, which was the cause of death according to post mortem examinations. The Court agreed with the shortcomings in the post mortem examination identified by an international forensic expert who had been commissioned by the applicant and who had drawn up his report on the basis of the post mortem reports prepared following the death.[667]

In *Akkum and Others v. Turkey*, the Court, examining whether the Government had explained the killings of the applicant's two relatives, assessed the oral evidence taken by the Commission's delegates and also took particular note of the investigation carried out at the domestic level.

---

664 *Salman v. Turkey*, cited above, § 102.
665 *Ibid.*
666 *Kişmir v. Turkey*, cited above, §§ 91-98. See also Appendix No. 13 for the applicant's observations.
667 *Ibid.*, § 85.

Having established that no meaningful investigation had been conducted at the domestic level capable, firstly, of establishing the true facts surrounding the killings and the mutilation of one of the bodies, and secondly, of leading to the identification and punishment of those responsible, the Court concluded that the Government had failed to account for the killings and for the mutilation in violation of Articles 2 and 3 of the Convention.[668]

It also appears from the Court's case-law that when a respondent Government fails to conduct a medical examination before placing a person in detention, it will to some extent have forfeited the argument that the injuries present at the time of release pre-dated the period of detention. Thus, in its judgment in the case of *Abdülsamet Yaman v. Turkey* the Court observed that the applicant had not been medically examined at the beginning of his detention and had not had access to a doctor of his choice while in police custody. Following his transfer from police custody, he had undergone two medical examinations which resulted in a medical report and the inclusion of a medical note in the prison patients' examination book. Both the report and the note referred to scabs, bruises, and lesions on various parts of the applicant's body.[669] Those injuries, in the absence of a plausible explanation from the respondent Government, were sufficient for the Court to conclude that they were the result of ill-treatment for which the Government bore responsibility in violation of Article 3 of the Convention.[670]

In conclusion, based on the case-law examined above, the Court expects a respondent Government to provide a satisfactory and convincing explanation for injuries and deaths caused in custody. It is not sufficient for a respondent Government to point to other potential causes without providing adequate evidence in support of its submissions. Any medical evidence submitted by a respondent Government will be scrutinised by the Court before it can be accepted as proof of the cause of injury or death in custody. It is also open to applicants to submit to the Court medical reports to rebut those put forward by the respondent Government. Furthermore, the Court itself can ask a forensic expert to comment on any medical evidence submitted by the parties. The Commission did just this in the *Salman v. Turkey* case mentioned above when it requested an expert opinion on the medical issues in the case "from Professor Cordner, Professor of Forensic Medicine at Monash University, Victoria (Australia) and Director of the Victorian Institute of Forensic Medicine".[671]

---

668 *Akkum and Others v. Turkey*, cited above, §§ 212-232.
669 *Abdülsamet Yaman v. Turkey*, cited above, § 45.
670 *Ibid.*, §§ 46-48.
671 See *Salman v. Turkey*, cited above, § 6.

11.5.2 Obligation to Assist the Court in Establishing Facts

As pointed out above, pursuant to Article 38 § 1 of the Convention, respondent Governments have an obligation to cooperate with the Court in the establishment of facts. Furthermore, according to Rule 44A of the Rules of Court, the parties to a case before the Court[672] have a duty to cooperate fully in the conduct of the proceedings and, in particular, to take such action within their power as the Court considers necessary for the proper administration of justice.

The Court has encountered difficulties in establishing the facts in a number of cases in which respondent Governments have failed to cooperate either by withholding documents or other evidence requested by the Court, or by failing to submit all the relevant documents in their possession. In this connection, the Court has stated that:

> "it is of the utmost importance for the effective operation of the system of individual petition, instituted under Article 34 of the Convention, that States should furnish all necessary facilities to make possible a proper and effective examination of applications".[673]

The Court acknowledged in its judgment in the case of *Timurtaş v. Turkey* that where an individual applicant accuses State agents of violating his or her rights under the Convention, it is in certain instances solely the respondent Government that has access to information capable of corroborating or refuting these allegations. The failure of a respondent Government to submit such information in its possession – or to submit it timely – without a satisfactory explanation may not only give rise to the drawing of inferences as to the well-foundedness of the applicant's allegations, but may also reflect negatively on the level of compliance by a respondent State with its obligations under Article 38 § 1 (a) of the Convention.[674] The case of *Timurtaş* concerned the disappearance of the applicant's son after the latter had allegedly been taken into unacknowledged custody by soldiers. The respondent Government denied that the applicant's son had been detained. The applicant submitted to the Commission a photocopy of a document which he argued was a post-operation military report. The report detailed the arrest and detention of his son by the soldiers who took part in the operation. When requested by the Commission to submit the original of the document, the respondent Government argued that a document with the same reference number did indeed exist but that they could not submit it to the Commission as it

---

672   Indeed, the duty to cooperate with the Court is extended in Rule 44A to Contracting Parties which are not even parties to the case at hand.

673   *Tanrıkulu v. Turkey* [GC], no. 23763/94, 8 July 1999, § 70.

674   *Timurtaş v. Turkey*, cited above, § 66.

contained military secrets. In the Government's opinion, the photocopy of the original document had been manipulated by the applicant to insert the name of his son. The Court stated in its judgment that the Government was in a pre-eminent position to assist the Commission by providing access to the document which it claimed was the genuine one; it was insufficient for the Government to rely on the allegedly secret nature of the document. In light of the respondent Government's failure to submit the original document, the Court drew an inference as to the well-foundedness of the applicant's allegations and accepted that the photocopied document was indeed a photocopy of the authentic post-operation report. Consequently, the Court found it established that the applicant's son had indeed been detained by the soldiers and had died in their custody.[675]

The approach adopted by the Court in the case of *Timurtaş* has become established practice, and the Court continues to draw inferences from the failures of respondent Governments to submit documents and other evidence as to the well-foundedness of applicants' allegations. Furthermore, on 13 December 2004 a new Rule was added to the Rules of Court in light of the approach adopted by the Court in *Timurtaş*.[676] According to this Rule:

> "[w]here a party fails to adduce evidence or provide information requested by the Court or to divulge relevant important information of its own motion or otherwise fails to participate effectively in the proceedings, the Court may draw such inferences as it deems appropriate".

It was not until the adoption of the judgment in the case of *Akkum and Others v. Turkey* on 31 May 2005 that a respondent Government's failure to cooperate with the Court by withholding relevant documents led the Court to shift the burden to that Government to disprove an applicant's allegations. This case, in so far as relevant, concerned the killing of two of the applicants' relatives in an area where a military operation had taken place, as well as the mutilation of the ears of one of those relatives. When the documents submitted by the parties proved insufficient to establish the facts of the case, the Commission held a fact-finding mission in Turkey and heard, *inter alia*, a number of military personnel who had taken part in the operation. Their testimonies made it clear that there existed another military report which was potentially capable of shedding light on the events in question but which the Government had not made available to the Commission. The Commission requested that the Government submit the report, but the Government failed to respond. The applicants, for their part, argued that in the circumstances of the case, the Government was required to provide a plausible explanation of

---

675   *Ibid.*, § 86.
676   Rule 44C of the Rules of Court.

how their relatives had been killed. In support of their arguments, they referred to the judgment of the Inter-American Court of Human Rights in the case of *Godinez Cruz v. Honduras*, in which that court held the following:

> "in proceedings to determine human rights violations the State cannot rely on the defense that the complainant has failed to present evidence when it cannot be obtained without the State's cooperation" (judgment of 20 January 1989, Inter-Am. Ct. H. R. Ser. C No. 5, § 141).

Moreover, the Human Rights Committee has also adopted a similar approach. The applicants referred to *Barbato v. Uruguay* (Human Rights Committee Communication No. 84, 1981, § 9.6), in which it had been considered that:

> "with regard to the burden of proof, the Committee has already established in other cases that the said burden cannot rest alone on the complainant, especially considering that the author and the State Party do not always have equal access to the evidence and that frequently the State Party has access to the relevant information".

The Court accepted the applicants' arguments and held that it was inappropriate to conclude that they had failed to submit sufficient evidence in support of their allegations, given that such evidence was in the hands of the respondent Government. The Court considered it legitimate to draw a parallel between the situation of detainees, for whose well-being the State is responsible,[677] and the situation of persons found injured or dead in an area within the exclusive control of the authorities of the State. According to the Court, that parallel was based on:

> "the salient fact that in both situations the events in issue lie wholly, or in large part, within the exclusive knowledge of the authorities. It is appropriate, therefore, that in cases such as the present one, where it is the non-disclosure by the Government of crucial documents in their exclusive possession which is preventing the Court from establishing the facts, it is for the Government either to argue conclusively why the documents in question cannot serve to corroborate the allegations made by the applicants, or to provide a satisfactory and convincing explanation of how the events in question occurred, failing which an issue under Article 2 and/or Article 3 of the Convention will arise".[678]

Observing that the Government had failed to make any argument from which it could be deduced that the documents withheld by them contained no information bearing on the applicants' claims, the Court went on to examine the investigation carried out at the national level in order to establish whether the respondent Government had discharged its burden. Having established that the domestic investigation was defective in many ways, the Court found that

---

677   See Section 11.5.1 above.
678   *Akkum and Others v. Turkey*, cited above, § 211.

the Government had failed to account for the killings and also for the mutilation of one of the bodies, in violation of Articles 2 and 3 of the Convention.

Similarly, in the case of *Çelikbilek v. Turkey*, the Court, referring to the *Akkum and Others* judgment, shifted the burden to the Government to prove that the documents it withheld could not serve to corroborate the applicant's allegations. In this case the applicant alleged that his brother had been taken into police custody and killed there. Despite the Commission's, and subsequently the Court's, numerous requests that the Government submit copies of the custody records to enable them to verify whether the applicant's brother had indeed been taken into custody, the Government failed to submit those records. The Court held:

> "in cases such as the present – where it is the non-disclosure by the Government of crucial documents in their possession which puts obstacles in the way of the Court's establishment of facts –, it is for the Government to argue conclusively why the documents in question cannot serve to corroborate the allegation made by the applicant".[679]

Noting that the Government had not presented any such arguments, the Court found that the applicant's brother had indeed been arrested and detained by agents of the State as alleged by the applicant. Noting further that no explanation had been put forward by the Government to explain the killing, the Court concluded that the Government had failed to account for the killing in violation of Article 2 of the Convention.[680]

The judgments in the cases of *Akkum and Others v. Turkey* and *Çelikbilek v. Turkey*, mentioned above, brought the Court's case-law in the area of burden of proof in line with the case-law of the Inter-American Court of Human Rights as well as that of the Human Rights Committee. In this connection, it must be pointed out that according to the Rules of Procedure of the Inter-American Commission on Human Rights:

> "[t]he facts alleged in the petition, the pertinent parts of which have been transmitted to the State in question, shall be presumed to be true if the State has not provided responsive information during the maximum period set by the Commission under the provisions of Article 38 of these Rules of Procedure, as long as other evidence does not lead to a different conclusion".[681]

It remains to be seen whether the Rules of Court in Strasbourg will be modified in the light of the Court's new approach to the burden of proof.

---

679   *Çelikbilek v. Turkey*, no. 27693/95, 31 May 2005, § 70.
680   *Ibid.*, §§ 71-72.
681   Article 39 of the Rules of Procedure of the Inter-American Commission on Human Rights.

11.5.3 Concluding Remarks

There is an understandable difficulty in obtaining evidence in ill-treatment cases. Because of the nature of ill-treatment, perpetrators are usually the only persons to witness it and they are therefore in a position to cover up their criminal actions. Such a cover-up will make it very difficult to establish the accuracy of allegations even if the authorities do have the will to investigate them. In certain circumstances, perhaps less frequent, perpetrators will not be deterred from ill-treating people publicly and will not even make attempts to cover up their actions because of the tolerance displayed by the authorities towards such actions. In such cases the authorities will not secure the evidence implicating State agents in the ill-treatment. Whatever the reasons, the fact remains that in most instances the victim will have difficulties supporting his or her case with "hard" evidence. It is in light of this fact that the Court's unique rules of evidence pertaining to the burden of proof must be examined. Burden-shifting compensates for the superior situation of a respondent Contracting Party *vis-à-vis* an individual and maximises the opportunity for the Court to establish the truth.

Needless to say, a respondent Government will not bear the burden of disproving each allegation of ill-treatment made against it. As pointed out elsewhere, the Court will have weeded out the frivolous allegations in its examination of the admissibility of an application. The rules discussed above relating to the burden of proof are employed by the Court only after it has decided that the allegations are not manifestly ill-founded. Furthermore, the Court will also require the applicant to be consistent in his or her allegations throughout the proceedings. For example, in the *Akkum and Others v. Turkey* and *Çelikbilek v. Turkey*, discussed above, the applicants were consistent in their allegations throughout the proceedings before the Convention institutions and did everything within their power to substantiate those allegations. These two cases can be contrasted with the case of *Toğcu v. Turkey*, which concerned the disappearance of the applicant's son after the latter had allegedly been detained by police officers. In his application form and later observations the applicant presented seriously contradictory versions of events leading up to his son's alleged detention by the police. The Government, for its part, failed to submit to the Court a number of important documents including custody records. The Court stated that it was faced with a situation in which it was unable to establish what had taken place and that this inability had emanated from, on the one hand, the contradictory information submitted by the applicant, and, on the other hand, the incomplete investigation file submitted by the Government. While noting the difficulties for an applicant to obtain the necessary evidence from the hands of the respondent Government, the Court concluded that to shift the burden of proof onto a respondent Government under circumstances similar to those in the case of *Akkum and Others* required by implication that the applicant have already made out a *prima facie* case. In light of the contradictory versions of events put forward by the applicant, the Court concluded that he failed to make out his case to the extent necessary for the burden to shift to the Government to explain that the documents withheld by them contained no relevant information concerning his son's disappearance.[682]

11.6 Standard of Proof

The Commission held in the *Greek Case* that the standard of proof it adopted when evaluating the material it had obtained was "proof beyond reasonable doubt".[683] This standard was also adopted by the Court in its judgment in the inter-State case of *Ireland v. the United Kingdom*, in which it stated the following:

> "...to assess [the] evidence, the Court adopts the standard of proof 'beyond reasonable doubt' but adds that such proof may follow from the coexistence of sufficiently strong, clear and concordant inferences or of similar unrebutted presumptions of fact. In this context, the conduct of the Parties when evidence is being obtained has to be taken into account".[684]

"Reasonable doubt" was explained by the Commission in the *Greek Case* in the following terms:

> "A reasonable doubt means not a doubt based on a merely theoretical possibility or raised in order to avoid a disagreeable conclusion, but a doubt for which reasons can be drawn from the facts presented".[685]

The high standard adopted by the Court has been the focus of intense criticism from a substantial number of the Court's own judges over the years. For example, eight of the seventeen judges of the Grand Chamber in the case of *Labita v. Italy* stated, *inter alia*, the following in their dissenting opinion:

> "The majority of the Court considered that the applicant has not proved 'beyond all reasonable doubt' that he was subjected to ill-treatment in Pianosa as he alleged. While we agree with the majority that the material produced by the applicant constitutes only prima facie evidence, we are nonetheless mindful of the difficulties which a prisoner who has suffered

---

682 *Toğcu v. Turkey*, cited above, §§ 96-97.
683 *The Greek Case*, Yearbook of the Convention, 1969, p. 196, § 30.
684 *Ireland v. the United Kingdom*, cited above, § 161.
685 § 30.

256

ill-treatment on the part of those responsible for guarding him may experience, and the risks he may run, if he denounces such treatment... We are accordingly of the view that the standard used for assessing the evidence in this case is inadequate, possibly illogical and even unworkable since, in the absence of an effective investigation, the applicant was prevented from obtaining evidence and the authorities even failed to identify the warders allegedly responsible for the ill-treatment complained of. If States may henceforth count on the Court's refraining in cases such as the instant one from examining the allegations of ill-treatment for want of sufficient evidence, they will have an interest in not investigating such allegations, thus depriving the applicant of proof 'beyond reasonable doubt'... Lastly, it should be borne in mind that the standard of proof 'beyond all reasonable doubt' is, in certain legal systems, used in criminal cases. However, this Court is not called upon to judge an individual's guilt or innocence or to punish those responsible for a violation; its task is to protect victims and provide redress for damage caused by the acts of the State responsible. The test, method and standard of proof in respect of responsibility under the Convention are different from those applicable in the various national systems as regards responsibility of individuals for criminal offences...".[686]

Similarly, Judge Bonello stated in his dissenting opinion in the case of *Sevtap Veznedaroğlu v. Turkey* that

"[p]roof 'beyond reasonable doubt' reflects a maximum standard relevant and desirable to establish *criminal* culpability. No person shall be judicially deprived of liberty, or otherwise penally censured, unless his guilt is manifest 'beyond reasonable doubt'. I subscribe to that stringent standard without hesitation. But in other fields of judicial enquiry, the standard of proof should be proportionate to the aim which the search for truth pursues: the highest degree of certainty, in criminal matters; a workable degree of probability in others... Confronted by conflicting versions, the Court is under an obligation to establish (1) on whom the law places the burden of proof, (2) whether any legal presumptions militate in favour of one of the opposing accounts, and (3) 'on a balance of probabilities', which of the conflicting versions appears to be more plausible and credible. Proof 'beyond reasonable doubt' can, in my view, only claim a spurious standing in 'civil' litigation, like the adversarial proceedings before this Court. In fact, to the best of my knowledge, the Court is the only tribunal in Europe that requires proof 'beyond reasonable doubt' in non-criminal matters".[687]

A review of the Court's case-law on the subject provides little guidance as to the nature of the "reasonable doubt" standard. However, the same review of the case-law reveals that in most cases the doubts which have prevented the Court from finding allegations to be substantiated were attributable to a lack of evidence which could only have been obtained with the cooperation of the

---

686   *Labita v. Italy* [GC], cited above.
687   *Sevtap Veznedaroğlu v. Turkey*, cited above.
688   See Erdal, pp. 73-79.

respondent Contracting Party.[688] It is submitted that the application of this criminal law standard adopted from common law legal systems, in isolation from a number of other principles in those legal systems which are intertwined with this standard, may not always result in the establishment of the true facts of a case. In this connection, three principles associated with the standard of proof in common law legal systems are relevant for the purposes of illustration. Firstly, in the legal systems where the standard of proof "beyond reasonable doubt" is employed, the burden of proving the guilt of the accused rests solely on the prosecution, and the accused person does not have to prove his or her innocence. This is not so in Convention proceedings: the applicant does not have the legal burden in its technical sense, and therefore the burden of proof continually shifts.[689]

The second prominent principle of the common law legal systems connected with the standard of proof "beyond reasonable doubt" is the defendant's right to silence. By virtue of this right, an accused person enjoys the freedom from compulsion to incriminate him or herself while at the same time enjoying the right not to have adverse inferences drawn from his or her silence. On the other hand, a respondent Government in Convention proceedings does not enjoy such freedoms. As pointed out above, Contracting Parties have obligations under Article 38 § 1 (a) of the Convention to furnish all necessary facilities to assist the Court in establishing the facts of cases. The failure of a respondent Government to cooperate with the Court may give rise to the drawing of inferences as to the well-foundedness of the applicant's allegations and, in certain circumstances, to the shifting of the burden to the Government.

Finally, the standard of proof "beyond reasonable doubt" is applied in conjunction with a rule of evidence whereby only the most relevant evidence is admissible. In Convention proceedings, on the other hand, no evidence is inadmissible, and therefore it is easy for the respondent party to create doubts in the minds of the Court's judges by adducing evidence which would be inadmissible in a court of law in common law legal systems.

The Court acknowledged the criticisms in its judgment of 6 July 2005 in the case of *Nachova and Others v. Bulgaria* and stated the following:

> "In assessing evidence, the Court has adopted the standard of proof 'beyond reasonable doubt'. However, it has never been its purpose to borrow the approach of the national legal systems that use that standard. Its role is not to rule on criminal guilt or civil liability but on Contracting

---

689   Both in the area of exhaustion of domestic remedies and in the area of establishment of facts as explained above in Sections 2.4.2 and 11.5, respectively.

States' responsibility under the Convention. The specificity of its task under Article 19 of the Convention – to ensure the observance by the Contracting States of their engagement to secure the fundamental rights enshrined in the Convention – conditions its approach to the issues of evidence and proof. In the proceedings before the Court, there are no procedural barriers to the admissibility of evidence or pre-determined formulae for its assessment. It adopts the conclusions that are, in its view, supported by the free evaluation of all evidence, including such inferences as may flow from the facts and the parties' submissions. According to its established case-law, proof may follow from the coexistence of sufficiently strong, clear and concordant inferences or of similar unrebutted presumptions of fact. Moreover, the level of persuasion necessary for reaching a particular conclusion and, in this connection, the distribution of the burden of proof are intrinsically linked to the specificity of the facts, the nature of the allegation made and the Convention right at stake. The Court is also attentive to the seriousness that attaches to a ruling that a Contracting State has violated fundamental rights".[690]

This new approach has already been followed in the judgment of 29 September 2005 in the case of *Mathew v. the Netherlands*, in which the Court added that the term "beyond reasonable doubt" has an autonomous meaning in the context of Convention proceedings.[691] However, the term remains undefined, and the Court has yet to state with precision the nature of the standard in Convention proceedings.

---

690   *Nachova and Others v. Bulgaria*, cited above, § 147.
691   *Mathew v. the Netherlands*, cited above, § 156.

BIBLIOGRAPHY

Alleweldt, R., *Schutz vor Abschiebung bei drohender Folter oder unmenschlicher oder erniedrigender Behandlung oder Strafe*, Springer, 1996

Aoláin, F.N., 'The European Convention on Human Rights and its Prohibition on Torture' in S. Levinson (ed.) *Torture*, Oxford University Press, 2004

Arai-Takahashi, Y., 'Uneven, But in the Direction of Enhanced Effectiveness – A Critical Analysis of "Anticipatory Ill-treatment" under Article 3 ECHR' (2002) 20 *Netherlands Quarterly of Human Rights*

Bassiouni, M.C., *Introduction to International Criminal Law*, Transnational Publishers, Inc., 2003

Erdal, U., 'Burden and Standard of Proof in Proceedings under the European Convention' (2001) 26 *EL Rev. Human Rights Survey*

Foley, C., *Combating Torture Handbook: A Manual for Judges and Prosecutors*, Human Rights Centre of the University of Essex, 2003

Giffard, C., *The Torture Reporting Handbook: How to document and respond to allegations of torture within the international system for the protection of human rights*, Human Rights Centre of the University of Essex, 2000

Giffard, C. and Rodley, N., 'The Approach of International Tribunals to Medical Evidence in Cases Involving Allegations of Torture' in M. Peel and V. Iacopino (eds.) *The Medical Documentation of Torture*, Greenwich Medical Media Limited, 2002

Harris, D.J., O'Boyle, M. and Warbrick C., *Law of the European Convention on Human Rights*, Butterworths, 1995

Janis, M., Kay, R. and Bradley, A., *European Human Rights Law Text and Materials*, Oxford University Press, 1995

Jones, D. R. and Smith, S. V., 'Medical Evidence in Asylum and Human Rights Appeals' (2004) 16/3 *International Journal of Refugee Law*

Leach, P., *Taking a Case to the European Court of Human Rights*, 2nd edn, Oxford University Press, 2005

Mahoney, P., 'Determination and Evaluation of Facts in Proceedings Before the Present and Future European Court of Human Rights' in S. Busutill (ed.), *Mainly Human Rights: Studies in Honour of J. J. Cremona*, Fondation Internationale Malte, 1999

Myjer, E., Mol, N., Kempees, P., van Steijn, A. and Bockwinkel, J., 'Introduire une plainte auprès de la Cour européenne des Droits de d'Homme: onze malentendus fréquents', in *Annales du droit luxembourgeois,* No. 14(2004), Bruyland, Bruxelles, 2005, p. 11 *et seq.*

Mole, N., '*Issa v. Turkey*: Delineating the Extra-territorial Effect of the European Convention on Human Rights' (2005) 1 *E.H.R.L.R.*

Mowbray, A. R., *The development of positive obligations under the European Convention on Human Rights by the European Court of Human Rights,* Oxford, 2004

O'Boyle, M., 'Comment on Life after Bankovic', in F. Coomans and M.T. Kamminga (eds.), *Extraterritorial Application of Human Rights Treaties,* Intersentia Antwerp-Oxford, 2004

Ovey, C. & White, R.C.A., *Jacobs & White: The European Convention on Human Rights,* 3rd edn, Oxford University Press, 2002

Peel, M. and Iacopino, V. (eds.) *The Medical Documentation of Torture,* Greenwich Medical Media Limited, 2002

Reid, K., *A Practitioner's Guide to the European Convention on Human Rights,* 2nd edn, Sweet and Maxwell, 2004

Rodley, N. S., 'The Definition(s) of Torture in International Law' (2002) 55 *Cur'nt Leg. Probs.* 467

Suntinger, W., 'The Principle of Non-Refoulement: Looking Rather to Geneva than to Strasbourg?' (1995) 49 *Austrian J. Public Intl.* 203

Uildriks, N., 'Police Torture in France' (1999)17 *Netherlands Quarterly of Human Rights*

van Dijk, P. and van Hoof, G.J.H., *Theory and Practice of the European Convention on Human Rights,* Kluwer Law International, 1998

INDEX

A

abuse of the right of application *see* **Admissibility Criteria**

Admissibility

      chamber decisions of   6.1, 6.2

      consequences of   6.3, 6.4

      decisions of   4.4, 6.1

      estoppel   2.4.1, 2.4.2

      Government's objections joined to the merits of the case 6.2

      joint procedure   1.7, 1.7.3, 5.1, 5.2, 8.1.1, 9.1

      procedure   1.7, 1.14, 2.1, 2.4.1, 4.4, 5.2, 6.1

Admissibility Criteria

      abuse of the right of application   2.7

      anonymous applications   2.8

      applications 'substantially the same as matter already examined by the Court'   2.9

      applications 'already submitted to another procedure of international investigation or settlement'   2.9

      compatibility *see* Compatibility of Applications

      exhaustion *see* Exhaustion of Domestic Remedies

      manifestly ill-founded   2.6 6.1

      six-month *see* Six-Month Rule

advisory opinions *see* **Grand Chamber**

anonymous applications *see* **Admissibility Criteria**

application form   1.7.1, 1.8, 1.10, 2.8, 3.1.3, 4.1, 4.2, 4.3, 7.2, Appendix 4

      arrest and interrogation   2.6.3, 10.2.1, 11.4.1, 11.5.1, 11.5.2,

Article 3

      absolute nature   10.1, 10.2, Appendix 10

      degrading treatment and punishment   2.6.2, 2.6.3 (a), 7.2.1, Appendix 10

      inhuman treatment and punishment   2.6.2, 2.6.3 (a), 7.2.1, Appendix 10

      terrorism   2.6.2 (b), 10.2, 11.4.4

      torture   2.6.2 (b), 2.6.3, 10.2, Appendix 10

      victim's behaviour, relevance of   2.6.3, 10.2.1

B

Blindfolding   2.6.3 (e)

Burden of Proof

About the Authors

Uğur Erdal (LL.B. (Hons.) in English Law and LL.M. in International Human Rights Law, from the University of Essex in the United Kingdom; BA in Turkish Law, from the University of Dokuz Eylül in Izmir, Turkey) is a lawyer at the Council of Europe.

Hasan Bakırcı (LL.B. in Turkish Law and LL.M (distinction) in Public Law, from the University of Marmara in Istanbul, Turkey; Mst (distinction) in International Human Rights Law, from the University of Oxford, in the United Kingdom) worked as a case lawyer at the Secretariat of the European Commission of Human Rights between 1996 and 1998. He has been working at the Registry of the European Court of Human Rights since November 1998. He is a human rights lawyer and lectures in various Universities in Turkey as well as at training seminars in a number of Council of Europe member States.

APPENDICES

Council of Europe
Conseil de l'Europe

Convention for the Protection
of Human Rights
and Fundamental Freedoms
as amended by Protocol No. 11

with Protocol Nos. 1, 4, 6, 7, 12 and 13

The text of the Convention had been amended according to the provisions of Protocol No. 3 (ETS No. 45), which entered into force on 21 September 1970, of Protocol No. 5 (ETS No. 55), which entered into force on 20 December 1971 and of Protocol No. 8 (ETS No. 118), which entered into force on 1 January 1990, and comprised also the text of Protocol No. 2 (ETS No. 44) which, in accordance with Article 5, paragraph 3 thereof, had been an integral part of the Convention since its entry into force on 21 September 1970. All provisions which had been amended or added by these Protocols are replaced by Protocol No. 11 (ETS No. 155), as from the date of its entry into force on 1 November 1998. As from that date, Protocol No. 9 (ETS No. 140), which entered into force on 1 October 1994, is repealed.

Registry of the European Court of Human Rights
September 2003

Convention for the Protection of Human Rights and Fundamental Freedoms

Rome, 4.XI.1950

The governments signatory hereto, being members of the Council of Europe,

Considering the Universal Declaration of Human Rights proclaimed by the General Assembly of the United Nations on 10th December 1948;

Considering that this Declaration aims at securing the universal and effective recognition and observance of the Rights therein declared;

Considering that the aim of the Council of Europe is the achievement of greater unity between its members and that one of the methods by which that aim is to be pursued is the maintenance and further realisation of human rights and fundamental freedoms;

Reaffirming their profound belief in those fundamental freedoms which are the foundation of justice and peace in the world and are best maintained on the one hand by an effective political democracy and on the other by a common understanding and observance of the human rights upon which they depend;

Being resolved, as the governments of European countries which are like-minded and have a common heritage of political traditions, ideals, freedom and the rule of law, to take the first steps for the collective enforcement of certain of the rights stated in the Universal Declaration,

Have agreed as follows:

Article 1 – Obligation to respect human rights

The High Contracting Parties shall secure to everyone within their jurisdiction the rights and freedoms defined in Section I of this Convention.

SECTION I – RIGHTS AND FREEDOMS

Article 2 – Right to life

1   Everyone's right to life shall be protected by law. No one shall be deprived of his life intentionally save in the execution of a sentence of a court following his conviction of a crime for which this penalty is provided by law.

2   Deprivation of life shall not be regarded as inflicted in contravention of this article when it results from the use of force which is no more than absolutely necessary:

   a   in defence of any person from unlawful violence;

   b   in order to effect a lawful arrest or to prevent the escape of a person lawfully detained;

   c   in action lawfully taken for the purpose of quelling a riot or insurrection.

Article 3 – Prohibition of torture

No one shall be subjected to torture or to inhuman or degrading treatment or punishment.

Article 4 – Prohibition of slavery and forced labour

1   No one shall be held in slavery or servitude.

2   No one shall be required to perform forced or compulsory labour.

3   For the purpose of this article the term "forced or compulsory labour" shall not include:

   a   any work required to be done in the ordinary course of detention imposed according to the provisions of Article 5 of this Convention or during conditional release from such detention;

   b   any service of a military character or, in case of conscientious objectors in countries where they are recognised, service exacted instead of compulsory military service;

c   any service exacted in case of an emergency or calamity threatening the life or well-being of the community;

d   any work or service which forms part of normal civic obligations.

Article 5 – Right to liberty and security

1   Everyone has the right to liberty and security of person. No one shall be deprived of his liberty save in the following cases and in accordance with a procedure prescribed by law:

a   the lawful detention of a person after conviction by a competent court;

b   the lawful arrest or detention of a person for non-compliance with the lawful order of a court or in order to secure the fulfilment of any obligation prescribed by law;

c   the lawful arrest or detention of a person effected for the purpose of bringing him before the competent legal authority on reasonable suspicion of having committed an offence or when it is reasonably considered necessary to prevent his committing an offence or fleeing after having done so;

d   the detention of a minor by lawful order for the purpose of educational supervision or his lawful detention for the purpose of bringing him before the competent legal authority;

e   the lawful detention of persons for the prevention of the spreading of infectious diseases, of persons of unsound mind, alcoholics or drug addicts or vagrants;

f   the lawful arrest or detention of a person to prevent his effecting an unauthorised entry into the country or of a person against whom action is being taken with a view to deportation or extradition.

2   Everyone who is arrested shall be informed promptly, in a language which he understands, of the reasons for his arrest and of any charge against him.

3   Everyone arrested or detained in accordance with the provisions of paragraph 1.c of this article shall be brought promptly before a judge or other officer authorised by law to exercise judicial power and shall be entitled to trial within a reasonable time or to release pending trial. Release may be conditioned by guarantees to appear for trial.

4   Everyone who is deprived of his liberty by arrest or detention shall be entitled to take proceedings by which the lawfulness of his detention shall be decided speedily by a court and his release ordered if the detention is not lawful.

5   Everyone who has been the victim of arrest or detention in contravention of the provisions of this article shall have an enforceable right to compensation.

Article 6 – Right to a fair trial

1   In the determination of his civil rights and obligations or of any criminal charge against him, everyone is entitled to a fair and public hearing within a reasonable time by an independent and impartial tribunal established by law. Judgment shall be pronounced publicly but the press and public may be excluded from all or part of the trial in the interests of morals, public order or national security in a democratic society, where the interests of juveniles or the protection of the private life of the parties so require, or to the extent strictly necessary in the opinion of the court in special circumstances where publicity would prejudice the interests of justice.

2   Everyone charged with a criminal offence shall be presumed innocent until proved guilty according to law.

3   Everyone charged with a criminal offence has the following minimum rights:

a   to be informed promptly, in a language which he understands and in detail, of the nature and cause of the accusation against him;

b   to have adequate time and facilities for the preparation of his defence;

c   to defend himself in person or through legal assistance of his own choosing or, if he has not sufficient means to pay for legal assistance, to be given it free when the interests of justice so require;

d   to examine or have examined witnesses against him and to obtain the attendance and examination of witnesses on his behalf under the same conditions as witnesses against him;

e   to have the free assistance of an interpreter if he cannot understand or speak the language used in court.

Article 7 – No punishment without law

1   No one shall be held guilty of any criminal offence on account of any act or omission which did not constitute a criminal offence under national or international law at the time when it was committed. Nor shall a heavier penalty be imposed than the one that was applicable at the time the criminal offence was committed.

2   This article shall not prejudice the trial and punishment of any person for any act or omission which, at the time when it was committed, was criminal according to the general principles of law recognised by civilised nations.

Article 8 – Right to respect for private and family life

1   Everyone has the right to respect for his private and family life, his home and his correspondence.

2   There shall be no interference by a public authority with the exercise of this right except such as is in accordance with the law and is necessary in a democratic society in the interests of national security, public safety or the economic well-being of the country, for the prevention of disorder or crime, for the protection of health or morals, or for the protection of the rights and freedoms of others.

Article 9 – Freedom of thought, conscience and religion

1   Everyone has the right to freedom of thought, conscience and religion; this right includes freedom to change his religion or belief and freedom, either alone or in community with others and in public or private, to manifest his religion or belief, in worship, teaching, practice and observance.

2   Freedom to manifest one's religion or beliefs shall be subject only to such limitations as are prescribed by law and are necessary in a democratic society in the interests of public safety, for the protection of public order, health or morals, or for the protection of the rights and freedoms of others.

Article 10 – Freedom of expression

1   Everyone has the right to freedom of expression. This right shall include freedom to hold opinions and to receive and impart information and ideas without interference by public authority and regardless of frontiers. This article shall not prevent States from requiring the licensing of broadcasting, television or cinema enterprises.

2   The exercise of these freedoms, since it carries with it duties and responsibilities, may be subject to such formalities, conditions, restrictions or penalties as are prescribed by law and are necessary in a democratic society, in the interests of national security, territorial integrity or public safety, for the prevention of disorder or crime, for the protection of health or morals, for the protection of the reputation or rights of others, for preventing the disclosure of information received in confidence, or for maintaining the authority and impartiality of the judiciary.

Article 11 – Freedom of assembly and association

1   Everyone has the right to freedom of peaceful assembly and to freedom of association with others, including the right to form and to join trade unions for the protection of his interests.

2   No restrictions shall be placed on the exercise of these rights other than such as are prescribed by law and are necessary in a democratic society in the interests of national security or public safety, for the prevention of disorder or crime, for the protection of health or morals or for the protection of the rights and freedoms of others. This article shall not prevent the imposition of lawful restrictions on the exercise of these rights by members of the armed forces, of the police or of the administration of the State.

Article 12 – Right to marry

Men and women of marriageable age have the right to marry and to found a family, according to the national laws governing the exercise of this right.

Article 13 – Right to an effective remedy

Everyone whose rights and freedoms as set forth in this Convention are violated shall have an effective remedy before a national authority notwithstanding that the violation has been committed by persons acting in an official capacity.

Article 14 – Prohibition of discrimination

The enjoyment of the rights and freedoms set forth in this Convention shall be secured without discrimination on any ground such as sex, race, colour, language, religion, political or other opinion, national or social origin, association with a national minority, property, birth or other status.

Article 15 – Derogation in time of emergency

1   In time of war or other public emergency threatening the life of the nation any High Contracting Party may take measures derogating from its obligations under this Convention to the extent strictly required by the exigencies of the situation, provided that such measures are not inconsistent with its other obligations under international law.

2   No derogation from Article 2, except in respect of deaths resulting from lawful acts of war, or from Articles 3, 4 (paragraph 1) and 7 shall be made under this provision.

3   Any High Contracting Party availing itself of this right of derogation shall keep the Secretary General of the Council of Europe fully informed of the measures which it has taken and the reasons therefor. It shall also inform the Secretary General of the Council of Europe when such measures have ceased to operate and the provisions of the Convention are again being fully executed.

Article 16 – Restrictions on political activity of aliens

Nothing in Articles 10, 11 and 14 shall be regarded as preventing the High Contracting Parties from imposing restrictions on the political activity of aliens.

Article 17 – Prohibition of abuse of rights

Nothing in this Convention may be interpreted as implying for any State, group or person any right to engage in any activity or perform any act aimed at the destruction of any of the rights and freedoms set forth herein or at their limitation to a greater extent than is provided for in the Convention.

Article 18 – Limitation on use of restrictions on rights

The restrictions permitted under this Convention to the said rights and freedoms shall not be applied for any purpose other than those for which they have been prescribed.

SECTION II – EUROPEAN COURT OF HUMAN RIGHTS

Article 19 – Establishment of the Court

To ensure the observance of the engagements undertaken by the High Contracting Parties in the Convention and the Protocols thereto, there shall be set up a European Court of Human Rights, hereinafter referred to as «the Court». It shall function on a permanent basis.

Article 20 – Number of judges

The Court shall consist of a number of judges equal to that of the High Contracting Parties.

Article 21 – Criteria for office

1   The judges shall be of high moral character and must either possess the qualifications required for appointment to high judicial office or be jurisconsults of recognised competence.

2   The judges shall sit on the Court in their individual capacity.

3   During their term of office the judges shall not engage in any activity which is incompatible with their independence, impartiality or with the demands of a full-time office; all questions arising from the application of this paragraph shall be decided by the Court.

Article 22 – Election of judges

1   The judges shall be elected by the Parliamentary Assembly with respect to each High Contracting Party by a majority of votes cast from a list of three candidates nominated by the High Contracting Party.

2   The same procedure shall be followed to complete the Court in the event of the accession of new High Contracting Parties and in filling casual vacancies.

Article 23 – Terms of office

1   The judges shall be elected for a period of six years. They may be re-elected. However, the terms of office of one-half of the judges elected at the first election shall expire at the end of three years.

2   The judges whose terms of office are to expire at the end of the initial period of three years shall be chosen by lot by the Secretary General of the Council of Europe immediately after their election.

3   In order to ensure that, as far as possible, the terms of office of one-half of the judges are renewed every three years, the Parliamentary Assembly may decide, before proceeding to any subsequent election, that the term or terms of office of one or more judges to be elected shall be for a period other than six years but not more than nine and not less than three years.

4   In cases where more than one term of office is involved and where the Parliamentary Assembly applies the preceding paragraph, the allocation of the terms of office shall be effected by a drawing of lots by the Secretary General of the Council of Europe immediately after the election.

5   A judge elected to replace a judge whose term of office has not expired shall hold office for the remainder of his predecessor's term.

6   The terms of office of judges shall expire when they reach the age of 70.

7   The judges shall hold office until replaced. They shall, however, continue to deal with such cases as they already have under consideration.

Article 24 – Dismissal

No judge may be dismissed from his office unless the other judges decide by a majority of two-thirds that he has ceased to fulfil the required conditions.

Article 25 – Registry and legal secretaries

The Court shall have a registry, the functions and organisation of which shall be laid down in the rules of the Court. The Court shall be assisted by legal secretaries.

Article 26 – Plenary Court

The plenary Court shall

a   elect its President and one or two Vice-Presidents for a period of three years; they may be re-elected;

b   set up Chambers, constituted for a fixed period of time;

c   elect the Presidents of the Chambers of the Court; they may be re-elected;

d   adopt the rules of the Court, and

e   elect the Registrar and one or more Deputy Registrars.

Article 27 – Committees, Chambers and Grand Chamber

1   To consider cases brought before it, the Court shall sit in committees of three judges, in Chambers of seven judges and in a Grand Chamber of seventeen judges. The Court's Chambers shall set up committees for a fixed period of time.

2   There shall sit as an ex officio member of the Chamber and the Grand Chamber the judge elected in respect of the State Party concerned or, if there is none or if he is unable to sit, a person of its choice who shall sit in the capacity of judge.

3   The Grand Chamber shall also include the President of the Court, the Vice-Presidents, the Presidents of the Chambers and other judges chosen in accordance with the rules of the Court. When a case is referred to the Grand Chamber under Article 43, no judge from the Chamber which rendered the judgment shall sit in the Grand Chamber, with the exception of the President of the Chamber and the judge who sat in respect of the State Party concerned.

Article 28 – Declarations of inadmissibility by committees

A committee may, by a unanimous vote, declare inadmissible or strike out of its list of cases an application submitted under Article 34 where such a decision can be taken without further examination. The decision shall be final.

Article 29 – Decisions by Chambers on admissibility and merits

1   If no decision is taken under Article 28, a Chamber shall decide on the admissibility and merits of individual applications submitted under Article 34.

2   A Chamber shall decide on the admissibility and merits of inter-State applications submitted under Article 33.

3   The decision on admissibility shall be taken separately unless the Court, in exceptional cases, decides otherwise.

Article 30 – Relinquishment of jurisdiction to the Grand Chamber

Where a case pending before a Chamber raises a serious question affecting the interpretation of the Convention or the protocols thereto, or where the resolution of a question before the Chamber might have a result inconsistent with a judgment previously delivered by the Court, the Chamber may, at any time before it has rendered its judgment, relinquish jurisdiction in favour of the Grand Chamber, unless one of the parties to the case objects.

Article 31 – Powers of the Grand Chamber

The Grand Chamber shall

a   determine applications submitted either under Article 33 or Article 34 when a Chamber has relinquished jurisdiction under Article 30 or when the case has been referred to it under Article 43; and

b   consider requests for advisory opinions submitted under Article 47.

Article 32 – Jurisdiction of the Court

1   The jurisdiction of the Court shall extend to all matters concerning the interpretation and application of the Convention and the protocols thereto which are referred to it as provided in Articles 33, 34 and 47.

2   In the event of dispute as to whether the Court has jurisdiction, the Court shall decide.

Article 33 – Inter-State cases

Any High Contracting Party may refer to the Court any alleged breach of the provisions of the Convention and the protocols thereto by another High Contracting Party.

Article 34 – Individual applications

The Court may receive applications from any person, non-governmental organisation or group of individuals claiming to be the victim of a violation by one of the High Contracting Parties of the rights set forth in the Convention or the protocols thereto. The High Contracting Parties undertake not to hinder in any way the effective exercise of this right.

Article 35 – Admissibility criteria

1   The Court may only deal with the matter after all domestic remedies have been exhausted, according to the generally recognised rules of international law, and within a period of six months from the date on which the final decision was taken.

2   The Court shall not deal with any application submitted under Article 34 that

   a   is anonymous; or

   b   is substantially the same as a matter that has already been examined by the Court or has already been submitted to another procedure of international investigation or settlement and contains no relevant new information.

3   The Court shall declare inadmissible any individual application submitted under Article 34 which it considers incompatible with the provisions of the Convention or the protocols thereto, manifestly ill-founded, or an abuse of the right of application.

4   The Court shall reject any application which it considers inadmissible under this Article. It may do so at any stage of the proceedings.

Article 36 – Third party intervention

1   In all cases before a Chamber or the Grand Chamber, a High Contracting Party one of whose nationals is an applicant shall have the right to submit written comments and to take part in hearings.

2   The President of the Court may, in the interest of the proper administration of justice, invite any High Contracting Party which is not a party to the proceedings or any person concerned who is not the applicant to submit written comments or take part in hearings.

Article 37 – Striking out applications

1   The Court may at any stage of the proceedings decide to strike an application out of its list of cases where the circumstances lead to the conclusion that

a   the applicant does not intend to pursue his application; or

b   the matter has been resolved; or

c   for any other reason established by the Court, it is no longer justified to continue the examination of the application.

However, the Court shall continue the examination of the application if respect for human rights as defined in the Convention and the protocols thereto so requires.

2   The Court may decide to restore an application to its list of cases if it considers that the circumstances justify such a course.

Article 38 – Examination of the case and friendly settlement proceedings

1   If the Court declares the application admissible, it shall

a   pursue the examination of the case, together with the representatives of the parties, and if need be, undertake an investigation, for the effective conduct of which the States concerned shall furnish all necessary facilities;

b place itself at the disposal of the parties concerned with a view to securing a friendly settlement of the matter on the basis of respect for human rights as defined in the Convention and the protocols thereto.

2 Proceedings conducted under paragraph 1.b shall be confidential.

Article 39 – Finding of a friendly settlement

If a friendly settlement is effected, the Court shall strike the case out of its list by means of a decision which shall be confined to a brief statement of the facts and of the solution reached.

Article 40 – Public hearings and access to documents

1 Hearings shall be in public unless the Court in exceptional circumstances decides otherwise.

2 Documents deposited with the Registrar shall be accessible to the public unless the President of the Court decides otherwise.

Article 41 – Just satisfaction

If the Court finds that there has been a violation of the Convention or the protocols thereto, and if the internal law of the High Contracting Party concerned allows only partial reparation to be made, the Court shall, if necessary, afford just satisfaction to the injured party.

Article 42 – Judgments of Chambers

Judgments of Chambers shall become final in accordance with the provisions of Article 44, paragraph 2.

Article 43 – Referral to the Grand Chamber

1 Within a period of three months from the date of the judgment of the Chamber, any party to the case may, in exceptional cases, request that the case be referred to the Grand Chamber.

2 A panel of five judges of the Grand Chamber shall accept the request if the case raises a serious question affecting the interpretation or application of the Convention or the protocols thereto, or a serious issue of general importance.

3   If the panel accepts the request, the Grand Chamber shall decide the case by means of a judgment.

Article 44 – Final judgments

1   The judgment of the Grand Chamber shall be final.

2   The judgment of a Chamber shall become final

a   when the parties declare that they will not request that the case be referred to the Grand Chamber; or

b   three months after the date of the judgment, if reference of the case to the Grand Chamber has not been requested; or

c   when the panel of the Grand Chamber rejects the request to refer under Article 43.

3   The final judgment shall be published.

Article 45 – Reasons for judgments and decisions

1   Reasons shall be given for judgments as well as for decisions declaring applications admissible or inadmissible.

2   If a judgment does not represent, in whole or in part, the unanimous opinion of the judges, any judge shall be entitled to deliver a separate opinion.

Article 46 – Binding force and execution of judgments

1   The High Contracting Parties undertake to abide by the final judgment of the Court in any case to which they are parties.

2   The final judgment of the Court shall be transmitted to the Committee of Ministers, which shall supervise its execution.

Article 47 – Advisory opinions

1   The Court may, at the request of the Committee of Ministers, give advisory opinions on legal questions concerning the interpretation of the Convention and the protocols thereto.

2   Such opinions shall not deal with any question relating to the content or scope of the rights or freedoms defined in Section I of the Convention and the protocols thereto, or with any other question which the Court or the Committee of Ministers might have to consider in consequence of any such proceedings as could be instituted in accordance with the Convention.

3   Decisions of the Committee of Ministers to request an advisory opinion of the Court shall require a majority vote of the representatives entitled to sit on the Committee.

Article 48 – Advisory jurisdiction of the Court

The Court shall decide whether a request for an advisory opinion submitted by the Committee of Ministers is within its competence as defined in Article 47.

Article 49 – Reasons for advisory opinions

1   Reasons shall be given for advisory opinions of the Court.

2   If the advisory opinion does not represent, in whole or in part, the unanimous opinion of the judges, any judge shall be entitled to deliver a separate opinion.

3   Advisory opinions of the Court shall be communicated to the Committee of Ministers.

Article 50 – Expenditure on the Court

The expenditure on the Court shall be borne by the Council of Europe.

Article 51 – Privileges and immunities of judges

The judges shall be entitled, during the exercise of their functions, to the privileges and immunities provided for in Article 40 of the Statute of the Council of Europe and in the agreements made thereunder.

SECTION III – MISCELLANEOUS PROVISIONS

Article 52 – Inquiries by the Secretary General

On receipt of a request from the Secretary General of the Council of Europe any High Contracting Party shall furnish an explanation of the manner in which its internal law ensures the effective implementation of any of the provisions of the Convention.

Article 53 – Safeguard for existing human rights

Nothing in this Convention shall be construed as limiting or derogating from any of the human rights and fundamental freedoms which may be ensured under the laws of any High Contracting Party or under any other agreement to which it is a Party.

Article 54 – Powers of the Committee of Ministers

Nothing in this Convention shall prejudice the powers conferred on the Committee of Ministers by the Statute of the Council of Europe.

Article 55 – Exclusion of other means of dispute settlement

The High Contracting Parties agree that, except by special agreement, they will not avail themselves of treaties, conventions or declarations in force between them for the purpose of submitting, by way of petition, a dispute arising out of the interpretation or application of this Convention to a means of settlement other than those provided for in this Convention.

Article 56 – Territorial application

1   Any State may at the time of its ratification or at any time thereafter declare by notification addressed to the Secretary General of the Council of Europe that the present Convention shall, subject to paragraph 4 of this Article, extend to all or any of the territories for whose international relations it is responsible.

2   The Convention shall extend to the territory or territories named in the notification as from the thirtieth day after the receipt of this notification by the Secretary General of the Council of Europe.

3   The provisions of this Convention shall be applied in such territories with due regard, however, to local requirements.

4   Any State which has made a declaration in accordance with paragraph 1 of this article may at any time thereafter declare on behalf of one or more of the territories to which the declaration relates that it accepts the competence of the Court to receive applications from individuals, non-governmental organisations or groups of individuals as provided by Article 34 of the Convention.

Article 57 – Reservations

1   Any State may, when signing this Convention or when depositing its instrument of ratification, make a reservation in respect of any particular provision of the Convention to the extent that any law then in force in its territory is not in conformity with the provision. Reservations of a general character shall not be permitted under this article.

2   Any reservation made under this article shall contain a brief statement of the law concerned.

Article 58 – Denunciation

1   A High Contracting Party may denounce the present Convention only after the expiry of five years from the date on which it became a party to it and after six months' notice contained in a notification addressed to the Secretary General of the Council of Europe, who shall inform the other High Contracting Parties.

2   Such a denunciation shall not have the effect of releasing the High Contracting Party concerned from its obligations under this Convention in respect of any act which, being capable of constituting a violation of such obligations, may have been performed by it before the date at which the denunciation became effective.

3   Any High Contracting Party which shall cease to be a member of the Council of Europe shall cease to be a Party to this Convention under the same conditions.

4   The Convention may be denounced in accordance with the provisions of the preceding paragraphs in respect of any territory to which it has been declared to extend under the terms of Article 56.

Article 59 – Signature and ratification

1   This Convention shall be open to the signature of the members of the Council of Europe. It shall be ratified. Ratifications shall be deposited with the Secretary General of the Council of Europe.

2   The present Convention shall come into force after the deposit of ten instruments of ratification.

3   As regards any signatory ratifying subsequently, the Convention shall come into force at the date of the deposit of its instrument of ratification.

4   The Secretary General of the Council of Europe shall notify all the members of the Council of Europe of the entry into force of the Convention, the names of the High Contracting Parties who have ratified it, and the deposit of all instruments of ratification which may be effected subsequently.

     Done at Rome this 4th day of November 1950, in English and French, both texts being equally authentic, in a single copy which shall remain deposited in the archives of the Council of Europe. The Secretary General shall transmit certified copies to each of the signatories.

Protocol to the Convention for the Protection of Human Rights and Fundamental Freedoms

Paris, 20.III.1952

The governments signatory hereto, being members of the Council of Europe,

Being resolved to take steps to ensure the collective enforcement of certain rights and freedoms other than those already included in Section I of the Convention for the Protection of Human Rights and Fundamental Freedoms signed at Rome on 4 November 1950 (hereinafter referred to as "the Convention"),

Have agreed as follows:

Article 1 – Protection of property

Every natural or legal person is entitled to the peaceful enjoyment of his possessions. No one shall be deprived of his possessions except in the public interest and subject to the conditions provided for by law and by the general principles of international law.

The preceding provisions shall not, however, in any way impair the right of a State to enforce such laws as it deems necessary to control the use of property in accordance with the general interest or to secure the payment of taxes or other contributions or penalties.

Article 2 – Right to education

No person shall be denied the right to education. In the exercise of any functions which it assumes in relation to education and to teaching, the State shall respect the right of parents to ensure such education and teaching in conformity with their own religious and philosophical convictions.

Article 3 – Right to free elections

The High Contracting Parties undertake to hold free elections at reasonable intervals by secret ballot, under conditions which will ensure the free expression of the opinion of the people in the choice of the legislature.

Article 4 – Territorial application

Any High Contracting Party may at the time of signature or ratification or at any time thereafter communicate to the Secretary General of the Council of Europe a declaration stating the extent to which it undertakes that the provisions of the present Protocol shall apply to such of the territories for the international relations of which it is responsible as are named therein.

Any High Contracting Party which has communicated a declaration in virtue of the preceding paragraph may from time to time communicate a further declaration modifying the terms of any former declaration or terminating the application of the provisions of this Protocol in respect of any territory.

A declaration made in accordance with this article shall be deemed to have been made in accordance with paragraph 1 of Article 56 of the Convention.

Article 5 – Relationship to the Convention

As between the High Contracting Parties the provisions of Articles 1, 2, 3 and 4 of this Protocol shall be regarded as additional articles to the Convention and all the provisions of the Convention shall apply accordingly.

Article 6 – Signature and ratification

This Protocol shall be open for signature by the members of the Council of Europe, who are the signatories of the Convention; it shall be ratified at the same time as or after the ratification of the Convention. It shall enter into force after the deposit of ten instruments of ratification. As regards any signatory ratifying subsequently, the Protocol shall enter into force at the date of the deposit of its instrument of ratification.

The instruments of ratification shall be deposited with the Secretary General of the Council of Europe, who will notify all members of the names of those who have ratified.

Done at Paris on the 20th day of March 1952, in English and French, both texts being equally authentic, in a single copy which shall remain deposited in the archives of the Council of Europe. The Secretary General shall transmit certified copies to each of the signatory governments.

Protocol No. 4 to the Convention for the Protection of Human Rights and Fundamental Freedoms securing certain rights and freedoms other than those already included in the Convention and in the first Protocol thereto

Strasbourg, 16.IX.1963

The governments signatory hereto, being members of the Council of Europe,

Being resolved to take steps to ensure the collective enforcement of certain rights and freedoms other than those already included in Section I of the Convention for the Protection of Human Rights and Fundamental Freedoms signed at Rome on 4th November 1950 (hereinafter referred to as the "Convention") and in Articles 1 to 3 of the First Protocol to the Convention, signed at Paris on 20th March 1952,

Have agreed as follows:

Article 1 – Prohibition of imprisonment for debt

No one shall be deprived of his liberty merely on the ground of inability to fulfil a contractual obligation.

Article 2 – Freedom of movement

1   Everyone lawfully within the territory of a State shall, within that territory, have the right to liberty of movement and freedom to choose his residence.

2   Everyone shall be free to leave any country, including his own.

3   No restrictions shall be placed on the exercise of these rights other than such as are in accordance with law and are necessary in a democratic society in the interests of national security or public safety, for the maintenance of ordre public, for the prevention of crime, for the protection of health or morals, or for the protection of the rights and freedoms of others.

4   The rights set forth in paragraph 1 may also be subject, in particular areas, to restrictions imposed in accordance with law and justified by the public interest in a democratic society.

Article 3 – Prohibition of expulsion of nationals

1   No one shall be expelled, by means either of an individual or of a collective measure, from the territory of the State of which he is a national.

2   No one shall be deprived of the right to enter the territory of the state of which he is a national.

Article 4 – Prohibition of collective expulsion of aliens

Collective expulsion of aliens is prohibited.

Article 5 – Territorial application

1   Any High Contracting Party may, at the time of signature or ratification of this Protocol, or at any time thereafter, communicate to the Secretary General of the Council of Europe a declaration stating the extent to which it undertakes that the provisions of this Protocol shall apply to such of the territories for the international relations of which it is responsible as are named therein.

2   Any High Contracting Party which has communicated a declaration in virtue of the preceding paragraph may, from time to time, communicate a further declaration modifying the terms of any former declaration or terminating the application of the provisions of this Protocol in respect of any territory.

3   A declaration made in accordance with this article shall be deemed to have been made in accordance with paragraph 1 of Article 56 of the Convention.

4   The territory of any State to which this Protocol applies by virtue of ratification or acceptance by that State, and each territory to which this Protocol is applied by virtue of a declaration by that State under this article, shall be treated as separate territories for the purpose of the references in Articles 2 and 3 to the territory of a State.

5   Any State which has made a declaration in accordance with paragraph 1 or 2 of this Article may at any time thereafter declare on behalf of one or more of the territories to which the declaration relates that it accepts the competence of the Court to receive applications from individuals, non-governmental organisations or groups of individuals as provided in Article 34 of the Convention in respect of all or any of Articles 1 to 4 of this Protocol."

Article 6 – Relationship to the Convention

As between the High Contracting Parties the provisions of Articles 1 to 5 of this Protocol shall be regarded as additional Articles to the Convention, and all the provisions of the Convention shall apply accordingly.

Article 7 – Signature and ratification

1   This Protocol shall be open for signature by the members of the Council of Europe who are the signatories of the Convention; it shall be ratified at the same time as or after the ratification of the Convention. It shall enter into force after the deposit of five instruments of ratification. As regards any signatory ratifying subsequently, the Protocol shall enter into force at the date of the deposit of its instrument of ratification.

2   The instruments of ratification shall be deposited with the Secretary General of the Council of Europe, who will notify all members of the names of those who have ratified.

In witness whereof the undersigned, being duly authorised thereto, have signed this Protocol.

Done at Strasbourg, this 16th day of September 1963, in English and in French, both texts being equally authoritative, in a single copy which shall remain deposited in the archives of the Council of Europe. The Secretary General shall transmit certified copies to each of the signatory states.

Protocol No. 6 to the Convention for the Protection of Human Rights and Fundamental Freedoms concerning the abolition of the death penalty

Strasbourg, 28.IV.1983

The member States of the Council of Europe, signatory to this Protocol to the Convention for the Protection of Human Rights and Fundamental Freedoms, signed at Rome on 4 November 1950 (hereinafter referred to as "the Convention"),

Considering that the evolution that has occurred in several member States of the Council of Europe expresses a general tendency in favour of abolition of the death penalty;

Have agreed as follows:

Article 1 – Abolition of the death penalty

The death penalty shall be abolished. No-one shall be condemned to such penalty or executed.

Article 2 – Death penalty in time of war

A State may make provision in its law for the death penalty in respect of acts committed in time of war or of imminent threat of war; such penalty shall be applied only in the instances laid down in the law and in accordance with its provisions. The State shall communicate to the Secretary General of the Council of Europe the relevant provisions of that law.

Article 3 – Prohibition of derogations

No derogation from the provisions of this Protocol shall be made under Article 15 of the Convention.

Article 4 – Prohibition of reservations

No reservation may be made under Article 57 of the Convention in respect of the provisions of this Protocol.

Article 5 – Territorial application

1   Any State may at the time of signature or when depositing its instrument of ratification, acceptance or approval, specify the territory or territories to which this Protocol shall apply.

2   Any State may at any later date, by a declaration addressed to the Secretary General of the Council of Europe, extend the application of this Protocol to any other territory specified in the declaration. In respect of such territory the Protocol shall enter into force on the first day of the month following the date of receipt of such declaration by the Secretary General.

3   Any declaration made under the two preceding paragraphs may, in respect of any territory specified in such declaration, be withdrawn by a notification addressed to the Secretary General. The withdrawal shall become effective on the first day of the month following the date of receipt of such notification by the Secretary General.

Article 6 – Relationship to the Convention

As between the States Parties the provisions of Articles 1 and 5 of this Protocol shall be regarded as additional articles to the Convention and all the provisions of the Convention shall apply accordingly.

Article 7 – Signature and ratification

The Protocol shall be open for signature by the member States of the Council of Europe, signatories to the Convention. It shall be subject to ratification, acceptance or approval. A member State of the Council of Europe may not ratify, accept or approve this Protocol unless it has, simultaneously or previously, ratified the Convention. Instruments of ratification, acceptance or approval shall be deposited with the Secretary General of the Council of Europe.

Article 8 – Entry into force

1   This Protocol shall enter into force on the first day of the month following the date on which five member States of the Council of Europe have expressed their consent to be bound by the Protocol in accordance with the provisions of Article 7.

2   In respect of any member State which subsequently expresses its consent to be bound by it, the Protocol shall enter into force on the first day of the month following the date of the deposit of the instrument of ratification, acceptance or approval.

Article 9 – Depositary functions

The Secretary General of the Council of Europe shall notify the member States of the Council of:

a   any signature;

b   the deposit of any instrument of ratification, acceptance or approval;

c   any date of entry into force of this Protocol in accordance with articles 5 and 8;

d   any other act, notification or communication relating to this Protocol.

In witness whereof the undersigned, being duly authorised thereto, have signed this Protocol.

Done at Strasbourg, this 28th day of April 1983, in English and in French, both texts being equally authentic, in a single copy which shall be deposited in the archives of the Council of Europe. The Secretary General of the Council of Europe shall transmit certified copies to each member State of the Council of Europe.

Protocol No. 7 to the Convention for the Protection of Human Rights and Fundamental Freedoms

Strasbourg, 22.XI.1984

The member States of the Council of Europe signatory hereto,

Being resolved to take further steps to ensure the collective enforcement of certain rights and freedoms by means of the Convention for the Protection of Human Rights and Fundamental Freedoms signed at Rome on 4 November 1950 (hereinafter referred to as "the Convention"),

Have agreed as follows:

Article 1 – Procedural safeguards relating to expulsion of aliens

1   An alien lawfully resident in the territory of a State shall not be expelled therefrom except in pursuance of a decision reached in accordance with law and shall be allowed:

a   to submit reasons against his expulsion,

b   to have his case reviewed, and

c   to be represented for these purposes before the competent authority or a person or persons designated by that authority.

2   An alien may be expelled before the exercise of his rights under paragraph 1.a, b and c of this Article, when such expulsion is necessary in the interests of public order or is grounded on reasons of national security.

Article 2 – Right of appeal in criminal matters

1   Everyone convicted of a criminal offence by a tribunal shall have the right to have his conviction or sentence reviewed by a higher tribunal. The exercise of this right, including the grounds on which it may be exercised, shall be governed by law.

2   This right may be subject to exceptions in regard to offences of a minor character, as prescribed by law, or in cases in which the person

concerned was tried in the first instance by the highest tribunal or was convicted following an appeal against acquittal.

Article 3 – Compensation for wrongful conviction

When a person has by a final decision been convicted of a criminal offence and when subsequently his conviction has been reversed, or he has been pardoned, on the ground that a new or newly discovered fact shows conclusively that there has been a miscarriage of justice, the person who has suffered punishment as a result of such conviction shall be compensated according to the law or the practice of the State concerned, unless it is proved that the non-disclosure of the unknown fact in time is wholly or partly attributable to him.

Article 4 – Right not to be tried or punished twice

1   No one shall be liable to be tried or punished again in criminal proceedings under the jurisdiction of the same State for an offence for which he has already been finally acquitted or convicted in accordance with the law and penal procedure of that State.

2   The provisions of the preceding paragraph shall not prevent the reopening of the case in accordance with the law and penal procedure of the State concerned, if there is evidence of new or newly discovered facts, or if there has been a fundamental defect in the previous proceedings, which could affect the outcome of the case.

3   No derogation from this Article shall be made under Article 15 of the Convention.

Article 5 – Equality between spouses

Spouses shall enjoy equality of rights and responsibilities of a private law character between them, and in their relations with their children, as to marriage, during marriage and in the event of its dissolution. This Article shall not prevent States from taking such measures as are necessary in the interests of the children.

Article 6 – Territorial application

1   Any State may at the time of signature or when depositing its instrument of ratification, acceptance or approval, specify the territory or territories to which the Protocol shall apply and state the extent to which it undertakes that the provisions of this Protocol shall apply to such territory or territories.

2   Any State may at any later date, by a declaration addressed to the
     Secretary General of the Council of Europe, extend the application of
     this Protocol to any other territory specified in the declaration. In respect
     of such territory the Protocol shall enter into force on the first day of the
     month following the expiration of a period of two months after the date of
     receipt by the Secretary General of such declaration.

3   Any declaration made under the two preceding paragraphs may, in
     respect of any territory specified in such declaration, be withdrawn or
     modified by a notification addressed to the Secretary General. The
     withdrawal or modification shall become effective on the first day of the
     month following the expiration of a period of two months after the date of
     receipt of such notification by the Secretary General.

4   A declaration made in accordance with this Article shall be deemed to
     have been made in accordance with paragraph 1 of Article 56 of the
     Convention.

5   The territory of any State to which this Protocol applies by virtue of
     ratification, acceptance or approval by that State, and each territory to
     which this Protocol is applied by virtue of a declaration by that State
     under this Article, may be treated as separate territories for the purpose
     of the reference in Article 1 to the territory of a State.

6   Any State which has made a declaration in accordance with paragraph 1
     or 2 of this Article may at any time thereafter declare on behalf of one or
     more of the territories to which the declaration relates that it accepts the
     competence of the Court to receive applications from individuals, non-
     governmental organisations or groups of individuals as provided in
     Article 34 of the Convention in respect of Articles 1 to 5 of this Protocol.

Article 7 – Relationship to the Convention

As between the States Parties, the provisions of Article 1 to 6 of this
Protocol shall be regarded as additional Articles to the Convention, and
all the provisions of the Convention shall apply accordingly.

Article 8 – Signature and ratification

This Protocol shall be open for signature by member States of the
Council of Europe which have signed the Convention. It is subject to
ratification, acceptance or approval. A member State of the Council of

Europe may not ratify, accept or approve this Protocol without previously or simultaneously ratifying the Convention. Instruments of ratification, acceptance or approval shall be deposited with the Secretary General of the Council of Europe.

Article 9 – Entry into force

1   This Protocol shall enter into force on the first day of the month following the expiration of a period of two months after the date on which seven member States of the Council of Europe have expressed their consent to be bound by the Protocol in accordance with the provisions of Article 8.

2   In respect of any member State which subsequently expresses its consent to be bound by it, the Protocol shall enter into force on the first day of the month following the expiration of a period of two months after the date of the deposit of the instrument of ratification, acceptance or approval.

Article 10 – Depositary functions

The Secretary General of the Council of Europe shall notify all the member States of the Council of Europe of:

a   any signature;

b   the deposit of any instrument of ratification, acceptance or approval;

c   any date of entry into force of this Protocol in accordance with Articles 6 and 9;

d   any other act, notification or declaration relating to this Protocol.

In witness whereof the undersigned, being duly authorised thereto, have signed this Protocol.

Done at Strasbourg, this 22nd day of November 1984, in English and French, both texts being equally authentic, in a single copy which shall be deposited in the archives of the Council of Europe. The Secretary General of the Council of Europe shall transmit certified copies to each member State of the Council of Europe.

Protocol No. 12 to the Convention for the Protection of Human Rights and Fundamental Freedoms

Rome, 4.XI.2000

The member States of the Council of Europe signatory hereto,

Having regard to the fundamental principle according to which all persons are equal before the law and are entitled to the equal protection of the law;

Being resolved to take further steps to promote the equality of all persons through the collective enforcement of a general prohibition of discrimination by means of the Convention for the Protection of Human Rights and Fundamental Freedoms signed at Rome on 4 November 1950 (hereinafter referred to as "the Convention");

Reaffirming that the principle of non-discrimination does not prevent States Parties from taking measures in order to promote full and effective equality, provided that there is an objective and reasonable justification for those measures,

Have agreed as follows:

Article 1 – General prohibition of discrimination

1   The enjoyment of any right set forth by law shall be secured without discrimination on any ground such as sex, race, colour, language, religion, political or other opinion, national or social origin, association with a national minority, property, birth or other status.

2   No one shall be discriminated against by any public authority on any ground such as those mentioned in paragraph 1.

Article 2 – Territorial application

1   Any State may, at the time of signature or when depositing its instrument of ratification, acceptance or approval, specify the territory or territories to which this Protocol shall apply.

2   Any State may at any later date, by a declaration addressed to the Secretary General of the Council of Europe, extend the application of this Protocol to any other territory specified in the declaration. In respect of such territory the Protocol shall enter into force on the first day of the month following the expiration of a period of three months after the date of receipt by the Secretary General of such declaration.

3   Any declaration made under the two preceding paragraphs may, in respect of any territory specified in such declaration, be withdrawn or modified by a notification addressed to the Secretary General of the Council of Europe. The withdrawal or modification shall become effective on the first day of the month following the expiration of a period of three months after the date of receipt of such notification by the Secretary General.

4   A declaration made in accordance with this article shall be deemed to have been made in accordance with paragraph 1 of Article 56 of the Convention.

5   Any State which has made a declaration in accordance with paragraph 1 or 2 of this article may at any time thereafter declare on behalf of one or more of the territories to which the declaration relates that it accepts the competence of the Court to receive applications from individuals, non-governmental organisations or groups of individuals as provided by Article 34 of the Convention in respect of Article 1 of this Protocol.

Article 3 – Relationship to the Convention

As between the States Parties, the provisions of Articles 1 and 2 of this Protocol shall be regarded as additional articles to the Convention, and all the provisions of the Convention shall apply accordingly.

Article 4 – Signature and ratification

This Protocol shall be open for signature by member States of the Council of Europe which have signed the Convention. It is subject to ratification, acceptance or approval. A member State of the Council of Europe may not ratify, accept or approve this Protocol without previously or simultaneously ratifying the Convention. Instruments of ratification, acceptance or approval shall be deposited with the Secretary General of the Council of Europe.

Article 5 – Entry into force

1   This Protocol shall enter into force on the first day of the month following the expiration of a period of three months after the date on which ten member States of the Council of Europe have expressed their consent to be bound by the Protocol in accordance with the provisions of Article 4.

2   In respect of any member State which subsequently expresses its consent to be bound by it, the Protocol shall enter into force on the first day of the month following the expiration of a period of three months after the date of the deposit of the instrument of ratification, acceptance or approval.

Article 6 – Depositary functions

The Secretary General of the Council of Europe shall notify all the member States of the Council of Europe of:

a   any signature;

b   the deposit of any instrument of ratification, acceptance or approval;

c   any date of entry into force of this Protocol in accordance with Articles 2 and 5;

d   any other act, notification or communication relating to this Protocol.

In witness whereof the undersigned, being duly authorised thereto, have signed this Protocol.

Done at Rome, this 4th day of November 2000, in English and in French, both texts being equally authentic, in a single copy which shall be deposited in the archives of the Council of Europe. The Secretary General of the Council of Europe shall transmit certified copies to each member State of the Council of Europe.

Protocol No. 13 to the Convention for the Protection of Human Rights and Fundamental Freedoms Concerning the abolition of the death penalty in all circumstances

Vilnius, 3.V.2002

The member States of the Council of Europe signatory hereto,

Convinced that everyone's right to life is a basic value in a democratic society and that the abolition of the death penalty is essential for the protection of this right and for the full recognition of the inherent dignity of all human beings;

Wishing to strengthen the protection of the right to life guaranteed by the Convention for the Protection of Human Rights and Fundamental Freedoms signed at Rome on 4 November 1950 (hereinafter referred to as "the Convention");

Noting that Protocol No. 6 to the Convention, concerning the Abolition of the Death Penalty, signed at Strasbourg on 28 April 1983, does not exclude the death penalty in respect of acts committed in time of war or of imminent threat of war;

Being resolved to take the final step in order to abolish the death penalty in all circumstances,

Have agreed as follows:

Article 1 – Abolition of the death penalty

The death penalty shall be abolished. No one shall be condemned to such penalty or executed.

Article 2 – Prohibitions of derogations

No derogation from the provisions of this Protocol shall be made under Article 15 of the Convention.

Article 3 – Prohibitions of reservations

No reservation may be made under Article 57 of the Convention in respect of the provisions of this Protocol.

Article 4 – Territorial application

1   Any state may, at the time of signature or when depositing its instrument of ratification, acceptance or approval, specify the territory or territories to which this Protocol shall apply.

2   Any state may at any later date, by a declaration addressed to the Secretary General of the Council of Europe, extend the application of this Protocol to any other territory specified in the declaration. In respect of such territory the Protocol shall enter into force on the first day of the month following the expiration of a period of three months after the date of receipt by the Secretary General of such declaration.

3   Any declaration made under the two preceding paragraphs may, in respect of any territory specified in such declaration, be withdrawn or modified by a notification addressed to the Secretary General. The withdrawal or modification shall become effective on the first day of the month following the expiration of a period of three months after the date of receipt of such notification by the Secretary General.

Article 5 – Relationship to the Convention

As between the states Parties the provisions of Articles 1 to 4 of this Protocol shall be regarded as additional articles to the Convention, and all the provisions of the Convention shall apply accordingly.

Article 6 – Signature and ratification

This Protocol shall be open for signature by member states of the Council of Europe which have signed the Convention. It is subject to ratification, acceptance or approval. A member state of the Council of Europe may not ratify, accept or approve this Protocol without previously or simultaneously ratifying the Convention. Instruments of ratification, acceptance or approval shall be deposited with the Secretary General of the Council of Europe.

Article 7 – Entry into force

1   This Protocol shall enter into force on the first day of the month following the expiration of a period of three months after the date on which ten member states of the Council of Europe have expressed their consent to be bound by the Protocol in accordance with the provisions of Article 6.

2   In respect of any member state which subsequently expresses its consent to be bound by it, the Protocol shall enter into force on the first day of the month following the expiration of a period of three months after the date of the deposit of the instrument of ratification, acceptance or approval.

Article 8 – Depositary functions

The Secretary General of the Council of Europe shall notify all the member states of the Council of Europe of:

a   any signature;

b   the deposit of any instrument of ratification, acceptance or approval;

c   any date of entry into force of this Protocol in accordance with Articles 4 and 7;

d   any other act, notification or communication relating to this Protocol;

In witness whereof the undersigned, being duly authorised thereto, have signed this Protocol.

Done at Vilnius, this 3rd day of May 2002, in English and in French, both texts being equally authentic, in a single copy which shall be deposited in the archives of the Council of Europe. The Secretary General of the Council of Europe shall transmit certified copies to each member state of the Council of Europe.

PRACTICE DIRECTION[1]

INSTITUTION OF PROCEEDINGS[2]

(individual applications under Article 34 of the Convention)

I. General

1. An application under Article 34 of the Convention must be submitted in writing. No application may be made by phone.

2. An application must be sent to the following address:

> The Registrar
> European Court of Human Rights
> Council of Europe
> F – 67075 STRASBOURG CEDEX.

3. An application should normally be made on the form[3] referred to in Rule 47 § 1 of the Rules of Court. However, an applicant may introduce his complaints in a letter.

4. If an application has not been submitted on the official form or an introductory letter does not contain all the information referred to in Rule 47, the Registry may ask the applicant to fill in the form. It should as a rule be returned within 6 weeks from the date of the Registry's letter.

5. Applicants may file an application by sending it by facsimile ("fax")[4]. However, they must send the signed original copy by post within 5 days following the dispatch by fax.

6. The date on which an application is received at the Court's Registry will be recorded by a receipt stamp.

7. An applicant should be aware that the date of the first communication setting out the subject-matter of the application is considered relevant for the purposes of compliance with the six-month rule in Article 35 § 1 of the Convention.

8. On receipt of the first communication setting out the subject-matter of the case, the Registry will open a file, whose number must be mentioned in all subsequent correspondence. Applicants will be informed thereof by letter. They may also be asked for further information or documents.

---

1. Issued by the President of the Court in accordance with Rule 32 of the Rules of Court on 1 November 2003.
2. This practice direction supplements Rules 45 and 47 of the Rules of Court.
3. The relevant form can be downloaded from the Court's website (www.echr.coe.int).
4. Fax no. +00 33 (0)3 88 41 27 30; other facsimile numbers can be found on the Court's website.

9.   (a) An applicant should be diligent in conducting correspondence with the Court's Registry.

(b) A delay in replying or failure to reply may be regarded as a sign that the applicant is no longer interested in pursuing his application.

10.   Failure to satisfy the requirements laid down in Rule 47 §§ 1 and 2 and to provide further information at the Registry's request (see paragraph 8) may result in the application not being examined by the Court.

11.   Where, within a year, an applicant has not returned an application form or has not answered any letter sent to him by the Registry, the file will be destroyed.

II. Form and contents

12.   An application must contain all information required under Rule 47 and be accompanied by the documents referred to in paragraph 1 (h) of that Rule.

13.   An application should be written legibly and, preferably, typed.

14.   Where, exceptionally, an application exceeds 10 pages (excluding annexes listing documents), an applicant must also file a short summary.

15.   Where applicants produce documents in support of the application, they should not submit original copies. The documents should be listed in order by date, numbered consecutively and given a concise description (e.g. letter, order, judgment, appeal, etc.).

16.   An applicant who already has an application pending before the Court must inform the Registry accordingly, stating the application number.

17.   (a) Where an applicant does not wish to have his or her identity disclosed, he or she should state the reasons for his or her request in writing, pursuant to Rule 47 § 3.

(b) The applicant should also state whether, in the event of anonymity being authorised by the President of the Chamber, he or she wishes to be designated by his or her initials or by a single letter (e.g. "X", "Y", "Z", etc.).

PRACTICE DIRECTION[1]

REQUESTS FOR INTERIM MEASURES

(Rule 39 of the Rules of Court)

Applicants or their legal representatives[2] who make a request for an interim measure pursuant to Rule 39 of the Rules of Court, should comply with the requirements set out below.

Failure to do so may mean that the Court will not be in a position to examine such requests properly and in good time.

I. Requests to be made by facsimile, e-mail or courier

Requests for interim measures under Rule 39 in urgent cases, particularly in extradition or deportation cases, should be sent by facsimile or e-mail[3] or by courier. The request should, where possible, be in one of the official languages of the Contracting Parties. All requests should bear the following title which should be written in bold on the face of the request:

"Rule 39 – Urgent/Article 39 – Urgent"

Requests by facsimile or e-mail should be sent during working hours[4] unless this is absolutely unavoidable. If sent by e-mail, a hard copy of the request should also be sent at the same time. Such requests should not be sent by ordinary post since there is a risk that they will not arrive at the Court in time to permit a proper examination.

If the Court has not responded to an urgent request under Rule 39 within the anticipated period of time, applicants or their representatives should follow up with a telephone call to the Registry during working hours.

II. Making requests in good time

Requests for interim measures should normally be received as soon as possible after the final domestic decision has been taken to enable the Court and its Registry to have sufficient time to examine the matter.

However, in extradition or deportation cases, where immediate steps may be taken to enforce removal soon after the final domestic decision has been given, it is advisable to make submissions and submit any relevant material concerning the request before the final decision is given.

---

1. Issued by the President of the Court in accordance with Rule 32 of the Rules of Court on 5 March 2003.
2. Full contact details should be provided.
3. To the e-mail address of a member of the Registry after having first made contact with that person by telephone. Telephone and facsimile numbers can be found on the Court's website (www.echr.coe.int).
4. Working hours are 8am – 6pm, Monday -Friday. French time is one hour ahead of GMT.

Applicants and their representatives should be aware that it may not be possible to examine in a timely and proper manner requests which are sent at the last moment.

III. Accompanying information

It is essential that requests be accompanied by all necessary supporting documents, in particular relevant domestic court, tribunal or other decisions together with any other material which is considered to substantiate the applicant's allegations.

Where the case is already pending before the Court, reference should be made to the application number allocated to it.

In cases concerning extradition or deportation, details should be provided of the expected date and time of the removal, the applicant's address or place of detention and his or her official case-reference number.

PRACTICE DIRECTION[1]

WRITTEN PLEADINGS

I. Filing of pleadings

General

1.   A pleading must be filed with the Registry within the time-limit fixed in accordance with Rule 38 and in the manner described in paragraph 2 of that Rule.

2.   The date on which a pleading or other document is received at the Court's Registry will be recorded on that document by a receipt stamp.

3.   All pleadings, as well as all documents annexed thereto, should be submitted to the Court's Registry in 3 copies sent by post with 1 copy sent, if possible, by fax.

4.   Secret documents should be filed by registered post.

5.   Unsolicited pleadings shall not be admitted to the case file unless the President of the Chamber decides otherwise (see Rule 38 § 1).

Filing by facsimile

6.   A party may file pleadings or other documents with the Court by sending them by facsimile ("fax")[2].

7.   The name of the person signing a pleading must also be printed on it so that he or she can be identified.

II. Form and contents

Form

8.   A pleading should include:

   (a) the application number and the name of the case;

   (b) a title indicating the nature of the content (e.g. observations on admissibility [and the merits]; reply to the Government's/the applicant's observations on admissibility [and the merits]; observations on the merits; additional observations on admissibility [and the merits]; memorial etc.).

---

1. Issued by the President of the Court in accordance with Rule 32 of the Rules of Court on 1 November 2003.
2. Fax no. +00 33 (0)3 88 41 27 30; other facsimile numbers can be found on the Court's website (www.echr.coe.int).

9.   A pleading should normally in addition

(a) be on A4 paper having a margin of not less than 3.5 cm wide;

(b) be wholly legible and, preferably, typed;

(c) have all numbers expressed as figures;

(d) have pages numbered consecutively;

(e) be divided into numbered paragraphs;

(f) be divided into chapters and/or headings corresponding to the form and style of the Court's decisions and judgments ("Facts" / "Domestic law [and practice]" / "Complaints" / "Law"; the latter chapter should be followed by headings entitled "Preliminary objection on ..."; "Alleged violation of Article ...", as the case may be);

(g) place any answer to a question by the Court or to the other party's arguments under a separate heading;

(h) give a reference to every document or piece of evidence mentioned in the pleading and annexed thereto.

10.   If a pleading exceeds 30 pages, a short summary should also be filed with it.

11.   Where a party produces documents and/or other exhibits together with a pleading, every piece of evidence should be listed in a separate annex.

Contents

12.   The parties' pleadings following communication of the application should include:

(a) any comments they wish to make on the facts of the case; however,

(i) if a party does not contest the facts as set out in the statement of facts prepared by the Registry, it should limit its observations to a brief statement to that effect;

(ii) if a party contests only part of the facts as set out by the Registry, or wishes to supplement them, it should limit its observations to those specific points;

(iii) if a party objects to the facts or part of the facts as presented by the other party, it should state clearly which facts are uncontested and limit its observations to the points in dispute;

(b) legal arguments relating first to admissibility and, secondly, to the merits of the case; however,

(i) if specific questions on a factual or legal point were put to a party, it should, without prejudice to Rule 55, limit its arguments to such questions;
(ii) if a pleading replies to arguments of the other party, submissions should refer to the specific arguments in the order prescribed above.

13. (a) The parties' pleadings following the admission of the application should include:

(i) a short statement confirming a party's position on the facts of the case as established in the decision on admissibility;
(ii) legal arguments relating to the merits of the case;
(iii) a reply to any specific questions on a factual or legal point put by the Court.

(b) An applicant party submitting claims for just satisfaction at the same time should do so in the manner described in the practice direction on filing just satisfaction claims.[1]

14.   In view of the confidentiality of friendly-settlement proceedings (see Article 38 § 2 of the Convention and Rule 62 § 2), all submissions and documents filed within the framework of the attempt to secure a friendly settlement should be submitted separately from the written pleadings.

15.   No reference to offers, concessions or other statements submitted in connection with the friendly settlement may be made in the pleadings filed in the contentious proceedings.

III. Time-limits

General

16.   It is the responsibility of each party to ensure that pleadings and any accompanying documents or evidence are delivered to the Court's Registry in time.

Extension of time-limits

17.   A time-limit set under Rule 38 may be extended on request from a party.

18.   A party seeking an extension of the time allowed for submission of a pleading must make a request as soon as it has become aware of the circumstances justifying such an extension and, in any event, before the expiry of the time-limit. It should state the reason for the delay.

19.   If an extension is granted, it shall apply to all parties for which the relevant time-limit is running, including those which have not asked for it.

---

1 Not yet issued; for the time being see Rule 60.

IV. Failure to comply with requirements for pleadings

20.   Where a pleading has not been filed in accordance with the requirements set out in paragraphs 8-15 of this practice direction, the President of the Chamber may request the party concerned to resubmit the pleading in compliance with those requirements.

21.   A failure to satisfy the conditions listed above may result in the pleading being considered not to have been properly lodged (see Rule 38 § 1 of the Rules of Court).

Submitting a Complaint to the European Court of Human Rights: Eleven Common Misconceptions[1]

Egbert Myjer
Nico Mol
Peter Kempees
Agnes van Steijn
Janneke Bockwinkel[2]

Compared with many of the domestic systems of procedural law existing in Europe, the procedure of the European Court of Human Rights (ECHR) is quite straightforward and easy to use. Nonetheless, even Strasbourg procedure requires some understanding on the part of practitioners. Just as in domestic proceedings, an error can harm the interests of the applicant and, at worst, result in the loss of the case.

Many of the problems which applicants and their counsel encounter in proceedings before the ECHR can be traced back to a limited number of simple misconceptions. The Dutch judge recently appointed to the Court and the Dutch lawyers working in the Registry of the Court explain below how these problems can be avoided.

Misconception 1: The ECHR is an appellate body

Cases regularly occur in which applicants (or their lawyers) submit an application to the Court alleging that the domestic courts have incorrectly determined the facts of a case or have overlooked essential submissions of the applicant. Often such an application is based on the submission that Article 6 of the European Convention on Human Rights has been violated.

The function of the Court is to ensure observance of the Convention and its protocols. The Court does not have the function of rectifying errors made by domestic judges in applying domestic law. Nor does the Court take the place of domestic courts in assessing the evidence. It is incorrect to view the Court as a court of 'fourth instance' to which all aspects of a case can be referred[3].

---

[1] This article originally appeared in French in: Myjer, E., Mol, N., Kempees, P., van Steijn, A., and Bockwinkel, J. "Introduire une plainte auprès de la Cour européenne des Droits de d'Homme: onze malentendus fréquents" in *Annales du droit luxembourgeois*, volume 14-2004, p. 11 *et seq.* (Bruyland, Bruxelles, 2005).
[2] Professor Myjer is a judge of the European Court of Human Rights; Mr Mol, Mr Kempees and Ms Van Steijn are legal secretaries of the Court (Article 25 of the Convention); and Ms Bockwinkel is a trainee judge seconded to the Court by the Netherlands Ministry of Justice.
[3] See the recent case of *Baumann v Austria*, no. 76809/01, § 49, 7 October 2004.

Complaints that the domestic courts should have arrived at a different decision (i.e. a decision more favourable to the applicant) are declared inadmissible as being manifestly ill-founded.

It makes no difference if the complaint is couched in terms of a violation of Article 6 of the Convention. This article guarantees only a fair and public hearing of certain well-defined categories of disputes before an independent and impartial tribunal. It does not also guarantee that domestic proceedings will arrive at the correct result.

Misconception 2: An initial letter is in any event sufficient to comply with the six-month period.

The Court regularly receives letters submitting a complaint in general terms shortly before the expiry of the period prescribed by Article 35 § 1 of the Convention; sometimes these letters include a statement that the grounds of the complaint will be explained in more detail later. Often a copy of a judgment of a domestic court is enclosed with the letter.

How an application must be lodged is described in detail in a practice direction. This, together with other invaluable information, can be found on the Court's website[4].

Although the Court is indeed prepared to accept a simple letter for the purposes of compliance with the six-month rule, the letter must provide a sufficient description of the complaint: in other words, it must in any event set out the facts on which the application is based and specify the rights which are alleged to have been violated, whether or not with references to articles of the Convention and its protocols.

The Court treats the date of dispatch of the letter containing this information as the date of introduction of the application[5]. For this purpose, the Court is, in principle, prepared to accept the date of the letter itself, unless of course there is an inexplicable difference between the date of the latter and the date of dispatch as evidenced by the postmark. If the letter is undated and the postmark is illegible, the date of introduction will be the date of receipt at the Registry of the Court.

---

[4] http://www.echr.coe.int/
[5] See as a recent example *Latif et al. v. the United Kingdom* (admissibility decision), no. 72819/01, 29 January 2004.

A faxed application will be accepted provided that the signed original copy, bearing original signatures, is received by post within 5 days thereafter.

The six-month period prescribed by Article 35 (1) of the Convention is an absolute time-limit. No procedure for rectification of default is available.

An initial letter which merely states that an application will be submitted does not qualify as submission of an application, even if the documents from the file of the domestic proceedings are enclosed: it is therefore not sufficient to allege that the domestic proceedings were unfair and then refer to an enclosed file of the proceedings. Nor is it possible to expand the scope of a complaint after the expiry of the six-month period.

It should be noted for the sake of completeness that the six-month period runs from the day on which the applicant (or his counsel) becomes aware or could have become aware of the last domestic judgment. In principle, the period is therefore calculated from the date of the pronouncement, if public; where, however, the domestic law prescribes notification in written form the period is calculated from the date of service or dispatch of the judgment[6]. It is for the applicant to convince the Court that it should use a different date.

Misconception 3: An application may be submitted within six months of a judgment on application for review or a judgment in a non-admissible appeal

Cases sometimes occur in which an applicant lodges an appeal or appeal in cassation against a judgment or decision against which no appeal lies and then submits an application to the Court. There are also cases in which an applicant applies for an extraordinary remedy before applying to the Court.

In such cases the Court calculates the period of six months from the decision given at the conclusion of the ordinary proceedings. The applicant is, after all, expected to have exhausted every 'effective remedy'. A remedy which is available to him only in certain exceptional circumstances, a request for leave to exercise a discretionary power or a remedy not provided by domestic law cannot be deemed to be an effective remedy. A judgment on an application for revision of a final judgment, a judgment given on an appeal lodged by a public authority to safeguard the quality of the case-law or a decision on a petition for a pardon do not therefore interrupt the six-month period[7]. Even the reopening of ordinary

---

[6] See the recent case of *Sarıbek v. Turkey* (admissibility decision), no. 41055/98, 9 September 2004.
[7] See the recent case of *Berdzenishvili v. Russia* (admissibility decision), no. 31679/03, 29 January 2004.

proceedings does not suspend the running of the period, unless this is actually followed by a new substantive hearing of the case[8].

Misconception 4: If a complaint has been made in a letter, it is not necessary to file the application form.

Rule 47 § 1 of the Rules of Court provides that individual applicants must make use of the form provided by the Registry unless the President of the Section concerned decides otherwise. This provision is strictly enforced.

The Registry sends the form to the applicant after receipt of the first letter. The form can also be found on the Court's website[9].

If the complaint has already been set out fully in a letter, it is not necessary to repeat it verbatim in the form. In such a case it is sufficient merely to refer to the letter in the form.

Forms that are incomplete or unsigned are returned to the applicant. The consequences of any delay that occurs as a result are borne by the applicant.

Misconception 5: A lawyer who states that he is acting on behalf of his client need not submit a written authority to act

Rule 45 § 2 of the Rules of Court states that representatives must submit a power of attorney or written authority to act. No distinction is made for this purpose between representatives who are registered as advocate and other representatives.

If counsel does not supply a written authority to act, the case cannot be heard by the Court. In such cases the Registry sends a reminder. This causes delay (which can sometimes be costly for the applicant).

The Registry supplies a model form of authority whose use is not mandatory (i.e. unlike the application form) but is nonetheless recommended. This model provides for express acceptance of the authority by the legal representative. This model too can be found on the Court's website[10].

Sometimes an applicant may have authorised a lawyer to act for him, but the lawyer's agreement is not evident from the documents. In such a case the Registry

---

[8] See, *inter alia, Bo ek v. the Czech Republic* (admissibility decision), no. 49474/99, 10 October 2000.
[9] See *supra* note 4.
[10] See *supra* note 4.

requests the applicant to arrange for his lawyer to acknowledge to the Court that he is acting. Until this has happened, the correspondence is continued with the applicant in person.

Misconception 6: The applicant has a full year in which to supplement his complaint by means of the application form, written authority and supporting documents

After receipt of the applicant's first communication, the Registry sends the applicant a letter enclosing the text of the Convention, the text of Rules 45 and 47 of the Rules of Court (detailing the formalities to be completed in respect of the application), a 'note for the guidance of persons wishing to apply to the Court' (explaining the admissibility criteria applied by the Court) and the application form with notes.

The last paragraph of the letter (English version) reads as follows:

> 'If the Registry receives no response from you, your complaints will be taken to have been withdrawn and the file opened in respect of the application will be destroyed – without further warning – one year after dispatch of this letter.'

The misconception occurs because the applicant (or his or her counsel) reads only this last paragraph. Elsewhere in the letter there is a warning about the consequences of unnecessary delay. The sanction imposed by the Court in this respect is that the date on which the application is filed is taken to be the date of the form (or an even later date if the form is not completed correctly) rather than the date of the letter of complaint. This may mean that the application is deemed to be filed after the six-month period.

The note for the guidance of prospective applicants (point 17) states that the Court wishes the form to be filed within six weeks. Although a request to extend this period may be made, the applicant is responsible for – and bears the risk of – ensuring that the Court receives a written document adequately explaining the complaint within six months of the last domestic decision[11].

After the Court has received the application, the applicant can be requested to supplement it, where necessary, with any missing documentary evidence or other information. The Registry may set a time-limit for this purpose. Although failure to comply with this time-limit does not necessarily invalidate the application, it is advisable to submit a reasoned request for an extension before the expiry of the period if it becomes clear that the time-limit cannot be met.

---

[11] See for example *Latif et al. v. the United Kingdom* (admissibility decision), see *supra* note 3.

It should be emphasised that the period of a year specified in the last paragraph of the letter of the Registry is definitely not the period available to the applicant. The applicant cannot derive any rights from it. The file is kept for one year after the last communication from the applicant. If the applicant does not communicate within this period the file will be destroyed in order to make space in the Court's already overfull archives for applications that are pursued with greater diligence.

A complainant who contacts the court again after a long period of silence may be required to explain his silence, even if it has lasted for less than a year. The Court may attach consequences to such silence.

Misconception 7: The entire proceedings can be conducted in the applicant's national language

Unlike the Court of Justice of the European Communities, the Court of Human Rights in Strasbourg has only two official languages, namely English and French (Rule 34 § 1 of the Rules of Court).

The original application and the supporting documents attached to it can be submitted in a language other than English or French provided that the language used is an official language of one of the Contracting Parties, i.e. the States that are party to the Convention[12] (Rule 34 § 2 of the Rules of Court).

Until recently an applicant was allowed to use such another language until the Court decided on the admissibility of his or her application. However, as preparations are under way to introduce a concentrated procedure without a separate admissibility decision, in anticipation of the entry into force of Protocol No. 14[13], the use of English or French has been made mandatory at an earlier stage in the proceedings, namely from the date on which the complaint is communicated to the respondent government.

The obligation subsequently to use one of the two official languages applies only to pleadings/observations submitted by or on behalf of the applicant. It follows that the applicant need not submit an unsolicited translation of documents from the domestic court file, unless of course these documents are drawn up in a language which is not an official language of one of the Contracting Parties.

---

[12] We would, for practical reasons, advise caution in the use of uncommon regional or minority languages, regardless of whether they have the status of official language in a particular area, and generally recommend the use of more widely used languages if possible.
[13] *Protocol No. 14 to the Convention for the protection of human rights and fundamental freedoms* (Strasbourg, 13 May 2004); Council of Europe Treaty Series/ Série des Traités du Conseil de l'Europe no. 194.

Voir Note explicative
See Explanatory Note

Numéro de dossier
File-number

COUR EUROPÉENNE DES DROITS DE L'HOMME
EUROPEAN COURT OF HUMAN RIGHTS

Conseil de l'Europe – *Council of Europe*
Strasbourg, France

REQUÊTE
APPLICATION

présentée en application de l'article 34 de la Convention européenne des Droits de l'Homme,
ainsi que des articles 45 et 47 du règlement de la Cour

*under Article 34 of the European Convention on Human Rights
and Rules 45 and 47 of the Rules of Court*

IMPORTANT: La présente requête est un document juridique et peut affecter vos droits et obligations.
This application is a formal legal document and may affect your rights and obligations.

I. LES PARTIES
THE PARTIES

A. LE REQUÉRANT / LA REQUÉRANTE
THE APPLICANT

(Renseignements à fournir concernant le/la requérant(e) et son/sa représentant(e) éventuel(le))
(Fill in the following details of the applicant and the representative, if any)

1. Nom de famille **Doe**
   Surname
   Sexe : masculin/féminin

2. Prénom(s) **John**
   First name(s)
   Sex: male / female **Male**

3. Nationalité **British**
   Nationality

4. Profession **Unemployed**
   Occupation

5. Date et lieu de naissance **1 January 1975, London, England**
   Date and place of birth

6. Domicile **123 Main Street, E00 0AB**
   Permanent address

7. Tel. N° **(0)20 1234-5678**

8. Adresse actuelle (si différente de 6.) **(Same)**
   Present address (if different from 6.)

9. Nom et prénom du/de la representant(e)* **Jane Smith**
   Name of representative

10. Profession du/de la représentant(e) **Attorney**
    Occupation of representative

11. Adresse du/de la représentant(e) **456 Main Street, E00 0AB**
    Address of representative

12. Tel. N° **(0) 20 8765-4321**   Fax N° **(0) 20 2345-6789**

B. LA HAUTE PARTIE CONTRACTANTE
THE HIGH CONTRACTING PARTY
(Indiquer ci-après le nom de l'Etat/des Etats contre le(lesquel(s) la requête est dirigée)
(Fill in the name of the State(s) against which the application is directed)

13. **United Kingdom**

---

*   Si le/la requérant(e) est représenté(e), joindre une procuration signée par le/la représentant(e).
     If the applicant appoints a representative, attach a form of authority signed by the applicant and his or
     her representative.

II. EXPOSÉ DES FAITS
STATEMENT OF THE FACTS

(Voir chapitre II de la note explicative)
(See Part II of the Explanatory Note)

14.   On 10 January 2002 my client (hereinafter referred to as "the applicant") was arrested in the city centre of X by officers from the Anti-Terrorist Branch on suspicion of involvement in terrorist activities (see appendix A for a copy of the record of arrest) and was taken to the City Hospital for a medical examination. According to the medical report drawn up at the end of the examination, there were no signs of any injuries on his body (see appendix B). The applicant was then placed in the detention facility of the police station. During his detention the applicant was questioned by police officers on a number of occasions. When he denied the allegations against him, the police officers became agitated and subjected him to serious ill-treatment which included being stripped naked, hosed down with pressurised cold water, suspended from his arms and being beaten with a truncheon on his chest. Also, electric shocks were administered to his toes. On 13 January 2002, while he was being ill-treated, the applicant was forced to sign a statement in which he confessed to having committed terrorism-related offences (see appendix C).

14.1 On 14 January 2002 the police officers took the applicant back to the City Hospital where they remained in the room while he was being examined by a doctor. When the doctor asked the applicant to remove his clothes, the police officers told him not to do so. As a result, the doctor stated in a medical report that there were no signs of any ill-treatment on the applicant (see appendix D). The applicant was then taken to the court house where he informed the judge of his ordeal and informed the judge that he had been forced to sign a confession under ill-treatment. The judge ordered his release (see appendix E for a copy of the order of release).

14.2 On his release the applicant was met outside the court building by his father and a lawyer who took him to the applicant's family doctor. The doctor recorded in his report that there were extensive bruises under his armpits which were compatible with the applicant's account of having been suspended from his arms, and the marks on his chest were compatible with having been beaten with an object. Furthermore, the doctor also observed that the applicant's toes bore signs of electric burns (see appendix F). According to the medical record, the injuries had been caused at least 24 hours previously.

14.3On the same day the applicant went back to the court where he submitted a petition to the prosecutor in which he detailed the ill-treatment to which he had been subjected (see appendix G for a copy of the petition). With his petition he also enclosed copies of the three medical reports (i.e. appendices B, D and F). He asked the prosecutor to investigate his allegations and prosecute the police officers responsible for the ill-treatment. He further informed the prosecutor that his father and his lawyer would be willing to testify to the effect that he had been released with injuries.

14.4On 21 January 2002 the prosecutor filed an indictment with the City Criminal Court in which he accused the applicant of membership in a terrorist organisation (see appendix H for a copy of the indictment). On 1 March 2002 a hearing was held in the City Criminal Court in the course of which the trial judge ordered the applicant's detention on remand pending the outcome of the trial (see appendix I for a copy of the verbatim record of the hearing). The trial continued until 1 March 2005 during which time there were 12 hearings. Throughout the trial the applicant professed his innocence and told the court that his confession had been extracted under ill-treatment (see appendix J for copies of the verbatim records of the 12 hearings). On 1 March 2005 the applicant was found guilty of the offences with which he had been charged and sentenced to a prison term of 12 years (see appendix K for a copy of the judgment). Within the statutory time limit the applicant appealed against his conviction and argued, *inter alia*, that the conviction was wrongful as it was based on the confession extracted from him under ill-treatment (see appendix L for a copy of the appeal petition). The applicant remained in detention on remand until his conviction was upheld by the Court of Appeal on 1 October 2005. The decision of the Court of Appeal was served on the applicant on 8 October 2005 (see appendix M for a copy of the Court of Appeal's decision). On 21 October 2005 the applicant was transferred to the County Prison to serve his prison sentence, and he is currently detained there.

14.5During his detention on remand in the City Prison between 1 March 2002 and 21 October 2005, the applicant was kept in a cell measuring 20 square metres (m^2) together with 19 other prisoners. As there were only 10 beds, the inmates had to take turns to sleep. There was only one window, measuring 75 x 120 cm. This window, which was the only source of fresh air and natural light, would only be open for two hours per day. The 20 prisoners had to share one toilet and one wash basin which were located in the corner of the cell and not enclosed by any sort of partition. The food would only be served once a day and was hardly edible. Moreover, the dirty crockery was not collected until the following day. As a result of the poor sanitary conditions, the cell was infested with rats, ants and lice. Once a fortnight the prisoners were allowed to take a shower which was limited to five minutes at most. The applicant was only allowed one hour of outdoor exercise in a small yard per day. As a result of the conditions in the prison the applicant's mental and physical health deteriorated and he is still suffering from serious health problems (see appendix N for the medical report, drawn up on 1 August 2005 showing the effects of the conditions of his detention). Although the problems the applicant suffered in the cell and his health problems were brought to the attention of the trial court as well as of the Court of Appeal on a number of occasions, no action was taken to remedy the situation, for example by moving the applicant to another prison or by releasing him pending the outcome of the trial.

14.6In the meantime, on 30 October 2004 the applicant sent a letter to the prosecutor and asked for information about the investigation into his allegations of ill-treatment (see appendix O for a copy of the applicant's letter). The applicant enclosed with his letter two statements which were drawn up by his father and the lawyer who had met him outside the court house upon his release and in which they detailed the applicant's injuries and stated that they had taken the applicant to the family doctor immediately after his release (see appendix T). In his letter of 1 January 2005 the prosecutor informed the applicant that the investigation was classified as confidential and for this reason he could not disclose any details (see appendix P for a copy of the prosecutor's letter). On 1 April 2005 the applicant received the decision of the prosecutor not to prosecute the police officers. The prosecutor's decision was based on a report that had apparently been drawn up on 15 November 2004 by the police chief of the police station where the applicant had been detained and ill-treated. According to the police chief's report, the police officers involved had been questioned by their commanding officer and had vehemently denied any wrongdoing. The prosecutor's decision also stated that according to the medical report of the City Hospital (appendix D), there were no signs of any injury on the applicant's body. As to the medical report obtained from the applicant's family doctor (appendix F), the prosecutor decided to exclude it since it had been drawn up by a private practitioner as opposed to a doctor employed by the State. The decision also stated that it would become final if no appeal was lodged against it within the statutory period of two weeks (see appendix Q for a copy of the prosecutor's decision not to prosecute the police officers). On 4 April 2005 the applicant appealed against the prosecutor's decision not to prosecute the police officers (see appendix R for a copy of the appeal petition). The appeal, which is the final remedy under domestic law, was dismissed on 1 September 2005 by the Assize Court (see appendix S for a copy of the decision). In accordance with the domestic procedure, the decision was served on the applicant on 30 September 2005.

III. EXPOSÉ DE LA OU DES VIOLATION(S) DE LA CONVENTION ET/OU DES PROTOCOLES ALLÉGUÉE(S), AINSI QUE DES ARGUMENTS À L'APPUI
STATEMENT OF ALLEGED VIOLATION(S) OF THE CONVENTION AND/OR PROTOCOLS AND OF RELEVANT ARGUMENTS

(Voir chapitre III de la note explicative)
(See Part III of the Explanatory Note)

15. The applicant submits that there have been three separate violations of

Article 3 of the Convention as well as a violation of Article 13 of the Convention on account of the treatment to which he was subjected since his arrest on 10 January 2002. These arguments will be separately dealt with below.

a) Violation of Article 3 on Account of the Ill-treatment in Police Custody

15.1   The applicant submits that the ill-treatment to which he was subjected whilst in the custody of the police officers was in breach of Article 3 of the Convention. In this connection the applicant refers to the established case-law of the European Court of Human Rights (hereinafter referred to as "the Court") according to which "where an individual is taken into police custody in good health but is found to be injured at the time of release, it is incumbent on the State to provide a plausible explanation of how those injuries were caused, failing which a clear issue arises under Article 3 of the Convention" (see, *inter alia, Selmouni v. France* [GC], no. 25803/94, 28 July 1999, § 87). The applicant was arrested and detained in police custody on 10 January 2002 (see appendix A) and remained there until his release on 14 January 2002 (see appendix E). According to the medical report drawn up on 10 January 2002, i.e. immediately after he was arrested and before he was placed in the police custody, his body bore no marks of ill-treatment (see appendix B). On the other hand, the report prepared by his family doctor within hours of his release on 14 January 2002 (see appendix F) details the extensive injuries on his body. It is submitted, therefore, that the injuries detailed in that medical report had been caused while the applicant was detained in the custody of the police.

15.2   The applicant argues that the medical report issued upon his release from police custody on 14 January 2002 (appendix D) cannot be relied on in evidence as discrediting his allegations of ill-treatment. That medical examination was carried out in the presence of police officers who had been responsible for the ill-treatment. Their presence prevented the applicant from informing the doctor about the ill-treatment and from showing the doctor his injuries. In this connection the applicant refers to the

Council of Europe's European Committee for the Prevention of Torture and Inhuman or Degrading Treatment or Punishment (CPT) Standards on Police Custody. According to these Standards, "medical examination of persons in police custody should be conducted out of the hearing, and preferably out of the sight, of police officers. Further, the results of every examination as well as relevant statements by the detainee and the doctor's conclusions should be formally recorded by the doctor and made available to the detainee and his lawyer". The Court has taken these Standards into account in evaluating medical reports in cases concerning allegations of ill-treatment (see, for example, *Akkoç v. Turkey*, nos. 22947/93 and 22948/93, 10 October 2000, § 118).

15.3   As regards the prosecutor's failure to take the medical report obtained from the applicant's family doctor (appendix F) into account because it was prepared by a private medical practitioner – as opposed to a doctor working for a State hospital – the applicant submits that medical reports drawn up by private medical practitioners are relevant for the Court's examinations of allegations of ill-treatment. Furthermore, the Court expects national investigating authorities to take such reports into account. In this connection the applicant refers to the Court's judgment in the case of *Dizman v. Turkey* in which the medical report obtained by Mr Dizman following his release formed the basis of the Court's conclusion that he had been ill-treated (*Dizman v. Turkey*, no. 27309/95, 20 September 2005, § 76). Like Mr Dizman had done, the applicant in the present application also brought the medical report to the attention of the investigating prosecutor and asked the prosecutor to prosecute the police officers. Furthermore, the applicant would draw the Court's attention to the fact that the independent medical report in question was obtained immediately after his release. There is no suggestion that the applicant suffered those injuries in that short time, i.e. after his release but before his examination by his family doctor. In any event, as can be seen in the applicant's petition submitted to the prosecutor on 14 January 2002 (appendix G), the applicant informed the prosecutor that his father and the lawyer were willing to testify to the effect that they had seen him released with injuries and had taken him immediately to the family doctor (see appendix T for copies of the statements). Furthermore, the medical report which states that the applicant's injuries were one day old places the timing of those injuries to the period of detention in police custody. No steps were taken by the prosecutor to question his father or the lawyer or to question the doctors who had drawn up the medical reports on 14 January 2002 to eliminate the contradictions between those reports.

15.4   In the light of the foregoing the applicant submits that he has satisfied the initial burden of proving that his injuries were caused in police custody. It follows, therefore, that the respondent Government's obligation is engaged to provide a plausible explanation of how the applicant's injuries were caused, failing which a clear issue arises under Article 3 of the Convention. To this end, the applicant maintains that the injuries were the consequence of the ill-treatment and reserves the right to respond to any arguments which may be advanced by the respondent Government and to adduce further evidence.

15.5   As regards the nature of his injuries, the applicant submits that they were serious and have been inflicted deliberately, thereby causing him very serious and cruel suffering (see *Ireland v. the United Kingdom*, no. 5310/71, 18 January 1978, § 167). The ill-treatment included being stripped naked, hosed down with pressurised cold water, being suspended from his arms and being beaten up with a truncheon on his chest. Also, electric shocks were administered to his toes. According to the Court, being suspended from the arms "could only have been deliberately inflicted; indeed, a certain amount of preparation and exertion would have been required to carry it out" (see *Aksoy v. Turkey*, no. 21987/93, 18 December 1996, § 64). Furthermore, the applicant draws the Court's attention to the fact that he was ill-treated in order to force him to sign a confession. In the light of the above, the applicant invites the Court to conclude that the ill-treatment to which he was subjected amounted to torture within the meaning of Article 3 of the Convention.

b)   Violation of Article 3 on Account of the Conditions of Detention on Remand

15.6   The applicant submits that his suffering on account of the conditions of his detention on remand in the City Prison between 1 March 2002 and 21 October 2005 went beyond the inevitable element of suffering or humiliation involved in a given form of legitimate treatment or punishment and reached the threshold of severity necessary to classify it as inhuman and degrading. In this connection the applicant refers to the findings of the CPT following its delegates' visit to the City Prison in 2004 while the applicant was being detained there. According to the CPT's report, the conditions in the prison were inhuman and degrading. Furthermore, it was stated in the CPT's report that 7 m² per prisoner was an approximate and desirable guideline for a detention cell, whereas the applicant was only afforded 1 m² of personal space.

15.7   Prison conditions similar to those the applicant endured in the City Prison have already been found by the Court to be inhuman and degrading. In this connection the applicant refers in particular to the Court's judgments in the cases of *Kalashnikov v. Russia* (no. 47095/99, 15 July 2002, § 97) and *Labzov v. Russia* (no. 62208/00, 28 February 2002, §§ 44-46) in which the Court found that personal space afforded to prisoners measuring between 0.9 - 1.9 m² and 1 m², respectively, in themselves gave rise to issues under Article 3 of the Convention. In the present application, the applicant was allowed 1 m² of personal space, in which he spent more than three years and seven months. The applicant submits that the fact that he was obliged to live, sleep and use the toilet in the same cell with so many other inmates is sufficient to cause distress or hardship of an intensity exceeding the unavoidable level of suffering inherent in detention, and arouse in him feelings of fear, anguish and inferiority capable of humiliating and debasing him.

15.8   The applicant invites the Court to take into account the cumulative effects of the conditions of his detention. As evidenced in the medical report of 1 August 2005 (appendix N) the conditions in the City Prison have adversely affected the applicant's mental and physical health.

15.9   In the light of the above, the applicant maintains that there has been a separate violation of Article 3 of the Convention on account of the unacceptable conditions of his detention.

c)   **Violation of Article 3 on Account of the Lack of an Effective Investigation**

15.10   According to the Court's established case-law, "where an individual raises an arguable claim that he has been seriously ill-treated by the police or other such agents of the State unlawfully and in breach of Article 3, that provision, read in conjunction with the State's general duty under Article 1 of the Convention to 'secure to everyone within their jurisdiction the rights and freedoms defined in [the] Convention' requires by implication that there should be an effective official investigation. This investigation, as with that under Article 2, should be capable of leading to the identification and punishment of those responsible" (*Assenov v. Bulgaria*, no. 24760/94, 28 September 1998, § 102; see also more recently *Bekos and Koutropoulos v. Greece*, no. 15250/02, 13 December 2005, §§ 53-57).

15.11   Modalities of an effective investigation into allegations of ill-treatment, as indentified in the Court's case-law, are summarised in the Court's judgment in the case of *Batı and Others v. Turkey* (nos. 33097/96 and 57834/00, 3 June 2004, §§ 133-137). According to the Court in *Batı and Others*, and in so far as relevant for the purposes of the present application, investigating authorities faced with allegations of ill-treatment must

show due diligence by promptly initiating an investigation

and by taking reasonable steps to expedite the investigation;

- take reasonable steps to secure the evidence;

- carry out the investigation in an independent and impartial manner; and

- enable the victim's effective access to the investigation.

15.12   In the present application no steps appear to have been taken in the investigation prior to the drafting of the report by the police chief on 15 November 2004, i.e. more than two years after the applicant brought his complaints to the prosecutor's attention (see appendix Q for a copy of the decision not to prosecute). Furthermore, no steps appear to have been taken between 15 November 2004 until 1 April 2005 when the prosecutor rendered his decision not to prosecute the police officers. Indeed, the report prepared by the police chief following his questioning of the police officers responsible for the ill-treatment remains the only step taken in the investigation which continued for a period of almost three years. Similarly, no consideration has been given by the trial court judge to the allegations of ill-treatment repeatedly voiced by the applicant in the course of the trial (see appendix J for copies of the verbatim records). It cannot be said, therefore, that the investigating authorities have acted promptly or that they have shown due diligence to expedite the investigation.

15.13   No steps have been taken by the prosecutor to secure the evidence. For example, no thought was apparently given to questioning the applicant or to having him examined by a doctor to obtain an additional medical certificate with a view to eliminating the contradictions between the two medical reports (see appendices D and F for copies of the medical reports). Similarly, no attempt has been made by the prosecutor to question the applicant's father and the lawyer who had met the applicant outside the court house upon his release and taken him to the family doctor (see appendix T).

15.14   It cannot be said that the investigation was independent or impartial. The police officers whom the applicant accused of having ill-treated him were questioned by their superior. On account of the hierarchical connection, the police chief cannot be regarded as an independent or impartial investigator. Strikingly, no steps were taken by the prosecutor to question the police officers directly.

15.15 Finally, there has been no public scrutiny of the investigation. In particular, the applicant has not been given any information about the investigation despite his request thereto (see appendix O). The applicant submits that the denial of information and access to the documents in the investigation file cannot be justified on account of the allegedly confidential nature of the investigation.

15.16 In the light of the foregoing, the applicant argues that the investigating authorities failed to carry out an effective investigation into his allegations of ill-treatment in violation of the positive obligation inherent in Article 3 of the Convention.

d) Violation of Article 13 on Account of a Lack of an Effective Remedy

15.17 The applicant submits that he has been denied an effective remedy in respect of his Convention complaints of ill-treatment. He maintains that the allegations of ill-treatment which he brought to the attention of the prosecutor was substantiated by adequate evidence and he had, therefore, an arguable claim for the purposes of Article 13 of the Convention (see, in particular, *Boyle and Rice v. the United Kingdom*, nos. 9659/82 and 9658/82, 27 April 1998, § 52-55). The authorities thus had an obligation to carry out an effective investigation into his allegations against the police officers. However, and as set out above, all his attempts to have criminal proceedings instituted against the police officers responsible for the ill-treatment have failed, and the authorities have thus deprived him of an effective remedy in violation of Article 13 of the Convention.

IV. EXPOSÉ RELATIF AUX PRESCRIPTIONS DE L'ARTICLE 35 § 1 DE LA CONVENTION
STATEMENT RELATIVE TO ARTICLE 35 § 1 OF THE CONVENTION

(Voir chapitre IV de la note explicative. Donner pour chaque grief, et au besoin sur une feuille séparée, les renseignements demandés sous les points 16 à 18 ci-après)
(See Part IV of the Explanatory Note. If necessary, give the details mentioned below under points 16 to 18 on a separate sheet for each separate complaint)

16. Décision interne définitive (date et nature de la décision, organe – judiciaire ou autre – l'ayant rendue)
Final decision (date, court or authority and nature of decision)

16.1 As regards the applicant's complaint concerning the ill-treatment to which he was subjected while in the custody of the police, the applicant applied to the prosecutor and asked the prosecutor to investigate his allegations (see appendix G). He also appealed against the prosecutor's decision not to prosecute the police officers (see appendix R). The appeal was rejected by the Assize Court on 1 September 2005, and the decision was communicated to the applicant on 30 September 2005 (see appendix S).

16.2 As regards the complaint concerning the conditions of his detention in the City Prison, the applicant informed the trial judge throughout the trial of the problems he was encountering in the prison (appendix J for copies of the verbatim records of the hearings). Furthermore the applicant also mentioned these problems in his appeal to the Court of Appeal (see appendix L). The appeal was rejected on 1 October 2005, and the decision was served on the applicant on 8 October 2005 (see appendix M).

15. Autres décisions (énumérées dans l'ordre chronologique en indiquant, pour chaque décision, sa date, sa nature et l'organe – judiciaire ou autre – l'ayant rendue)
Other decisions (list in chronological order, giving date, court or authority and nature of decision for each of them)

17.1 City Criminal Court's judgment of 1 March 2005 in which the applicant was convicted and sentenced to 12 years' imprisonment (appendix K).

168. Dispos(i)ez-vous d'un recours que vous n'avez pas exercé? Si oui, lequel et pour quel motif n'a-t-il pas été exercé?
Is there or was there any other appeal or other remedy available to you which you have not used? If so, explain why you have not used it.

18.1 The appeal against the prosecutor's decision not to prosecute and the appeal against the decision of the City Criminal Court judgment constitute the final domestic remedies within the meaning of Article 35 § 1 of the Convention.

Si nécessaire, continuer sur une feuille séparée
Continue on a separate sheet if necessary

V. EXPOSÉ DE L'OBJET DE LA REQUÊTE
STATEMENT OF THE OBJECT OF THE APPLICATION

(Voir chapitre V de la note explicative)
(See Part V of the Explanatory Note)

179. By introducing this application the applicant primarily seeks to obtain a finding from the Court that his rights under Articles 3 and 13 of the Convention have been violated. In the applicant's opinion, the most appropriate form of redress would be to re-open the investigation into his allegations of ill-treatment and to grant him a re-trial, disregarding the confession extracted from him under torture.

The applicant reserves the right to submit in due course his claims under Article 41 of the Convention for his costs and expenses associated with the bringing of his application as well as for his pecuniary and non-pecuniary damages.

VI. AUTRES INSTANCES INTERNATIONALES TRAITANT OU AYANT TRAITÉ L'AFFAIRE
STATEMENT CONCERNING OTHER INTERNATIONAL PROCEEDINGS

(Voir chapitre VI de la note explicative)

(See Part VI of the Explanatory Note)

20. Avez-vous soumis à une autre instance internationale d'enquête ou de règlement les griefs énoncés dans la présente requête? Si oui, fournir des indications détaillées à ce sujet.
Have you submitted the above complaints to any other procedure of international investigation or settlement? If so, give full details.

20.1 The applicant has not submitted his complaints to another procedure of international   investigation   or   settlement.

VII. PIÈCES ANNEXÉES

(PAS D'ORIGINAUX, UNIQUEMENT DES COPIES ; PRIERE DE N'UTILISER NI AGRAFE, NI ADHESIF, NI LIEN D'AUCUNE SORTE)

LIST OF DOCUMENTS

(NO ORIGINAL DOCUMENTS, ONLY PHOTOCOPIES, DO NOT STAPLE, TAPE OR BIND DOCUMENTS)

(Voir chapitre VII de la note explicative. Joindre copie de toutes les décisions mentionnées sous ch. IV et VI ci-dessus. Se procurer, au besoin, les copies nécessaires, et, en cas d'impossibilité, expliquer pourquoi celles-ci ne peuvent pas être obtenues. Ces documents ne vous seront pas retournés.)
(See Part VII of the Explanatory Note. Include copies of all decisions referred to in Parts IV and VI above. If you do not have copies, you should obtain them. If you cannot obtain them, explain why not. No documents will be returned to you.)

181. a) Record of Arrest of 10 January 2002

b) Medical report drawn up at the City Hospital on 10 January 2002

c) The confession extracted from the applicant under torture on 13 January 2002

d) Medical report drawn up at the City Hospital on 14 January 2002

e) Judge's order of release of 14 January 2002

f) Medical report drawn up by the family doctor on 14 January 2002

g) Complaint petition submitted to the prosecutor on 14 January 2002

h) Indictment of 21 January 2002

i) Verbatim record of the first hearing held on 1 March 2002

j) Verbatim records of the 12 hearings

k) City Criminal Court's judgment of 1 March 2005 convicting the applicant

l) The applicant's petition of appeal against his conviction

m) Decision of the Court of Appeal dismissing the appeal

n) Medical report of 1 August 2005

o) The applicant's letter of 30 October 2004 addressed to the prosecutor

p) The prosecutor's reply of 1 January 2005

q) The prosecutor's decision of 1 April 2005 not to prosecute the police officers

r) The petition of appeal of 4 April 2005 against the prosecutor's decision not to prosecute

s) Assize Court's decision of 1 September 2005 dismissing the applicant's appeal

t) Statements drawn up by the applicant's father and the lawyer.

VIII.DÉCLARATION ET SIGNATURE
DECLARATION AND SIGNATURE

(Voir chapitre VIII de la note explicative)
(See Part VIII of the Explanatory Note)

Je déclare en toute conscience et loyauté que les renseignements qui figurent sur la présente formule de requête sont exacts.
I hereby declare that, to the best of my knowledge and belief, the information I have given in the present application form is correct.

Lieu/*Place* ....

Date/*Date* 30 March 2006

(Signature du/de la requérant(e) ou du/de la représentant(e))
(Signature of the applicant or of the representative)

APPENDIX 7

ANNEX I OF THE ISTANBUL PROTOCOL: PRINCIPLES ON THE EFFECTIVE INVESTIGATION AND DOCUMENTATION OF TORTURE
AND OTHER CRUEL, INHUMAN OR DEGRADING TREATMENT OR PUNISHMENT

ANNEX I

Principles on the Effective Investigation and Documentation of Torture and Other Cruel, Inhuman or Degrading Treatment or Punishment132

The purposes of effective investigation and documentation of torture and other cruel, inhuman or degrading treatment (hereafter referred to as torture or other ill-treatment) include the following: clarification of the facts and establishment and acknowledgement of individual and State responsibility for victims and their families, identification of measures needed to prevent recurrence and facilitation of prosecution or, as appropriate, disciplinary sanctions for those indicated by the investigation as being responsible and demonstration of the need for full reparation and redress from the State, including fair and adequate financial compensation and provision of the means for medical care and rehabilitation.[132]

States shall ensure that complaints and reports of torture or ill-treatment shall be promptly and effectively investigated. Even in the absence of annex press complaint, an investigation should be undertaken if there are other indications that torture or ill-treatment might have occurred. The investigators, who shall be independent of the suspected perpetrators and the agency they serve, shall be competent and impartial. They shall have access to, or be empowered to commission, investigations by impartial medical or other experts. The methods used to carry out such investigations shall meet the highest professional standards, and the findings shall be made public.

The investigative authority shall have the power and obligation to obtain all the information necessary to the inquiry.[133] Those persons conducting the investigation shall have at their disposal all the necessary budgetary and technical resources for effective investigation. They shall also have the authority to oblige all those acting in an official capacity allegedly involved in torture or ill-treatment to appear and testify. The same shall apply to any witness. To this end, the investigative authority shall be entitled to issue summonses to witnesses, including any officials allegedly involved, and to demand the production of evidence. Alleged victims of torture or ill-treatment, witnesses, those conducting the investigation and their families shall be protected from violence, threats of violence or any other form of intimidation that may arise pursuant to the investigation. Those potentially implicated in torture or ill-treatment shall be removed from any position of control or power, whether direct or indirect, over complainants, witnesses and their families, as well as those conducting the investigation.

Alleged victims of torture or ill-treatment and their legal representatives shall be informed of, and have access to, any hearing as well as to all information relevant to the investigation and shall be entitled to present other evidence.

Inc cases in which the established investigative procedures are inadequate because of insufficient expertise or suspected bias or because of the apparent existence of a pattern of abuse, or for other substantial reasons, States shall ensure that investigations are undertaken through an independent commission of inquiry or similar procedure. Members of such a commission shall be

---

[132] The Commission on Human Rights, init s resolution 2000/43, and the General Assembly, init sresolution5 5/89, drew the attention of Governments to the Principles and strongly encouraged Governments to reflect upon the Principles as a useful tool in efforts to combat

[133] Under certain circumstances professional ethics may require information to be kept confidential. These requirements should be respected.

chosen for their recognized impartiality, competence and independence as individuals. In particular, they shall be independent of any suspected perpetrators and the institutions or agencies they may serve. The commission shall have the authority to obtain all information necessary to the inquiry and shall conduct the inquiry as provided for under these Principles.[134]

A written report, made within a reasonable time, shall include the scope of the inquiry, procedures and methods used to evaluate evidence as well as conclusions and recommendations based on findings of fact and on applicable law. On completion, this report shall be made public. It shall also describe in detail specific events that were found to have occurred and the evidence upon which such findings were based, and list the names of witnesses who testified with the exception of those whose identities have been withheld for their own protection. The State shall, within a reasonable period of time, reply to the report of the investigation, and, as appropriate, indicate steps to be taken in response.

Medical experts involved in the investigation of torture or ill-treatment should behave at all times in conformity with the highest ethical standards and in particular shall obtain informed consent before any examination is undertaken. The examination must follow established standards of medical practice. In particular, examinations shall be conducted in private under the control of the medical expert and outside the presence of security agents and other government officials.

The medical expert should promptly prepare an accurate written report. This report should include at least the following:

(a) The name of the subject and the name and affiliation of those present at the examination; the exact time and date, location, nature and address of the institution (including, where appropriate, the room) where the examination is being conducted (e.g. detention center, clinic, house); and the circumstances of the subject at the time of the examination (e.g. nature of any restraints on arrival or during the examination, presence of security forces during the examination, demean our of those accompanying the prisoner, threatening statements to the examiner) and any other relevant factors;

(b) A detailed record of the subject's story as given during the interview, including alleged methods of torture or ill-treatment, the time when torture or ill-treatment is alleged to have occurred and all complaints of physical and psychological symptoms;

(c) A record of all physical and psychological findings on clinical examination, including appropriate diagnostic tests and, where possible, colour photographs of all injuries;

(d) An interpretation as to the probable relationship of the physical and psychological findings to possible torture or ill-treatment. A recommendation for any necessary medical and psychological treatment and further examination should be given;

(e) The report should clearly identify those carrying out the examination and should be signed.

The report should be confidential and communicated to the subject or a nominated representative. The views of the subject and his or her representative about the examination process should be solicited and recorded in the report. It should also be provided in writing, where appropriate, to the authority responsible for investigating the allegation of torture or ill-treatment. It is the responsibility of the State to ensure that it is delivered securely to these persons. The report should not be made available to any other person, except with the consent of the subject or on the authorization of a court empowered to enforce such transfer.

---

[134] See footnote above.

ANNEX II

Diagnostic tests

Diagnostic tests are being developed and evaluated all the time. The following tests were considered to be of value at the time of the writing of this manual. However, when additional supporting evidence is required, investigators should attempt to find up-to-date sources of information, for example by approaching one of the specialized centers for the documentation of torture (see chapter V.E.).

1. Radiological imaging

In the acute phase of injury, various imaging modalities may be quite useful in providing additional documentation of skeletal and soft tissue injury. Once the physical injuries of torture have healed, however, the residual sequelae are generally no longer detectable by the same imaging methods. This is often true even when the survivor continues to suffer significant pain or disability from his or her injuries. Reference has already been made to various radiological studies in the discussion of the examination of the patient or in the context of various forms of torture. The following is a summary of the application of these methods. However, the more sophisticated and expensive technology is not universally available or at least not to a person in custody.

Radiological and imaging diagnostic examinations include routine radiographs (x-rays), radioisotopic scintigraphy, computerized tomography (CT), nuclear magnetic resonance imaging (MRI) and ultrasonography (USG). Each has advantages and disadvantages. X-rays, scintigraphy and computerized tomography use ionizing radiation, which may be a concern in cases of pregnant women and children. Magnetic resonance imaging uses a magnetic field. Potential biologic effects on foetuses and children are theoretical, but thought to be minimal. Ultrasound uses so und waves, and n o biologic risk is known.

X-rays are readily available. Excluding the skull, all injured areas should have routine radiographs as the initial examination. While routine radiographs will demonstrate facial fractures, computerized tomography is a superior examination as it demonstrates more fractures, fragment displacement and associated soft tissue injury and complications. When periosteal damage or minimal fractures are suspected, bone scintigraphy should be used in addition to x-rays. A percentage of x-rays will be negative even when there is an acute fracture or early osteomyelitis. It is possible for a fracture to heal, leaving no radiographic evidence of previous injury. This is especially true in children. Routine radiographs are not the ideal examination for evaluation of soft tissue.

Scintigraphy is an examination of high sensitivity, but low specificity. It is an inexpensive and effective examination used to screen the entire skeleton for disease processes such as oesteomyelitis or trauma. Testicular torsion canal so be evaluated, but ultrasound is better suited to this task. Scintigraphy is not a method to identify soft tissue trauma. Scintigraphy can detect an acute fracture within twenty-four hours, but it generally takes two to three days and may occasionally take a week or more, particularly in the case of the elderly. The scan generally returns to normal after two years. However, it may remain positive incases of fractures and cured osteomyelitis for years. The use of bone scintigraphy to detect fractures at the epiphysis or metadiaphysis (ends of long bones) in children is very difficult because of the normal uptake of the radiopharmaceutical at the epiphysis. Scintigraphy is often able to detect rib fractures that are not apparent on routine x-ray films.

(a) *Application of bone scintigraphy to the diagnosis of Falanga*

Bone scans can be performed either with delayed images at about three hours or as a three-phase examination. The three phases are the radionucleide angiogram (arterial phase), blood pool images (venous phase, which is soft tissue) and delayed phase (bone phase). Patients examined soon after *falanga* should have two bone scans performed at one-week intervals. A negative first delayed scan and positive second scan indicate exposure to *falanga* within days before the first scan. In acute cases, two negative bone scans at an interval of one week do not necessarily mean that *falanga* did not occur, but that the severity of the *falanga* applied was below the sensitivity level of the scintigraphy. Initially, if three-phase scanning is done, increased uptake in the radionucleide angiogram phase and the blood pool images and no increase uptake in the bone phase would indicate hyperaemia compatible with soft tissue injury. Trauma in the foot bones and soft tissue can also be detected with magnetic resonance imaging.[135]

(b) *Ultrasound*

Ultrasound is inexpensive and without biological hazard. The quality of an examination depends on the skill of the operator. Where computerized tomography is not available, ultrasound is used to evaluate acute abdominal trauma. Tendonopathy can also be evaluated by ultra sound, and it is a method of choice for testicular abnormalities. Shoulder ultrasound is carried out in the acute and chronic periods following suspension torture. In the acute period, oedema, fluid collection on and around the shoulder joint, lacerations and haematomas of the rotator cuffs can be observed by ultrasound. Re-examination with ultrasound and finding that the evidence in the acute period disappears over time strengthen the diagnosis. In such cases, magnetic resonance imaging, scintigraphy and other radiological examinations should be carried out together, and their correlation should be examined. Even lacking positive results from other examinations, ultrasound findings alone are adequate to prove suspension torture.

---

[135] See footnotes 82-84; also refer to standard radiology and nuclear medicine texts for further information.

(c) *Computerized tomography*

Computerized tomography is excellent for imaging soft tissue and bone. However, magnetic resonance imaging is better for soft tissue than bone. Magnetic resonance imaging may detect an occult fracture before it can be imaged by either routine radiographs or scintigraphy. Use of open scanners and sedation may alleviate anxiety and claustrophobia, which are prevalent among torture survivors. Computerized tomography is also excellent for diagnosing and evaluating fractures, especially temporal and facial bones. Other advantages include alignment and displacement of fragments, especially spinal, pelvic, shoulder and acetabular fractures. It cannot identify bone bruising. Computerized tomography with and without intravenous infusion of a contrast agent should be the initial examination for acute, sub-acute and chronic central nervous system (CNS) lesions. If the examination is negative, equivocal or does not explain the survivor's CNS complaints or symptoms, proceed to magnetic resonance imaging. Computerized tomography with bone windows and a pre- and post-contrast examination should be the initial examination for temporal bone fractures. Bone windows may demonstrate fractures and ossicular disruption. The pre-contrast examination may demonstrate fluid and cholesteatoma. Contrast is recommended because of the commonvascul ar anomalies that occur in this area. For rhinorrhea, injection of a contrast agent into the spinal canal should follow a temporal bone. Magnetic resonance imaging may also demonstrate the tear responsible for leakage of the fluid. When rhi norrhea is suspected, a computerized tomography of the face with soft tissue and bone windows should be performed. Then a computerized tomography should be obtained after a contrast agent is injected into the spinal canal.

(d) *Magnetic resonance imaging*

Magnetic resonance imaging is more sensitive than computerized tomography in detecting central nervous system abnormalities. The time course of central nervous system haemorrhage is divided into immediate, hyperacute, acute, sub-acute and chronic phases and central nervous system haemorrhage has ranges that correlate with imaging characteristics of the haemorrhage. Thus, the imaging findings may allow estimation of the timing of head injury and correlation to alleged incidents. Central nervous system haemorrhage may completely resolve or produce sufficient haemosiderin deposits that the computerized tomography will be positive even year s later. Haemorrhage in soft tissue, especially in muscle, usually resolves completely, leaving no trace, but, rarely, it can ossify. This is called heterotrophic bone formation or *myositis ossificans* and is detectable with computerized tomography.

2. Biopsy of electric shock injury

Electric shock injuries may, but do not necessarily, exhibit microscopic changes that are highly diagnostic and specific for electric current trauma. Absence of these specific changes in a biopsy specimen does not mitigate against a diagnosis of electric shock torture, and judicial authorities must not be permitted to make such an assumption. Unfortunately, if a court requests that a petitioner alleging electric shock torture submit to a biopsy for confirmation of the allegations, refusal to consent to the procedure or a negative result is bound to have a prejudicial impact on the court. Furthermore, clinical experience with biopsy diagnosis of torture-related electrical injury is limited, and the diagnosis can usually be made with confidence from the history and physical examination alone.

This procedure is, therefore, one that should be done in a clinical research setting and not promoted as a diagnostic standard. In giving informed consent for biopsy, the person must be informed of the uncertainty of the results and permitted to weigh the potential benefit against the impact upon an already traumatized psyche.

(a) Rationale for biopsy

There has been extensive laboratory research measuring the effects of electric

shocks on the skin of anaesthetized pigs.[136] [137] [138] [139] [140] [141] This work has shown that there are histologic findings specific to electrical injury that can be established by microscopic examination of punch biopsies of the lesions. However, further discussion of this research, which may have significant clinical application, is beyond the scope of this publication. The reader is referred to the above-cited references for additional information.

Few cases of electric shock torture of humans have been studied histologically.[142] [143] [144] [145] Only in one case, where lesions were excised probably seven days after the injury, were alterations in the skin believed to be

[136] Thomsen et al., "Early epidermal changes in he at and electrically injured pig skin: a light microscopic study", *Forensic Science International* (17 1981:133-43).
[137] Thomsen et al., "The effect of direct current, sodium hydroxide, and hydrochloric acid on pig epidermis: a light microscopic and electron microscopic study", *Acta path microbiol. immunol. Scand* (sect. A 91 1983:307-16).
[138] H. K. Thomsen, "Electrically induced epidermal changes: a morphological study of porcine skin after transfer of low-moderate amounts of electrical energy", dissertation (University of Copenhagen, F.A.D.L. 1984:1-78).
[139] T. Karlsmark et al., "Tracing the use of torture: electrically induced calcificationo f collageni npi g skin", *Nature* (301 1983:75-78).
[140] T. Karlsmark et al., "Electrically-induced collagen calcification inp ig skin. A histopathologic and histochemical study", *Forensic Science International* (39 1988:163-74).
[141] T. Karlsmark, "Electrically induced dermal changes: a morphological study of porcine skin after transfer of low to moderate amounts of electrical energy", dissertation, University of Copenhagen, *Danish Medical Bulletin* (37 1990:507-520).
[142] L. Danielsen et al., "Diagnosis of electrical skin injuries: a review and a description of a case", *American Journal of Forensic Medical Pathology* (12 1991:222-226).
[143] F. Öztop et al., " Signs of electrical torture on the skin", *Treatment and Rehabilitation Centers Report 1994* (HumanRi ghts Foundationo f Turkey, HRFT Publication, 11 1994:97-104).
[144] L. Danielsen, T. Karlsmark, H. K. Thomsen, "Diagnosis of skin lesions following electrical torture", *Rom J. Leg. Med* (5 1997:15-20).
[145] H. Jacobsen" Electrically induced deposition of metal on the human skin", *Forensic Science International* (90 1997:85-92).

diagnostic of the electrical injuries observed (deposition of calcium salts on dermal fibres in viable tissue located around necrotic tissue). Lesions excised a few days after alleged electrical torture in other cases have shown segmental changes and deposits of calcium salts on cellular structures highly consistent with the influence of an electrical current, but they are not diagnostic since deposits of calcium salts on dermal fibres were not observed. A biopsy taken one month after alleged electrical torture showed a conical scar, 1-2 millimeters wide, with an increased number of fibroblasts and tightly packed, thin collagen fibres, arranged parallel to the surface, consistent with but not diagnostic of electrical injury.

(b) *Method*

After receiving informed consent from the patient, and before biopsy, the lesion must be photographed using accepted forensic methods. Under local anaesthesia, a 3-4 millimetre punch biopsy is obtained, and placed in buffered formalin or a similar fixative. Skin biopsy should be performed as soon as possible after injury. Since electrical trauma is usually confined to the epidermis and superficial dermis, the lesions may quickly disappear. Biopsies can be taken from more than one lesion, but the potential distress to the patient must be taken into account.[146] Biopsy material should be examined by a pathologist experienced in dermatopathology.

(c) *Diagnostic findings for electrical injury*

Diagnostic findings for electrical injury include vesicular nuclei in epidermis, sweat glands and vessel walls (only one differential diagnosis: injuries via basic solutions) and deposits of calcium salts distinctly located on collagen and elastic fibres (the differential diagnosis, calcinosis cutis, is a rare disorder only found in 75 of 220,000 consecutive

human skin biopsies, and the calcium deposits are usually massive without distinct location on collagen and elastic fibres).[147]

Typical, but not diagnostic, findings for electrical injury are lesions appearing in conical segments, often 1-2 millimetres wide, deposits of iron or copper on epidermis (from the electrode) and homogenous cytoplasm in epidermis, sweat glands and vessel walls. There may also be deposits of calcium salts on cellular structures in segmental lesions or no abnormal histologic observations.

---

[146] S. Gürpinar, "Korur Fincanci ü, Insan Haklari Ihlallari ve Hekim Sorumlulu»u" (Human Rights Violations and Responsibility of the Physician), *Birinci Basamak Icin Adli Tip El Kitabi* (Handbook of ForensicMedicine for General Practitioners) (Ankara, Turkish Medical Association, 1999).

[147] Danielsen et al. (1991).

IN THE EUROPEAN COURT OF HUMAN RIGHTS

Application No. 25424/05

<u>Ramzy</u>   Applicant

v.

The Netherlands   Respondent

WRITTEN COMMENTS
BY

AMNESTY INTERNATIONAL LTD., THE ASSOCIATION FOR THE PREVENTION OF TORTURE, HUMAN RIGHTS WATCH, INTERIGHTS, THE INTERNATIONAL COMMISSION OF JURISTS, OPEN SOCIETY JUSTICE INITIATIVE AND REDRESS

PURSUANT TO ARTICLE 36 § 2 OF THE EUROPEAN CONVENTION ON HUMAN RIGHTS AND RULE 44 § 2 OF THE RULES OF THE EUROPEAN COURT OF HUMAN RIGHTS

22 November 2005

I. INTRODUCTION

1.   These written comments are respectfully submitted on behalf of Amnesty International Ltd, the Association for the Prevention of Torture, Human Rights Watch, INTERIGHTS, the International Commission of Jurists, Open Society Justice Initiative and REDRESS ("the Intervenors") pursuant to leave granted by the President of the Chamber in accordance with Rule 44 § 2 of the Rules of Court.[1]

2.   Brief details of each of the Intervenors are set out in Annex 1 to this letter. Together they have extensive experience of working against the use of torture and other forms of ill-treatment around the world. They have contributed to the elaboration of international legal standards, and intervened in human rights litigation in national and international fora, including before this Court, on the prohibition of torture and ill-treatment. Together the intervenors possess an extensive body of knowledge and experience of relevant international legal standards and jurisprudence and their application in practice.

II. OVERVIEW

3.   This case concerns the deportation to Algeria of a person suspected of involvement in an Islamic extremist group in the Netherlands. He complains that his removal to Algeria by the Dutch authorities will expose him to a "real risk" of torture or ill-treatment in violation of Article 3 of the European Convention on Human Rights (the "Convention"). This case, and the interventions of various governments, raise issues of fundamental importance concerning the effectiveness of the protection against torture and other ill-treatment, including in the context of the fight against terrorism. At a time when torture and ill-treatment – and transfer to states renowned for such practices – are arising with increasing frequency, and the absolute nature of the torture prohibition itself is increasingly subject to question, the Court's determination in this case is of potentially profound import beyond the case and indeed the region.

4.   These comments address the following specific matters: (i) the absolute nature of the prohibition of torture and other forms of ill-treatment under international law; (ii) the prohibition of transfer to States where there is a substantial risk of torture or ill-treatment ("*non-refoulement*")[2] as an essential aspect of that prohibition; (iii) the absolute nature of the *non-refoulement* prohibition under Article 3, and the approach of other international courts and

---

[1] Letter dated 11 October 2005 from Vincent Berger, Section Registrar to Helen Duffy, Legal Director, INTERIGHTS. The World Organization Against Torture (OMCT) and the Medical Foundation for the Care of the Victims of Torture provided input into and support with this brief.

[2] "Other ill-treatment" refers to inhuman or degrading treatment or punishment under Article 3 of the Convention and to similar or equivalent formulations under other international instruments. "*Non-refoulement*" is used to refer to the specific legal principles concerning the prohibition of transfer from a Contracting State to another State where there is a risk of such ill-treatment, developed under human rights law in relation to Article 3 of the Convention and similar provisions. Although the term was originally borrowed from refugee law, as noted below its scope and significance in that context is distinct. The term "transfer" is used to refer to all forms of removal, expulsion or deportation.

human rights bodies; (iv) the nature of the risk required to trigger this prohibition; (v) factors relevant to its assessment; and (vi) the standard and burden of proof on the applicant to establish such risk.

5.   While these comments take as their starting point the jurisprudence of this Court, the focus is on international and comparative standards, including those enshrined in the UN Convention against Torture and Other Cruel, Inhuman or Degrading Treatment or Punishment ("UNCAT"), the International Covenant on Civil and Political Rights ("ICCPR"), as well as applicable rules of customary international law, all of which have emphasised the absolute, non-derogable and peremptory nature of the prohibition of torture and ill-treatment and, through jurisprudence, developed standards to give it meaningful effect. This Court has a long history of invoking other human rights instruments to assist in the proper interpretation of the Convention itself, including most significantly for present purposes, the UNCAT.[3]   Conversely, the lead that this Court has taken in the development of human rights standards in respect of *non-refoulement*, notably through the *Chahal v. the United Kingdom* (1996) case, has been followed extensively by other international courts and bodies, and now reflects an accepted international standard.[4]

III. THE 'ABSOLUTE' PROHIBITION OF TORTURE AND ILL-TREATMENT

6.   The prohibition of torture and other forms of ill-treatment is universally recognised and is enshrined in all of the major international and regional human rights instruments.[5]   All international instruments that contain the prohibition of torture and ill-treatment recognise its absolute, non-derogable character.[6]   This non-derogability has consistently been reiterated by human rights courts, monitoring bodies and international criminal tribunals, including this Court, the UN Human Rights Committee ("HRC"), the UN Committee against Torture ("CAT"), the Inter-American Commission and Court, and the International Criminal Tribunal for

---

[3] *Aydin v. Turkey* (1997); *Soering v. the United Kingdom* (1989); *Selmouni v. France* (1999); and *Mahmut Kaya v. Turkey* (2000). For full reference to these and other authorities cited in the brief see Annex 2 Table of Authorities.

[4] See e.g. CAT Communication *T.P.S. v. Canada* (2000); Inter-American Commission on Human Rights, *Report on the Situation of Human Rights of Asylum Seekers Within the Canadian Refugee Determination System* (2000); UN Special Rapporteur on Torture, *Reports to General Assembly* (2005, §§ 38–39; 2004, § 28; and 2002, § 32).

[5] Universal Declaration of Human Rights (Article 5); ICCPR (Article 7); American Convention on Human Rights (Article 5); African Charter on Human and Peoples' Rights (Article 5), Arab Charter on Human Rights (Article 13), UNCAT and European Convention for the Prevention of Torture and Inhuman or Degrading Treatment or Punishment. The prohibition against torture is also reflected throughout international humanitarian law, in e.g. the Regulations annexed to the Hague Convention IV of 1907, the Geneva Conventions of 1949 and their two Additional Protocols of 1977.

[6] The prohibition of torture and ill-treatment is specifically excluded from derogation provisions: see Article 4(2) of the ICCPR; Articles 2(2) and 15 of the UNCAT; Article 27(2) of the American Convention on Human Rights; Article 4(c) Arab Charter of Human Rights; Article 5 of the Inter-American Convention to Prevent and Punish Torture; Articles 3 of the Declaration on the Protection of All Persons from Being Subjected to Torture and Other Cruel, Inhuman or Degrading Treatment or Punishment.

the Former Yugoslavia ("ICTY").[7]

7.   The prohibition of torture and other forms of ill-treatment does not therefore yield to the threat posed by terrorism. This Court, the HRC, the CAT, the Special Rapporteur on Torture, the UN Security Council and General Assembly, and the Committee of Ministers of the Council of Europe, among others, have all recognised the undoubted difficulties States face in countering terrorism, yet made clear that all anti-terrorism measures must be implemented in accordance with international human rights and humanitarian law, including the prohibition of torture and other ill-treatment.[8] A recent United Nations World Summit Outcome Document (adopted with the consensus of all States) in para. 85 reiterated the point.

8.   The absolute nature of the prohibition of torture under treaty law is reinforced by its higher, *jus cogens* status under customary international law. *Jus cogens* status connotes the fundamental, peremptory character of the obligation, which is, in the words of the International Court of Justice, "intransgressible."[9] There is ample international authority recognising the prohibition of torture as having *jus cogens* status.[10] The prohibition of torture also imposes obligations *erga omnes,* and every State has a legal interest in the performance of such obligations which are owed to the international community as a whole.[11]

9.   The principal consequence of its higher rank as a *jus cogens* norm is that the principle or rule cannot be derogated from by States through any laws or agreements not endowed with the same normative force.[12] Thus, no treaty can be made nor law enacted that conflicts with a *jus cogens* norm, and no practice or act

---

[7] See HRC General Comment No. 29 (2001); CAT 's Concluding observations on the Reports of: the Russian Federation (2001, § 90), Egypt (2002, § 40), and Spain (2002, § 59); Inter-American cases, e.g. *Castillo-Petruzzi et al. v. Peru* (1999, § 197); *Cantoral Benavides v. Peru* (2000, § 96); *Maritza Urrutia v. Guatemala,* (2003, § 89); this Court's cases, e.g. *Tomasi v. France,* (1992); *Aksoy v. Turkey,* (1996); and *Chahal v. the United Kingdom,* (1996); ICTY cases, e.g. *Prosecutor v. Furundzija* (1998).

[8] This Court, see e.g. *Klass and Others v. Germany* (1978); *Leander v. Sweden* (1987) and *Rotaru v. Romania* (2000); HRC, General Comment No. 29 (2001, § 7), and Concluding observations on Egypt's Report, (2002, § 4); CAT Concluding observations on Israel's Report (1997, §§ 2-3 and 24); Report to the General Assembly (2004, § 17) and *Statement in connection with the events of 11 September 2001* (2001, § 17); General Assembly Resolutions 57/27(2002), 57/219 (2002) and 59/191 (2004); Security Council Resolution 1456 (2003, Annex, § 6); Council of Europe Guidelines on Human Rights and the Fight Against Terrorism (2002); Special Rapporteur on Torture, *Statement to the Third Committee of the GA* (2001). Other bodies pronouncing on the issue include, for example, Human Rights Chamber for Bosnia and Herzegovina (see e.g. *Boudellaa and others v. Bosnia and Herzegovina and the Federation of Bosnia and Herzegovina,* 2003, §§ 264 to 267).

[9] Advisory Opinion of the ICJ on the *Legal Consequences of the Constructions of a Wall in the Occupied Palestinian Territory,* (2004, § 157). See also Article 5,3 Vienna Convention on the Law of Treaties (1969) which introduces and defines the concept of "peremptory norm."

[10] See e.g. the first report of the Special Rapporteur on Torture to the UNHCR (1997, § 3); ICTY judgments *Prosecutor v. Delalic and others* (1998), *Prosecutor v. Kunarac* (2001, § 466), and *Prosecutor v. Furundzija* (1998); and comments of this Court in *Al-Adsani v. the United Kingdom* (2001).

[11] See ICJ Reports: *Barcelona Traction, Light and Power Company, Limited,* Second Phase (1970, § 33); *Case Concerning East Timor* (1995, § 29); *Case Concerning Application of the Convention on the Prevention and Punishment of the Crime of Genocide* (1996, § 31). See also Articles 40-41 of the International Law Commission's Draft Articles on State Responsibility ("ILC Draft Articles") and the commentary to the Draft Articles. See ICTY case *Prosecutor v. Furundzija,* (1998, § 151); Inter-American Commission on Human Rights, *Report on Terrorism and Human Rights,* (2000, § 155); and HRC General Comment 31(2004, § 2).

[12] See Article 53 of the Vienna Convention on the Law of Treaties 1969; also ICTY *Furundzija* (1998, §§ 153-54).

committed in contravention of a *jus cogens* norm may be "legitimated by means of consent, acquiescence or recognition"; any norm conflicting with such a provision is therefore void.[13] It follows that no interpretation of treaty obligations that is inconsistent with the absolute prohibition of torture is valid in international law.

10.   The fact that the prohibition of torture is *jus cogens* and gives rise to obligations *erga omnes* also has important consequences under basic principles of State responsibility, which provide for the interest and in certain circumstances the obligation of all States to prevent torture and other forms of ill-treatment, to bring it to an end, and not to endorse, adopt or recognise acts that breach the prohibition.[14] Any interpretation of the Convention must be consistent with these obligations under broader international law.

IV. THE PRINCIPLE OF *NON-REFOULEMENT*

11.   The expulsion (or '*refoulement*') of an individual where there is a real risk of torture or other ill-treatment is prohibited under both international conventional and customary law. A number of States, human rights experts and legal commentators have specifically noted the customary nature of *non-refoulement*[15] and asserted that the prohibition against *non-refoulement* under customary international law shares its *jus cogens* and *erga omnes* character. As the prohibition of all forms of ill-treatment (torture, inhuman or degrading treatment or punishment) is absolute, peremptory and non-derogable, the principle of *non-refoulement* applies without distinction.[16] Indicative of the expansive approach to the protection, both CAT and HRC are of the opinion that *non-refoulement* prohibits return to countries where the individual would not be directly at risk but from where he or she is in danger of being expelled to another country or territory where there would be such a risk.[17]

12.   The prohibition of *refoulement* is explicit in conventions dedicated specifically to torture and ill-treatment. Article 3 of UNCAT prohibits States from deporting an individual to a State "where there are substantial grounds for believing that he would be in danger of being subjected to torture." Article 13(4) of the Inter-American Convention to Prevent and Punish Torture provides, more broadly, that deportation is prohibited on the basis that the individual "will be subjected to torture or to cruel, inhuman or degrading treatment, or that he will be tried by special or ad hoc courts in the requesting State."

---

[13] Jennings and Watts, *Oppenheim's International Law* (Vol. 1, Ninth ed.) 8 (1996). See also Article 53, Vienna Convention.
[14] See ILC Draft Articles (40 and 41 on *jus cogens*; and Articles 42 and 48 on *erga omnes*); see also Advisory Opinion of the ICJ on the *Legal Consequences of the Constructions of a Wall in the Occupied Palestinian Territory*, (2004, § 159). In respect of the *erga omnes* character of the obligations arising under the ICCPR thereof, see Comment 31 (2004, § 2).
[15] See E. Lauterpacht and D. Bethlehem (2001, §§ 196-216).
[16] See e.g. HRC General Comment No. 20 (1992, § 9).
[17] CAT General Comment No. 1(1996, § 2); *Avedes Hamayak Korban v. Sweden* (1997); and HRC General Comment 31(2004).

13.   The principle of *non-refoulement* is also explicitly included in a number of other international instruments focusing on human rights, including the EU Charter of Fundamental Rights and Inter-American Convention on Human Rights ("I-ACHR").[18] In addition, it is reflected in other international instruments addressing international cooperation, including extradition treaties, and specific forms of terrorism.[19] Although somewhat different in its scope and characteristics, the principle is also reflected in refugee law.[20]

14.   This principle is also implicit in the prohibition of torture and other ill-treatment in general human rights conventions, as made clear by consistent authoritative interpretations of these provisions. In *Soering* and in subsequent cases, this Court identified *non-refoulement* as an 'inherent obligation' under Article 3 of the Convention in cases where there is a "real risk of exposure to inhuman or degrading treatment or punishment." Other bodies have followed suit, with the HRC, in its general comments and individual communications, interpreting Article 7 of the ICCPR as implicitly prohibiting *refoulement*.[21]   The African Commission on Human Rights and the Inter-American Commission on Human Rights have also recognised that deportation can, in certain circumstances, constitute such ill-treatment.[22]

15.   The jurisprudence therefore makes clear that the prohibition on *refoulement*, whether explicit or implicit, is an inherent and indivisible part of the prohibition on torture or other ill-treatment. It constitutes an essential way of giving effect to the Article 3 prohibition, which not only imposes on states the duty not to torture themselves, but also requires them to "prevent such acts by not bringing persons under the control of other States if there are substantial grounds for believing that they would be in danger of being subjected to torture."[23] This is consistent with the approach to fundamental rights adopted by this Court, and increasingly by other bodies, regarding the positive duties incumbent on the

---

[18] Article 19 EU Charter of Fundamental Rights; Article 22(8) I-ACHR; Article 3(1) Declaration on Territorial Asylum, Article 8 Declaration on the Protection of All Persons from Enforced Disappearances, Principle 5 Principles on the Effective Prevention and Investigation of Extra-legal, Arbitrary and Summary Executions, and Council of Europe Guidelines.

[19] Article 9 International Convention against the Taking of Hostages, Article 3 European Convention on Extradition, Article 5 European Convention on the Suppression of Terrorism, and Article 4(5) Inter-American Convention on Extradition contain a general clause on *non-refoulement*. See also Article 3 Model Treaty on Extraditions.

[20] The principle of *non-refoulement* applicable to torture and other ill-treatment under human rights law is complementary to the broader rule of *non-refoulement* applicable where there is a well founded fear of 'persecution' under refugee law, which excludes those who pose a danger to the security of the host State. However, there are no exceptions to *non-refoulement*, whether of a refugee or any other person, when freedom from torture and other ill-treatment is at stake. See Articles 32 and 33 of the Convention Relating to the Status of Refugees, 1951, *Chahal* case (1996, § 80), the New Zealand case of *Zaoui v. Attorney General* (2005); and Lauterpacht and Bethlehem (2001, §§ 244 and 250).

[21] See HRC General Comments No. 20 (1990, at § 9), and No. 31 (2004, §12). For individual communications, see e.g. *Chitat Ng v. Canada*, (1994, § 14.1); *Cox v. Canada* (1994); *G.T. v. Australia* (1997).

[22] See African Commission on Human Rights, *Modise v. Botswana*, and I-A Comm. HR *Report on Terrorism and Human Rights* (2004).

[23] Report of the Special Rapporteur to the Third Committee of the GA (2001, § 28).

state.[24] Any other interpretation, enabling states to circumvent their obligations on the basis that they themselves did not carry out the ill-treatment would, as this Court noted when it first considered the matter, 'plainly be contrary to the spirit and intention of [Article 3].'[25]

The Absolute Nature of the Prohibition on *Refoulement*

16.   The foregoing demonstrates that the prohibition on *refoulement* is inherent in the prohibition of torture and other forms of ill-treatment. UN resolutions, declarations, international conventions, interpretative statements by treaty monitoring bodies, statements of the UN Special Rapporteur on Torture and judgments of international tribunals, including this Court, as described herein, have consistently supported this interpretation. It follows from its nature as inherent to it, that the *non-refoulement* prohibition enjoys the same status and essential characteristics as the prohibition on torture and ill-treatment itself, and that it may not be subject to any limitations or exceptions.

17.   The jurisprudence of international bodies has, moreover, explicitly given voice to the absolute nature of the principle of *non-refoulement*. In its case law, this Court has firmly established and re-affirmed the absolute nature of the prohibition of *non-refoulement* under Article 3 of the Convention.[26] In paragraph 80 of the *Chahal* case, this Court made clear that the obligations of the State under Article 3 are "equally absolute in expulsion cases" once the 'real risk' of torture or ill-treatment is shown. The CAT has followed suit in confirming the absolute nature of the prohibition of *refoulement* under Article 3 in the context of particular cases.[27]   Likewise, other regional bodies have also interpreted the prohibition on torture and ill-treatment as including an absolute prohibition of *refoulement*.[28]

Application of the non-refoulement *principle to all persons*

18.   It is a fundamental principle that *non-refoulement*, like the protection from torture or ill-treatment itself, applies to *all persons* without distinction. No characteristics or conduct, criminal activity or terrorist offence, alleged or proven, can affect the right not to be subject to torture and ill-treatment, including through *refoulement*. In the recent case of *N. v. Finland* (2005), this Court reiterated earlier findings that "[a]s the prohibition provided by Article 3 against torture, inhuman or degrading treatment or punishment is of absolute character, *the activities of the individual in question, however undesirable or*

---

[24] See Special Rapporteur on Torture Report (1986, § 6) and Report (2004, § 27); HRC General Comments No. 7 (1982) and No. 20 (1992); Articles 40–42 and 48 of the ILC Draft Articles; ICTY *Furundzija* judgment (1998, § 148).
[25] *Soering v. UK* (1989, § 88).
[26] *Soering v. UK* (1989, § 88); *Ahmed v. Austria* (1996 § 41); *Chahal v. UK* (1996).
[27] See CAT *Tapia Paez v. Sweden*, (1997, at § 9.8) and *Pauline Muzonzo Paku Kisoki v. Sweden* (1996).
[28] See *Modise* case and *Report on Terrorism and Human Rights*.

dangerous, cannot be a material consideration (emphasis added)." The same principle is reiterated in other decisions of this Court and of other bodies.[29]

Application of the non-refoulement *principle in the face of terrorism or national security threat*

19. The jurisprudence of other regional and international bodies, like that of this Court, rejects definitively the notion that threats to national security, or the challenge posed by international or domestic terrorism, affect the absolute nature of the prohibition on *non-refoulement*. In *Chahal*, this Court was emphatic that no derogation is permissible from the prohibition of torture and other forms of ill-treatment and the obligations arising from it (such as *non-refoulement*) in the context of terrorism. This line of reasoning has been followed in many other cases of this Court and other bodies including the recent case of *Agiza v. Sweden* in which CAT stated that "the Convention's protections are absolute, even in the context of national security concerns."[30]

20. Thus no exceptional circumstances, however grave or compelling, can justify the introduction of a "balancing test" when fundamental norms such as the prohibition on *non-refoulement* in case of torture or ill-treatment are at stake. This is evident from the concluding observations of both HRC and CAT on State reports under the ICCPR and UNCAT, respectively.[31] On the relatively few occasions when states have introduced a degree of balancing in domestic systems, they have been heavily criticised in concluding observations of CAT,[32] or the HRC.[33] This practice follows, and underscores, this Court's own position in the *Chahal* case where it refused the United Kingdom's request to perform a balancing test that would weigh the risk presented by permitting the individual to remain in the State against the risk to the individual of deportation.

Non-Refoulement as *Jus Cogens*

21. It follows also from the fact that the prohibition of *refoulement* is inherent in the prohibition of torture and other forms of ill-treatment, and necessary to give effect to it, that it enjoys the same customary law, and *jus cogens* status as the general prohibition. States and human rights legal experts have also specifically asserted that the prohibition against *non-refoulement* constitutes

---

[29] *See inter alia Ahmed v. Austria* (1996); and CAT *Tapia Paez v. Sweden* (1997, § 14.5); *M. B. B. v. Sweden* (1998, § 6.4).

[30] See CAT *Agiza v. Sweden* (2005, § 13.8); *Aemei v. Switzerland* (1997, § 9.8); *M.B.B. v. Sweden*, §6.4; *Arana v. France*, (2000, § 11.5).

[31] E.g. CAT's Concluding Observations on Germany (2004), commending the reaffirmation of the absolute ban on exposure to torture, including through *refoulement*, even where there is a security risk.

[32] See CAT's Concluding Observations on Sweden's Report (2002, §14); and on Canada's Report (2005, § 4(a)).

[33] See also HRC Concluding Observations on Canada's Report (1999, §13) condemning the Canadian *Suresh* case, which upheld a degree of balancing under Article 3, based on national law, and *Mansour Ahani v. Canada*, (2002, § 10.10) where HRC also clearly rejected Canada's balancing test in the context of deportation proceedings.

customary international law, and enjoys *jus cogens* status.[34] As noted, one consequence of *jus cogens* status is that no treaty obligation, or interpretation thereof, inconsistent with the absolute prohibition of *refoulement*, has validity under international law.

22. Certain consequences also flow from the *jus cogens* nature of the prohibition of torture itself (irrespective of the status of the *non-refoulement* principle), and the *erga omnes* obligations related thereto. The principle of *non-refoulement* is integral – and necessary to give effect – to the prohibition of torture. To deport an individual in circumstances where there is a real risk of torture is manifestly at odds with the positive obligations not to aid, assist or recognise such acts and the duty to act to ensure that they cease.[35]

V. THE OPERATION OF THE RULE
The General Test

23. When considering the obligations of States under Article 3 in transfer cases, this Court seeks to establish whether *"substantial grounds are shown for believing that the person concerned, if expelled, faces a real risk of being subjected to torture or to inhuman or degrading treatment or punishment in the receiving country."*[36] This test is very similar to those established by other bodies. Article 3 (1) of the UNCAT requires that the person not be transferred to a country where there are *"substantial grounds for believing that he would be in danger of being subjected to torture."* The HRC has similarly affirmed that the obligation arises *"where there are substantial grounds for believing that there is a real risk of irreparable harm."*[37] The Inter-American Commission for Human Rights has likewise referred to *"substantial grounds of a real risk of inhuman treatment."*[38]

24. The legal questions relevant to the Court's determination in transfer cases, assuming that the potential ill-treatment falls within the ambit of Article 3, are: first, the nature and degree of the risk that triggers the *non-refoulement* prohibition; second, the relevant considerations that constitute 'substantial grounds' for believing that the person faces such a risk; third, the standard by which the existence of these 'substantial grounds' is to be evaluated and proved. The comments below address these questions in turn.

---

[34] See Lauterpacht and Bethlehem (2001, § 195); Bruin and Wouters (2003, § 4.6); Allain (2002); Report of Special Rapporteur on Torture to the GA (2004); IACHR Report on the Situation of Human Rights of Asylum Seekers within the Canadian Refugee Determination System (2000, § 154). There has also been considerable support among Latin American States for the broader prohibition of *non-refoulement* in refugee law as "imperative in regard to refugees and in the present state of international law [thus it] should be acknowledged and observed as a rule of *jus cogens*" (Cartagena Declaration of Refugees of 1984, Section III, § 5).

[35] ILC Draft Articles, Article 16.

[36] *N v. Finland* (2005).

[37] HRC General Comment 31 (2004).

[38] *Report on Terrorism and Human Rights* (2002), *Report on the Situation of Human Rights of Asylum Seekers within the Canadian Refugee Determination System*, (2000, § 154).

25.   A guiding principle in the analysis of each of these questions, apparent from the work of this Court and other bodies, is the need to ensure the effective operation of the *non-refoulement* rule. This implies interpreting the rule consistently with the human rights objective of the Convention; the positive obligations on States to prevent serious violations and the responsibility of the Court to guard against it; the absolute nature of the prohibition of torture and ill-treatment and the grave consequences of such a breach transpiring; and the practical reality in which the *non-refoulement* principle operates. As this Court has noted: "The object and purpose of the Convention as an instrument for the protection of individual human beings require that *its provisions be interpreted and applied so as to make its safeguards practical and effective.*" [39]

Nature and Degree of the Risk

26.   This Court, like the CAT, has required that the risk be "real", "foreseeable", and "personal".[40] There is no precise definition in the Convention case law of what constitutes a "real" risk, although the Court has established that "mere possibility of ill-treatment is not enough",[41] just as certainty that the ill-treatment will occur is not required.[42] For more precision as to the standard, reference can usefully be made to the jurisprudence of other international and regional bodies which also apply the 'real and foreseeable' test. Notably, the CAT has held that the risk "must be assessed on grounds that go beyond mere theory or suspicion", but this does not mean that the risk has to be "highly probable".[43]

27.   The risk must also be "personal". However, as noted in the following section, personal risk may be deduced from various factors, notably the treatment of similarly situated persons.

Factors Relevant to the Assessment of Risk

28.   This Court and other international human rights courts and bodies have repeatedly emphasised that the level of scrutiny to be given to a claim for *non-refoulement* must be "rigorous" in view of the absolute nature of the right this principle protects.[44] In doing so, the State must take into account "all the relevant considerations" for the substantiation of the risk.[45] This includes both the human rights situation in the country of return and the personal background and the circumstances of the individual.

---

[39] *Soering v. the United Kingdom*, (1989, § 87), emphasis added.
[40] CAT General Comment 1 (1997); *Soering v. the United Kingdom* (1989, § 86); *Shamayev and 12 others v. Russia* (2005).
[41] See *Vilvarajah*, (1991, § 111).
[42] *Soering*, (1989, § 94).
[43] See e.g. CAT *X.Y.Z. v. Sweden* (1998); *A.L.N. v. Switzerland* (1998); *K.N. v. Switzerland*; and *A.R. v. The Netherlands* (2003).
[44] *Chahal v. the United Kingdom*, 91996, § 79); *Jabari v. Turkey* (2000, § 39).
[45] UNCAT Article 33 (2).

General Situation in the Country of Return
29.   The human rights situation in the state of return is a weighty factor in virtually all cases.[46] While this Court, like CAT,[47] has held that the situation in the state is not sufficient *per se* to prove risk, regard must be had to the extent of human rights repression in the State in assessing the extent to which personal circumstances must also be demonstrated.[48] Where the situation is particularly grave and ill-treatment widespread or generalised, the general risk of torture or ill-treatment may be high enough that little is required to demonstrate the personal risk to an individual returning to that State. The significant weight of this factor is underlined in Article 3(2) of UNCAT: "For the purpose of determining whether there are such grounds, the competent authorities shall take into account all relevant considerations including, where applicable, the existence in the State concerned of a consistent pattern of gross, flagrant or mass violations of human rights."

Personal Background or Circumstances
30.   The critical assessment in *non-refoulement* cases usually turns on whether the applicant has demonstrated "specific circumstances" which make him or her personally vulnerable to torture or ill-treatment. These specific circumstances may be indicated by previous ill-treatment or evidence of current persecution (e.g. that the person is being pursued by the authorities), but neither is necessary to substantiate that the individual is 'personally' at risk.[49] A person may be found at risk by virtue of a characteristic that makes him or her particularly vulnerable to torture or other ill-treatment. The requisite 'personal' risk does not necessarily require information specifically about that person therefore, as opposed to information about the fate of persons in similar situations.

Perceived Association with a Vulnerable Group as a Strong Indication of the Existence of Risk
31.   It is clearly established in the jurisprudence of the CAT that, in assessing the "specific circumstances" that render the individual personally at risk, particular attention will be paid to any evidence that the applicant belongs, or is *perceived* to belong,[50] to an identifiable group which has been targeted for torture

---

[46] As held by CAT, the absence of a pattern of human rights violations "does not mean that a person cannot be considered to be in danger of being subjected to torture in his or her specific circumstances." See e.g. *Seid Mortesa Aemei v. Switzerland* (1997).
[47] CAT has explained that although a pattern of systematic abuses in the State concerned is highly relevant, it "does not as such constitute sufficient ground" for a situation to fall under Article 3 because the risk must be 'personal'.
[48] *Vilvarajah* (1991, § 108).
[49] See eg. *Shamayev and 12 otehrs v. Russia* (2005, § 352); *Said v. the Netherlands* (2005, § 48-49).
[50] It is not necessary that the individual *actually* is a member of the targeted group, if believed so to be and targeted for that reason. See CAT *A. v. The Netherlands* (1998).

or ill-treatment. It has held that regard must be had to the applicant's political or social affiliations or activities, whether inside or outside the State of return, which may lead that State to identify the applicant with the targeted group.[51]

32. Organisational affiliation is a particularly important factor in cases where the individual belongs to a group which the State in question has designated as a "terrorist" or "separatist" group that threatens the security of the State, and which for this reason is targeted for particularly harsh forms of repression. In such cases, the CAT has found that the applicant's claim comes within the purview of Article 3 even in the absence of other factors such as evidence that the applicant was ill-treated in the past,[52] and even when the general human rights situation in the country may have improved.[53]

33. In this connection, it is also unnecessary for the individual to show that he or she is, or ever was, personally sought by the authorities of the State of return. Instead, the CAT's determination has focused on the assessment of a) how the State in question treats members of these groups, and b) whether sufficient evidence was provided that the State would believe the particular individual to be associated with the targeted group. Thus in cases involving suspected members of ETA, Sendero Luminoso, PKK, KAWA, the People's Mujahadeen Organization and the Zapatista Movement, the CAT has found violations of Article 3 on account of a pattern of human rights violations against members of these organisations, where it was sufficiently established that the States concerned were likely to identify the individuals with the relevant organisations.[54]

34. In respect of proving this link between the individual and the targeted group, the CAT has found that the nature and profile of the individual's activities in his country of origin or abroad[55] is relevant. In this respect, human rights bodies have indicated that a particularly important factor to be considered is the extent of publicity surrounding the individual's case, which may have had the effect of drawing the negative attention of the State party to the individual. The importance of this factor has been recognized both by this Court and the CAT.[56]

Standard and Burden of Proving the Risk

35. While the Court has not explicitly addressed the issue of standard and burden of proof in transfer cases, it has held that in view of the fundamental character of the prohibition under Article 3, the examination of risk "must

---

[51] See CAT General Comment 1 (1997, § 8 (e)).
[52] Gorki Ernesto Tapia Paez v. Sweden (1997).
[53] See Josu Arkauz Arana v. France (2000), finding that gross, flagrant or mass violations were unnecessary in such circumstances.
[54] See inter alia CAT, Cecilia Chipana v. Venezuela (1998); Ahmed Hussein Mustafa Kamil Agiza v. Sweden (2005); Kaveh Yaragh Tala v. Sweden (1998); Seid Mortesa Aemei v. Switzreland (1996).
[55] See e.g. Seid Mortesa Aemei v. Switzerland (1997); M.K.O. v. The Netherlands (2001).
[56] N v. Finland (2005, § 165); Venkadajalasarma v. the Netherlands (2004); Said v. the Netherlands (2005, § 54); Thampibillai v. the Netherlands (2004, § 63). See also CAT Sadiq Shek Elmi v. Australia (1999, § 6.8).

necessarily be a thorough one".[57] It has also imposed on States a positive obligation to conduct a 'meaningful assessment' of any claim of a risk of torture and other ill-treatment.[58] This approach is supported by CAT,[59] and reflects a general recognition by this and other tribunals that, because of the specific nature of torture and other ill-treatment, the burden of proof cannot rest alone with the person alleging it, particularly in the view of the fact that the person and the State do not always have equal access to the evidence.[60] Rather, in order to give meaningful effect to the Convention rights under Article 3 in transfer cases, the difficulties in obtaining evidence of a risk of torture or ill-treatment in another State – exacerbated by the inherently clandestine nature of such activity and the individual's remoteness from the State concerned – should be reflected in setting a reasonable and appropriate standard and burden of proof and ensuring flexibility in its implementation.

36.   The particular difficulties facing an individual seeking to substantiate an alleged risk of ill-treatment have been recognized by international tribunals, including this Court. These are reflected, for example, in the approach to the extent of the evidence which the individual has to adduce. The major difficulties individuals face in accessing materials in the context of transfer is reflected in the Court's acknowledgment that substantiation only "to the greatest extent practically possible" can reasonably be required.[61] Moreover, CAT's views have consistently emphasised that, given what is at stake for the individual, lingering doubts as to credibility or proof should be resolved in the individual's favour: "even though there may be some remaining doubt as to the veracity of the facts adduced by the author of a communication, [the Committee] *must ensure that his security is not endangered*.[62] In order to do this, it is not necessary that all the facts invoked by the author should be proved."[63]

37.   An onus undoubtedly rests on individuals to raise, and to seek to substantiate, their claims. It is sufficient however for the individual to substantiate an 'arguable' or *'prima facie'* case of the risk of torture or other ill-treatment for the *refoulement* prohibition to be triggered. It is then for the State to dispel the fear that torture or ill-treatment would ensue if the person is transferred. This approach is supported by a number of international tribunals addressing questions of proof in transfer cases. For example, the CAT suggests that it is sufficient for the individual to present an *'arguable case'* or to make a *'plausible allegation'*; then it is for the State to prove the lack of danger in case of

---

[57] *Said v. the Netherlands* (2005, § 49), *N. v Finland* (2005); *Jabari v. Turkey* (2000, § 39).

[58] See *Jabari v. Turkey* (2000).

[59] E.g. CAT General Comment 1 (1997, § 9(b)).

[60] See e.g. HRC, *Albert Womah Mukong v. Cameroon* (1994); I-ACHR, *Velasquez Rodriguez v. Hondouras* (1988, § 134 et seq).

[61] E.g. *Said v. the Netherlands* (2005, § 49); *Bahaddar v. the Netherlands*, (1998, § 45).

[62] Emphasis added.

[63] *Seid Mortesa Aemei v. Switzerland* (1997).

return.[64] Similarly, the HRC has held that the burden· is on the individual to establish a *'prima facie'* case of real risk, and then the State must refute the claim with 'substantive grounds'.[65] Most recently, the UN Sub-Commission for the Promotion of Human Rights considered that once a general risk situation is established, there is a 'presumption' the person would face a real risk.[66]

38.   Requiring the sending State to rebut an arguable case is consistent not only with the frequent reality attending individuals' access to evidence, but also with the duties on the State to make a meaningful assessment and satisfy itself that any transfer would not expose the individual to a risk of the type of ill-treatment that the State has positive obligation to protect against.

An Existing Risk Cannot be Displaced by "Diplomatic Assurances"

39.   States may seek to rely on "diplomatic assurances" or "memoranda of understanding" as a mechanism to transfer individuals to countries where they are at risk of torture and other ill-treatment. In practice, the very fact that the sending State seeks such assurances amounts to an admission that the person would be at risk of torture or ill-treatment in the receiving State if returned. As acknowledged by this Court in *Chahal*, and by CAT in *Agiza*, assurances do not suffice to offset an existing risk of torture.[67] This view is shared by a growing number of international human rights bodies and experts, including the UN Special Rapporteur on Torture,[68] the Committee for Prevention of Torture,[69] the UN Sub-Commission,[70] the Council of Europe Commissioner on Human Rights,[71] and the UN Independent Expert on the Protection of Human Rights and Fundamental Freedoms while Countering Terrorism.[72] Most recently, the UN General Assembly, by consensus of all States, has affirmed "that diplomatic assurances, where used, do not release States from their obligations, under international human rights, humanitarian and refugee law, in particular the principle of *non-refoulement*."[73] Reliance on such assurances as sufficient to displace the risk of torture creates a dangerous loophole in the *non-refoulement* obligation, and ultimately erodes the prohibition of torture and other ill-treatment.

---

[64] CAT General Comment 1 (1997, § 5): *"The burden of proving a danger of torture is upon the person alleging such danger to present an 'arguable case'. This means that there must be a factual basis for the author's position sufficient to require a response from the State party."* In *Agiza v. Sweden* (2005, § 13.7) the burden was found to be on the State to conduct an *"effective, independent and impartial review"* once a 'plausible allegation' is made. Similarly, in *A.S. v. Sweden* (2000, § 8.6) it was held that if sufficient facts are adduced by the author, the burden shifts to the State *"to make sufficient efforts to determine whether there are substantial grounds for believing that the author would be in danger of being subjected to torture."*
[65] See HRC, *Jonny Rubin Byahuranga v Denmark*, (2004, §§ 11.2-3).
[66] UN Sub-Commission for the Promotion and Protection of Human Rights, Resolution 2005/12 on Transfer of Persons, (2005, § 4); see similarly, European Commission for Human Rights in the *Cruz Varas* case (1991).
[67] *Chahal v. the UK* (1996, § 105); *Agiza v. Sweden* (2005, § 13.4).
[68] See Report of Special Rapporteur on Torture to the General Assembly, (2004, § 40).
[69] See CPT 15th General Report, (2004-2005, §§ 39-40).
[70] See above note 70, at § 4.
[71] Report by Council of Europe Commissioner for Human Rights (2005, §§ 12-3).
[72] Report of the UN Independent Expert (2005, §§ 19-20).

40.   Moreover, assurances cannot legitimately be relied upon as a factor in the assessment of relevant risk. This is underscored by widespread and growing concerns about assurances as not only lacking legal effect but also as being, in practice, simply unreliable, with post-return monitoring mechanisms incapable of ensuring otherwise.[74] While effective system-wide monitoring is vital for the long-term prevention and eradication of torture and other ill-treatment, individual monitoring cannot ameliorate the risk to a particular detainee.

41.   The critical question to be ascertained by the Court, by reference to all circumstances and the practical reality on the ground, remains whether there is a risk of torture or ill-treatment in accordance with the standards and principles set down above. If so, transfer is unlawful. No 'compensating measures' can affect the peremptory *jus cogens* nature of the prohibition against torture, and the obligations to prevent its occurrence, which are plainly unaffected by bilateral agreements.

VI. CONCLUSION

42.   The principle of *non-refoulement*, firmly established in international law and practice, is absolute. No exceptional circumstances concerning the individual potentially affected or the national security of the State in question can justify qualifying or compromising this principle. Given the inherent link between the two, and the positive nature of the obligation to protect against torture and ill-treatment, no legal distinction can be drawn under the Convention between the act of torture or ill-treatment and the act of transfer in face of a real risk thereof. Any unravelling of the *refoulement* prohibition would necessarily mean an unravelling of the absolute prohibition on torture itself, one of the most fundamental and incontrovertible of international norms.

43.   International practice suggests that the determination of transfer cases should take account of the absolute nature of the *refoulement* prohibition under Article 3, and what is required to make the Convention's protection effective. The risk must be real, foreseeable and personal. Great weight should attach to the person's affiliation with a vulnerable group in determining risk. Evidentiary requirements in respect of such risk must be tailored to the reality of the circumstances of the case, including the capacity of the individual to access relevant facts and prove the risk of torture and ill-treatment, the gravity of the potential violation at stake and the positive obligations of states to prevent it. Once a *prima facie* or arguable case of risk of torture or other ill-treatment is

---

[73] See UN Declaration (2005, § 8).
[74] Courts in Canada (*Mahjoub*), the Netherlands (*Kaplan*), and the United Kingdom (*Zakaev*) have blocked transfers because of the risk of torture despite the presence of diplomatic assurances. There is credible evidence that persons sent from Sweden to Egypt (*Agiza & Al-Zari*) and from the United States to Syria (*Arar*) have been subject to torture and ill-treatment despite assurances: for more information on practice, see Human Rights Watch, 'Still at Risk' (2005); Human Rights Watch, 'Empty Promises' (2004).

established, it is for the State to satisfy the Court that there is in fact no real risk that the individual will be subject to torture or other ill-treatment.